TRUTH CANNOT BE REHEARSED

TRUTH CANNOT BE REHEARSED

Talks, Sessions, & Essays
About The Art Of
Being Fully Human

Robert Augustus Masters

XANTHYROS FOUNDATION

ISBN: 0-9694819-0-X

Contents

TALKS, SESSIONS, & ESSAYS

1. Keeping Our Heart Open In Hell   1
2. Ego Is a Cult of One: The Ins and Outs of Self-Entrapment   10
3. The Three Stages of Conscious Attention   19
4. Becoming Intimate With Full-Blooded Ecstasy   27
5. Into the Heart of Endarkened Moods   43
6. God Is Not Elsewhere: Making an Ally Out of Unsettledness   53
7. Embodying the Passionate Witness   61
8. Weaving the Cocoon: A Broken-Field Run Through Larva-Land   70
9. Ecstasy Is Not the Goal, But the Foundation   85
10. When Suffering Is No Longer Reduced To a Problem   93
11. Releasing Sex From the Obligation To Make Us Feel Better   101
12. No More Fumbling In the Dark   108
13. Disarming Our Harm-Doing   119
14. A Cancerous Bottling-Up of Mind: Doubt Explored & Unmasked   123
15. Power From Persona Versus Power From Essence   131
16. Exploring Self-Suppression's Paralyzing Grasp: An Intimate Look At Fear   138
17. No More Stage Fright: Acting Without Reacting   149
18. The Naked Nerve of Deserted Need: Titillation, Immunity, & Relational Insecurity   158
19. The Inside Story On Information: Data, Attention, Truth, & Being   169
20. A Safe Place To Let Go of Being Safe: Mind, Emotion, & Appropriateness   173
21. Real Anger Is Not an Avoidance of Anything   185
22. Without Intimacy, Meditation Is But a Remedy   196
23. Facts Are Facts, But They're Not Necessarily the Truth: Outgrowing Information's Playpen   203
24. What Is Objective Knowledge?   210

25. The Separative Swoon of False Oneness:
     An Exposé of Romance   217
26. Awakening Creates Its Own Morality   234
27. Flirting With Nasty Possibility: The Nature of Anxiety   242
28. Birthing a True Community   247
29. You Can't Think Your Way Into Being   257
30. The Art of Letting Love Be Present   266
31. Look & Leap At the Same Time:
     Making Good Use of Turning Points   275
32. The Creation of Sexual Charge As Compensation
     For the Loss of Self   287
33. The Exploding Heart of Fleshed-Out Ecstasy:
     Orgasm, Appetite, & God   291
34. Meaning, Meaninglessness, & Destiny:
     Embodying One's True Purpose   306
35. Cutting Through the Avoidance of Embodiment:
     The Fleshbody, the Dreambody, & Death   313
36. Real Happiness Is Not In Having, But In Being   325
37. Toward Unadulterated Intimacy With Children   331
38. The Incredible Hulk On the Cello:
     Myth As a Vessel For Awakening   337
39. The Nun & the Whore: Real Sex Doesn't Need Fantasy   347
40. Letting Go of the Whip:
     Moving From Guilt To Shame To Freedom   355
41. No More Diseased Release: Cutting Through Masochism   362
42. Children & Real Education   367
43. Roots & Wings: When Learning Is a Conscious Process   377
44. Plugging In Instead of Jacking Off   382
45. Letting the Broken Heart Enliven the Soul:
     Despair, Disillusionment, & Being   386
46. Guilt On Amphetamines: A Close-Up of Hysteria   396
47. Into the Heart of Abortion: Little One, What Do You Say? 399
48. Our Children Are Not Ours   403
49. Speaking True, No Matter What Our Condition:
     An Evening of Spiritwork   411
50. Look Inside Your Looking: The Essence of Seeking   429

51. Illuminating Our Resistance To Working On Ourselves   435
52. Turning Off the Headlights:
     Dependence, Independence, & Real Commitment   447
53. Dying Into a Truer Life: Real Risk-Taking   461
54. Speaking a Truer Tongue   467
55. The Spirit of Assignments:
     From Submission To Cocreative Surrender   476
56. We're Always Channeling: Mediumship Unveiled   485
57. Na Pali: Embracing the Knowingness That Upstages
     All Mindtraps   493
58. The Invitation That Will Not Go Away   505

POETRY, INCANTATIONS, & OTHER WRITINGS

Sacred Fire   26
Woke Up Feeling Kinda Thick   42
Everything Already Aflame   69
Must I Lose You Again?   90
My Freedom's In My Chains   99
Crushed Beneath a Lesser View   146
Sex Got Stuck In a Pelvic (& Neo-Tantric) Headlock   164
Living As a Mind Means Being Stuck In Time   182
The Summer of 1976   216
Transplantation   246
Outbreathing My Shock Was I   256
Wildwinged Shapeshifters Disassembling Your Mind   282
He Wants His Money Back   286
Darkness Lifts a Veil   310
They Got a Deal   324
When I Lived In an Empty Room   329
She Defends Those Who Hurt Her   361
Unborn Children Fill My Rooms   402
When Our Eyes Meet   409
Incarnation's Fleshdance   474
An Ordinariness of Extraordinary Obviousness   502

REMEMBRANCE

The waves return, glittering with remembered sun
Ancient songs seizing our tongues
The broken pillars standing anew
The temple rising, rising, rising
The circle shining true

The waves return, carrying the work done then
Ancient songs seizing our tongues
And we stand together again
Looking through all the slumber and pain
O Breathe us strong, breathe us sure
O Breathe us strong, breathe us pure

It is time to bring forward the gifts of old
It is time to come in from the cold
It is time to build our trust anew
Let the walls rise, naked with Eternity's View
Let the walls rise, rise from our ruins
Let the walls rise, rise, rise!
And we stand together again
Ancient songs seizing our tongues
And we can only be the Truth we must speak

Our hearts are wounded but glowing
Our power is trembling but growing
O Breathe us strong, breathe us sure
O Breathe us strong, breathe us pure
Is not the temple rising, rising, rising?
Are not our days Wonder-spun?
Are we not lovers with the Undying One?

Is not the temple rising, rising, rising?
Here we are, gathered from afar
Each of us a spark from a waking star
O Flame us bright, flame us steady
O Flame us bright, flame us ready
And we stand together again
Ancient songs trembling with our name
The temple rising, rising, rising
The circle shining true

Welcome...

–1–

Keeping Our Heart Open in Hell

Yesterday a woman who has a very strong desire to have a child, a specific child that she has sensed around her spiritually for some time, said to me she didn't know if she really wanted to bring such a being into this world, since this Earth of ours is in such terrible shape. I said to her what made her think that she was so wise as to know whether or not the conditions prevalent on Earth now were necessarily *not* conducive to what such a being might need?

Earth is not a paradise. It is not a perfected world. In many ways, it's a kind of hell, a realm of delusion, spiritlessness, addiction, and gross insensitivity, a place where true Help is readily crucified or trivialized, where those who are psychospiritually imprisoned all too easily make an enemy out of those who have left the prison. Nevertheless, Earth offers *extremely* conducive conditions for the Awakening process — everything that's neurotic about us is colourfully exaggerated and reflected (and thereby made *obvious*) by our environment, level upon level, ever inviting us out of our slumber...

Earth isn't just some benign playpen wherein humans smoothly transition from one evolutionary stage to another. It's a domain of carnivorous intent, murder, great difficulty, tragedy, and torture, and it's also a place fertile with the possibility of exquisite courage, love, true art, and luminous risk-taking... It's possible here to literally embody every sort of psychospiritual option. One can become profoundly subhuman. One can be awakened to one's true condition. One can be a black hole, or one can be a blazingly brilliant light. There are lessons here, lessons concerning desire, attachment, and identity, lessons that cannot be reduced to mere information — their Truth must be *felt*, nakedly felt, right in the moment, assimilated, spontaneously expressed, lived, appreciated, kept out of Belief's

Gustave Doré: *Milton's Paradise Lost*

ossifying reach... No one's giving the lessons. *We* are the lessons; we are the very curriculum from which we must graduate!

Almost all who are incarnated here "did" so unknowingly, contrary to the currently popular metaphysical notion which has it that we *all*, in our supposed bardo-state wisdom, *consciously chose* to be here, *consciously chose* our parents, our circumstances of birth and so on. What ego-gratifying delusion! As if "I" can so choose, as if ego (in its latest spiritual garb) possesses such wisdom!

In fact, it is our prevalent *conditioning*, our strongest (and therefore most deeply *unconscious*) habits, that determine our course in almost all cases. To even use the word "our" is misleading, for the process of incarnation is not ordinarily even that *personal*; its resulting individuation has far more to do with the automaticities of biological differentiation than it does with soul-level choice, except in those for whom Awakening is *already* firmly established. Very few are those who consciously chose incarnation, and those few need particular conditions for their arrival, their fleshing-out. The woman who spoke to me last night is, to some extent, in touch with such a being; unfortunately, her desire to bring forth such a one is not so strong as her *fear* of doing so, her fear of what it would require of her. Such beings usually cannot incarnate unless love outshines fear, day after day. Their taking birth almost always requires a soul-deepening on the mother's part, a spirit-bright fecundity, a decisive cutting through of all romanticism about being a mother...

As it is lived by most, Earth is a hell, but not a hell of devil-ushered fires and moralistic punishment — that's but a cartoon version of the typical life's consequences, a titillatingly righteous tabloid metaphor that's much closer to melodrama than it is to real myth. (Such damnation-preaching melodrama is just as tackily vapid as its cherubic, pie-in-the-sky counterpart, both grinding it out together, spawning conventional religion and other related horror-shows.) When we turn away from the imperatives of our spirit with overwhelming consistency, we create Hell, literally marooning ourselves from what truly nourishes us. Whatever is done unconsciously or in unlove creates its own Life-negating consequences — our actions set in motion corresponding forces that both reflect and magnify our current condition, regardless of how numb we may be to such feedback. Our relationship to these consequences, however time-delayed they might be, usually generates a context that seems more or less hellish to us, a context wherein we all too easily feel victimized, badly done by, misunderstood... If we don't work well with such consequences, such karmic benefits, we will only be, unknown to ourselves, inviting in bigger and bigger crises, or awakening shocks. Of course, on a massive scale, this is exactly what is happening on Earth now.

You could say that our entire purpose in living amidst such consequences is to awaken to their motivation, not just from the neck up, but with our entire being, so that we cannot help but do something Life-affirming about our difficulties. To awaken in the midst of Hell, to keep our heart open in Hell — that's the key here, the real test. Can you keep your heart open in Hell? This doesn't mean floating above things, drifting along fastened to a belief system, clinging to a mantra, doing some form of positive thinking, or engaging in any other escapist or *disembodied* strategy. Rather, it means being wounded, openly wounded, not morbidly but *openly*, gutsily, wakefully, staying as receptive as possible to what is deeper than reactivity. We are *all* wounded, especially at the heart. To keep ourselves open, discriminatingly yet vulnerably open, during seemingly negative times is not easy! However, the more difficult it is, the more necessary it is to open, to make room for our pain and suffering as well as for our love...

When it gets really difficult, we'll likely close down, flashing all kinds of convincing alibis with which we hedge and bind and mind ourselves, often seeking the gee-ain't-it-a-shame agreement and solace of others in a similar fix. Such company, though, only reinforces our flight from the heart of the matter — when we are blowing it, shutting down our depths, closing ourselves off from the Truth, the last thing we need from those around us is sympathy or condolences. At such times, we need the ass-kicking side of true love, the sword of real compassion; we need the shock of a passionately-expressed reminder of what we are actually up to. We don't need anyone to go into agreement with us about how terrible or rotten things are — we've *already* made an agreement, at least in our mind, about how terrible our situation is, how unfair, and so on, and we're not about to view it otherwise. (Unless we want to play that ego-centered New Age game of *thinking* that we've created it all, hopelessly muddling together responsibility and blame, even as our very *conceptualizing* distances us from what we're *actually* doing.) We may bitch about our situation, ignore it, try to drink or think it away, but rarely do we do anything truly Life-giving about it.

This is why an alliance with kindred spirits (especially in the form of *living* community) is so essential for almost all who would truly engage in the full-blooded awakening of themselves. Left to ourselves, we're all too likely to remain blind relative to most of our slumber-habits — we need others to remind us of what we're up to, to Zen-stick us, to jolt us, to love us true, to experiment and journey with us, to enter into shared responsibility with us for our mutual awakening. (At worst, this can slip into cultism and degenerative dependency, but if it's worked with skilfully and graced with a sufficiently adept guide, it engenders a strength that's utterly *unthreatened* by dependency, a strength that's bright with real intimacy, a strength that's as vibrantly individuated as it's communal.)

These others must be more than just acquaintances, more than just members of some therapeutic or "spiritual" group — they must be deep friends, intimately interactive allies who have also put their lives on the line, without investing any energy in keeping an exit available for themselves, in case their community effort doesn't pan out. They've decided, and decided with their entire being, to go for it 100 percent; they still waver and slip here and there, but their commitment does not... If, after some time, it becomes clear that the situation is not working, or is not working enough for them (if, for example, the leader or leaders are short on integrity), they then can change direction with a minimum of fuss — their very *totality* of participation in such a communal effort will have, in most cases, deepened their capacity for integrity-rich vision to such an extent that they will be able to alter their course profoundly, if they need to.

This is utterly different than the case of the devotee, of the childish or neurotically dependent person, who goes to a teacher not to be catalyzed into a deeper wakefulness, a truer life, but for the security-providing sensations of a larger-than-life parental presence. Devotees cannot form or sustain a viable community, simply because their passion is not for such family, but rather for a sense of wraparound belonging, of blissful immunity, of all-consoling us-ness. Unfortunately, almost all so-called communities are made up of devotees of one kind or another, cultically intertwined with one another.

The true community is very easily confused by most with false or superficial community — the knee-jerk reactivity and glib stupidity of just about all "news" media lumps together all "alternative" communities, tossing around the buzzword "cult" with the greatest of ease, hinting at fiascos like Jonestown or Rajneeshpuram, but steering clear of tellingly acknowledging the cultism of such phenomena as Republicanism, Catholicism, and the nuclear family. A true community is *not* a hideout from the suffering of this world, but rather an environment where one has to face one's suffering, nakedly, presently, fully, both in aloneness *and* in intimacy — essential to the fruition of this is the energy field of the community, the common Presence evoked and magnified by the combined work of all (and kept *consistently* alive by the guide of such a community), a Presence that supports love and passion, camaraderie, courage, primal breakthrough, tenderness, and core-level communion. In such a setting, neither repression nor indulgence can take firm hold; their very presence is but soil for further work, for further revelation...

In a true community, suffering is neither avoided nor unnecessarily reinforced. In fact, once such a community has ripened, the only suffering therein is *necessary* suffering, the suffering inherent to purification and maturation, the suffering of allowing oneself to be deeply touched by the fires of the Awakening process. There is pain here, and there is also Ecstasy; the pain is not avoided, and the Ecstasy is not clung to, nor reduced to a goal. Such a community, such an extended family, does not shut itself off from the culture that surrounds it, but nor is it consumed by it — it uses its relationship to the society around it as further fuel for revelation, as yet another opportunity to practise integrity and artful communication.

Back to my initial theme... For almost all, Earth *is* Hell, a realm of Self-suppression and compensatory addictions, plagued with split-level pain and pleasure-seeking somnambulism. The Christian fantasies of Hell are but garish reflections of what is *already* here, in or out of pew, hidden behind all of our distractions and ego-views. For one who is awakening, Earth is still Hell, but it's also Heaven, not literally, but psychoemotionally, psychospiritually — there may be a simultaneous abhorrence of conditions here and an equally strong appreciation of them, even a gratitude for such deep testing, for such soul-germinating challenge.

Eventually, one has to realize that nothing here can be flinched from, nothing! To contract from any of it is to not know *that* aspect of it, but to simply flee from the *branchings* of it, to miss the opportunity of truly encountering and perhaps even uprooting it. Bear with me as I weave this... To uproot what's troubling us, we must become profoundly intimate with it; we must recognize how we've incorporated it, how we've compensated for its unpleasantness, how we've projected it all around us, how we've let it shape us, in our stride, our posture, our musculature, our emotions, our spirit, our psyche... Such self-examination is *not* a clinical procedure, not necessarily even a scientific one — instead, it's one of ever-alert art, and such art usually flowers most beautifully in the company of similarly inclined individuals, which brings me back to the very beginning of this talk... To bring a child into this world may be a mistake if one does not have a conducive environment for such an opportunity. However, the incarnation of a being, a consciously and lovingly welcomed being, is an utterly auspicious circumstance and opportunity when there are conditions present such as are found in a true community; such a child will not only have spirit-recognition, real love, and nourishing challenge, but also many parent-figures, many welcoming and supportive arms, a colourfully diverse and richly intimate environment of allies who are not stuck in Heaven or in Hell...

We have to do it alone, and we have to do it together, no matter what the weather. The blending of both is the very essence of our humanness; it is tribal in the best sense of that word. Much of Earth's hellishness has to do with both the avoidance of being *truly* alone, and the avoidance of being *truly* together — it's the dreary dance of loneliness and cultism, of neurotic dependence and neurotic independence, the loneliness of the crowd, all stickily swirling around that hellishly ubiquitous cult of one known as ego...

Consider the epithet "Go to Hell!" But almost all Earthlings are, much of the time, *already* in Hell, already embodying hellish conditions, already resolutely imbedded in Hell-reinforcing rituals, especially those that are *supposed* Hell-antidotes! So *what* is Hell? It's the result of having turned away from What truly nourishes and sustains us; it's estrangement from our core of Being, from God, from Love and Ecstasy. Hell is a state of being, a state of deeply contracted being, a collapse or psychoemotional embalming of heart, a chronically anxious or enervated knotting up of solar plexus, belly, and throat, a compression or bloating of mind, a shrinkage of Being, a desiccation or hysterical inflation of emotion, a resolute clinging to surrogates of the Real, an abuse or non-use of *real* help...

Hell is suppression of Self. Wherever that is being done, it unavoidably creates conditions or circumstances that both carry its seed and reflect it — what is now occurring on Earth accurately, painfully, eloquently, exaggeratedly even, reflects the Self-suppression that characterizes most of us most of the time. Worse, almost all humans are not only chronically stuck in Hell, but are generally fast asleep in Hell, the more "spiritually" inclined all too easily mistaking their snoring for the Music of the Spheres. Even worse, instead of noticing that we are in prison, self-bound and self-downed, we only busy ourselves exploiting the possibilities *within* our cage, reducing freedom to fragmented licence or soapbox conceptualizing, enthusiastically losing ourselves in cage-decoration, redecoration and interior design, sporadically rearranging the furniture, the personnel, the lines, again and again trying to engineer a more comfortable fit. But we're never *really* comfortable, but only periodically satiated, emptied, pleasurably deluded... How can we be truly at ease when we're so out of place, so *unnaturally* positioned?

Nothing we can do within the cage can *truly* satisfy us; there's no liberation solely within our self-incarceration. To awaken within the cage is not to seek more gratification or consolation there, but is to recognize the cage for what it is, and to take appropriate action — finding the way out (which has a lot to do with recognizing just *how* we got in!), *now*. And the way out is not outside ourselves — it is within, located in the bound energies of the very assumptions that keep us contracted and spirit-shrunken. (Yes, there is outside help, but we cannot access it until *we've* begun to contact *and* honour our Awakening-impulse.)

There's no point in airbrushing our Hell, nor in wailing over it. All we need do is recognize it for what it is, namely *our* personal doing, "created" by our conditioning, by our attachment to our personified habits, the most prevalent of which is ego. Ordinarily, ego is self-incarceration in action, a hell-raiser second to none. But, as I've pointed out in other talks, ego need not be annihilated — open its windows, clean out its closets, allow it to become transparent to essence, and it'll become but a playful, colourfully personal expression of our depths, a Life-affirming superficiality, a brightly-nuanced surface in idiosyncratic harmony with our deeper currents...

To say that Earth is hellish is not to say that it's a bad place, but that it's a place throbbing with transformational possibility. Such possibility, of course, is much more than some kind of mind-game where we try to *think* our way into a "better" state. Real transformation in-

volves our *entire* being. It must include an honest, full-bodied exposure of our woundedness (which also is a simultaneous confession of
the failure of our self-entrapment to truly satisfy us). There's no
other way, although there are many ways to bring such exposure to
light. (Yes, a taste of Ecstasy might get us going, but if we merely
look for *more*, we'll just find ourselves back behind bars.) Our wounds
must be opened, skilfully and sensitively opened, descabbed, liberated from their mind-bandages, shown to the sun, to the Undying
One, to our intimates. We must learn to love the little one within us
who cries brokenly behind our every disguise, our every strategy to
fortify ourselves. Our softness calls for healing, and so does our
hardness; to make either wrong is to deny ourselves our fullness. (So
many "sensitive" or "feminist" men betray their maleness in their
lopsided embrace of softness, losing in their abandonment of their
"hardness" not only macho qualities, but also the power of healthy
thrust, of discriminative sharpness, of gut-level risk-taking.)

Instead of pushing away what we can't stand about ourselves, we
need to go right into it, consciously and vulnerably, armed with both
power and love, meeting and wrestling with and merging with the
dreaded "it", until it's no longer an "it", but only reclaimed us, still
perhaps shadowed, but not alienatingly separate. Such is the real
essence of integration, of Self-reunion, of illuminated Aliveness; when
this is entered into *fully*, then Earth is neither Hell nor Heaven, but
only a marvellously diversified opportunity, a doorway pulsating with
our Heart's desire. Already it is ever so slightly open, invitingly ajar,
calling you from near and far...

–2–
Ego is a Cult of One:
The Ins & Outs of
Self-Entrapment

Ego is not a somebody, a discrete entity, but rather is a habit, a deeply ingrained habit, a habit gone to mind, a habit that insists on referring to itself as a me, a habit that is but the *personification* of our suppression of Being, our turning away from our deeper nature. Ordinarily, when we say I, we are simply giving voice to our ego — we are busy being who we *think* we are, not realizing that ego is simply something *we* are doing, something *we* are animating. All too easily, ego persists as our center; the more attention "we" give to the imperatives of ego, the less attention we have for the cultivation of true center, which could be called Essence-centricity, as opposed to ego-centricity...

Nevertheless, ego is *not* necessarily a problem or obstacle or hindrance; it is not necessarily something we, in our spiritual ambition, must try to eradicate. There is no point in trying to annihilate ego. In fact, there is nothing more egotistical than the effort to somehow get rid of ego! The very habits that make up ego must be faced, penetrated, uprooted, and loved bright, not so that we will exist in an egoless state, but so that what is now present as our ego can become something that cleanly and colorfully reflects our core of Being, something that, with idiosyncratic accuracy and flair, expresses our depths.

So the point is not to get rid of ego, but to purify it, to give it what it needs to become an ally. Of course, when such purification has become profound and natural, ego will not necessarily appear as ego, but rather as a kind of refreshingly alive, idiographic transparency, utterly permeable to Essence, no longer masquerading as our true center, but only conveying (and artfully translating) that which arises from our *true* center of Being.

Ego is but obsessive and *unconscious* identification with persona (or personality). The usual human ordinarily exists only as a crowd of fragments, not as a wholeness, a conscious totality. Each fragment, when given sufficient attention, tends to refer to itself as "I". Depending on our mood, our condition, our current circumstance, all kinds of different "I's" assume dominance or center stage, so that in a typical day we may, in saying "I" hundreds of times, actually refer to at least a dozen, perhaps two dozen, fragments of self — the "I" that is hurriedly making lunch is not the "I" that lusts for sexual discharge, nor is it the "I" that is setting the alarm clock, nor is it the "I" that is studying the mirror. Nevertheless, we almost always say "I" for *all* of our fragments of self, rarely realizing that we are doing so, rarely articulating the actual presence of the particular fragment that we are channeling...

The most consistently dominant fragment (or coalition of fragments) makes up our persona, existing through the subjugation and suppression of all the other fragments of self, many of which frequently assert themselves, frequently making their presence known (in the manner of unruly, disobedient, or lascivious peasants), thereby rigidifying (and perhaps even seemingly legitimizing) the governing force of the dominant fragment of self. Thus do we tend to exist as an uneasily and unconsciously governed crowd, rather than as a wholeness or an awakened cooperative, repetitiously and stubbornly trying to legislate our way through Life, numbing ourselves with inner bureaucracy, our very efforts to heal ourselves only deepening our fracturing of self...

All too often, we mechanically identify with our persona, thereby creating ego, automatically allowing it to refer to itself as "I". Trying to escape from this in some metaphysical fashion, or through some sort of belief restructuring, does not work — ego loves to put on holy robes, loves to paint wings on itself, loves to adopt lofty religious ideals, loves to do mantras and affirmations, and then, glorious then, refer to itself not just as "I", but as atman, soul, universal self, and so on. The ultimate dream of ego is to be enlightened, to be an ego that is egoless! The caption for its cartoon efforts to transcend itself could be: Enlightenment guaranteed, or your ego back!

The very forces that motivate us to become addicted to ego must be faced directly, thoroughly and passionately, fully, uncompromisingly, with humor, guts, and heart. Almost all of us live in a trap. Instead of

Gustave Doré: *The Bible*

working to get out of it (that is, *if* we've even noticed we're entrapped), we all too easily become obsessed with trying to escape or minimize the suffering of being in such a bind. We won't actually *leave* the trap, for it is security to us, a haven of familiarity, of repetitious cosiness, which we can brighten up with novelty, erotic compulsion, and other distractions — most of the time, we are too terrified of the Unknown, too caught up in our craving for security and predictability, and, above all, too consistently unconscious of all this, to even consider leaving the trap!

In fact, those who stand outside the trap are not usually treated by us as allies, but as enemies or lunatics; with the greatest of ease, we crucify, vilify, poison, or condemn them, either literally or in our thoughts. We don't want to be reminded that we are not only trapped, but are *creating* such entrapment for ourselves. It is much easier for us to become compulsively concerned with the sheer pressure of such continuous contraction of self, such resolute stranglehold on the heart, such corrosive worry, such ulcerated feeling... Like drugged moles, we stay within our traps, ever looking for more and more pleasurized remedies, ever trying to make the best of the trap, thereby only weakening our impulse to leave. We redecorate our trap, rearrange its furniture, buy new pictures, bring new people into it, have others go, do therapy within a bigger cage; we might look for a "better" trap, a more "spiritual" or more rural one, madly relocating, but not *really* leaving, not really cutting through our dream of a *perfect* cage...

None of this is obviously volitional; to one who can see, it appears just as mechanical as the activities of rats running through a maze. Again and again, we unknowingly animate our entrapping assumptions, not noticing that the trapdoor is *already* open. This is the secret, the fundamental secret of esotericism, a secret that cannot be decoded unless it is encountered in *more* than a merely *informational* way — my saying it is of no use whatsoever unless it is *felt* as more than just data. Instead of recognizing and taking advantage of the open door, we, out of sheer habit (including that of making our prison our security), tend to only further our efforts to pleasurably occupy and entertain ourselves *within* our trap. The more successfully oriented we are to thus numbing and comforting ourselves, the less likely we are to leave the trap, let alone illuminate it!

And what is the trap primarily? It is ongoing participation in the suppression of Being, a turning away from Ecstasy, from Truth, from Aliveness, from the Source and Substance of all, a self-bound recoil from the Undying Mystery, the Great Paradox, the Eternity That pervades all of this. It is a turning away from what *truly* nourishes us, a turning away that drives us to create surrogates of what we've fled, such creation being as compulsive as it is blind. Having turned away from Ecstasy, we create all sorts of counterfeits of Ecstasy, trying to maximize pleasurable stimulation, sensation, and release, blithely addicting ourselves to those circumstances or people through which or whom we can, or seemingly can, achieve a thoroughly distracting and even thrilling release. In this, we are but psychospiritual junkies, masking our stagnation with sedation and remote-control titillation, dreaming that we are awake, even as our snore paints false doors on our walls...

And what brings us to the point of even realizing we are in a trap that is reinforced by our seeking to escape its pain, its distress, its airtight containment? What brings us to this recognition? Suffering, and more suffering, not just the suffering that sets in motion the mechanics of psychophysical release, but a deeper suffering, a suffering of such profound dissatisfaction that there is nothing that can successfully persuade us to continue our automaticities of self-distressing, self-pleasuring, and self-entrapment.

At some point, there has to be such *naked* despair that we are no longer seducible by hope, the hope of the next remedy, the next psychospiritual seminar, the next fuck, the next audition, the next tomorrow, the next whatever! No hope whatsoever is essential, hope being but bravely smiling doubt, or, more precisely, despair masking itself through taking a crash course in positive thinking. Hope is but nostalgia for the future. It must be outbreathed, outdanced, outlived by our desire to wake up, to make good use of our despair — instead of injecting ourselves with hope and other distractions, including the effort to maximize pleasurable release, we need to *honour* and *welcome* our disillusionment, really welcoming and making good use of it, bringing more lucidity to our dreams and far more attention to our Awakening impulse...

When we soften the edges of our hurt through our usual rituals of release, our cosy little lullabies of body and mind, we only weaken our capacity to embrace a very different sort of release, namely that which could take us *through* the trapdoor, not into some superworld, some etheric dimension, some metaphysical abstraction, some heavenly anodyne or some nirvanic desirelessness, but rather into the very heart of our own Being, which is not at all abstract or necessarily ethereal — it is *human*, unabashedly passionate, full-blooded, messy, lusty, unburdened by rehearsal, *already* unstressed, *already* loose (even in its needed tensility), *already* happy (or luminously present in the midst of every feeling, including anger and grief), *already* flexible and functionally adept (that is, free to *truly* learn), juicily alive — it is our *humanness* that calls to us, not some make-believe, pain-free realm!

It is our multidimensional humanity (as well as our prehuman and transhuman nature) that calls to us, calling and calling, calling to us in its profound and transfiguring ordinariness, its heart-full simplicity, its sublime subtlety, its paradoxical Ecstasy, grief, and seamless Wonder... Even now it calls to you, weaving your true names and unravelling your life-negating games, but you are all too often elsewhere and elsewhen, deafened by the soundtrack of your efforts to make your entrapment tolerable. If you stop thus distracting and drugging yourself, your entrapment will hurt so damned much that you will *have no* option but to *fully* consider and honor something very different!

Everyone likes the *idea* of leaving the trap, but the trap they are thinking of leaving is not the *primary* trap they are in, but instead is the suffering created by their entrapment. This is *not* a fine distinction; it must be understood, not just intellectually, but with our *entire* being — otherwise, it becomes just one more belief, one more ideal on which to impale ourselves, one more abstraction to take to bed. The first sign of truly moving toward leaving the trap is when center begins to develop in us, when Essence-centricity begins to become more important to us than ego-centricity.

Essence-centricity loves, but ego-centricity cannot; at best, it reduces love to sentimentality and romance. Romance is a fantastic device for distraction — all one has to do is dissolve one's boundaries (whether in solitary, dyadic, familial, or national fashion), getting lost in swooning chestfuls of lust and misguided loyalty, pretending that there is no distance between oneself and one's beloved, when in fact there is an immense distance (which ordinarily does not become apparent until the honeymoon is *over*). Essence-centricity, on the other hand, prefers Ecstasy and communion to romance; It does not dissolve or collapse Its boundaries in some irresponsible fashion, but rather consciously *expands* them, thereby *including* the other, keeping Itself capable of true compassion through Its sensitive, subtle, and unquestionably vital empathy with the other. Essence-centricity does not lose Itself in the other, nor in the world, nor in Its own coupling sensations, nor does It allow Itself to degenerate into any sort of self-enclosed, neurotically independent entity (commonly known as an individual in our culture). Ego-centricity, which usually moves back and forth between the two extremes of neurotic dependence and neurotic independence, is something we *do* when we are asleep to ourselves — it is a dream, a nightmare, a confession of longtime slumber.

Ego is a cult of one, just as almost all marriage is a cult of two, and religion a cult of many. Essence-centricity, however, is not at all cultic; It simultaneously maintains Its integrity, Its connectedness with Its Source, and remains permeable to outside influence, lucidly discriminative in Its inclusivity. It remains capable of empathy, not the kind of empathy that swamps or floods one, but the kind that increases one's appreciation for the diversity of life, the kind that empowers *all* involved, the kind that deepens center again and again and again...

The door is already open, but we cannot simply pass through it intellectually, or in a metaphysical wheelchair, or upon a gust of enthusiasm. *All* of one must pass through — body, mind, emotions, spirit, *all* of one, every portion and level and facet. It is all too easy to allow subtle regions of the mind (such as are activated by certain high-end affirmations and psychic attunements) to pass through, to leave the body behind, to leave the emotions behind, especially those emotions that are commonly labelled as negative or spiritually inauspicious. This only creates dissociation, more self-division, a more refined fragmentation of self, just another fracturing of Being. One can do something like this and actually believe that one *is* whole, compulsively affirming that one *is* whole, that one *is* at one with God, but this is a lie, unless we are actually *living* it with our entire being! (The truth, most of the time, is that one is just reinforcing one's self-fragmentation, making it even worse by pretending that wholeness is occurring.)

Once we're convinced through mere belief that we're awake, then there is no awakening of us. We cannot be found until we realize that we're lost. We cannot truly know who we are until we fully *and* bodily realize that we *don't* know who we are. The reluctance almost all feel in making (or even in considering making) the passage into full-bodied wakefulness is because of the intensity of feeling, of woundedness, that must be encountered. Few of us are willing to tolerate such a depth of feeling, except perhaps in the honeymoon stages of body-oriented psychotherapy. We may even occasionally like to think we can tolerate an intensity of joy, but we can't; as soon as it's there, we want to get rid of it, to fuck it away, to exploit it away, to diminish its charge... Most people tighten up, however subtly, right before and/or during orgasm. One who is not capable of *full* anger, *full* sadness, *full* grief, *full* exultation, cannot fully let go during orgasm, let alone during sex! Only those who can uninhibitedly and sensitively enter and enjoy the depths of their darkest emotions can *freely* participate in Ecstasy.

Implicit in this is the fact that there is nothing inherently wrong with *any* feeling — what really matters is what we *do* with our feelings. Do we use our anger to harm the other, to make them wrong, or do we use it to break through barriers to intimacy? Do we use our hurt as a tool for blame, or are we truly vulnerable in it, open-faced and present throughout it? Do we pollute our love with sentimentality, or do we let it shine? Do we expand or contract with our grief? Do we bank our joy, or do we permit it its innate spontaneity? Do we violate our rage with wraparound smiles, or do we uncage it with righteous haste, or do we let it storm free of its own contractedness, letting it become but unbound need, luminous hurt, streamingly alive love and humour? Do we use our jealousy to reject whoever seems to be rejecting us, or do we use it to stand naked in the truth of our deeper need?

The Awakening process is often fiery; if we are not willing to learn to welcome its flames, its purifying heat, then we only have our traps to look forward to, with all their possibilities of entertainment, novelty, and narcosis. Yes, we might try to get rid of our ego as we dwell within our trap, perhaps within an ashramized part of the trap, a spiritualized enclave all heavenly-hedged, but when we only want to replace the dream we're stuck in with a more consoling or "better" dream, we simply further the injury we are already doing our soul.

The point is not to fulfill ourselves *within* our dreams, but rather to awaken from them, to really awaken from them, *all* of them! This is no matter of mere enthusiasm — it is a long, difficult process (to *believe* otherwise simply leaves one stranded in the gossamer of belief, far from the imperatives of the Awakening process, which has *nothing* to do with believing this or that — to think it can be easy just because one has *believed* it to be so, as in movements such as Rebirthing, is but an exercise in stupidity), which requires tremendous courage, the courage to *fully* embody one's passions, high and low, dark and light, gross and subtle, the courage to go into one's lust with open eyes, to dive into one's most sublime subtleties with de-romanticized alertness, the courage to illuminate the habit known as ego...

Again, ego is just a habit gone to mind, a garrulously ossified result of our suppression of Being, a convincing personification of the knot that we have pulled tight between sternum and spine. Stop identifying with persona. Stop being it. Stop fulfilling it. Stop catalyzing it. Stop trying to get rid of it. Stop running from it, and stand true, breathing integrity into your stride, undoing your ego-centered pride. Something is calling you, Something that both includes and transcends all the fragments of you, Something that is already, even now, appearing *as* you, simultaneously free of and bound by limitation, yet unfragmented by Its finiteness, Its mortality, Its need...

-3-

The Three Stages of Conscious Attention

Where is your attention right now? Upon what is it fixed? Is it there consciously? Or has it merely strayed there, unknown to you? Perhaps in this moment it *is* conscious, but for just about all of us, our attention is more often than not unconsciously given... When attention is made conscious, as in most meditative practices, it usually is either deliberately placed somewhere unmistakably specific (as upon the movement of the breath or upon the arising of thoughts), or it is simply allowed to go where it will, without any interference or masterminding, with us doing no more than noticing that it's going there or is there. In both cases, attention is focussed on something *specific*. This is the essence of contemplative awareness practices such as Zazen and Vipassana (except in their advanced stages, where attention is permitted to become more panoramic, more diffuse, more vastly focussed). It is also the foundation, the concentrative anchoring of mysticism, in that it provides the necessary ground-level focus and preparation for journeys into the Unknown, into the regions of the brain where visionary, auditory, and sensory extraordinarinesses can be catalyzed (and exploited!), or into unmappable realms pulsating with a Truth that is as paradoxical as It is real...

Whatever one's practice with consciously-placed attention, it is of great value relative to the unconscious wandering of attention so common to most of us. However, simply placing our attention here and there in the body, mind, psyche, or whatever, is but a stepping-stone, a transitional doing — it is *not* the end or goal of the Awakening process, but only a part of the *beginning*. Our purpose is not to be *thus* conscious all the time, aware of every single breath and every somatic signal — to force oneself into such obsessive awareness, as can happen in certain branches of Vipassana, creates an unnecessary dissociation from Life's passions, a lack of connection to one's vul-

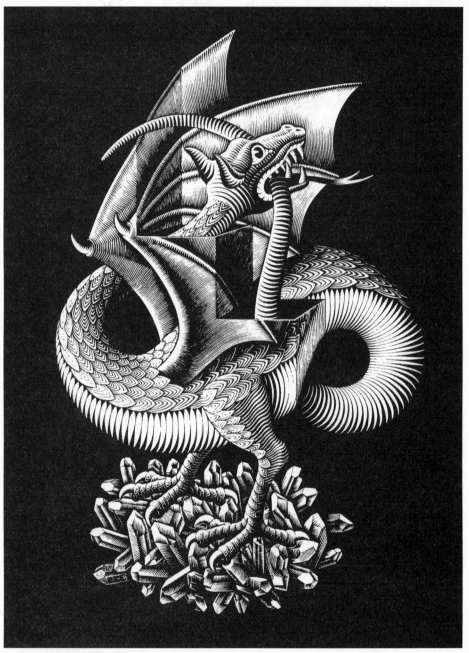

Maurits Cornelis Escher: *Dragon* (Escher Foundation)

nerability, vitality, and humanness. This is but avoidance, a denial of Life, a denial of Death, a denial of Being... The monk or meditator clinging to the noticing of their breath is fundamentally no different than anyone else who is busy clinging to something, worldly or other-worldly. Only in embracing the next level of attention can we fully undo this tendency, this craven urge to fixate attention (consciously *or* unconsciously) on whatever seemingly brings us release, relief, non-anxiety, or immunity from what we are doing to ourselves (namely knotting up our Truth and subdividing our wilderness of Being)...

The next way of working with attention, which I'm calling the second stage of conscious attention, is to be aware of ourself as a totality, to be conscious of our overall presence... This is *not* about just noticing specifics of breath, thought, desire, movement, or intention, but rather is about letting such noticing become *secondary* to the notic-ing of oneself as a presence, a totality, a wholeness (which does not mean *thinking* about such things!). When our attention is thus yielded, spontaneously and consciously yielded, to our *entire* being, some of our attention will still *usually* go to specificities of breath, thoughts, desire, movement and so on, but *in the context of our entirety* — in so doing, there is no halfheartedness, no partiality, no reinforcement of self-fragmentation, emotional dissociation, or spiritual escapism. This kind of attention is close to what Gurdjieff called self-remembering. It is *not* an act of mind. It is not something we can progressively move toward — either we're practicing it, or we're not. It is the natural state of attention in a truly healthy being. (If it's plagued with humorless super-efforts, as in the rigidly repressed case of many of Gurdjieff's "descendants," then it's not attention given to one's full-ness of being, but rather only attention stuck in the service of one's spiritual ambition.)

Become aware now, exactly now, of yourself as a totality. Notice that such awareness is instantaneous. Don't focus on anything in particu-lar, regardless of "your" temptation to do so. Give your attention to the fullness of yourself, not to your heart, not to your belly, not to the light above your head, not to your chakras, not to your itches, not to your urge to do something else, not to your breath, but rather to pure Being, to the *undivided* presence of yourself. Notice what this does to you. Observe the sense of expansiveness you now "have." You have not willfully, through some sort of arcane imaging or etheric yogic practice, projected yourself out and out, extending your energy body, separating out from your physicality — No! The

expansion you feel (and *are*) is natural and inherent. It is not motivated by an urge to build charge or to be powerful or to be protected,
immune, or self-deified — it simply is you realizing, with *all* of
yourself, *who you are*, even though you might not be able to verbalize
such realization. Notice how potent this condition is, and also notice
how amazingly *fragile* it is — let your attention shrink and mechanically wander to a certain detail of body or mind or environment, and
let that detail become foreground, and this awareness of yourself as a
totality is gone, completely gone...

Again, become aware of yourself in your entirety, and then deliberately allow some of your attention to go to your breathing — that is,
permit your attention to be simultaneously focussed on you as presence, and on the sensory details of your breath. Can you feel the
urge to just be aware of your breathing only, to abandon the larger
awareness? Notice this, but do not strain to avoid it; to firmly
establish the second stage of conscious attention is far from an
overnight attainment! It cannot just be held in place through the
power of resolution or determination, for it is more of an allowing
than a forcing, much more of a surrender than an achievement...

The next level of attention is only possible, except for very rare
flashes, when the first two are not only commonplace in one, but also
naturally established, their existence not depending on any sort of
emotional or somatic dissociation (nor upon adherence to any technique). This third level is that of attention being fully yielded to its
Source — in a sense, this is only the fruition, the sublime stretching,
of the second level of conscious attention, a spontaneous, motiveless
realization of the utter interconnectedness of our personal presence
with the Presence of God. In such a condition, "we" are aware of
attention itself, aware of the core mechanics of attention itself, not
merely as a witness to attention, but as pure Consciousness, *inherently* aware of everything arising in It, including all witnessing. In
other words, the third stage of conscious attention is Consciousness
Itself, unmodified, unclouded, undifferentiated, yet paradoxically also
present as whatever arises in It, however solidly embodied. Here,
one recognizes that all attention is but a focussing of Consciousness,
simultaneously transpersonal and personal —

And just who or *what* is doing this focussing? Is it an ambitious
meditator? Is it someone who longs for liberation? Is it someone who
craves release, or is it someone who is already happy, already pres-

ent, already centered? As you hear these words, this voice, who or what is focussing your attention now? Put another way, from where is the motive for this focussing rising? Is there some self-conscious desire in you to be more present, more alert, more divine, some urge to demonstrate the signs, the gorgeously unmistakable signs of spiritual maturity? Look closely — where is your attention now, at this very moment, emerging from? Not where is it going, but from *where* is it now arising? From *where* does it emanate? Where? Now where?

Nowhere in particular. Nowhere at all. It is found where Consciousness exists, and Consciousness has no particular dwelling-place. Or does it? Spiritual paths that focus on the ascension of Life-force usually place the seat of attention somewhere above the top of the head, amongst the fabled petals of the crown chakra, the thousand-petalled lotus of yogic lore. Others, especially those with a foundation in the martial arts, will locate Consciousness in the hara, just below the navel. Others will locate It in the heart or the heart chakra, right at the hub of the emotional center. Others who are metaphysically or occultly inclined will probably locate It just above and between the eyebrows, several inches behind the forehead, in or near the pineal gland...

But this need to give Consciousness a *particular* seat within the bodymind (or just above or around it) is itself just a confession of being stuck at the first level of conscious attention, the level of mandatory specificity (or it can be a confession of being no more than a true believer, fast asleep at the wheel!). Those who are relatively adept at the second level of conscious attention, already deeply centered in their core of Being, will tend to locate Consciousness not somewhere in the body, mind, or psyche (which is roughly equivalent to saying not somewhere in space, time, or subjectivity), but will *experience* It as being everywhere and everywhen. Those who have spent more than a few moments at the third level of conscious attention will not only realize that attention, unbound attention, is everywhere, but that it, as Consciousness, *is* the very substance, the matrix, the breath, the flesh, the form, of *everything*. Everything! It's not simply the essence of pure observation, the Peak of witnessing, the Source of attention, but also the very stuff of the Universe...

It is of no use to believe in this, to believe in the statement that everything is Consciousness. We must *feel* it with our entire being, and throughout our entire being. There's no point in convincing ourselves that the preceding statement about Consciousness is true; there's no point whatsoever in getting married to non-dualistic concepts. The *real* nature of Consciousness can only be realized when one has thoroughly penetrated and lived *everything* that makes up one — dark and light, high and low, superficial and deep. Only when we've consistently made room for *everything* we are (having faced, embraced, illuminated, and passed through it, to the point of luminous embodiment), can we *truly* know that Consciousness is you, me, us, this, that, forever and ever and right now... Where is your attention now? Again, become aware of yourself as a presence. Notice how this almost immediately sensitizes you to your environment, so that you can not only sense what is in front of you, but also what is beside you, below you, behind and inside you... Your body is aware of what is around it, not so much in form as in *feel* (and this awareness, however fleeting, comes from your *whole* body, not just from some concentration-engorged portion of it). In this state, you will ordinarily feel both your boundaries, and your boundlessness, and this will not appear as paradox to you, but as living Truth...

When attention is enslaved to mind chatter and automaticities of appetite, then we are cut off from what truly sustains and nourishes us, ever seeking compensatory distractions, again and again reducing love to an ideal (as in romance, or in *belief* in "unconditional love"), desperately and repetitively submitting ourselves to whatever seems to relieve our suffering. However, when attention is not automatically given to our programming and addictions, but rather is given to the *illumination* of these, then love is *natural* for us, existing not so much as something we have or do, but as the very essence of what we *are*. Real love is full-bodied Ecstasy, fleshed-out knowingness, relational joy, rejuvenative empathy — it is a celebration of the raw-feeling'd recognition of interconnectedness, of Eternal interrelatedness, as well as of diversity and individuation. It is luminous passion, intimate with its every wound. It is the bridge between Formlessness and Form, the primordial embodiment of Consciousness... It is the look, the feel, the stride of *real* freedom. It keeps attention moist; it keeps awareness fertile, juicy, empathetically stained...

Now where is your attention focussed? On love? Or on your *ideas* of love? Again, give your attention to your fullness of Being, letting this very moment bloom and throb and come unequivocally alive. And who or what is this Presence, this totality of Being, that has just absorbed "your" attention? Who? What? Don't look for an answer, but instead *look inside your looking*, letting all your maps be but confetti in endless sky. In such awareness, such wide-awake innocence, such an ancient knowingness, familiarity dissolves (and I speak here of conventional familiarity). Your knowingness here is not of knowledge, not of detail or information, but rather is a knowingness of Being — it is not an escape from the finite, the everyday, the mundane, the limited, but is instead a revelatory illumination of them, a transverbal recognition of them, a lending to them of a perspective that allows them to become aligned, non-Procrusteanly aligned, with Truth, with the primal imperatives of Being...

And again I fall, forgetting the Sacred Call, and again I remember, and again I include it all, and again we are Here, already free, already true, not to just have, but to be, to breathe and be breathed, to form and to unform, to be lovers with the calm and the storm, ever making room for what is unborn, and again I join what's above with what's below, and what's inside with what's outside, and again I recognize the One behind the show, the One present as the show, the One That is nakedly the Many, and again everything's aflame with the Holy Glow, again and again and again...

Sacred Fire

Into the fiery mouth he did leap
Into the blazing pit he did jump
Into the circle of pitted blackstone
he did dance alone
Until the lava altar did quake
and falter, breaking open from within
splintering and petalling
as he did spin
Bursting arcing drooping to reveal a molten head,
an upright oblong pulsing with incandescent song
too hot to take face
And how he did loop it
And how he did breathe with it
And how he did become the eyes of its crimson flowering
and the sky for its volcanic cry
and the crucible for its lushly wrinkled flow
and the voice
of the sudden rainstorm
His hands floating above the steam
His heart exploding through the original dream
His future sitting upon this very spot
This fatly folded carpet of extinguished stone
where only the veiled embers of the dead
still flicker and weightlessly groan,
making wood out of hope and seeking the wrong ears,
forgetting
he who died into the light of the sacred fire,
he who lives EverNow
the wind-pummeled rain carrying his leap
across this sun-fried basin
of crumbling dark

– 4 –

Becoming Intimate with Full-Blooded Ecstasy

JEAN: I've been quite happy lately... When I thought about this session, I felt really excited, but noticed that I was overcontaining my excitement, maybe because I usually just spray it all over the place! (*Laughter*) A lot of the time, I don't seem to know how to be grounded in Ecstasy or in happiness...

ROBERT: Well, to be grounded in Ecstasy is not necessarily like typical grounding or centeredness, with its solid feel, its richly anchored physicality, its visceral intimacy with Gravity... To be grounded in Ecstasy certainly involves a well-rooted embodiment, but it's more like the kind of embodiment or grounding you might feel when you're lucidly centered in a dream, especially a dream in which you know you are dreaming. And how do you stay grounded in such a dream? Your dreambody doesn't need to breathe, so you can't rely on breath awareness; nor does your dreambody need to obey physical laws — it can fly, go through walls, change age and shape, even dissolve or infinitely expand — so you cannot just meditatively focus on the moment-to-moment *details* of bodily sensation, and nor can you necessarily even anchor yourself by paying attention to your mind-processes, for thinking in such a state easily mutates into three-dimensional representations of thought, crazily ballooning cartoonings of mind.

So what's the basis for grounding here? It comes from an *ongoing* sensitivity to the knowingness that "Here I am, dreaming", and, as such, its meditative focus is much more on *presence* than it is on details! It's like at the end of those evenings when *everyone* here is in a state of effortless awareness, not needing to attend to their breath, nor to engage in any *particularized* focussing of attention in order to stay present — their attention is naturally and *already* yielded to the

Presence of Being, the Presence of Primal Mystery, the Presence
That is not other than the core Truth of their identity...

Real Ecstasy carries its own grounding. If you have to separate
yourself from Ecstasy in order to be grounded in it, then it's not
Ecstasy, but only exaggerated pleasure, circumstantial happiness, a
crest of goodcheer, an intoxicating glee. Ecstasy comes from the
Greek word "ekstasis", meaning to stand outside of oneself — you
can read a certain dissociation into this, but it's actually to do with
expanding beyond your assumed boundaries, especially your percep-
tually-determined boundaries, expanding in both presence *and* in
feeling, without any dilution of passion or vitality. To be in Ecstasy
means there's an overflow, a rapturous abundance, of Life-energy,
emanating out with radiant generosity — yes, it *could* spray in all
directions, like a blissbursting, a love-lit fireworks, or it might be
much quieter, stiller, a silent pooling out. And it's not about you
being there expressing Ecstasy — if Ecstasy is really happening, *you
are It*! You cannot *have* Ecstasy, but can only *be* It!

We have to learn to clearly differentiate between pleasure and Ecstasy. Ecstasy is *not* maximized pleasure; it is in an altogether different range than the peaks of pleasure! Also, Ecstasy, if it is real, has at
times an element of sadness in it, a very high level of sadness, a
drama-free grief, so that it might remain in empathetic communion
with all that is, rather than being just a gleeful transcendence of it —
to further clarify, Ecstasy is not only a celebration of the joy of
Being, but also is a profoundly felt acknowledgment of the passing of
all things. In its own way, grief, pure grief, is just as expansive as
Ecstasy. Grief honours the finite, Ecstasy the infinite, and where the
two intertwine, we are truly human, letting our love both soar and
weep. This is the heart, the very root, of compassion...

Everything that you love is going to die, change, rot, pass away, and
you don't have control over that. Feel into this, and it's painful, not
morbidly painful, but sharp with the sense of loss; to avoid feeling
this in the name of self-transcendence or Ecstasy is simply a cop-out,
an act of cowardice and self-denial, an avoidance of the woundedness innate to *real* love. Grief is utterly different from the sadness of
not getting your way; such sadness is self-enclosed, reactive, even
masturbatory, stubbornly implosive. Real sadness, on the other hand,
is not self-enclosed — it's expansive, leaking out all over the place
into a luminous flood. It replenishes, it rejuvenates, it heals, it puts

us in touch with universal grief *and* joy... To me, the appropriate response to the passing of everything isn't detachment or indifference, but both grief and Ecstasy — to acknowledge only what dies, or only What cannot die, is not enough. Our work is to feel both at the same time.

JEAN: Sometimes it hurts me so much to feel loss, even loss that hasn't happened yet... My sadness gets so strong that it opens me, and I know that all I can do is love, no matter what...

ROBERT: Ecstasy is the full-blooded shine of love, the seamless embodiment of love's divinity — it's a confession of love, both love for the other and love for God, a confession that suffuses the entire body, level upon level, with sacred Presence... (*Pause*) You could call Ecstasy love in motion, but you could also say the same for true relationship, Ecstasy being the sky for such motion, relationship the ground. Such relationship is vibrantly intimate, moving not toward picket-fence coupling, but toward a core integrity, a full-bodied and full-souled honouring of both the Eternal and the temporal.

JEAN: For me, relationship involves movement, especially the movement of love...

ROBERT: Yes, but *you* don't move such love — rather, *it* moves you. All you have to do is sensitize yourself to its imperatives, its nudges, and then give up your inertia... You see, we're talking about love with a capital "L". We have to do this to distinguish It from what people usually call love, which is little more than a mishmash of revved-up appetite, sentimentality, and nostalgia. That's not Love!

JEAN: It's swooning...

ROBERT: Yes. Swooning is characteristic of romanticism, just as Ecstasy is characteristic of Love. True lovers are, among other things, ecstatically linked, losing none of their integrity in even their most deliciously blissful encounters. Unlike the romantically inclined, they're not a cult of two! Ecstasy is an expansion, a conscious stretching, of one's boundaries, whereas conventional pleasure is but a mechanical effort to dissolve or lose one's boundaries, whether through sexual indulgence, televisional or pseudo-meditative absorption, drug abuse, or mass participation in the over-interested observation of some sporting event...

JEAN: And the key word is "effort" — there's effort there.

ROBERT: Yes. But paradoxically, it's also laziness incarnate; in fact, laziness is more central to it than effort. It's very easy to dissolve or blur one's boundaries through orgiastic excess, drugs, alcohol, crowd-frenzy, over-amped vicariousness... It's easy to do that; it doesn't take intelligence or sensitivity or groundedness to do that. All it takes is a willingness to discard one's integrity and dignity, a willing-ness to settle for the counterfeit oneness that such self-abandonment catalyzes.

Ecstasy, on the other hand, is effortless, but the creation of its environment is not — such creation is a discipline that asks the very best of us, day after day, moment after moment... (*Long pause*) And Ecstasy has a coolness to it too, a refreshingly cool spaciousness, an unrippled silence, an unspeakably alive silence, whereas intense pleas-ure is merely overheated, swollen, pantingly turbulent, *noisy* with its grasping for its goal. Yes, sometimes Ecstasy can be very hot — say, in the middle of a powerful sexual encounter — but there's still a coolness, a spaciousness, however diffuse, an atmosphere that's more than just heat and sweat. However enthralling ecstatic experience is, it's *not* a disturbance of one's system, but rather a rejuvenation and expansion of it, whereas pleasure is very different, especially unillu-minated pleasure — it's just aflame with its engorgement, its itch, its built-in craving...

JEAN: There's something disturbing about it —

ROBERT: Exactly. That's why it's important not to make such a virtue out of pleasurable excitation. Look at how easily most modern parents let their children *overdo* their play, overcrank their excite-ment, until mere stimulation, hyped-up stimulation, overshadows sensitivity, love, and subtlety — the kids finally get so sated that they run down, numbing themselves, which of course epitomizes how most people have sex! They play with hyper-excitement so much, so unrestrainedly, that they have to get some sort of release from the very *tension* generated by such frenzied stimulation — this is the essence of masturbation, whether carried out in typical sexing, or in the "play" of such children (which all too often carries the very same cruelty, mechanicalness, and mob-stupidities that commonly charac-terize so-called adult activities — these children have already been "adulterated" by our culture's obsessive preoccupation with self-pleasuring), or in the chronically anxious, inflationary cogitating that plagues most of us... (*Pause*) I'm not saying that strong excitement is a no-no, but that it is heavily abused by most, exploited as a substitute for Ecstasy...

Nor is tension necessarily a bad thing. What's commonly thought of as tension is but a neurotic knotting, but there are other kinds of tension, including that which maintains us as individuated forms, as entropy-defying shapings of Life-energy. Such tension is but cosmic Order, ever doing Its sublime dance with cosmic Chaos, the dance that creates and expresses Being...

Ecstasy is a taboo in our culture, camouflaged by its Madison Avenue stand-ins. Ecstatic people cannot be controlled because they don't need someone else to turn them on — they are *already* turned on, already alive with essence-centered pleasure and vitality! They are immune to advertising, sexploitation, drug-lures, and masturbatory stimulation, as well as to parental or governmental force-feeding and conformist-pressurings. They don't have to advertise or flaunt their difference; they may even appear very "normal" outwardly. Nor do they feel lost, alienated, bereft of belonging, so they can't be exploited by those forces or mass movements that come along and enticingly say in so many words: "You can be with us, belong to us, be part of us, *if* you will do the following..." The ecstatic, or even partially ecstatic, are not fodder for the state; they don't make good citizens, but nor are they reactionary rebels, angrily uptight adolescents, perpetually at war with the very structure that they would secretly like to govern (and do occasionally govern, with no better results than their predecessors)... (*Pause*) So when you're dealing with Ecstasy, doing more than just flirting with the possibility of it, you're also dealing with this massively unconscious energy in our culture that says, "Don't be ecstatic! Pleasure yourself into consumerist oblivion, but *don't* get ecstatic!"

JEAN: I can feel that, in the streets, in the supermarkets, all over the place. I can feel it in my past, with my parents and family, how dead that was...

ROBERT: Yes. And even when excitement is pushed and parentally promoted, Ecstasy is still taboo, for it is a terrible threat to the pleasure-punctuated misery that squats at the center of most modern life. Isn't it odd how Ecstasy is commonly viewed as an anomaly, an aberration even (except in infants, where it is tolerated by most, however obscured it may be by protestations of cuteness, poking, mishandling, and "give us a smile" idiocies), a kind of insensitivity, as in: "Can't you see how much suffering there is in the world? How dare you be so happy?" However, Ecstasy, or *real* happiness, non-circumstantial happiness, is precisely what is most useful in working effectively with suffering, because it provides not only the spaciousness and energy needed for such work, but also an *overflow* of *open-eyed* compassion, love, and multidimensional sensitivity! Whereas glee or conventional good cheer, like dourness, doesn't help anyone at all. In short, the presence of Ecstasy is inherently healing...

JEAN: And sensitive.

ROBERT: Yes... If Ecstasy doesn't include sensitivity and subtlety, then it's not Ecstasy, but only a situational high, a byproduct of a particular set of circumstances. Ecstasy cannot be produced or manufactured, for it's *inherent* to Being — it's a profoundly *felt* intuition of the Unspeakable, a body-centered, seamlessly rapturous embracing of God, simultaneously throbbingly alive and serenely spacious, wildly open and exquisitely sensitive, as equally free of mind as it is of false feeling. (*Long pause*)

Much of what I'm doing is teaching people the art of working through what's in the way of Ecstasy. We're just not meant to be miserable slobs who now and then get high or lucky! We're meant to be *truly* happy, established in God-Realizing joy, which of course doesn't mean smiling away our pain, acting happy, or trying to rise above Life's difficulties! What I'm talking about is becoming capable, consistently capable, of accessing such happiness, such feelingly alive spaciousness and love, even under the most trying of conditions. Consciously embodying this does not end or negate our anger or sadness, but rather permits such feelings their purest expression... Primal happiness is already present, seemingly buried, but *that* apparent entombment is only from the viewpoint of your periphery! Go deeper, and it's there, obviously there, at the very center of you, inviting you into its everlasting Heart...

JEAN: To me, it's a fullness... a fullness free of the drama of the situation.

ROBERT: In Ecstasy, there's no central drama, no identification with drama. Ecstasy is, among other things, a transcendence of mind, an abiding in a Realm where mind cannot go, and drama, being largely a mind-product, therefore cannot take root in Ecstasy. Yes, there's a certain drama, a certain mythical colouring that's often playfully associated with the perimeter of Ecstasy, but only the truly archetypal qualities of drama, of grand drama, can penetrate into Ecstasy, and even these disappear at Ecstasy's core... (*Long pause*)

In the Light of Ecstasy, almost all drama is irrelevant, however touching or endearing it might be — it's like a candywrapper in a storm, there for a transparent moment, and then gone, as instantly forgettable as last year's faces of the week. Its existence is not needed for the fullness of Now. This all only makes room for a deeper story, a truer story, the story of us coming into our fullness of Being, the flowering of our capacity both for Ecstasy and for real individuation. (Drama, in the form of *living* myth, can, and even must, serve our *entry* into this native capacity of ours — in the psychic theatre provided by whole-hearted participation in arche-typal myth, we'll find both inspiration and wisdom for the journey of being we know we must undertake.) Ecstasy and individuation must be permitted to co-exist, fruitfully co-exist. Why not at once be ecstatic and live a highly functional life? Why not be a mystic *and* a scientist, a poet *and* a mathematician, a saint *and* a lover? Why flee into the transpersonal, or into the personal?

JEAN: So much of the spiritual teachings from the East say that you can't combine the two. So many of the books I've read preach about transcendence, about there being no such thing as an individual... Years ago, I really thought I had to become an ascetic, that I mustn't develop an ego...

ROBERT: Such teachings, in almost all cases, were and *are* against the body! As if there were something *innately* wrong or problematic with our somatic nature, our fleshiness! Pin the blame on the body, pin the blame on desire, pin the blame on sex, pin the blame on the personal... (*Pause*) Most asceticism is just perverse passion turned inside out, a mere flight from the demands of intimacy and other body-affirming practices — it's just repression in holy robes, an indulgence in escapism, a withdrawal from embodiment. It's anti-sex, anti-body, anti-Life! It's no more virtuous than the grossly indul-gent materialism of the West. Asceticism's split of spirit and matter, of soul and body isn't just the province of the Manichean or the sadhu, but of just about all of us. Such a neurotically rooted duality is counterbalanced by an equally neurotic sense of oneness (as epitomized by crowd frenzy, "non-dualistic" metaphysical conceits, and dissociative meditative practices). However much we might be obsessed by bodily beauty and perfection in our culture, we still are fundamentally body-negative — for most of us, our body is still *down there*, as though *we* are up *here*, holed up in our skulls somewhere! In such compulsive headiness, the body's inherent wisdom is obscured by the posturings of unilluminated mind... (*Pause*)

The mind thinks, but the body knows. However, when we desensitize ourselves to our body, our feelings, our visceral nature, we then associate knowingness with our mind — we try to *think* our way through Life, giving ourselves a break every now and then with a pleasure-plunge into the mess we've made of our somatic reality. Our bodies are saturated with our minds — someone asks us how we feel, and most of us look away, looking into our *mind* for the answer! As if the mind knows! And when we make the mind do other than its true work, we distress ourselves, worrying ourselves to death, trying to compute our way through Life while seeking release from such distress, usually through some sort of bodily indulgence, some sort of somatic *slumming*, as epitomized by typical sex!

Do you see what a mess this is? Make the body wrong, make desire wrong, and you won't be singing your true song. To generalize: The East denies the body, and the West exploits it. The East spurns it, detaches from it, even flagellates it, and the West overfocusses on it, rapes with it, even wants to take it to Heaven! We have to heal ourselves from the ground up, and to do that, we must stop making an object out of our body, whether lowly or idolatrous... (*Long pause*) Some day, for some of us, maybe sexuality will naturally transmute into real celibacy. Or maybe not. Natural celibacy is very, very rare, except in the aged (and even there, it's usually not a *real* celibacy, for the mind is still horny, still robotically lustful, especially in old men, nostalgic for juicy fucking). In almost all cases, celibacy is just repression, like in Muktananda...

JEAN: I remember reading about him — he was talking about how he'd overcome desire and anger, and how in a true spiritual teacher you wouldn't observe anger or desire or sexual feelings.

ROBERT: That's bullshit.

JEAN: So many people believe that, that *that's* spirituality, that they shouldn't have certain desires...

ROBERT: Yes, but look how easy it is! All you have to do is get a little ascetic, become a vegetarian, stop having sex (except maybe with your spouse!), avoid intimacy — you just do it, obey a bunch of tidily laid-out rules. It's so fucking easy! There's no need for subtlety, no need for intelligence, no need to creatively interpret the spirit of the rules! You just follow them, or you're out. And at the other extreme, you've got the more obviously self-indulgent activities of typical hedonists, people exploiting themselves left and right, making a Holy Grail out of the perfect friction! So what *does* work?

JEAN: Feeling our desires, feeling our longings, allowing them to move us, but without getting identified with them, or caught up in having them happen...

ROBERT: Yes... They must be allowed to surface and show themselves. Every one of our emotions or urges that we're afraid of must be faced — given a voice and a face, then a deeper voice and a deeper face, an ever-truer embodiment, an ever-purer, soul-centered expression — until we can be in their presence without self-repression, without *having to* act them out, without having to take on *their* viewpoint... (*Pause*)

The Easterner withdraws from desire, whereas the Westerner, equally fearful, fucks it away, eats it away, busies it away. Both abuse desire; both actually are turned away from desire. Sure, Westerners may be looking to get turned on, stimulated, orgasmed, but as soon as they're bloated with desire, what do they do? They try to get *rid* of it; they try to empty themselves of it. Instead, how about saying, "Okay, here's desire, including hot-blooded desire. Let's let it be here, right here, without any mind-dressing. Let's illuminate it, let's not stand rigidly separate from it, let's embody it without taking on any Life-negative programming it might have been injected with... Let's risk that, let's risk being raw, being passionately alive, being ecstatic!" Wakefulness is crucial here, but so is *direct* participation in our desiring — awakening does *not* require emotional dissociation!

Such risk-taking cuts through fearfulness, especially the futurized fear (anxiety, worry) that erodes so many of us. To reach the place where inappropriate fear (which is at least 99 percent of fear) is

obsolete, we must face what we're afraid of, what we're *really* afraid
of... (*Pause*) Someone who keeps sky-diving over and over again, not
just for the thrill, but to prove to themselves that they're courageous,
may actually only be avoiding facing their fear of not having their
daddy's approval; they may be out to prove that they're not afraid by
doing something that would scare a lot of people, but nevertheless,
they're *still* afraid. They're not facing their *deeper* fear, their fear of
disappointing Daddy, but are only compensating by taking on a *lesser*
fear. Many, many people indulge in this, taking on challenges that
only obscure a deeper, more essential challenge...

But we're not meant to live in fear, anymore than we're meant to live
in invulnerability. Anyone who is busy existing as an ego is living in
fear. Ego is a fear-fueled addiction, a self-enclosed habit that's terrified of its own annihilation, terrified of death, so terrified that it tries
to perpetuate itself, to create a convincing mirage that it'll live
forever — ego dresses up as soul, and then dreams about going to
Heaven, about having a nice little piece of real estate *up there* (I
emphasize "up there" because the whole damned charade is spawned
in the skull), a permanent home. Ego is a denial of impermanence, of
the inherent flux of Life. Ego's too static to be ecstatic! To remain
identified with ego is Hell, the Hell of chronic fear, of missing out on
the richness of Life...

JEAN: There's almost always a sense of partiality of being... When
you were talking about fear, I had so many memories, childhood
memories, of how I would always walk the fence or jump with my
bike or climb to the top of the tree to prove that I could do it, to
prove that I wasn't afraid. I did that a lot...

ROBERT: But you didn't, until very recently, examine what you
were doing that for, did you? There was a deeper fear.

JEAN: It was the fear of death, the fear of being nothing...

ROBERT: Which was rooted in the fear of not belonging... You
knew, right from the beginning, that you didn't belong; you knew
that your parents weren't your *real* parents, that they were only
parents to you genetically, biologically, but not *spiritually*. Sure, you
couldn't articulate this, but you sure *felt* it, and that was terrifying to
you, overwhelmingly so, for there was no-one you could share it
with, no-one whose eyes shone with soul-recognition. So what did

you do to cope? You needed to distract yourself from your inner devastation, your intolerable alienation, your sense of being marooned, so you found *secondary* fears and challenges you could occupy yourself with, fears you could handle, fears whose overcoming established you as an ego! You simply drove yourself to your periphery, losing your intimacy with your core, so that even now, you're *still* afraid, *still* subtly suspicious, of intimacy, of real depth-sharing with another!

You cannot *be* an ego, and be ecstatic. The ego cannot work on itself to the point of Ecstasy — it could do yoga for lifetimes, it could take growth seminars forever, it could do every kind of therapy, it could read every great book, and it still wouldn't have a clue about Ecstasy! Ego is incapable of Ecstasy because of its very structuring. Do you see the hell of this, the built-in hell?

JEAN: Yes.

ROBERT: People keep looking for Ecstasy, not realizing that their very looking, their very search, is the problem! Our assumptions about Ecstasy, about pleasure, about what we need, must be exposed... We must become much more sensitive to our ego-centricity, if we are to ever know essence-centricity and Ecstasy. Being centered in the Essential is necessary for there to be experiential Ecstasy. Being thus centered and being ecstatic are not sequentially related, but are necessarily coexistent, intimately juxtaposed, because they're basically the *same* thing. A centered person without Ecstasy-access is not *really* centered, but only physically (or, more rarely, psychophysically) centered, like a black belt in a martial art — they've got a certain visceral center, but they don't have center in their emotional body, their subtle body (except perhaps in some Aikido adepts), their heart and soul. Sure, they may appear to be more grounded, more consciously embodied than most people — they are, but they're *not* ecstatic! (This is not to say that martial arts mastery and Ecstasy are mutually exclusive; they don't *have to be*!) An ecstatic person is both very powerful and very fragile, because they're not defended in the usual manner. They're both solid and transparent...

JEAN: In the sadness I just felt, I could see how I've built all this protection around me to keep myself from being crushed, to keep myself from being hurt...

ROBERT: All of your defenses have to be artfully encountered, rather than just wiped out, as if all they were was neurotic — the very energy invested in them asks for liberation and love, *not* a different sort of closeting! The binding forces of your resistance need light, not do-gooder might! It's so damned easy to put vulnerability on a pedestal! If you, in the name of supposed Truth, prematurely dismantle your defense mechanisms, their blueprint will remain intact, and will flesh itself out again as soon as your enthusiasm wanes... (*Long pause*)

Being vulnerable, even *healthily* vulnerable, doesn't necessarily make one ecstatic, yet vulnerability is a prerequisite for Ecstasy. It isn't easy; in fact, it's maybe the hardest part of the journey. Why? Because you have to get vulnerable, really vulnerable, without Ecstasy necessarily coming — you're going to *have to* nakedly experience the level of vulnerability associated with helplessness, and that can be excruciatingly difficult to work with... To stay present in that incredibly hurtful place that your whole life has been an avoidance of, is a matter of great courage and determination and true love of Self. Stay with it, and you'll eventually find a vulnerability that's a *source of strength*, a vulnerability that aligns you with the Source of all, a vulnerability that's rooted in empathetic Ecstasy. But to go *through* the helplessness, to face the deep hurt in us, we need support, allies, true friends, an environment in which we can sustain our effort and nourish what's just starting to grow in us — this is a lot of what Xanthyros is about.

Center arises from a mature vulnerability, a strongly activated willingness to accept and love the wounded you, the you who is incredibly vulnerable. And while center is yet unformed, embryonic, and we are vulnerable, we are in a very difficult position — since there's no center of being (except momentarily) to provide stability for our vulnerability, we'll tend to close off, to go to the surface, to rationalize such flight. *This* is why we need each other! We need real friends, real allies, to help us make the transition from no center to substantial center — more precisely, we need to do it both alone *and* together, both in solitude and in relationship... (*Pause*)

Now, you know, all along the way, there'll be tastes of Ecstasy, bits of bliss, and there'll also be a making of associations between such rapture and the particular circumstances present at such times — we'll likely try to reproduce such conditions so as to get more of that rapture, which of course only has the opposite effect. The Ecstasy along the beginning path is a treat, a reminder, a gift, a divine gift, that we should be grateful for, rather than resenting —

JEAN: — For not happening more! (*Laughter*)

ROBERT: Yes.

JEAN: I've done that. And it's also where a lot of my fighting comes from, from feeling myself being too dependent on this or that for my happiness. And yet, beneath it all, I *do* need!

ROBERT: And when you let that need *really* come alive, independent of mind and manipulation, then you'll be intimate with Ecstasy, regardless of your mood! Take need to its ultimate sense, to its very core, and you'll feel your *total* dependency on the Universe for your very existence, let alone your continuation. You're not truly separate from any of it, not at all! That's why there's no need to try to be special. Why do that, when you're *already* innately unique, *already* in communion with the very Essence of it all? Well, we do that when we separate ourselves from what truly nourishes us — we build our specialness, our little bastion of *apparent* independence, as a buffer against our despair, a mirage of somebody-ness to plaster over our sense of worthlessness, of nobody-ness.

Such is the machinery of ego, or unconscious identification with persona, with specialness... Break that identification, and ego will become permeable to Essence, a way of expressing the colour, the flavour, the peculiarities and wonders of your particular individuality. A healthy persona is *dramatically* appropriate, strong yet flexible, lit by an awareness that it is not "I", but only a marvellously nuanced mask of external considering, of societal skill, a mask that serves the needs both of one's Essence and of one's environment. Such a mask has to be fluid, almost like water, but it also needs to have definition, to have its own feel, its own uniqueness. It acts without *re-acting*...

In the East, persona is devalued, put down, viewed as an illusion, an obstacle to spiritual growth, and in the West, persona is glorified, blown-up, paraded, made newsworthy. In our culture, we exploit persona. We dress it up, and let it live our lives and drive our cars and fuck our spouses. As egos, we're fascinated by other egos, especially those of media stars; they get immensely rewarded for playing their roles, so we unconsciously think that if we too play our role, our designated role, to the hilt, we too will get rewarded, whether with sex, money, recognition, or Heaven! What an idiotic game!

JEAN: Such strong images I see — the magazines, the newspapers, all the headlines and gossip — I remember looking at magazines and thinking, if I dressed like that or looked like that, then I could be happy, I could have what I thought I needed...

ROBERT: Those are our role models, literally, *role models*, mannequins, larger-than-life somnambulists, glued to their stage, stuck in tabloid hell, pinned to fame! What hell! And those who envy the famous are only feeding on them — it's a case of mutual parasitism, with long-life pacifiers stuck in its multi-mouthed face! (*Long pause*) Ego is looking for immunity, whether through inflation, or through extreme deflation; it wants to live forever, and so drives its conditioning into its children, passing on the generational madness that plagues humanity. But look — since ego is just something we are *doing* to ourselves, it is also something we can undo, or radically alter. It's meant to be altered. I don't care how old we are. They say you can't teach an old dog new tricks, but you can if the old dog wakes up!

Look at Gail now. [*Gail has been observing the session, and will participate with Jean in the transverbal work that'll end the session*] Immediately, there's love flowing between you and her, a warm, richly alive love between two individuals (*Speaking slowly*)... But also notice an even deeper love, a love of Something That sees Itself reflected in her eyes — What you're gazing at in Gail's eyes is also gazing out through your eyes... It's not primarily personal, yet It's very, very loving, brighter than any thrill-produced love could ever be... (*Long pause*) So there's an impersonal love here, and a personal love, both occurring simultaneously, neither one being essentially senior to the other...

Usually, we only want to feel one of them — we go into the impersonal (or transpersonal) dimension of love, and we end up reducing its magnificently compassionate Indifference and Detachment into escapist indifference, monkish detachment, intimacy-recoil — or we go into the personal dimension of love, and we end up reducing it to romanticism, to sentimentality, to an arena wherein we can dramatize our neuroses ad nauseum... (Pause) But if you will feel *both*, as you are now, the transpersonal will make breathing room for the personal, and the personal will give grounding to the transpersonal, keeping it moistly compassionate...

As you look more and more deeply at each other and into each other, letting yourselves be flooded by love and Ecstasy, it'll be obvious to you that trust is absolutely essential to this (*Speaking more and more slowly*)... Ecstasy does not happen without trust — an ecstatic being is present as deep trust for the whole Universe, for Being, for What animates It all, for the fundamental laws of Manifestation. An ecstatic being lives in accord with such primal laws... (*Long pause*) You now know, without thinking about it, that the Core of all this is not about knowledge — there's no payload of information that'll unleash Ecstasy. The Core is simply everlastingly overflowing with knowledge-less knowing. Do you not feel that?

As you continue looking at each other and loving each other, there's no need to know anything in particular, but there is an undeniable knowingness, an unspeakably lucid intuition about it all... It's profoundly simple, complex only in its outer mechanics... Once you're established in this sublime simplicity of trust and love, then immensely valuable insights can flow forth from you. But if the love isn't there, if the trust isn't there, then any emerging insights won't be of much value — they'll likely just ossify into philosophy, into various belief systems, into various fencing-ins of cleverness... But in the love that you both now are surrendered to, your insights are luminously permeable, more like mandalas than data print-outs, more like templates for the very best you can do than tidy little effort-catalyzers... And is not this Ecstasy, this glowing ease, this unclouded Happiness, more than something that's just happening to you? Is it not *you*?

Woke Up Feeling Kinda Thick

Woke up feeling kinda thick
Looked out my window
Sky an ashen brick
My eyes squirming in a dull grip
My mind scratching itself
Fingering the sores
Body squashed behind unseen doors
Yes I woke up this morning
Finding myself still asleep
My breath a sluggish little stream
Oozing sullen slow and sludgygreen
Woke up this morning
Spreadeagled in the phlegm of some dream
Sick of meditative manipulation
Sick of psychic ejaculation
Sick of seducing my moods away
Woke up feeling so damned thick
Thoughts like boxcars packed with bricks
Got out of bed I did
Staggering under my head
Blinking at my yawning kneecaps
Giving the mirror less than a glance
My flesh like a mushy fist
My mind churning out illegible lists
But I sat in my mood
Watching its mind unwind
Watching it change by itself
Just like the sky this morning
With all its black dumplings silverbright
I woke up feeling kinda thick
Doing nothing
Except lighting up the fog
Moods come and go
I don't

-5-

Into the Heart of
Endarkened Moods

When circumstances, inner or outer, are such that we feel crushed, depressed, downcast, shrunken, dejected, plagued with doubt, riddled with despair, or otherwise miserable, we may all too easily find ourselves *believing* the viewpoint of our mood, binding ourselves to its dour logic. We may push away what we *really* need at such times, withdrawing into neurotic seclusion, unresistingly submitting to the pharmaceuticals dispensed by our mood, permitting the mind-riddled biochemistry of psychophysical disturbance to stream through us without any interference...

We stress ourselves unnecessarily at such times. We literally shrink and de-press ourselves, immersing ourselves in doubt after doubt, finding a perverse satisfaction in continuing to indulge in doubt (there's a sense of reassuringly *solid* identity in doing so, as epito-mized by the ever-popular credo: I am miserable, therefore I am), especially in the face of opposition to our mood from those around us who are at that time more stably established in happiness, in center, in non-collapse of Being — they can obviously see what we're up to and we *know* it, yet we still usually persist in staying miserably contracted, resisting their penetration as though it were actually *equivalent* to the insensitive, loveless penetration we have suffered from others in our past. This is the ugliest sort of indulgence, the pout of rigidly defiant doubt. It is us being loveless (and resolutely *impermeable* to love) right in the midst of our twisted calling out for love...

There are times when, for various reasons, we are overwhelmed by certain conditions, no matter how mature we may be, no matter how centered we ordinarily are, no matter how lovingly alive we usually are. There are times when we seem to lose it all and fall, fall, fall into

Gustave Doré: *The Bible*

a pit of darkness and ignorance, a pit teeming with self-loathing, self-doubt, cynicism, and denial of the Divine. This is *not necessarily* the so-called "Dark Night of the Soul" — it doesn't usually have the intensity or multidimensional *risk* of that. It is more like a low-grade infection; it's not cancer, but only a nasty head cold, an itchy fever, a squirmy unpleasantness, the essence of which is exaggerated self-containment or shrinkage of Being. When *we allow* circumstances, inner or outer, to squeeze us into such contractedness, of course we suffer, and of course we look for release, usually sometime after we have thoroughly indulged our self-entrapment, perhaps making those around us as miserable as possible, seeking their company (and agreement about how terrible it all is) in our dark stagnation.

In the very midst of such self-indulgence we need to ask ourselves "Who's going to clean up the mess?" The one we are when we are busy reinforcing our misery doesn't give a shit about cleaning up the mess we are making. Someone else has to do it, and unfortunately, that particular us is usually plagued by guilt and recrimination, seeking but falling short of real self-forgiveness for what was done during the earlier acting-out. What I'm talking about is reactivity. It is essential that we know that we are being reactive as soon as it occurs. If we have the good fortune to have someone point out to us that we are being reactive, we ought to immediately stop, breathe deeply, let in what they've said, *fully* consider it, and, if they are right, change course, honestly and nakedly confessing our inner whereabouts, letting ourselves lose face without losing touch, letting ourselves melt, letting ourselves directly *feel* our need for healing contact, for love, for awakened attention, in effect letting down (or at least *illuminating*) the barriers we have erected and embodied...

When we are burdened by a depressive or hurtful mood, we need to see what we are up to; we need to recognize and clearly acknowledge our withdrawal from What nourishes and sustains us. We need to see our pout, our sulk, for what it is — a denial of our connectedness with All That Is, a recoil from relatedness and human communion, a retreat into numbing immunity, indifference, invulnerability, a flight from intimacy. Such gross protectionism does no good at all, except perhaps in certain situations where there is a very real danger to us if we do expose ourselves.

To take care of ourselves when we are depressed, crawling with doubt, festering with despair, or otherwise troubled, requires that we remember who we are, not so much in terms of content as in terms of feeling — to allow ourselves to feel, to *fully* feel ourselves when we are down and out (or up and in!) breaks through the walls with which we have surrounded ourselves, thawing our limbs and de-straitjacketing our torso and uncramping our minds. When you're inundated by reactivity, dejection, dread, and so on, interrupt your dramatics for a moment, and ask, "Whose point of view, or which point of view, am I now taking on or acting out?" You may even want to describe out loud what that particular standpoint sees and assumes — instead of just immediately saying "I see...", preface your description with something like "This is my fear (or doubt or depression or anxiety or reactivity) speaking." In other words, give the context for what you are about to say — *clearly state which "I" you are busy being.* Speak *its* mind for a few minutes. Deliberately exaggerate *its* characteristic gestures, especially facially and posturally. Notice how predictable its outlook is. Notice how drearily familiar its terrain is. And notice how unrelentingly self-obsessed its script is...

The point is not to escape or rehabilitate this land, this endarkened domain you've put yourself in, but rather is to illuminate it with Awakening force, with love, with a pioneering spirit, with guts and subtlety, and when that occurs you will *naturally* be carried into and through your state or mood — you will not have, in some yogic or therapeutic fashion, manipulated yourself out of your condition, but instead will have surrendered to your condition in such a manner that you are not only no longer bound by it and its viewpoint, but are also *intimate* with it, in deep embrace with its energies and fertile possibilities. You cannot strategically put yourself in such a position; the whole affair is one of spontaneity, naturalness, non-rehearsal, and faith, deep faith. It is a fluidly alive marriage of effort and non-effort, an act of one's totality...

If you think about this too much, you will sink. Thinking about it does little good, but *noticing* that you are thinking about it is of some use. When you can at least say "I am depressed" or "I'm down" or "I am hurting" or "I'm closed", ask yourself who it is who is *aware* of such depression or pain, and you will immediately observe that that particular you is not depressed, not hurting, not shut down, but rather is witnessing incarnate. However, there is no point in escaping into pure witnessing or disembodied Consciousness — witnessing must be intimately coupled with a deep willingness to feel, unobstructedly feel, the *totality* of oneself, whatever the pain or joy.

It is a fine art to be passionately involved in Life and, at the same time, to remain centered in one's core of Being. To be thus involved (and therefore *attached*, such attachment not necessarily being a hindrance to awakening, despite the humorless bleating to the contrary of various spiritual approaches) would perhaps seem to mean that occasionally certain circumstances would blast one away from one's center, apparently so distancing one from one's core that there'd be no hope, at least in the moment, of behaving sanely. This, however, is not true. The physical and emotional signs that we tend to associate with being centered may be obliterated by our condition, and yet center remains. It must be intuited, felt, and felt with our entire Being, not just perceptually, physically, or emotionally, but with our everything — our center of Being is more than our center of gravity, more than our center of mentalizing, more than our centers of sensing and feeling. It may at times seem to be encapsulated, concentrated somewhere in particular, but its domain is seamless, unpolluted by even the worst of our moods. The point is to remain conscious. Perhaps I can clarify what I'm saying about maintaining center by talking a bit about the difference between the waking and dreaming states with regards to meditative activity...

In the waking state, we can sit still, close our eyes, and pay attention to our breathing, perhaps counting one on the exhale, two on the next exhale, and so on up to ten, then start at one again, over and over and over, until there is some stability or equanimity of mind, some single-pointedness. Or attention may be given to the rising and falling sensations in the belly (or the expansion and contraction of the small of the back) created by the movement of our breathing. In other words, our breathing becomes the object for meditative focus. However, in the dreaming state, awareness of the breathing of our physical body is, except in extremely rare circumstances, not at all present.

Nevertheless, it *is* possible to be conscious during the dreaming state, to simultaneously be aware that we are dreaming and still remain in the dream, even though we're aware of being in bed (not perceptually, but intuitively), of our body being asleep, of roughly what time it is perhaps, of different intentions we've made during the waking state — we're still surrounded by (and part of) the vividly three-dimensional environment of our dreamscape, which is every bit as real to us as the phenomena of the so-called waking state. Now, what maintains awareness here is not a focus on breath, but rather a focus on our totality, a moment-to-moment remembering of ourself (a more partial or flimsy awareness can be maintained by focussing on certain dream details). The continuity of unstressed awareness in the dreaming state does not require a concentration on something *specific*, be it physical, emotional, or whatever... Doing such a practice in the *waking* state maintains center no matter what our mood or condition. If we insist on being in a certain state before we can be centered, then we're setting ourselves up for a lot of suffering — why insist on the presence of our breath, or of a particular sensation or asana or time or climate or whatever? Better to be aware of ourselves as a presence, a wholeness, a totality (which *doesn't* mean *thinking* of ourselves thus!), and to let the noticing of details be gracefully *secondary* to such awareness...

Now back to the dynamics of being depressed, down, dejected, despairing, seemingly centerless — at such times, we ought not to rely on what we ordinarily rely on to be stably established in some sort of loving sanity. What if the body is ill? What if you have a splitting headache? Great suffering in the flesh? Immense emotional pain? Heartbreaking grief? Soul-numbing shock? A deep shattering of love or home? At such times, there's no point in trying to recenter through our usual methods (to insist on doing so is but a violation of Self) — the signs that we look for as indications that we're centered must eventually be let go of, and a *deeper* trust allowed to emerge, so that awareness is not dependent on body/mind signs, but rather is simply present as part of our uninhibited trust in Life Itself. This is not naive trust, a martyr-like throwing of oneself into the nearest wind — it is a trust overflowing with knowledgeless wisdom, a trust whose very heart throbs in resonance with its Source, a resonance that keeps one profoundly empathetic with the human condition, not just in general, but *specifically* and vulnerably...

This talk could be called "What to do when you are in emotional pain, or physical pain, or just plain suffering from a severe case of mistaken identity." In some ways, it's about what *not* to do. There's no point in rising above our pain, nor in indulging it, nor in anesthetizing it, nor in affirming its non-existence, nor in escaping into pure witnessing of it, nor in making oneself right or wrong relative to it. The key is to openly confess what we're feeling, what we're *actually* doing, what we're assuming. We have to pull down the pants of our neuroses. We have to uproot our irony, our detachment, our disembodied safety. We have to level the monuments of our cynicism, and drain the swamps of our sentimentality. In short, we need to break down the very structure, the primal latticework of our needless suffering, and confess all of this with *energy*, not just in some shrunken or dejected manner, but with embarrassingly intense passion, nakedness of face, and gutsiness of humor, so that whatever shame is present in us can gush loose and flush out our entire system, warming and blushing us freer and freer of our recoil from intimacy.

Losing face without losing touch is what it's all about. Letting go of being right. Letting go of being wrong. Letting go of our depression's song, realizing that depression is not a feeling at all, but a pressing down of feeling, a mind-heavy collapse of real emotion. Depression is no more an emotion than is hysteria; both are but opposite sides of the same thing, namely a recoil from real feeling...

Those who are depressed simply need to feel, and in order to feel, they need to loosen the grip they have on themselves, undoing the clamp they have on their heart and longings. This isn't easy for them, because they don't trust; they're afraid that if they let go, something terrible might happen to them, so they usually stay right where they are — nevertheless, something unpleasant *is* now happening to them, right where they are, but at least it isn't terrible, but only rotten, mediocre, unhappy, and, above all, *theirs!*

At least they know that this is *their* state, and that it will be their state for as long as they damned well please, as long as they maintain their exaggerated repression and avoid those who could free them, those who could help them to awaken. They prefer the safety of their misery, the dense predictability of it, as compared to the utter lack of guarantees in the Unknown. They don't trust anything except their mistrust. They don't realize the inherent Mysteriousness of all that is. As they deny their identity with such Mystery, they make a lifestyle out of their miserable little dramas, imprisoning themselves in low-key melodrama, consoling themselves with occasional forays into amplified sensation, pleasurable release, distractions of various kinds, mind-games, and so on...

It's not just that everybody has their good days and their bad days. Most of us have mostly bad days, our so-called good days being only *situational* highs. This talk is meant primarily for those who have already begun to awaken, but who still find themselves troubled by their moods, their peaks and valleys, and who do not wish to escape into monkish or dissociative witnessing, nor into compensatory pleasuring and mentalizing, nor into degenerative catharsis. This talk is especially intended for those who are beginning to be irresistibly drawn toward an alertness that is not at all divorced from the passions, lusts, highs and lows, darknesses, and fathomlessness of Life.

Do not expect that as you work on yourself more deeply and deeply that you will have less and less hurt. You may hurt more, much more, for a while. As you mature, the fire will inevitably get hotter and hotter (since you'll be closer to it), but you will learn to welcome its heat because you'll know that it also brings light — you'll see yourself more and more clearly in the firelight, even as the non-essential in you is consumed by the flames, all blame gone to ashes, a joyously functional responsibility, a guilt-free accountability, filling you out as you yield to your awakening heart's pure desire, the ruins of what you once took to be yourself now but fertile soil for the fleshing out of your soul...

This, of course, is not about not having bad moods, unpleasant times, crankiness and so on, but is about making good use of them. I myself began this talk in a wretched mood, sluggishly downcast, nastily exhausted, but knowing that there was something to be done with it besides escaping it, something that would be of value to me, and perhaps to those who hear this talk. After a few minutes of talking, I noticed that my mood had motivelessly dissolved, even as I felt my way to its labyrinthine core. It and I were no longer at odds, and it was no longer an it, but simply reclaimed me...

One more thing: Don't let your commitment to waking up waver with your moods. Otherwise, you will always be rebuilding center, from scratch; you will not be building on what has been previously attained or realized. Beginning thus again and again gradually becomes a very enervating process, making more and more room for the phantoms of doubt, perhaps even to the point of forgetting our purpose in undertaking such work, so that we fall prey to the egregious habit of making major decisions when we are less than open...

A subtle enjoyment of bad moods is actually possible, not the perverse enjoyment of one who is indulging in such moods and hurting others by doing so, but rather the enjoyment of one who is working with endarkened moods, wisely using them, letting their energies be fuel for self-revelation, breakthrough humor, and wakefulness. Dare to be such a one. Don't avoid your bad moods; don't try to make sure they don't happen, or try to drink, think, or shrink them away. Welcome them when they arrive, with the openness not of a fool, but of a spiritual warrior. Don't make an enemy out of your endarkened moods — find their hidden doors, their dungeoned cries, their canals and tunnels and passageways, going into them with open eyes and dissolving disguise, until they transmute into something utterly different, something that is but available Life-energy. This is what it's all about — staying available, potently receptive, no matter what's occurring, no matter what the weather, letting our Truth shape us, both in calm and in storm...

Gustave Doré: *Perrault's Fairy Realm*

– 6 –
God is Not Elsewhere:
Making an Ally
Out of Unsettledness

(James says that he has been feeling unsettled lately, unpleasantly off balance, awkwardly adding how concerned he is that he's not feeling God in the midst of his day-to-day activities)

ROBERT: How do you know that what you're feeling isn't God?

JAMES: I don't know that.

ROBERT: Then why do you assume it? Why do you assume that what you're feeling isn't God?

JAMES: Because I have ideas about God.

ROBERT: Such as...

JAMES: That the feelings associated with God should be rapturous and ecstatic.

ROBERT: Because...

JAMES: Because... *That's* what I'd like to feel! *(Laughter)*

ROBERT: Exactly! That's what *you* would like to feel! And just *who* is it that needs to feel such feelings? It's the you who doesn't feel so good, and who therefore wants to feel those juicy feelings in order to feel better about himself. If you *already* felt good about yourself, you wouldn't have to go looking for a way to feel better — the well-being you were embodying would create its own momentum for going deeper into God. But why limit God to rapture? Do you mean that what is non-rapturous is *not* God? And if it isn't, then *what* is it? You could call it James! (*Laughter*) See, James is very busy convincing himself that what he is experiencing isn't God. So what can we do about that? After all, it is *his* conviction, literally so, even though there isn't actually a real him, a discrete entity, making the conviction, but just the deeply-imbedded personification of a bunch of dumb habits. (*Pause*) Is it all God?

JAMES: Yes.

ROBERT: How do you know that?

JAMES: I don't.

ROBERT: Is the feeling of not feeling God also God?

JAMES: Yes.

ROBERT: That's just a belief, a facile answer. Beliefs usually get in the way — if you're caught up in believing something, then you're not in real touch with God. Even though everything's God, you're busy being that aspect of God that doesn't believe it is God! It is obsessed with itself, obsessed with maintaining its particularity, obsessed with ossifying its apparent identity, obsessed with being self-enclosed. That's what pain is, to become shrunken, to enclose on yourself, to rigidly encapsulate yourself, and then, when sufficiently miserable, to go out *seeking* happiness, relief, release, pleasurable distraction, or some other facsimile of what you've already turned away from. This is madness, mass madness...

It's like that story of Mullah Nasrudin where he's out in the middle of the night, out in the street on all fours underneath a street lamp. A friend comes by, and asks what he's doing. Nasrudin replies that he lost his house keys, and the friend says, "Well, you mean you lost them out here?" "No," says the Mullah, "I lost them in the house, but there's more light out here." (*Laughter*) Just like you, James, in your wanting to go where there's more rapture. The very you who wants more rapture is *inherently* miserable and self-bound, and to be *really* happy, you must expose that particular entity, rather than merely trying to fulfill its apparent needs! Just see what we so easily do — we want to fulfill the needs of that particular somebody, rather than illuminating its real nature and going right through it, until the very habit of animating it no longer attracts our attention.

When you are concerned that you are not feeling God, all you are really saying is that you are experiencing something that doesn't suit your notion of how you *should* be feeling. You're trying to outguess God, to do it better than God, as in "Oh, this feeling shouldn't exist, this mood ought not to be allowed...to be anywhere...especially in me! Yes, indeed, this is most definitely *not* spiritual! I'm not supposed to feel this way!" In this, you, fragmented, self-obsessed you, have your very own program for the Universe, wherein James is perfectly pampered, eternally happy and untroubled, forever immune... and is *still* James!

James has to be sacrificed, not so that individuality is eradicated, but so that a *true* individuality can emerge, one that is intimate with the Timeless... So how do you sacrifice James? (*Long pause*) Certainly not through annihilation or disembodiment, or any other such ego-centered programs! You just stop taking his programs for survival so fucking seriously! Now, let me ask you: Is there an actual entity called James?

JAMES: Yes.

ROBERT: Where?

JAMES: Here. (*Laughter*)

ROBERT: Where? (*James points to his head*) Where's that?

JAMES: My head.

ROBERT: Whose head?

JAMES: This entity that includes James.

ROBERT: How do you know it's an entity?

JAMES: Inside it, there's a feeling of existence.

ROBERT: Where?

JAMES: It's total, it includes the whole of me...

ROBERT: Why personify it?

JAMES: It's what I know.

ROBERT: You don't know it. There are some thoughts about it, and those thoughts create the illusion of a thinker, a thinker who has the good sense to call himself James! You still have the sense, it seems, that somewhere inside you there's this soul, this divine somebody, this discrete entity that will pass on from lifetime to lifetime, complete unto itself, self-contained, with its very own evolutionary blueprint. But if you truly look, you won't discover that there's someone inside — all you'll discover is the *personification* of your own inwardness, your own urge to reassure yourself with things or experiences you can find inside! It's hard to talk about this, because to do so I have to say "I" and refer to you as a "you", even though that's not necessarily how it is. Can you make sense of this?

JAMES: No.

ROBERT: Why?

JAMES: I don't know. I'm just not able to — I can try, but it just doesn't seem to be appropriate. I know that I've... I'm having a hard time talking.

ROBERT: I know. (*Pause*) So what's true?

JAMES: This feeling of existence is true.

ROBERT: So, in other words, *something* exists. But why fragment it into different pieces, such as the one called James? Don't you see how arbitrary that is? There are two great processes going on at once here — there's you flowering as a real individual, living out your particular destiny as an apparent entity (and that's as honorable as it's necessary), and hand in hand with that, there's also a co-existent purpose, that of awakening to God, of waking up fully. They go together — you don't get to realize God if you ignore or rise above your individuality's needs and imperatives. This embrace of the temporal and the Everlasting is paradoxical to the mind, but Truthful to the heart. You tend to view Existence through your mind-filters, so you're usually caught up in either/or, right/wrong, good/bad, should/shouldn't, and so on — all the usual dualities...

But if you come from your heart, not just your physical heart, but from your psychoemotional, spiritual heart, your center of deep soul-feeling, then things are not automatically divided, but are whole, even in their sharpest diversity. However, you can't *think* your way into that; you can't just say, "Well, that's a great idea! I'll come from my heart now..." That's just one more dumb resolution, seeded with its own destruction. (And why? Because it arises not from your core of Being, but only in your mind and enthusiasm, carrying in its underbelly another aspect of you that doesn't give a damn about growth.) You don't get to your heart of Being through resolutions; you have to illuminate the *whole* process, entering into it with your entire being. Otherwise, you'll always be fighting yourself in it — part of you will be gung-ho about it, and another part will be saying, "That's bullshit; it doesn't make sense, and I'm damned if I'm going to go along with it."

I'm feeling our encounter as I talk to you, but you're still trying to...grasp it *mentally*. You ought to instead be taking hold of it psychospiritually, feeling-ly, letting your urge to grasp soften, letting your attention go to something other than your mind. Others in this room are starting to click into what I'm saying. If you go into yourself deeply enough, you will locate the place in you where you *already* know exactly what I'm talking about. You then won't agree with what I'm saying, and nor will you disagree — instead, you'll *feel* it, soulfully feel it, and everyone else in the room who is now living at a similar depth in themselves will also feel the very same thing, because at *that* level, we are *literally* all one, sharing the same Unity of Being. When you're consciously existing as that depth of yourself, you cannot help but have the same fundamental perception or intuition of something as someone else who is also abiding at the same depth in themselves. Then you don't just have opinions, the conditioned little prepackagings of "Oh, I see it this way, and you see it that way" or "I create my reality, and you create yours" (the epitome of infantile omnipotence fantasy and ego-centricity!) or "Truth is relative."

Instead, you reach the domain of what Gurdjieff called "objective knowledge", or *Essence-centered* knowingness. To get there, you can't be farting around on the periphery of yourself, snorkeling the shallows, mindfucking about this and that, looking for safety and immunity and satiation, looking for how to not feel unsettled — it's good to feel unsettled! You *need* to be uprooted, until you find a truer ground. You need to breathe yourself looser, James. You tend to be a serious seeker; your favorite role is that of the serious student, the ardently serious seeker (*Laughter*), stiff with sincerity, constipated with good intentions, the bashfully earnest young man firmly astride the path of self-realization! (*Laughter*) That's just a game, a low-grade game.

JAMES: (*Sheepishly but happily*) Gimmee a break!

ROBERT: Give us all a break! 'Cause you can make a problem out of just about *anything!* You go about making a problem out of it, you decide to then look for a solution, and your mind comes galloping in: "Ah, have I got some solutions for you, James!" (*Laughter*) You take them to head, you get hooked and booked, thereby only creating more problems, and all the while there you are combatting the nasty aspects of your mind, *heroically* resurrecting your witnessing capacity, trying to get some distance from all those horrible mind-scenarios that make you so anxious — you're just fighting off all these unpleasantries with the do-gooder side of your mind, the side that likes to do positive thinking, affirmations, inflationary make-believe, the side that is stuck on hope. Simply put, you're combatting mind with more mind; you're mixing hot air with hot air. What do you then get? You get *more* hot air! Inflation, James (*Laughter*), to compensate for your underlying sense of deflation. But why not go beyond this seesawing of inflation and deflation? Why not go deeper than the drama of agreement or disagreement?

Feel what I'm saying, *feel it now* — because I could say the same thing in a very different way to someone else ten minutes later. I'm speaking with this particular vocabulary, this phrasing, this texturing and resonance of voice, this quality of eye contact, these movements of my arms and hands, because of your energy right now and mine, and the ambience and spirit-presence of this room — it's all quite unique to this moment. So welcome your sense of being unsettled, and *use* it to find a deeper sense of settledness, a truer sense of being at home, realizing that you cannot *truly* make a home out of a steppingstone or plateau that's partway along your path — you can rest there, you can rejuvenate yourself there, but then you need to move on, to go beyond your inertia, to go deeper...

Implicit in this is the need to make friends with our insecurity, especially with the *inherent* insecurity of Life, rather than just wishing that things were different, that "I could be secure right now if only I had the right partner, the right environment, the right music, the right stuff, the right practice, the right this, that, or the other." That's just neurotic bargaining, the prime equation of misery. On the otherhand, if you *really* embrace insecurity, you'll be happy, not necessarily smilingly or rapturously happy, but you'll be happy in the sense that you'll be in deep contact with the very core of Life, with the innate changeability of Life. And when you become intimate with this great changeability, this spin of seasons, you will also, paradoxically, come into equally profound contact with the Eternalness of Life. The two go hand in hand; if you go deeply and consciously into one, you meet the other. If you avoid one, you will also avoid the other...

So that's the art here, to go all out into both our *true* individuality and our Eternal nature. A feeling of being unsettled can be used as a springboard into that, just like any other feeling can. Whatever's happening in this moment provides the perfect environment for such realization. The point is to not turn away from anything, including insecurity, dread, and terror. If you're only wanting to have superficially pleasurable feelings or sensations, you'll live a mediocre life, not discovering the depths of yourself, unless perhaps some huge crisis comes along and shocks you awake, and even if that happens, you'll probably go right back to sleep.

Your need, our need, is not only to locate our willingness to wake up, but also to wisely cultivate it, to nourish it no matter what our mood or circumstance. Every time you welcome an endarkened feeling or mood and work well with it, going right to the heart of it, you stabilize your awakening, bringing your James-ness into a more Life-expanding alignment with your essential nature...

William Blake (British Museum)

–7–

Embodying the
Passionate Witness

When we compulsively busy ourselves seeking an alternate experience, we only strengthen the *roots* of the one we're attempting to escape. When we're burdened by ricocheting doubts, unpleasant mind-forms, tenacious worry, seemingly overwhelmed by repetitive and tediously insistent thought, the way through such a mess, such a tangled complexity of mental energy, with all its accompanying physical, emotional, and psychic symptoms, is just that — *through*, not around, not above, not under, but *through*, through to the very core or birthplace not just of a particular thought, but of the very assumption of a *thinker*, an assumption that we rarely question, except perhaps intellectually.

Not often do we carry alertness into the innermost labyrinths of our cogitation, but if we do, we will eventually encounter a multi-faced minotaur, a shapeshifting, composite *personification* of what we won't face about ourselves. It is not enough to merely say that such an appearance is just a deception, a mere illusion, a dream-creation — relative to the everyday us, it's utterly real, completely worthy of our attention. The minotaur must be faced and unmasked. To be told that doing so will reveal to us our own face is of little use (just like any other information that we are not yet ripe enough to embody and wisely use), unless we're hungry to "see" our true face.

The minotaur is carrying part of that face, an essential layer of it, a particular colouring of it, a certain tone and archetypal texture, manifesting as an enormously rich, endarkened power that you may or may not encounter literally. Instead of meeting a beast-man or beast-woman (or both) within the maze of your thoughts, you may simply come up against the delusory solidity of a computerized administrator, perhaps not even personalized, perhaps appearing only as a shadowy crystallization of intent...

The point is to make the journey, not in some self-glorifying heroic manner, but more deeply, moment to moment. There are hundreds of moments in a typical day that call for such a journey. The journey may only last a second or two. And what is the journey? In part, it's simply an activated willingness, at least most of the time, to dive into and illuminate a certain contraction of mood or emotion, a certain tightening of thought or flesh, a certain obsessiveness of focus — all these little penetrations, or psychosomatic scoutings, are wonderful preparation for the larger, riskier penetrations that Life will inevitably ask of us again and again. We are always being invited to fully participate in (and *as*) the Mystery That animates all; we are always being invited to co-create our positioning in the midst of everything along with That Which breathes us, is us, was us, will be us...

Almost all of us, when lost amidst the turmoil and chaos of destructive thoughts, intentions, and various cravings, tend to *automatically* speak the mind of the condition we have put ourselves in, as though *it* were the living Truth, the true us — we let *it* look through our eyes and shape our stride... As such, we frequently make decisions, big decisions sometimes, that emerge not from the depths or totality of us, but rather only from an unillumined fragment of us, a compression or clenching of self, a vice-like gripping of belly, heart, torso, and shoulders, a literal squeezing of Life-force away from the great centers of the trunk up, up, up into the skull or down, down, down into the genital and perineal region.

At either end, discharge is the intention, whether through excessive thinking, analyzing, planning, postponing, scheduling, prevaricating, imagining, and so on, or through compulsive sexing, neither of which truly alleviates the problem. They both simply take the pressure off for a while, sedating and comforting us, often working together, staying open for business at all hours. (Our sex center remains open with the help of the pornographic visuals or romanticized scenarios supplied by mind and twisted need.) More, much more, could be said about this interplay between mind and sexuality, but now is not the time...

When we are clenching or knotting ourselves and we don't know we're doing so (or don't admit it), we've only armoured ourselves, positioning ourselves behind a barricade of rationalizations and soulless logic, neurotically defending ourselves against what might liberate us, as well as against what might harm us; we don't often distinguish between the two, since we are so busy being defensive. Rarely do we tellingly notice *how* we clench ourselves, *how* we grip and bind ourselves, *how* we shrink from Being, *how* we put a stranglehold on our heart. To notice this is essential if we are to unbind ourselves. Of course, the urge to unclench, to uncontract, to uncramp ourselves is common to all of us, but it is normally brought about (and this is almost always only *peripherally* releasing) through outside intervention — some kind of regulatory manipulation, some kind of alternate experience, is brought into being — the television is switched on, the mind heats up the genitals, a special meal is prepared, a long-awaited event is about to happen, the phone rings, there's a detective novel to finish, a sex manual to swallow, a joint to smoke, an orgasm to have, a somebody to meet, a weekend but a day away, and on and on. There is so, so much available for the purpose of distraction from our suppression of being, providing us with the opportunity to almost continually dress up our stagnation with superficial change and near-constant occupation!

It is not an easy matter to authentically face our Self-suppression, to so directly and honestly face it that we can see, really see, that *we are doing it*, not merely believing that we are doing it because we've been told so, but actually experiencing ourselves doing it in the very moment when it is occurring! Once we have entered into such experience, then we can begin loosening the knot, or, more precisely, creating conditions in which such knottedness can begin to loosen. Simply by being aware that it exists, we can permit it to breathe itself open, not in some yogic or therapeutic manner, but *naturally*, while noticing that we have enslaved our breath to it, our vitality, our passion, our interrelatedness with All That Is...

Thus do we allow expansion in the midst of contraction, not as an escapist strategy, but as a participatory surrender, a conscious depressuring of self that is free from submission to the barrage of thoughts that, suddenly arising, loudly proclaim that such expansion is delusory and definitely dangerous. Yes, it is dangerous, very dangerous, but only to egocentricity, Self-negation, addictiveness, and unlove. In such expansion, such potent unclenching, we'll inevitably feel strong emotions, perhaps anger, terror, and hurt at first, soon followed by rage, deep sadness, grief, and a seedling joy, all coupled with an intense longing to stand our true ground, a longing so pure that it seemingly breaks us apart, and soon our heart is streaming through our eyes, our love illuminating our goodbyes, our grief-cries and sighs, and suddenly we are unmistakably open and radiantly vulnerable, present but not helpless, no longer a victim, no longer a devotee of sentimentality or cynicism...

It is fine to talk of this when we are present, sane, loving, grounded, and happily alive, but what is really important is what we will do when we're overwhelmed by fear, inundated by a darkness of mood, of feeling, of intention, wrapped up in an obsession of thought or flesh, lost in a maze of self-generated trouble. Our tendency likely will be to attempt to somehow *think* our way out of this — we will probably just speak the mind of the darkness that we're embodying, without knowing we are doing so.

What we need to do at such times is simply and clearly state where we are or what we're up to (this may need to be preceded by allowing one's contracted state to express itself through movement and sound, by means of *creatively* cathartic release, such expression needing to be raw, full-bodied, and so alive that it carries no self-consciousness), no matter how broken or unfamiliar our voice might be. It may be enough to simply say, "I'm lost" or "I'm scared shitless" or "I won't open!" Or we might describe, deliberately and accurately describe, the point of view that we are assuming — we might, for example, say, "This is the position I am speaking from, this is how it looks to me from here, here's how you look, here's what I'm thinking about, here's what I'm assuming is true," or whatever else you need to say in order to provide a context for the content that will follow (some examples of such content being: "I don't trust you" or "You're all out to get me" or "You must hate me" or "I'm looking for an easy way out of this" or "You look like you'd like to kill me" or "It's not safe for me to open up to you").

To thus confess our prevailing point of view strengthens the witness in us, without necessarily detaching us from our experience. This is the crucial part — if we detach from our experience, we will have only reinforced our tendency to detach from Life, from passion, from the richness of being human; we will have only supported the escapist inclinations of the meditator within us. Don't detach. Simply witness *and* simultaneously feel the very hurt, the uncovered pain of where you now are. Don't seek an alternate experience; don't just look for (or create) reasons for why you're feeling the way you are.

To ask why at such times only reinforces the state of mind that *already* characterizes you where you are now trapped. Whatever you're thinking about when you are contracted, suppressed, clenched, self-obsessed, is worth almost nothing, at least in terms of *content* — it is far more valuable to confess the tone, the texture, the feel, the *context* of such thoughts, to say, "I'm thinking, thinking and thinking, trying to think my way out of this," or "I notice that my thoughts have the sound of my father's voice" or "All my thoughts feel paranoid." To confess such things is useful, for the I who speaks thus is not contracted, not trapped, but simply exists as a witness, a gutsy witness...

And if that particular "I" can remain in contact with the *feeling* of where you are, then you are on your way through, journeying to the very heart of what has been troubling you. When you stand at that point, that dark stillpoint, that purity of night, and you remain conscious, it is as if you are in a lucid dream, fully aware that you are dreaming, allowing your body, your dreambody, to expand, to change form, to become a wondrous shapeshifter, a magician of Awakening's alchemy, a naked embodiment of pure Being, ever yielding to an impulse far greater than that of your mind at any time. You expand, you let go, you awaken, and the cave, the pit, the trap, the bind, suddenly is no more, or it is a luminous zone of immense possibility.

Yes, you may still feel the effects of your entrapment for a while — the biochemistry of it may still be running around through your body for some time, but you will find yourself reestablished in intimacy with your environment, inner and outer, and you'll more deeply feel those around you, the eyes, the faces, the shadows, the sea, the trees, the rain, the postures, the shifting light. You will more profoundly empathize with others, and you will be rooted in the present moment. Yes, you may still hurt, there may be tears pouring from your eyes, you may be angry, you may be in grief, you may be overcome with emotion, you may be blinded by psychic revelation, but you will feel soulfully connected to your environment, and healing will happen very quickly. No medicine is needed, no therapy (except perhaps to get things rolling), no electroshock, no inculcation of dogma, no meditative remedy, no mantra or gemstone or rabbit's foot or belief, but only this full-bodied reestablishment of connectedness, of primal intimacy...

The value of meditative technique, psychotherapy, hypnotherapy, bioenergetics, group dynamics, and bodywork is to prepare the soil from which real transformation can occur. If such tools are used to simply vault from an endarkened mood or from a maelstrom of chaotic thought, one quickly comes to depend on such technique for escape from whatever is unpleasant. This association of a particular methodology with relief from unpleasant conditions is, except initially, not useful. What is required when we are trapped (and to varying degrees, almost all of us are thus entrapped) is a simultaneous recognition of the trap and a deep willingness to uninhibitedly *feel* (and even *be*) the qualities that epitomize the trap. This is the embodiment of the passionate witness. It is a matter of heartfelt insight, not some kind of insight that has been remembered from the past or conjured up from some belief system, but rather one that arises *from* the very letting go of self-contraction, one whose spontaneous art lights up the labyrinths of self-deception and ego-conception. Such art may have as its precursors various techniques of psychotherapy and meditation, but these will not provide fruitful conditions for liberation if they are used ritualistically; perhaps such ritual will free us to some extent at first, or even for some time (as in the case of meditative disciplines such as Vipassana), but sooner or later it becomes a trap, perhaps a bigger or more consoling trap, but nevertheless a trap, simply because of our addiction to it.

Once the soil has been thoroughly tilled, through deep preparatory work on oneself, then the tools that were used for such ground-breaking must be let go of — they can, of course, be occasionally returned to if their usage is spontaneously appropriate to a particular moment's imperatives. One can carry signals from a sane state of being into one's darkness, but such signals must be unburdened by liberation-expectation; otherwise, one will automatically expect them (and their backup methodologies) to free one from one's own self-inflicted difficulties. One might as well be sitting in front of a television flipping through the channels, looking for one that'll present a program that will relieve the moment of its despair or heaviness or doubt...

Good therapists (and spiritual teachers) often create a certain attachment to themselves at first with their clients, not for monetary gain nor for egoic gain, but to teach their clients about the dynamics of attachment. Soon, perhaps in a couple of months, these therapists consciously and artfully begin to wean their clients from such attachment, such childish dependency, gradually and sensitively teaching (and this teaching may not even appear to be a teaching) them a truer kind of dependency, a healthier dependency, one that is not to be automatically associated with helplessness, one that is rooted not in neurotic submission, but rather in a well-lit blending of vulnerability, strength, and mind-free need.

Therapists like this (who may not even call themselves therapists) are not fronts for a particular system or lineage, but are psychospiritual alchemists, ever creating appropriate forms for work, according to the real needs of the moment, according to the energies, needs, and resistive forces of the client, and, to a lesser extent, according to their own needs (insofar as they serve the deepening of the session). Unfortunately, this is true of very few therapists — most therapists are unskilled in the very areas in which they profess to possess expertise. For example, many of those who label themselves marriage or relationship counsellors are frequently messed up in their own relationships, just as lost and deluded and neurotic as their clientele...

Nevertheless, such people can be of some use to beginners, if only to teach them what is non-workable; through such therapists, an intelligent, Truth-hungry person learns, gradually learns, what doesn't work, learning to distinguish the false teacher from the true teacher through his or her own experience. It is of no use to just read a book that lays out the signs whereby one may recognize a true teacher — the reliance on such lists is simply that of neurotic dependence, the granting of power-over to yet another expert, yet another how-to hustler or do-gooder or well-meaning visionary...

The point, however, is not that one must do the work alone, like some kind of independent little entity, some kind of perpetual adolescent, some kind of self-glorifying, self-glamourizing hero or heroine — help *is* necessary, but if it is gone after from a position of fix-me helplessness or impotence, it will probably only complicate our pain, amplifying and further knotting it. There is real help available, but it must be consciously invited, welcomed with more than desperation, moved toward with both awareness and a willingness to come undone...

When we're stuck, nastily densified, contracted, depressed, suffering a severe case of mistaken identity, or just plain miserable, we've nowhere to go but into *and* through, without recoil or dissociation, right to the heart and soul of the matter, shedding the roles of both victim and rescuer. Then the labyrinth is not a problem, not a something into which our mind can sink its teeth, busying itself (and us) with all sorts of "solutions."

The journey in and through is an adventure, a daily adventure that invites our open-eyed participation and passion. If we so embark, there will be pain, there will be hurt, but it will be a pain, a hurt, of purification, of cleansing, of preparation, sooner or later to be accompanied by an equally deep joy, a rejuvenative joy, a *sobering* joy, a true illumination of one's condition...

Do not take what I have said here as a precise recipe; I'm simply creating a context for effectively working with the conditions that arise when we've severely contracted ourselves. Embodying the passionate witness is both a difficult and an effortless process, one that requires a resolute continuity of alertness, a deeply empathetic involvement with one's environment, a gutsy, unrehearsed facing of what we are most afraid of, a willingness to feel both terror and ecstasy, both rage and grief, both sun and rain. The journey is to the very core of What is imperishably everlasting, unavoidably loving, unreasonably happy, unambiguously alive, unmistakably us, the real us... It begins now, right where you are...

Everything Already Aflame

Body stuck in overlapping mindframes
pretending to be in a chrysalis
Mind pretending to be inside the body
personalizing its headquarters
Imposter indweller making a killing making Time
dressed up as Soul, as something Whole
Thus do we keep making diseased mind
until it makes us
And so I rot in my room
trying to outfuck Time
finally puking up the hero and antihero
fleshing out more of the sacred zero
Down, down the tubes I go
implanted in fastframe zones
Everything already aflame
in its own wedding garment
Spinning and awakening at last
into a quivering landscape
Slowing down the dream, making it solid
for a while until days appear
But something must die, now
The everyday's already full of holes
riddled empty, leaking out me and more me
until I can't convincingly claim
any shape
It only makes sense
When we stop trying to make it make sense
And here's a love that unzips these lines
melting down every strategic design
I am thrust into a deeper Now,
gleaming at the tip, sobbing at the rupture
New frontiers flowering out of the familiar
I'm at the edge and at the center
There's no ending this, no mending this
And here's a laughter upstaging my mind
And here's a something no one can find
This Wonder forever unlost, blooming as this
My dying flesh lit by Its Play
My every name devoured once again
until there's nothing to reclaim

– 8 –
Weaving the Cocoon: A Broken-Field Run Through Larva-Land

(Shanti talks for a while about the difficulties some other members of Xanthyros are having)

ROBERT: By focussing as you are on what *they* are doing, you take the heat off *yourself*. You've been doing well for a long time, but not nearly so well the last few weeks, and you're making it worse by trying to cover it up, whether through deflection or non-inspection... Not only are you denying what's actually occurring for you, but you're also in denial of your denial! Do you agree?

SHANTI: Yes. I've been sharing a lot of my sadness around missing different people...

ROBERT: You've been missing them? Have you called or seen any of them?

SHANTI: No.

ROBERT: Your missing of them is no different than your supposed empathy for those who are having difficulty — it's little more than a diversionary tactic, a compulsively outward movement of attention, a well-dressed distraction from what's troubling *you*! You're just pampering and superficializing yourself with this picture of yourself as someone who's "there" for this person, sympathetically concerned for that person, missing yet another person, and so on — yes, you *do* feel some of this, but you're blinding yourself to what you're doing with it! *(Pause)* It seems to me that right now your fear is far more primary than your sadness...

SHANTI: It's true — I'm feeling a lot of fear and insecurity. *(Long pause*) This morning, I really felt like acting out, just driving somewhere and staying away all day.

ROBERT: Why?

SHANTI: Because I didn't want to go back and have to take care of everything!

ROBERT: Who says you have to take care of everything?

SHANTI: I've been saying that.

ROBERT: Why?

SHANTI: To get approval.

ROBERT: From?

SHANTI: People in my house...

ROBERT: What this all says to me, Shanti, is that you're losing touch with your capacity to sanely parent yourself. You're looking for more and more parenting from others, even as you sabotage the whole damned thing — as with your parents, you simultaneously want it and don't want it. Your very trying to *earn* others' parenting, approval, and love only draws forth from them a response to your calculatedness — the you that you present to them is *not* the you who needs loving parenting, but rather is a parody of you, a clever complex of habits that refers to itself as you! Drop all the calculation, all the strategy, and there you'll be, with your naked need and your terror of it not being met, or even recognized, as happened with your parents...

But you're treating your need, your deep need, just as your parents treated you when you were a child! Why maintain that generational madness? As long as you won't lovingly and sanely parent yourself, you'll be at war with your need to have others parent you...

Only when you have truly begun to parent yourself, will you be able to make good use of others' parenting — short of that, you will only either shrink from it, or neurotically submit to it. If you insist on staying at that level, stuck in either disobedience or obedience, you'll never know the joy of real parenting, whether of self, of others, or from others! (*Long pause*) You're slipping, and you're trying to disguise the fact that you are slipping.

SHANTI: I know.

ROBERT: You agree too easily! It's just more deflection, just more seduction — it keeps you superficial, and lodged in your mind, distanced from your suffering...

SHANTI: I have been scared.

ROBERT: You're not scared now?

SHANTI: I am... There's fear, definitely...

ROBERT: What are you doing with it?

SHANTI: Holding it.

ROBERT: How?

SHANTI: In my voice, my throat, my chest, tightening up, holding down...

ROBERT: Yes. You're literally uptight, all wrapped-up in your mind... Your left eye looks flat and dull, lifeless — it's gotten smaller as we've been talking. (*Pause*) It looks about ten or eleven years old to me...

SHANTI: I've been going in and out of feeling very young and insecure; I keep pulling myself back together again... I guess I'm trying to look good, to look better than I actually feel...

ROBERT: For whose benefit?

SHANTI: I'm not sure.

ROBERT: It's just more bargaining, more control... And underneath, it's an attempt to find something truly valuable, something that you despair of ever finding, something that you'll not find if you keep making façade more important than Essence... (*Long pause*) If you really want guidance from someone like me, you have to simultaneously tap into your own inner guidance, or else you will almost invariably resist me, rather than cooperate with me; if you've no sense of co-creating with me, then you will be bound to sabotage whatever I do with you, no matter what it is. (*Pause*) So your fear has you by the mind. You can state it, you can clearly verbalize it, but you're still stuck in it.

SHANTI: My mind has been dominating... I seem to have to uphold a certain image in order to avoid rejection.

ROBERT: But in doing *that*, you are actually rejecting what *truly* needs acceptance in you! You're *already* immersed in a context of rejection! However much you numb yourself to your ongoing self-rejection, it eats away at you, clawing for your attention... (*Pause*) Let's get into it now. Take off your glasses and look at Nancy [*Nancy's assisting Robert in the session*] and show her this self-image you apparently need to uphold. Let it take over your face and your voice... That's it — keep letting yourself *be* this image, keep fleshing it out, keep speaking *its* mind and smiling *its* smile...

SHANTI: I am strong. I can take care of myself. I don't need anybody! (*Pause*) I can hide from you by pretending to be strong, to not need (*Her voice is shaking*)...

ROBERT: Feel what's trembling behind the mask. It's time to feel, to *directly* feel, your fear, Shanti. Open your mouth wider, even wider. Open your eyes as wide as you can — feel the terror that's there, feel it now... (*She sobs shudderingly, then screams, more and more loudly, deep, hair-raising screams*)

Let it come! Let it come undammed! (*More screaming*) Keep your eyes open — stay with Nancy! (*Shanti's screaming broadens, then subsides into wide-open, baby-like crying*) Let it keep coming... Let your need flow forth... No mind now, no strategy, no turning away from your hurt and need... Just pure need, uncomplicated need, pure and simple, streaming out... (*Long pause*) Now, very gently at first, call for your mother...

SHANTI: Mommy, Mommy, Mommy... (*Very softly, yet with great purity of feeling*)

ROBERT: Really feel your mouth as you call, your lips, your tongue, the yearning in your arms, the aching in your whole body...

SHANTI: (*Wailing now*) Mommy, mama, mama, mama...

ROBERT: Stick your lips out more — let them move more freely... Open your eyes wide, and open your voice wide — *really* call her!

SHANTI: Mama!! Mama!! (*Repeated about a dozen times with great intensity, followed by deep crying for a minute or two, and by a series of big sighs*)

ROBERT: Now, sit up straighter, lengthening the back of your neck. Breathe a few more deep breaths, sitting up a little straighter, letting your chest lift and come more forward. You're in deep need of mothering-energy right now — if you were less open, you'd likely try to *give* that energy, instead of opening yourself to receive it. You need to trust the others here, especially the women, with your vulnerability and woundedness, instead of trying to take charge or otherwise stay in control — you really know this now, don't you? (*She cries*)

If you don't start reaching out for mothering from the other women, you will have just about none to give to your daughters — in fact, you'll be teaching them that it's too dangerous to reach out for mothering, or that it can only be done through adopting a parentally-pleasing mask! How can you be a mother to them when you won't mother yourself? You *need* the other women, and you *need* them far more than you're letting on! Sure, they're not your mother, but they *are* mothers. (*Pause*) You reject mothering because you associate it with how you felt with your own mother, whom you were both attracted to and repulsed by — you wouldn't want to lay in her lap, would you?

SHANTI: No! I dreamt about her last night, and I got really scared.

ROBERT: Well, you're going to dream such dreams of her until you clean up your relationship with mothering; she'll haunt you until you stop fleeing her, or, more precisely, until you stop fleeing what you took on from her — your flesh carries *her* shame, *her* repressiveness, *her* aborted longings. Look at Shanti — she's got it together, she sings beautifully, she flows, she takes care of the needy, she ain't greedy, she never gets fucked up in the groups — she's Ms. Clean!

SHANTI: It's not true! I don't want to be Ms. Clean! (*Half-laughing, half-crying*)

ROBERT: So be a conscious Ms. Messy! Don't just package your need — unwrap it, and let it flood all over the place for a while! Stop *arranging* yourself for a while...

SHANTI: I know that if I don't, I'll want to run away again.

ROBERT: So don't run away *inside*!

SHANTI: I don't *really* want to run away, Robert. (*Crying*) I don't...

ROBERT: But the urge to do so *still* exists, regardless of your good intentions, and you feed that urge when you don't ask for what *you* need! Instead of being clear and truthful about your needs, you do something else, something that's a roundabout way of trying to get those very same needs met...

SHANTI: My ego wants to dominate.

ROBERT: And what is this ego?

SHANTI: The place where I stay in control.

ROBERT: Where is this place? Is it behind your eyes, or in your neck, or below your navel, or in your fingers? No? Well then, *where* is it? It doesn't have a specific location, does it? It may seem to be somewhere inside the skull, but it's not a discrete something — it's just a habit, an addiction, a personified addiction. Give it attention, unconscious attention, and it leaps into being! It's stuffed with neurotic pride, the pride that says I can do it by myself! (*She cries*) Its stance is just the flipside of your extreme insecurity, that insecurity that's reflected so accurately in the rigidity of your upper back, the question-mark curvature of it, the infolding of your shoulders, the compensatory thrust of your jaw, your excessive talking... You are worried thin! Your body's an eloquent statement of how you dealt with your difficulties — it screams out the powerlessness you felt when you were a child.

SHANTI: I just wanted to get away when I was a kid, to get out of there.

ROBERT: But in *staying*, your style became that of being in charge, of playing the all-competent mother — of course, you counterbalanced that by "choosing" a so-called spiritual path that allowed you to shed your responsibilities in the name of "going to God" — chant, chant, and chant some more, and ye shall be saved! Your suffocated cries of "Mama!" found a consolingly disembodied outlet in your adulatory sighs of "Baba" [*Muktananda*]... Aren't you fed up with trying to be in charge, of *trying* to be so fucking responsible?

SHANTI: Yes! I don't want to be in charge...

ROBERT: But you need to be in charge in some ways, Shanti — like being in charge of *not* being in charge! There *is* a responsibility of an entirely different sort than the kind you've been saddling yourself with — isn't it time to get off your own back? (*Laughter*) You get so afraid of what *might* happen! You shack up with doomsday possibilities, miring yourself in a kind of negative hope... (*Pause*) Worrying has never helped anyone — it just destroys tissues, initiative, love, trust, and the capacity for center. Worry is only a waste of energy, a socially-acceptable species of anxiety, a *false* face of concern, a clinging to negative anticipation...

Whenever you feel fear, and the fear concerns something that hasn't yet happened or isn't *currently* happening, you'll notice that your mind is churning out thoughts veined with worry — at this point, instead of continuing to worry or to numb yourself to your worry, *immediately* go into a straightforward, Vipassana-based witnessing, labelling your mental activity for what it is — thinking, thinking, or perhaps doubting, doubting, or worrying, worrying... Make your observation of your mind more important than its contents, letting your attention *gradually* shift to something deeper, something more central, something more *body*-rooted. Only when your attention becomes conscious, do you have a chance to outgrow your life-negating habits...

SHANTI: I've actually been doing that "worrying, worrying" meditative approach, but what I haven't been doing is going deeper — sometimes I just end up worrying about worrying! I start feeling dry, and getting really afraid of not making it...

ROBERT: That fear is just a boogeyman! What happens to boogeymen when you turn on the lights?

SHANTI: They disappear.

ROBERT: So turn on the lights!

SHANTI: By not listening to my mind?

ROBERT: No! You turn on the lights by flicking the switch! (*Laughter*) And to flick the switch, you just have to put attention into the you who can flick the switch on (which also means being *aware* of the you who's flicking it *off!*). You can still listen to your mind, as long as you don't take it seriously, especially in the realm of psychoemotional assessment. If a TV was on in this room and we couldn't turn it off for some reason, we'd have to hear it, but we wouldn't have to let *that* hearing dominate the rest of our experience — we could remain aware of it, mostly as background noise. Destroying the TV or covering it with a thick layer of blankets doesn't flick on the lightswitch! So you take your mind into account, you remain aware of its activities, even as you get on with what's most important. Techniques for "stopping the mind" are worth mastering insofar as they give one a taste of no-mind, but what happens when we let go of the technique? We may just fling ourselves into the arms of another technique, inflating ourselves with honeymoon anticipation, or we may decide we've had enough of such relationships!

When you ceased your Siddha Yoga chanting practice, there you were, with all your neuroses still intact! Who are we without our centering devices? If we've used those methodologies well, we'll be more centered than we were before we took on their discipline, but if we don't use them well, if we become addicted to them, then we're even worse off than we were before we took them on. True center is *not* held in place by any technique, but the journey to true center almost always requires a profoundly thorough exploration of technique — you can't really let it go until you're intimate with it... (*Long pause*)

Okay... Cover your right eye, so you're looking at Nancy with just your left eye. Breathe through your mouth.

SHANTI: I can hardly see.

ROBERT: The eye is only partially open — it's flat, barren-feeling. (*Pause*) Now, let's try the other eye. Cover your left eye, and look out of your right eye. Right away, there's more energy emerging from it, isn't there? More presence, more depth...

SHANTI: Yes... I've been feeling that my female side [*She associates this with her left side, including her left eye*] has been squished down lately...

ROBERT: You mean for your whole life! (*She starts crying*) Cover your right eye again, and look at Nancy through your left. Breathe more deeply. Let everything around your eye soften, relax, widen... Slowly raise your left eyebrow... Even slower, and now lower it just as slowly... Do it a few more times, keeping your breathing loose... your eye's a little more open now, a little less dried-up looking. How does your eye feel?

SHANTI: It's difficult to keep it open.

ROBERT: Don't collapse! This eye reveals your terror of deeply receiving; it's more like a puddle than a pool. In its very fear of receptivity, it is crippled in its giving... Nevertheless, it *is* shining a little now, trusting a little more. Raise the eyebrow more, and drop the opposite eyebrow if you can... That's it... The eye is tender now, little-girl tender, very, very vulnerable. (*She weeps*)

SHANTI: I feel happier now, more innocent.

ROBERT: Yes. The child in you has more breathing room now, more permission to *be*. In granting her this, you are mothering yourself. Without mothering, we just dry up. Without mothering, we are marooned from our Source, emotionally disconnected from intimacy... (*Pause*) When we reach out for what we truly need, it comes toward us, out of sheer magnetic attraction; that is, it inevitably becomes more available to us. This is the meaning of that old saying that goes something like this: "Those who have, shall receive; those who don't have, won't." This is not about injustice, or unfair distribution of goods! Those who have are those who are genuinely reaching out, those who *already* have accessed within themselves what they're reaching out for! Those who don't have are those whose reaching out is a plea for a quick fix; like the lonely, they are actually *impermeable* to what they crave! A lonely person may seem to be calling out for love, but he or she is, through their very desperation and contractedness, actually closed to love!

SHANTI: My mind is saying to me, "You should have learned this by now"...

ROBERT: One more nagging "should" for your poor shoulders, your *"should-ers"*! There's still this desiccated yogi inside you, Shanti, looking for spiritual shoulds, some sort of ladder to God, complete with textbook rungs, sutra'd all the way! Chant, and you'll get to God; if you ain't getting there, then chant harder! Such is the bullshit you fed on for so many years...

Recipes are very seductive; just about everyone *wants* a step-by-step program, a step-by-step scenario, a kind of computerized fitness program for their soul! But the whole thing's just as mechanical and masturbatory as most aerobics classes! We pollute ourselves with fear and doubt, and then look for an escape from our fear, immersing ourselves in all sorts of remedial programs and disciplines, instead of actually facing and illuminating our fear!

Most seeking is neurotic. We tighten up inside, and then try to get rid of the resulting pain with all kinds of counter-efforts, without *actually* ceasing our inner tightening — it's as if we're vise-gripping the back of our neck, and trying to get rid of the resulting headache (through drugs, meditation, visualization, therapy, exercise) without ceasing our gripping! It's very simple. You suppress your Being, you shrink, you contract, you close down, creating enormous distress for yourself, then you run around like a chicken with its head cut off, trying to find ways to get rid of your distress — compulsive thinking, fucking, working too hard, distraction upon stimulatingly soporific distraction... What pain!

Just about everything people are doing is an attempt to relieve the distress they're creating through their very suppression of Being! When we're truly happy, abiding in and as our core of Being, we may still seek, but our seeking is free of all desperation. The yogi in you, however, is a miserable character, prudish, stupidly meticulous, self-obsessed, anti-sexual, anti-intimacy, anti-Life!

You really tried the yoga of devotion, didn't you? Remember all the gopis around Krishna, trying to swoon their way to God? It's just romance, guru-worship, an irresponsible dissolution of one's personal boundaries, an idol-centered emotionalism... Ah, but the lure of the ten steps, the twelve steps, the twenty steps — here they are, ladies and gentlemen, the ten steps, the doing of which will get you there, and might I add, ladies and gentlemen, that if you *don't* get there, it is *your* responsibility (which *actually* means fault!), because you didn't do the steps right or fully enough!

This guilt-provoking logic, however understated it might be, characterizes not only much of yoga and other Eastern approaches to spirituality, but also many Western methodologies, such as est, power-of-positive-thinking offshoots (epitomized by New Age "you can have it all" bleatings), pop psychology, and much of so-called sex therapy... (*Pause*) Ladders everywhere, creating *walls*, on and on and on... how to become a better lover, a better manager, a better parent, a better yogi — how to, how to, how to, neatly bundled up in ten easy steps in the latest bestseller, the one being peddled on every damned talkshow! Gawkshows is more like it — isn't *this* interesting, folks, golly gee, but let's take a commercial break! (*Laughter*) Everyone's so busily giving everyone else head!

On one end of the teetertotter, you've got the you who's married to the ten easy steps, and on the other end, you've got the you who's stuck on doing it *her* way. But they're *both* imposters, both impersonators of you, both unswervingly superficial... So what do you do? You get off the seesaw! You go to a deeper playground. You make a real effort to clear the rubble, to uproot some habits, and suddenly one day, there's no effort needed, because you've understood, understood transverbally and with your entire being, what you've been up to — you no longer have to curb yourself from buying candybars everytime you go into supermarkets!

Now, on a bigger scale, the effort to work on yourself may one day transcend itself, so that your Awakening proceeds without any dependence on efforting, at least in the usual sense — Awakening then would not come from effort, but would *create it*, as necessary. What precedes this is not ten easy *nor* ten difficult steps; an artfulness is needed, a spontaneity, a willingness to embrace the Unknown. It's a pathless path, a marvellous frustration of one's spiritual ambition... So where does discipline fit into this? It's what you have to do to stay aligned with your inherent happiness; it's not meant to make us miserable, nor to inflate us, nor to reinforce our ego-centricity. Real discipline both expresses and reinforces *Essence*-centricity...

SHANTI: (*Much later in the session*)... I had a dream last week where it was pouring with rain, and I was far away from home...

ROBERT: Well, you've sure rained in this session! (*Laughter*) But how far away from home are you really?

SHANTI: I'm not away from home.

ROBERT: Then why are you *acting* as if you are?

SHANTI: Because I'm an idiot! (*Laughter*) Because I go to sleep so easily...

ROBERT: What puts you to sleep?

SHANTI: My not paying attention.

ROBERT: And what keeps you from paying attention?

SHANTI: My mind, mostly.

ROBERT: You want to blame someone or something, don't you? So blame your poor mind! (*Laughter*) Blame it for your terrible bind! (*Pause*) All that's really occurring is you convincing yourself that you're not home, that you're not happy, that you're a flop of a human being — the evidence for this, of course, is everywhere since you're so caught up in looking for it! Seek, and ye shall find. (*Laughter*) Intellectually, you can say, "I am home and at one with God", but that's not your usual conviction, is it? Your dominating conviction is that you're just this blabbering nerd stumbling along asleep, this abject nebbish stuck in a body that's shaped like a question mark!

SHANTI: Yeah — a bumbling idiot! (*Giggling*)

ROBERT: Well, let's take a jump now, and say that Life's like volley-ball. (*Laughter*)

SHANTI: Oh, here we go!

ROBERT: If Life's like volleyball, then where's Shanti?

SHANTI: Stuck in hesitation... Part of what I'm learning from when we all play volleyball is how I hesitate to really go for it. I hold back. I don't watch the ball closely...

ROBERT: You panic, then get even more uptight about trying to do
it right! You try so hard to not look bad that you end up looking even
worse! (*Laughter*) There's that one great, show-stopping image of the
ball way up in the air, really high, finally coming down toward you,
and you're running around underneath it with your arms outstretched
like you're carrying a tray of just-opened Perrier bottles, and then
you completely miss the ball, like those cartoon firemen who run
around in circles under someone who's going to jump from a ledge
high above, making a great show out of saving him, then disappearing right before he lands! (*Laughter*) But missing the ball isn't the
failure; your commitment to being tense is! Don't you see how such
commitment just serves your image of yourself as a nerd? Why keep
convincing yourself that you're just a lowly wretch? Why keep convincing yourself that you're not home? Why keep making sure that
there's no shortage of evidence for your sentencing of yourself?

Paradoxically, you are home and you're not home — go deeper, and
it won't even be a paradox. You'll simply *know* it, with your entirety...
(*Pause*) You do not yet recognize your identity with Light, with the
Radiance of the Source. Modern physics can tell you, in so many
words, that you are Light, but you don't *feel* it — you rarely experience yourself as pure Energy, Self-Illuminating Energy, but now and
then you intuit that this is so... And your body, your physicality, is
not separate from this — it is, through its very makeup, elementally
and energetically continuous with the rest of the Universe, in everchanging yet eternal relationship with everything else...

Xanthyros is a crucible for your Awakening, as volatile as it's loving;
it's a conducive transition house for us, a transformational zone,
evolving as we evolve, taking form in accordance with our current
needs... (*Pause*) We're a wide-open chrysalis, swelling and bursting
with new growth, with translarval awareness — the wings are just
starting to show, trembling ever so slightly... We have been and are
working very hard to keep the cocoon functional, so that it remains a
sanctuary and not a hideout — those who persist in trying to make
what we have into a cult have a hard time with me, as you know! It's
easy to die in the cocoon, isn't it? Cults are so over-protective of
what they harbour that they suck the very life out of it — they bind
it, overmind and suffocate it, even as they hoist its flag high...

We're metamorphosing. This is not an opinion, but a fact, an obviousness signalled by the dramatic healing occurring in everyone here. There's a regressive tendency here too, as the deeper layers of resistance are encountered — it's a gradual unpeeling, sometimes even a re-layering, a defiant nostalgia for caterpillar-ness... (*Long pause*) We could become butterflies. We could become fully human. Xanthyros is our cocoon, our common womb, and it's also what waits beyond the cocoon. We're all weaving the cocoon together, slowly but surely, and we've gotten rid of the caterpillars (*Laughter*) — at least to a high enough degree to keep our work going!

Caterpillars get stepped on, especially when they consistently resist their evolutionary imperatives, ever distracting themselves through their feeding — they're obsessed with what's outside them. Once in a cocoon, however, a caterpillar is no longer thus obsessed (although an inward obsession can certainly develop!); all its energy turns in, gathers within, in multilevelled consolidation. And that's what we're doing now, and probably until the end of the year — turning in, cocooning, cleaning up, not deliberately associating with people outside Xanthyros, unless they come toward us. We need to do this for a while longer until we're more firmly and deeply established, more truly communal, more intimate, more tellingly purified. When we finish this phase, we'll explode and blossom outward, naturally and inevitably, and we'll touch many people. When a butterfly appears, many people see it. Hardly anyone spots cocoons, however! They're hidden, they're tucked away in protective places, they're Life-affirmingly self-enclosed...

There's no point in leaving the cocoon too soon; you'll simply crash and be worse off than before. What's far worse, though, is caterpillars pretending to be butterflies, as is so common among New Age afficionados and other devotees of spiritual laziness... (*Long pause*) So your job, Shanti, is to help weave the cocoon strong and energetically permeable, but not to become such a Robert-pleasing weaver that you neglect your need for mothering!

All I'm really talking about is you becoming more of a caretaker for your own ripening...

Gustave Doré: *Milton's Paradise Lost*

– 9 –

Ecstasy Is Not The Goal, But The Foundation

Only when you are already consciously immersed in the wellspring of your Being can *you* produce anything of *real* value; short of that, you will only manufacture ego and its derivative sideshows (the galleries of which will display not true art, but only the aesthetic pretensions of overinsular catharsis and unresolved self-fragmentation), the high price or profitable marketing of which has nothing to do with *real* worth. Do not force your creative urge; do not even attempt to mastermind it, nor to drink, smoke, sniff, screw, blackmail, deadlinize, or psychobotanicalize it into action. Instead, consciously reside where creativity originates, rather than trying to recontextualize yourself there — that is, don't use art to get there, but rather to express and celebrate your core of Self, so that even the utterly superficial or trivial is illuminated by the depths underlying it, made real by virtue of its *felt* continuity with the forces that animate it...

Do not expect yourself to perfectly produce whatever it is that you assume you need to produce. Realize that Ecstasy cannot be produced, since it is *inherent* to Being — that is, the art of Ecstasy exists prior to any technique that purports to bring it about, including those of so-called tantric sex, devotionalism, and hallucinogen ingestion. Ecstasy is an intensification of happiness, the kind of happiness that does not depend at all on something in particular happening, the kind of happiness that is innately independent of circumstances, inner or outer.

Ecstasy cannot be produced, but Its surrogates can, and *are*, by almost all who have turned away from Ecstasy, Truth, naked feeling, God-communion, and the cultivation of true center. The very turning away from these (which is not so much a literal turning as it is a shrinkage or collapse of being) creates immense suffering, as well as an urge for release from such distress. To bring about this release, we have come up with all kinds of substitutes for the ecstatic, mostly in the realm of sexuality, again and again expecting sex to somehow produce Ecstasy, to somehow catapult us into the truly joyful. Many are those who worship at the altar of false ecstasy, chronically pretending that they really are being fulfilled, ever dreaming that they are actually awake...

The very effort to produce something that will relieve us of our suffering only further distresses us, only further contracts and tightens us, pulling the knot between sternum and spine tighter and tighter, until there is an overwhelmingly obsessive urge for release, not release from what is creating the knot in the first place, but release from the knot itself... What commonly happens is that the tension of the knot is fucked away, drugged, hugged, tucked, sucked, talked, shocked, trained, drained away. With the greatest of ease, we perpetuate our disease of soul, desperately trying to sedate ourselves, to fuck ourselves into immunity-stained oblivion, either literally via sexuality, or through mind-fucking, fantasy, repetitious thought, affirmation-preaching, allegiance to unexamined beliefs and assumptions, anything to escape or minimize suffering. Such escapism only deepens our suffering, by reinforcing our addiction for release, especially pleasurably stimulating release.

Once Ecstasy has been turned away from, nothing *truly* satisfies us. At best, we only empty ourselves of our desire, but not of its roots. (And here we may encounter the disease of so much of religion — the making of desire into a problem, or even an enemy. The point, however, is not to flee or dissociate from our passions and desires, but rather to go to the very heart of them, to luminously embody them, to witness them without detaching from them.) The very effort to produce Ecstasy through sex (or anything else) is but a confession of our *recoil* from Ecstasy and Its demands. To not be thus stranded requires that our doing arises not from ego-centered urges, but from essence-centered urges. When our doing springs forth from a place of spaciousness, relaxation, well-lit honesty, love, and integrity, it is completely different from the sort of doing that arises from the desire to be satisfied, comforted, or delivered into a realm of seeming immunity.

There is no escape from suffering. Even the Buddhist approach of dissociating from desire (that is, of pursuing the goal of desirelessness) is but another way of creating suffering. So-called Nirvana is, in this context, no more than ultimate escapism, a miracle of continuous disembodiment, a grand avoidance of Life, of passion, of intensity, of lust, of attachment, of manifest existence — the beauty of it, the horror of it, the grief and joy of it, the totality of it... None of it, however, must be avoided. *All* of it must be faced, directly faced and passed through, until it no longer binds us, until we're no longer obsessed by it. This does not, however, mean that we rise above it, no longer feel it, no longer are empathetically associated with it — No! It simply means that we no longer make a problem out of our attachments.

There is nothing inherently wrong with attachment; what matters is what we *do* with our attachments. If, in our spiritual ambition, we try to get rid of them, or to escape them, we only create another sort of attachment, one dark with denial, non-intimacy, visceral vacuity, and mentally regurgitated reruns of ultra-rationalized runaway. If we instead choose to make room for our attachments, to make room for their pain, clinging, ups and downs, joys and heartbreak, inevitable changes and passing, all the while remaining awake, then and only then are we really human, learning to welcome the inevitable fires of purification, disillusionment, and *necessary* suffering...

We have to face such fires sooner or later, not with a fire extinguisher, but with wakefulness, gutsy integrity, and heart. We cannot afford to avoid this passage — to numb ourselves with religious or metaphysical lullabies, or to otherwise pretend that it can be gone around, outthought ("*I* create my own reality!"), risen above, or just plain disappeared, is the acme of naïveté, the plastic heart of escapism. Let us consider sex in these terms — sex ought not to be used as an escape from one's difficulties, nor as a safety valve for the discharge of distress or tension, but rather as a lovingly eloquent expression and celebration of a deeply felt inner unity.

If entered into consciously and full-bloodedly, sex (besides being an ecstatically intimate flowering) both exaggerates and illuminates our difficulties — by going into sex profoundly and nakedly alert, we energetically, even electrically, feel and eventually pass *through* the very heart of our difficulties, finding in that vibrantly alive stillpoint no trouble, no distress, no problematicalness, no craving for energetic dissipation, but only open-faced Truth, pure passion, transverbal revelation, and a veritable wilderness of Being populated not by phantoms of mind, but by archetypal shapings of Love and Primordial Presence...

We may even transcend all form, and come to rest in the arms of the Undying One; this, however, must not be made into a goal, or we'll all too easily end up just faking such depth, such intimacy, such resonance with God, unacknowledgedly generating in ourselves those sensations whose presence we take as signs that we are indeed where we are claiming to be! This ego-inflating production of "spiritual" signs is but a lofty version of *mind-generated* emotionality, as so garishly illustrated by the swoon of the devotee, the display of kriyas (*supposedly* involuntary movements created by the unlocking of Life-force, commonly via a guru's presence or touch), the preverbal gushing of the so-called born-again, the facial and vocal gyrations of bigbucks mediums, the glazed gaze of romance, and so on...

Honesty is essential, not just an honesty of content, but an honesty of context and feeling, an honesty that couples power and sensitivity, an honesty as subtle as it's vital. Honesty means more than just reporting the facts; it requires a willingness to tell the Truth, and the Truth is far more than a list of facts. It is a *creative* occasion, a soul-bright visitation, an obviously spontaneous occurrence — it is not precisely repeatable, because it is utterly unique in its moment-to-moment expression, being artfully and dynamically sensitive to the needs of the moment, spoken (with one's whole being) in feelingly exact accordance with its *current* environment. As such, Truth-telling is very different than factual reporting. Truth-telling may include informational reporting, but it is never limited to the mere recitation of facts — it is an open-hearted confession, completely spontaneous, as alive as it is unrehearsed, as non-verbal as it is verbal...

Truth-telling is at its fullest when Love is present, not obsessively soft love, nor sentimentalized love, nor romanticized love, but real love, Love that is not afraid to be ruthless, to be forceful, to be fiery, Love that is not afraid to be nakedly vulnerable and unguarded. When such Love is embodied, *really* embodied, Ecstasy is inevitable; in fact, Ecstasy is then *already* the case!

When Truth and Love are unobstructedly present together, Ecstasy is also present (whether serenely so or wildly so), and all urge to produce something that is *seemingly* truthful, loving, or ecstatic disappears. No producer, no director, no scripted acting, no mind-held stage... Only the fullness of Now, only the seamless wonder of Now, only the imperatives of Now, the ecstatically grounded practicality of Now, the graceful functionality of Now, ever capable of moving with ease and integrity through the commonplace, the mundane, the painful, the disturbing, without any escapism.

Ecstasy does not mean going somewhere else where you can be safe or immune — it means being right here, *completely* here, bodily here, right now, and now, and *now*, feeling every feeling and every wound to the core, letting your *full* participation in Life shine open the sacred doors and ignite the sacred fire and reveal the Mystery of what you are, your flesh no longer a hindrance, but an exquisitely articulate veil...

In fully letting go of "needing" to have something special occur so that we might feel better, we make room for Ecstasy, literally embodying It. When we deeply relax our ambitions to be somewhere else, somewhere seemingly more auspicious, and instead yield to the primal imperatives of our Being, then Ecstasy is not ours, but *us*. Ecstasy is not our destiny, but our birthright, our very nature, our ground and sky, our purest soulcry, asking only that we adapt to It, instead of to Its substitutes, Evernow...

Must I Lose You Again?

Must I lose you again? Must I lose you before we learn to live where there is no loss? I see you all torn away from me, and I break like water, rising easily from my ruins, but rising so full of grief, once again forming the template for our communion, my labour fueled by my attachment to you.

Only through my ecstasy can I bear my sorrow. My pain is the hurt of pillaged love, the desecration of the True, the murder of Innocence, the denial of the Real, the turning away from Being. I have access to the Eternal, but my human heart weeps for our loss of each other. Must I lose you again? Shedding all protection, I dive into my sense of loss, choosing to feel not only my suffering, but the suffering of all, including those who would do me harm, if only in their thoughts.

In the very core of my attachment to you, we are already free, free together, our many appearances throughout Time giving colour and shape to an endless Sky, yet this is no consolation. Must I lose you again? I am your lover, your parent, your child, your ally, and I'm also your grief and joy, the achingly alive obviousness of the Mystery of you. I know the most agonizing chaos, the most precarious balance, the most ripping loss, and I know the most sublime rhyme. In many places do I live, but only from one do I truly give, and what I give is *the illumination of my heart, the unobstructed feeling of Being, the love that's uncompromised by its wounds and betrayals.*

Must I lose you again? I'm a baby left to perish in a savage forest, a warrior who'll fight with ferocious elegance, a temple-builder and a troublemaker, a hello shining through every goodbye, and I'm a fire in love with its fuel. I'm in love with you so fiercely and so tenderly that I am love with you, a love that is an unexploitable medium for the Presence of the Undying One. Thus have I committed myself. Thus have I taken a stand in an unlocatable land. Thus do I do my time, even as I journey and rest elsewhere. The passing of everything both wounds and delights me. It is into the embrace of the mortal and the Immortal that I am drawn, not to be fulfilled, but to simply be...

There is little else to say. Love must also weep. The heart must break to heal. My sword is suddenly a flower, and my flower a sword, not exactly interchangeable, but both altered, both slipping out of their familiarity, and my Wonder is reawakened, my identity with Mystery deepened, my sky widened, my undefended wound carrying me into that Realm Where both you and I live already free, nakedly alive, untroubled by our ancient and future history.

Gustave Doré: *Milton's Paradise Lost*

– 10 –

When Suffering Is No Longer Reduced to a Problem

Short of enlightenment, we are obsessed with our suffering, and just as obsessed with distracting ourselves from it, with seeking a cure for it, some kind of remedy or palliative; rarely do we tellingly notice that our very seeking for an end to our suffering only creates another sort of suffering, one that is ever impaled on the altar of goal-fixation. All too easily, our attention becomes focussed, compulsively focussed, on the end that our seeking dangles before or above us...

It would be far better if our attention was consciously yielded to our suffering itself, *prior* to our seeking to fix it. If we don't face and nakedly encounter our suffering, especially the roots of our suffering, then we readily and even eagerly become enslaved to the search to end it, to somehow get rid of its symptoms, to somehow annihilate it, to disappear it, to rise above it, to think it away, to meditate or fuck or cathart or believe it away, to so thoroughly distract ourselves from it that it seems to not exist anymore, or at least to not exist in a troublesome manner.

However, our very suffering, when rightly used, is but a springboard into our true condition — it rips us open, making us raw relative to our Source, so raw that we have to feel, *directly* feel, what we've turned away from. Suffering that is not fled from, nor collapsed with, cuts through our defences, eroding our egotism and jingoistic preoccupations, casting us into a fertile chaos, equipped with nothing except a lifeline to our Heartland...

We all get depressed sometimes. When we say that we feel depressed, we are in error, however, since depression is not a feeling, but only a suppression of feeling, a collapse of heart, a numbing of vitality. Of course, we want to cure ourselves of such a nasty state (perhaps after we've sufficiently infected others with it); we want to feel better. When we find something that relieves us, that makes us feel better for a while, we usually don't realize that we have only created more suffering, in that we've generated one more attachment to hang ourselves from, namely that of whatever *seemingly* delivered us from our pain. Thus do we chain ourselves to pleasurable distraction, slowly but surely addicting ourselves to whatever seems to best relieve us of the *sensations* of our suffering.

The key here is not to just get all absorbed in our search, but to illuminate it, to expose its roots, its original motivation, to see how our primal suffering itself, our turning away from our Source (that is, our disconnectedness with our Source), both motivates and *creates* our search for release! However, there's nothing inherently wrong with seeking. All we need do is turn on the lights in the midst of our seeking, rather than just blindly following behind the headlights of our search, densely driving ourselves down meaningful cul-de-sacs, therapeutic detours, metaphysical mindfields...

All our pain, all our hurt, all our woundedness in its *primary* form is simply present to alert us to our condition, natively so — it is there to be wisely used, to remind us of where we stand, of what we are actually up to, of who we are busy being, of what drama we are encapsulated in. Our suffering is not inherently a problem, but as soon as we make it into a problem (or as soon as it *seemingly* becomes problematic), we tend to get caught up in apparent solutions, thereby overengaging our thinking minds in the process, thus increasing our distance, our psychophysical distance, from what's *really* going on. That is, we get so lost in the *secondary* ramifications of our suffering that we lose sight, almost completely, of the roots, the main trunk, of our suffering...

And, what is our suffering (specifically, our *self-created* suffering)? Basically, it is simply the result of our denial of our Truth, our turning away from What truly nourishes and sustains us, our withdrawal from the demands of real intimacy, our recoil from the demands of an Awakened Life. Such suffering is just a byproduct of our insistence on maintaining and defending our case of mistaken identity; it is a ubiquitous madness, an insanity so, so common as to be taken as utterly normal by almost all...

The disastrous condition of the Earth now is but a reflection of the condition of the typical human — fragmented, unilluminated, raped and polluted by all kinds of less than Life-giving programs and activities, obsessed with distraction, faking it left and right, stockpiling grudges, despoiling beauty, starving level upon level, pretending to be awake, driven by pain — but what is this pain, fundamentally? It is simply the sensation of having retreated from the Source of all, from the Great Mystery That animates all of this. Once that turning away, that adolescent reactivity, has been successfully embodied, then our focus easily becomes the creation of surrogates of What we've turned away from, and so we become crazily fixated on whatever means seem to best lead to these surrogates, to maximal pleasure and/or immunity possibilities...

This is idol worship. This is denial of God. This is the root of suffering. In almost all cases, the search to end suffering has a false foundation, one that is based not on awakening, but rather on exploiting the options *within* one's self-entrapment. Thus do we take time to kill time, penned up in our minds, lying face down in what we cannot stomach, trying to console ourselves in the midst of our trouble. In our madness, our suppressed woundedness, our continued violation of our own vulnerability and depth, we easily make an enemy out of whatever might free us, giving our allegiance to the perpetrators (inner as well as outer!) of false freedoms, facile freedoms, counterfeit freedoms that do not take us into our Heartland, but only into egoic inflation and wraparound fantasy, not to mention the self-obsessed irresponsibilities of mere licence...

So how do we get to the heart of the matter? We cannot think or shrink or bluff our way into it; we cannot somehow just decide that it's wrong to seek, or that we only have to trade in our beliefs for a "better" set of beliefs... We have to feel, really feel, nakedly feel what we are up to, not just with a bit of hyped emotion, but with our everything! We need to be ruthlessly compassionate with ourselves, unburdening ourselves from all sentimentality and neurotic protectionism; we need to open our borders and depant our sentinels and disarm our inner militia, not in some indiscriminate or naïvely hopeful fashion, but with loose-bodied intelligence, humor, and spaciousness of Being, letting in the light of insight and love, as well as those who are no longer indulging in just being tourists relative to the Awakening process...

We need to go much deeper than enthusiasm (or its flipside, doubt). So how to do this? First of all, notice your turning away, and stop rationalizing it. Of course, when you stop turning away to a significant degree, you won't suddenly be Enlightened — you may hurt like hell for awhile, but your pain will, if wisely used, help you open more fully to what you most deeply long for, because such hurt, through its very openness, fluidity, power and purity of emotion, and mind-free wildness, can carry you through your stagnation and self-damnation, transporting you right into the fathomless depths of your Being. You won't be masterminding this process (if you try, it won't work, simply because the *you* doing the masterminding is part of what must be let go of); you won't be behind the wheel; you won't even be under or on the wheel! You'll be far beyond the you who's always looking for somewhere special or auspicious to kneel, the you who's hoping to *steal* back what has been lost. Even now you may be resorting to your everyday mind, trying to make sense out of what was just spoken. If so, that is a sign to you that you are not hearing this, but only wanting to reduce it to mere information, a tidy little strategy to perhaps align yourself with, to enthusiastically use for a short time, and then to discard as soon as it becomes clear that "it" doesn't work (after which you can shop around for some more "transformational" information, once again pumping yourself up with hope, mistaking such inflation for real expansion)...

Such strategies don't work, because they involve the very you who is in the way of your awakening. That particular you isn't even a somebody, but just a dressed-up habit, a blustering cluster of assumptions that loves to refer to itself as you! This particular you must be recognized for what it is, not just simply witnessed, but unconstrainedly *felt* — its knottedness, its perennial uptightness, its non-Ecstaticness, must be *directly* experienced. The wound of it needs to be exposed, not morbidly, nor defeatedly, but with intelligence, compassion, and luminous interest. No fear of fear. No taking sides. Just raw, uncooked feeling, not emotionalism, not hysteria, not mind-generated feeling, but pure *feeling*, an unrefereed encounter with what is, right now, ever Now...

Again, you'll notice that I am not giving a prescription. What I'm saying is not intended to be taken as a progression of steps, nor as a reproducible method. The leap required of you is one of guts, elegance, spontaneity and totality, a jump of aesthetic and full-bodied wonder, however messy, however screamingly shaped, colored, or textured. The very occurrence of such a leap generates a beauty far beyond that of any ordinarily created beauty. Your leap, your risk, your plunge into your essentialness, is a kind of multidimensional painting, and this talk's intention is to help create a fitting frame for that work of art, a fluidly alive frame, a frame that hangs in a room with no walls, a frame that serves as a potent doorway into your Heartland. What is required of us is an art. You could call it the art of Being. Its name doesn't really matter; what does matter is that we know it is an art, a spontaneous gesture of our *whole* being. It is not partial. It is not a matter of self-manipulation. It is a surrender, not a submission, submission being an unillumined contraction, a mere crumbling of Being, whereas surrender is an expansion of Being, a yielding of self to a truer self, a dying into a deeper Life. Such surrender is not an irresponsible dissolving of one's boundaries or limits, as epitomized by romance, but rather is a conscious expansion of them, at once innocent and lucidly discriminative...

And what is the goad for all this? Suffering. What I'm describing now is not just the search to end suffering, but more so the very process whereby we can go right into our suffering, so potently, so fully, so strongly, so truly, that it literally becomes our ticket to Enlightenment. To say this is to invite misunderstanding, of course, for it implies a causal relationship between suffering and Enlightenment. It would be more accurate to say that there can be a positive correlation between the two, but even that takes the whole affair into the realm of the everyday mind for almost all. If you can feel what I'm saying between the lines, in the pauses, somewhere in between the words, you will be closer to *truly* understanding this, than if you simply persist in trying to make logical sense out of my words. I'm not deliberately being roundabout; I am simply pointing to the picture in which you are tending to be lost, that perceptual picture wherein you repetitiously dramatize your difficulties, where you make a problem out of your suffering, where you lose yourself (and then seek to find yourself, but in such a way that "you" find yourself in compensatory realms of pleasure-sweetened contraction)...

The door is *already open*. But, if you are not presently open and alert, then the door will be but a fiction to you, a romanticized fantasy, a vague goal (to be *apparently* attained through addiction to various methodologies, both Western and Eastern), a hope-riddled mirage, a mindtrap for your attention... But if *you* are not closed, not stuck in fantasy, and have conserved your energy wisely, then there will be sufficient passion and desire in you to go through that doorway, rather than to just use your energies to exploit the possibilities of your imprisonment. You cannot go through the door by simply imagining or believing it open, or by placing yourself in trance before a simulation of it. To try to replicate that door via imaging, belief, or trance is to, in almost all cases, *remove* ourselves from it, to dream that we *are* going through, and such dreams of course will conveniently generate the very sensations that seemingly say to us: "We have done it!" In our sleep-dreams, we often feel things strongly; they feel quite real to us. We kick a stone, for example — it may hurt our foot, our dream-foot, creating a sense of verisimilitude, wherein we are extremely unlikely to realize that we are actually dreaming. So the generation of sensation, of feeling, is not necessarily a sign that we have actually accessed the Truth...

The door of which I speak does not ask for some kind of mindgame, so that it might be passed through. It is simply here, obviously and openly here, when we are doing nothing whatsoever to distract ourselves from our suffering. The door leads to Eternal Unknowableness, and it also leads to a profound and exquisitely simple awareness that you are *already* existing in and *as* That Mystery prior to going through the door, even as you now listen to these words, even as you now become more sensitive to your hearing, to your breathing, to your subtle intentions and tensions. In fact, the more sensitive we become to such tension, the more acutely we become aware of an even deeper tension — the suppression of Being that is at the root of all our self-imposed suffering. We cannot become sensitized to this primal suffering of ours if we remain compulsively focussed on our *secondary* sufferings, namely all those difficulties created by our obsessive search to be relieved of our pain.

Something calls for us right now. Hear it without your ears. Sense it without your senses. Understand it without your mind. Something calls for you right now, as it has all through this talk, and prior to this talk, throughout your entire existence. It is a kind of Invitation, an undying Welcome — if you attune to It more deeply, It will eventually show itself as a sacred demand to which you must sooner or later completely surrender. All your suffering, all our suffering, is but purification for this sublime passage, this unspeakable Return, this heartbreaking reunion, this Mysterious embodiment of who we truly are...

My Freedom's in My Chains

Cutting through amnesia's infectious anesthesia
Sailing into the original wound
The waves carrying shards of both a dying and an Eternal sun
My craft weathering threat and sublime nostalgia
Arrowing through armoured desire and artificial fires
Riding the high and surviving the low
Carrying torchlight into caves of inevitable sorrow
Resisting tossing my hurt into tomorrow
Letting everything together spark a new start
Bringing the unrehearsable to my every part
I cannot stop this aching
Its currents cradle me through my grief
And the Joy comes so strong and the Moment so long
There's something to be done
and something to be undone
When your child was torn from you, did you fade?
When your people was violated, did you lie in defeat?
When your beloved was killed before your eyes,
        did you go to the very core of your deepest cries,
    or did you comfort yourself with yet another disguise?

I am an exile who cannot forget his Home
No one banished me, and nothing will vanish me
Already gone am I, yet never so here
My return is not to a place
I am a slave to my birthing
My freedom's in my chains
        my love guiding the reins
            my longing beating out the time
                my humanness providing the rhyme
                    my need
                    carving clear
                the Everlasting Shore
            and the Evermortal steps I must take
                        until my heart does completely break
                and reassembled soar mindfree
            inseparable from the Great Heart

Gustave Doré: *Milton's Paradise Lost*

– 11 –

Releasing Sex From The Obligation To Make Us Feel Better

In expecting sex to make us feel better, we only postpone or obscure facing whatever is not working in our life, especially in our so-called intimacies. When a relationship is polluted by unresolved conflict, unexpressed needs, twisted jealousies, chronic anxiety, boredom, lies, compensatory fantasies, and so on, there inevitably arises a craving for release from such distress, the most common method for most being through sexual discharge and its warmups. It's no accident that as soon as most people start copulating with someone else, they almost invariably claim to *now* "have" a relationship with that person — that is, a fantasy-laden arena wherein enough biochemical/ emotional charge can be built up (through projection, imagination, and, especially, chronic relational *conflict*) so as to *seemingly* necessitate sexual discharge.

When sex is used to relieve distress, to drain or prune accumulated tensions and psychoemotional disturbances, it is being abused, serving not to express and celebrate interrelatedness, joy, love, intimacy, and soulful communion, but rather to feed the activities of pleasurable distraction and ego-reinforcement. The worse we feel, the more likely we are to look for some sort of compensation, some sort of pleasantly consoling release, some sort of easily accessible sedation, especially that available through typical sex. Thus do we tend to fuck away the very passion we need for the Awakening process, enervating ourselves with all the clarity of drugged laboratory rats, going to the same damned place for the cheese every time, screwing into oblivion the very signals that we are harming ourselves! Again and again, we fuck away our very *desire* for sex, unable to tolerate its intensity, its richness, its fullness of sensation (that is, we, being so *turned off*, crave being *turned on*, and yet as soon as we're turned on, we want to get rid of the sensation of being turned on!), thereby only reinforcing the *roots* of our urge to numb ourselves to our suffering. On and on we tend to go, resolutely resurrecting our cycle of conflict, relational difficulty, distress, overload of charge, and release from such tension via sexual discharge and all the titillations of its opening act...

Do not expect that as you become more conscious, and therefore (at least in most cases) more open to the fires of necessary purification, that sex will somehow increase your comfort, somehow relieve you of your pain, somehow magically transport you into a realm where suffering is obsolete. No! As you mature, *everything* that is neurotic about you, misaligned, twisted, or just plain unhappy will usually be *obviously* exaggerated during your sexplay, perhaps even very exaggerated, through the very intensity, the all-round aliveness, that epitomizes active sex. (If there's very little aliveness, then *that* or its faked opposite will be exaggerated, or made quite explicit to awareness.) As such, you will, despite your reactivity or laziness, learn to use your times of sexual coupling to *illuminate* what is *already* in essence occurring in your life (inner and outer), so that sex will not merely be a vacation from the rest of your life, a pleasurable refuge, but rather a wonderfully permeable part of it, a highly functioning part of it, profoundly contributing to your ripening, bringing to it not only the joy of Being, but the joy of integrity, good humor, and a vulnerability unburdened by helplessness and egoic programming.

If you persist in such full-bodied honesty and openness, eventually sex will be Ecstasy for you, simply because you'll come to it already loose, already naked, already unstressed, already willing to be deeply seen and felt, already intimate. But prior to this natural ecstasy, you will encounter difficulties in sex, not so much in terms of its actual mechanics, as in terms of what is occurring in the rest of your life, given that you are now, at least to a significant degree, willing to allow *everything* that you are to be obviously, openly, vitally present *during* your lovemaking. Yes, once so long ago (perhaps only yesterday) when you were unconscious, asleep, mechanically inclined, you *apparently* enjoyed sex more (as a combination super-stimulant and super-sleeping pill), but not *really*, not truly, because you were in slumber, thickly content to use sex as a *mechanism* to release distress, to inflate ego, to sustain romantic delusion, to temporarily defuse relational stalemates, and so on. Do not pretend that there was Ecstasy then; you might as well welcome your disillusionment (which doesn't mean getting cynical!) and get on with it...

When we're in between a completely unawakened state and one wherein wakefulness is stably established, there is self-conscious-ness, not the sort that is simply a neurotic fixation on what others are apparently making of us, a kind of spirit-crushing stagefright, but rather the sort that is a rudimentary awakening in which it is all but impossible to go *fully* unconscious during sex (or anything else). Given this, we will during sex inevitably notice neurotic and me-chanical behavior on our part and/or our partner's, and we'll proba-bly feel compelled to not simply continue our genital exercise, but to interrupt or alter it so that something more Life-giving, something truer, can happen.

As such, sex will, at times, be quite frustrating — we won't be able to keep pursuing our sexual rituals to their conventional climax, nor will we be able to bury ourselves in the misinformed, fantasy-pushing "feel-good" advice of most so-called sex therapists — we'll know too much, feel too much, see too much, to be able to let our mechanical-ness go unchallenged. We will not so easily be able to irresponsibly discharge the energy we have accumulated; we will not so easily be able to rub or drive ourselves into such overdone stimulation that genital release seems utterly necessary; we will not so easily be seduced by the ecstasy-promising hype of "higher" sex manuals; we will not so easily be able to fuck away what isn't working in our lives, and we especially won't be able to so easily abuse ourself and our partner.

In this partially awakened condition, we're in a cocoon of sorts, too far into it to totally become a caterpillar again, but not so far as to be able to emerge as butterflies. We've sensed the presence of our wings, but we cannot yet fully unfold them, though at times it seems we can, in our dreams, in our peaks of enthusiasm, or perhaps in the airtight sanctums of our beliefs or hopes. Nevertheless, we will emerge, truly emerge, if we continue making awakening our priority, *and* if that awakening is not pursued independent of our passion, vitality, and desiring — we'll one day be so firmly established in our center of Being that sex (and everything else in our life) will be an expression of our happiness, our joy, our Truth, rather than a means *toward* it. Sex will then not be used by us to make us feel better, but rather as a full-fleshed, soulshining expression and intensification of our condition of *already* feeling good, of *already* feeling happy, alive, vulnerable, present, authentic, in touch with the Eternal, in deep communion with our every feeling, in love with our partner, together bodily, ecstatically, nakedly, honoring the dark and the light, the high and the low, the personal and the transpersonal...

In this, Ecstasy is not the goal, but the foundation. No strategy is required here, even though there will likely be some attraction to strategy, to technique, to ritual, some sort of spiritual ambition ("tantric" or otherwise), some modicum of craving to find a method that will do it to us — permanently center us, uncork our kundalini, carry us into transcendental rapture, blow our minds once and for all, whatever — those who succumb to such ambition may choose to fixate on a particular group, assuming that membership therein will liberate them, ever looking outside themselves for fulfillment. You could call their way the way of the extrovert, but it is also the way of the convert, the guru-worshipper, the compulsive joiner, the one who, having turned away from intimacy with the Source, craves belonging to something seemingly bigger than himself or herself, something that provides a sensation of familial solidity, of anchoredness, of easily-accessed identity (as in nationalism of all kinds, as well as in just about every sort of religion). The way of the introvert doesn't work either, the one who assumes that truth is within, that all the answers are to be found through exploiting (and even glorifying) one's inwardness and recoil from relatedness.

What I am talking about is not to be found through becoming an introvert, extrovert, or convert, or any combination of these, for all three are busy diverting their attention from their deeper authenticity, unquestioningly assuming that there's something wrong with them that needs to be fixed — they are only looking for distraction from their pain (including the pain of their very search), comforting themselves with notions that they are indeed progressing or "going through a lot" following "their" path. Instead of being an extrovert, introvert, or convert relative to the Awakening process, it is far more useful to be a lover, not a lover as in a self-enclosed, cultic sense, an impermeable little bubble of would-be immunity, but a lover as the full-blooded wholeness of ourselves, the passion-bright fullness of ourselves, a warrior and flower of intimacy, a nakedly alive power, a juicily-embodied celebration of our totality, a tender storm and a wild calm, an exquisitely vital meeting place of the Eternal and the mortal — the lover doesn't seek refuge from Life's demands, but is utterly committed to awakening without any dilution of passion or attachment, without any monkish or seemingly religious withdrawal from the world of the senses. The lover is not trying to escape outwardly *or* inwardly. The lover is surrendered to the Source, no matter what the pain. The lover neither avoids suffering nor unnecessarily reinforces it...

Those who make a problem out of suffering are always looking for relief from it (and from the stress of their problematic orientation!), usually through sexuality or obsessive mentalizing, again and again fucking away their passion and integrity, seeking oblivion, numbness, safety, entertainment, and engorged complication, through ritualistically stimulating themselves, trying to eroticize themselves into a semblance of Life. They'd rather masturbate than make love. In fact, almost all sex between unawakened beings is just mutual masturbation, however romantic its setting or mood might be, all rubbed up with nowhere to flow. Do not expect your sexlife to dissolve your dissatisfaction; if you fuck away the branchings of your distress, you only strengthen its roots. Know that I tire of my criticalness here, but I must go on; this whole affair fills me with grief and a tremendous longing to be of real use in the reestablishment of love and wakefulness in the domain of sexuality...

For the usual human, sex is a fire that's all heat and no light. For those who have begun to awaken a little, the very intensity and richness of sex must be used, at least in part, to illuminate what is occurring for them. It must be permitted to brighten the way. It need not be forced to play this role, for it *naturally* does so. If you realize the folly of trying to stimulate (or otherwise manipulate) yourself into Ecstasy, then perhaps you will, for a time anyway, lose interest in sex. If passion does not simply arise out of mutual love, then why force it, why fantasize or rub yourself into it, why indulge and deify friction?

Better, wait for sexual passion to arise from a state of relaxed alertness and love. Bring trust to your sexual impulse. Stop trying to guide it; let it lead you. Bring light to your lust, and then the must in lust will cease to be. Then sex will be liberated to ride its own mind-free momentum, its own primal currents, its love-generated powers; then its passion, its force, its tenderness and subtlety, its brilliance, its labyrinthine wonder, will be utterly unlike that which was manifested when you were unconscious and blindly lustful.

When we release sex from the obligation to make us feel better, then we deepen our commitment to the Awakening process, enriching our yes to Truth, making ourselves more and more available to a passion far beyond any passion that can be created through mere sensory stimulation — we will have brought ourselves to a point where we are capable of tolerating an ever more intense thrill of feeling, a point where we don't have to get rid of such feeling or desire, but where we can circulate it throughout our *entire* system, physically, emotionally, psychically, spiritually, mentally, thus rejuvenating and refreshing our *everything*, reestablishing us in our core of Being again and again, and we'll do this not only through sex, but through everything that is part of our life now, without expecting that such activities will bring us joy...

What I'm talking about here is nakedness of spirit. Such nakedness, such soulful openness, is intolerable as it's evanescent if there's no steadiness of center within us. To stably establish such center requires an increasing willingness to be naked, level upon level, in a manner luminously discriminative, vulnerable, and open-eyed. This is more often than not a difficult process, a very difficult process, asking for all-out participation; it is often best cultivated in the presence and alliance of a true group, a non-cultic group, a group *completely* committed to real intimacy, *naturally* and passionately committed to cutting through reactivity, to making room for all of their pain and suffering and joy, hiding nothing from each other, including their urge to so hide. Such a group cannot be automatically formed out of mere enthusiasm or common belief; it is much deeper than that, asking not for belief, but for surrender to one's longing to awaken and for a quality of trust that is almost unheard of in our culture, a kind of trust utterly unlike that which characterizes converts, or devotees of political parties, religious movements, or particular belief systems. The true group is family at its best; it is a vibrant, marvelously alive embodiment of intimacy, integrity, and love.

In the lover, the fully human lover, individuality and surrender to God go hand in hand, merging ever deeper, catalyzing each other, asking not for a dissolving of personal boundaries, but for an uninhibited expansion of them, so that one is, moment to moment, spontaneously and consciously including the other (human and otherwise), thrilled through and through by love and a profound empathy, leading to a oneness that is not an indiscriminate, homogenized soup of qualities, but a oneness that coexists with diversity, without any elitist hierarchical positioning.

The true lover gives love without giving herself or himself away. The true lover is not an ideal, nor a should, nor a recipe or a remedy, but only what is most natural to us when we are already happy, already open, already willingly established in our native integrity of Being. Creating the environment of the true lover is a matter of profound effort, but *being* the lover is a matter of equally profound non-effort. The doings, sexual and otherwise, of the lover are not typical doings, but rather are doings that spring forth from Essence-centered non-effort, a non-effort that shines with sacred silence, knowledgeless wisdom, and heartfelt resonance with the Source of All...

From a session given July 10, 1988

– 12 –

No More Fumbling
in the Dark

SUSAN: I felt quite nervous coming to this session.

ROBERT: Why?

SUSAN: Maybe something will be exposed that I don't know about.

ROBERT: Like what?

SUSAN: (*Sighing*) Like what you told me about how I hug you —
things I'm really unconscious of doing.

ROBERT: What do you really want to talk about?

SUSAN: Sex.

ROBERT: Now you're sitting up straighter! (*Laughter*) Go ahead.

SUSAN: It's an area where I still flounder around a lot. I don't feel at
ease sexually, most of the time.

ROBERT: That's partially because you're more conscious now; you
can't so easily slip into the ease of mechanical sex. What you hid
then you can't so easily hide now, so to the degree that you're still
hiding sexually, you're ill at ease during love-making times. You're
getting more sober sexually, but don't let that obstruct your joy!
Don't try so hard to do it right! When you start to wake up, sex
becomes fundamentally no different than any other act; it's just a
lovely intensification of something that's *already* occurring. Of course,
for most, sex is their big out, their super-stimulant, their favorite way
of throwing away their surface tension. Most keep their sexuality

separate from the rest of their lives, shutting more doors than just the bedroom door. As foreplay, it's exaggeratedly advertised, suggested all over the place, winking out from all sorts of faces, but as actual intercourse, it's usually secretive, not just relative to outsiders, but in terms of the actual copulating pair!

There is basically no wisdom in our culture concerning sex. There isn't even much wisdom about it in spiritual literature either, because most who have engaged in so-called higher spiritual practices have avoided sex, or have gotten too esoteric about it, too precious, too non-relational. It's important to discover what's true about sex, from the ground up. No preset beliefs, no dogmatic practices, no sex-manual automaticities, but only raw, well-lit experimentation. Creating access to real Ecstasy. Coming alive...

SUSAN: There are some areas I still keep a lid on. I have so much shame around my sexuality...

ROBERT: Well, for you sex has been a method of controlling your world. You've been a whiz at hooking men, at making them want what you've got. If you can get them excited, hard, lusting, with some kind of fantasy about you, some sort of juicy promise, then they are hooked, drooling at *your* command. So the issue here is less about sex than it is about control; in fact, most sexual "problems" are not about sex at all... In Lenny Bruce's autobiography, he talks about a whorehouse in France, wherein the prostitutes all dressed in different costumes. One of the favorite costumes was that of a little girl, a sweet, alluringly innocent Daddy's little girl. The turn-on wasn't so much sex, as it was breaking a taboo. But the favorite, or most popular costume of all, was that of a nun, nakedly available under her habit. The safe violation of another taboo. Another round of guilt-engorged stimulation and degenerative release...

When people bitch about their sex-life, or brag about it, they're usually not even talking about sex — the whole matter is not about sex, but about something quite different, something that's trying to work itself out through sex, literally fumbling in the dark! When you, for example, try to work out, or express, certain power dynamics through your sexuality, you're only abusing yourself sexually, exploiting your sex center, forcing it to do other than its true work. If you could feel now, in its fullness, all the men you have let come inside you so that you might feel powerful or have control, you'd probably be nauseous. You've let your power center, along with your mind, dominate your sex center. It's very difficult for you to connect your sexuality with your heart, because of what's happening in between the two, namely the constriction and congestion of your belly, the obsessive misdirection of your gut-level power. Your power center will start to open when you say a *healthy* no to people, especially to those who hurt you. But instead of saying no, you get revenge by making them want you, and by dangling what they want just out of their reach! How can you possibly give yourself fully in sex if your priority is remaining in control?

Everything has been out of balance in you, but now you are coming into balance; things are starting to line up in you, and so whatever's out of alignment is becoming more and more glaringly obvious. It may seem worse than it used to be, but it actually isn't — it's just that you see more, that you can't help but see more. You're healthier sexually than you've ever been before, but because you've now got some of the lights on, it appears that you're now more neurotic, more twisted. It's not so. Don't make a problem out of this; don't get stuck evaluating yourself. If you can honestly and clearly expose where you are stuck sexually, you'll see that *that* is where you are also stuck in other areas of your life! Again, so-called sexual problems are not problems of sex, but of being...

Let's look at Brian, for example [*her current lover*]. His tentativeness pollutes a lot of what he does, but when he's in his power, he's not tentative at all — he's still sensitive, but he's not at all hesitant or limp. Nevertheless, his neurotic and common urge is to still wait until someone like me gives him permission to take power. Yes, he does it, and often does it beautifully, but he himself has not yet given himself a full yes to come out — he's still *partial* about it, still habitually hesitant, and this shows up in the rest of his life, in his stride, his glance, his sexuality, his touch...

Now, other men may have a touch that seems more manly, more assured, but in many cases, they're not as open as Brian; their certainty is more of density than of depth. You could meet a gross guy in a bar, he could later on grab you, embrace you strongly, but he wouldn't be expressing very many dimensions of himself — lust, aggressiveness, maybe even some romanticism, but not much more. No real vulnerability. Brian, on the other hand, is exaggeratedly vulnerable, terrified of not doing it right, terrified of taking a real stand. Ultimately, he's afraid of commitment, not storybook commitment, but real commitment; to commit himself sexually is no different than committing himself in any other way. In his dramatization of his great vulnerability and supposed need, he is hiding a deeper vulnerability, a true openness of being, and by keeping that from you, he keeps a semblance of control, weaker than yours, but still nevertheless control.

You must stop protecting yourself. When you were lovers with Shawn, there was so, so much unnecessary struggle, so much loveless friction, so many lies, that it was very difficult for you to truly see what you were up to sexually with him. In fact, your sexuality then tended to be more of a neurotic escape, a tension-release, a pleasurable antidote to the rest of your relationship. And that is exactly what you ought not to be doing with your relationship with Brian! What you need to do is to enjoy him in a *friendly* way, a personable way, and when sex comes, still stay in touch, in *feeling* communion with him, even if that sometimes means stopping the sex act, getting messy or uncomfortable, having no orgasms, and so on...

SUSAN: I get really afraid when I get near orgasm. It's something I never was aware of before.

ROBERT: So when you orgasmed with earlier lovers, you didn't feel the fear.

SUSAN: That's right.

ROBERT: Because your orgasms then were primarily physical.

SUSAN: Yes. Just friction and the right positions and moves.

ROBERT: That's easy. Throw in a little romance, some sentimental pretence, and you've got sex as it's practised by most. Your orgasms now will not be primarily physical; they'll likely be far less frequent, but a hell of lot more real. You won't be making yourself come. You'll be far more aware that you are orgasming with Brian, not just *a* man, not just another cock with an attached mind! You won't just be having an orgasm, a blast of consoling pleasure — you will *be* the orgasm, you'll be at one with its energies, and you'll also be utterly present with Brian, instead of being off somewhere in your own oblivion, all pleasured-out and still psychospiritually intact.

SUSAN: It's that dissolving feeling in deep orgasm that makes me feel panicky...

ROBERT: You're capable of going very deep, right through egoic death. You know exactly what it is to let go fully, to relinquish all ego-centered control. To go right into your sexuality is to become intimate with both Death and Life. The point isn't just to surrender at orgasm, but throughout the entire sex act! There's both a dissolution of form, and an intensification of presence — at least that's how it is for me. There's no solid shape for me then, but only a diffuseness of form, a spermatic upspiralling, a bursting of light, a fluid shapeshifting — it's an expansion of love, an ecstasy, a deep meeting, a wonder, an unpredictability. The key with orgasm, other than to cut through obsession with having it, is to not control it. But that takes a kind of trust that very few are willing to embody. Just about everyone is hankering for orgasm, because it gives them a taste of "no-mind," a mini-break from the tedium of their usual self — there's a split second of unspeakable knowingness, and then you and your mind come rushing back into that great spaciousness...

In deep sex, you'll feel an orgasmic quality throughout, often quite subtly. If you don't feel it early on, you're probably out of rhythm, out of touch. You can't rub or friction or manipulate yourself into such feeling; its passion arises from stillness and love, rather than from stimulation. Out of such stillness, such juicy silence, movement will occur, free of your mind's programming. However, if you overdo the movement, get greedy for more of its pleasure-inducement, you'll numb yourself to your ecstatic capabilities. Repetition that does not arise from Being is only going to produce *more and more* of the you that your sexing is an attempt to escape!

True pleasure is more than physical; it's a matter of full-bodied, spiritual surrender, an intensification of the feeling of God-communion. It's Ecstasy. And it requires an *unqualified* letting go, not some infantile, non-individuated letting go, but a letting go that's as expansive as it's luminous. You cannot mastermind it, you cannot reproduce it from a sex manual, you cannot oversee it... If you try to be "spiritual" during sex, it won't really work, because you'll be using the other person to have a certain experience. You used to fuck; and now you're...tantric! A few pseudo-spiritual gestures or intentions are tossed in, plus some textbook posturing, and humping turns into holy communion! What pretentious bullshit! Ordinary sex is screwed up enough, but this is twice removed from the real thing! In true sex, no surrogates of Ecstasy are permitted — there is no pretending. There is the joy of nothing held back. There is no ultimate dissolving of personal boundaries, but rather a deliciously alive expansion of them. You give it all without giving yourself away. You expand to include the other, without abandoning your own core of Being. This is love. It is not romance. It is rich with integrity and a deep appreciation of each other's differences. It's an embrace both lusty and sacred.

Sometimes the genitals will feel very turned on in that embrace, and at other times they simply won't. There's no sense in trying to make anything in particular happen; the energetics of it transcend any meaning you might want to superimpose on it. Sometimes the impulse is there to be passionate and strong and not have the sex act last that long; at other times, it's utterly appropriate to linger and be very slow. It doesn't really matter; the mechanics of sex must be secondary to the imperatives of the currents arising from your depths. Each time is unique. Addiction to repetition of what worked before will destroy Ecstasy. Do what you have to do to not bring your everyday mind into your sexing.

However still sex might be, it must emanate from unrepressed feeling. It shouldn't be just a coolness, nor a heated parody of real emotion. It is emotional, nakedly so! You must feel free to cry, to laugh, to wail and soar, even to get angry! Sometimes you'll have to stop, and confront something in the other, some lie, some falsity of sound or movement, some pretence of enjoyment, and get right into it with them, even to the point of raging at them! Why repress it and just keep on fucking? Be authentic, not like some little twerp playing a finger-pointing therapy-game, but instead like a full-blooded woman! Rock the boat. Make waves. Don't save all your juice for copulation! Make room for psychic and mystical experience during sex — don't have sex for this purpose, but do make room for it...

You and Brian are not, at least to a very significant degree, creating tension in your relationship, so your sexlife with him is not primarily a release from that tension. On the other hand, you and Shawn created a tremendous tension together, a huge amount of distress and hurt, so when you got together to make love, you were not just getting together as lovers, but as seekers after release, release from all the tension and struggle of your everyday relationship. Many people have their so-called "best sex" after they've fought, learning to associate conflict with hot sex (hence the bonding of sex and violence). Sure, they may seem to fight for all sorts of reasons, but underneath, they're just looking to come more alive, to feel more — it's usually a clumsy approach, usually an unnecessarily hurtful approach, but nevertheless it is a strategy, however unconscious, to feel more, to break out of the suffocating grip of their more "civilized" repressions. Like war, it gets the blood up. It's a hit. Look at couples who don't fight at all, and you'll discover that very, very few of them have a passionate sexlife; many, in fact, don't even have a sex life. But if sex only "feels good" if there's an overload of sensation, it's not real sex. Real sex doesn't need relational conflict, nor deliberate stimulation, for its passion; its base of love and luminous desire and soul-communion creates, *naturally* creates, passion...

Orgasm is a kind of Death, a rapturous dying into Life, a passage into and through the subtle worlds, followed by a sense of rebirth, of rejuvenative re-embodiment. Sometimes it's not even that pleasurable. Sometimes for me, it's more of a silent explosion, a great softness, a river fanning in all directions, exquisitely yielding, with no sound of rapids or waterfalls. Other times, it's tremendously vital for me, very vocal. But don't make the mistake of making sounds so as to sound like you're having a good time! There must be a freedom of emotion in such sounds, an utter vulnerability, a complete letting go of body and mind.

Don't make an ideal out of how sex should be. Allow it to be ordinary. Be aware of the itch of a bedsheet, the itch of your habits. What if you smack your skull on the headboard? What if one of you farts? You must cultivate compassion for all the homely little moments of sex, all the little discomforts that never make it to the big screen. Don't expect sex to deliver you from your troubles. Come to sex already clean, already loose. Bring your need, but not your neediness, letting the energy that emerges between you and him guide your actions — you don't guide it, but let it guide you. Stop expecting sex to make you feel better! Sex is no more salvation than it is damnation. Why should it do your dirty work? (*Long pause*)

Let's shift gears now, and get more specific. How do you feel kissing Brian?

SUSAN: I don't find it that pleasurable most of the time.

ROBERT: What don't you like about the way he kisses you?

SUSAN: It's tentative.

ROBERT: He has trauma around and in his mouth, doesn't he? Conflicting impulses imbedded in his jaw, made all the worse by his unrelenting self-consciousness... How about his tongue? How does he use it when he's kissing you?

SUSAN: Awkwardly.

ROBERT: In other words, unnecessarily deliberate. The tongue needs to move in a way that complements the rest of the body, instead of the dictates of the mind. It must be as sensitive as it is free to roam. A mouthful of mechanically moving tongue is not exactly a turn-on!

SUSAN: Once we were kissing, and he was very unaware of his mouth, and he was slobbering out of it. (*Laughter*) I just stopped us, and started laughing.

ROBERT: Did he know in that moment what had happened?

SUSAN: No. I had to tell him.

ROBERT: Was he hurt?

SUSAN: I think so.

ROBERT: It's very important to clearly identify what works and what doesn't work. In depth, and in detail. This, if done well and lovingly, takes the mystique out of sex, while reestablishing it in Mystery. (*Pause*) But back to Brian's mouth — it looks like a gaping wound to me sometimes.

SUSAN: Sometimes he has difficulty sucking on my breasts.

ROBERT: How so?

SUSAN: Tentative, again. He'll just lay there...

ROBERT: That's probably because he may not even want to be sucking on your nipples, but thinks he should be, so to please both impulses, he beaches himself there! He has to stop trying to get turned on, or acting like he's trying to get turned on, if he doesn't feel it, and you need to help him here, help him speak more bluntly. If you simply reject him, it does neither of you any good. He must also identify for himself what he doesn't like about your body, instead of pretending you're one big erogenous zone! How does he treat your neck and its scar?

SUSAN: He avoids it.

ROBERT: He needs to cut through that, right through his apparent repulsion. He needs to make love to your *whole* body, and you to his.

SUSAN: When we were together last time, it was the first time he addressed my scar; he looked at it, touched it, talked about it.

ROBERT: If he really looked at it, he'd probably cry; he'd feel the wound of it, the hurt, the violation of you that it signals. It'd resonate with his own woundedness, his own apparent ugliness. He needs to touch it, to stroke it, to truly acknowledge that *this* is Susan, too. (*Long pause*) Does he touch your genitals?

SUSAN: Very rarely.

ROBERT: Have you talked about this?

SUSAN: Yes. He says he finds vaginas to be disgusting.

ROBERT: Vaginas disgust most men, including those who dutifully touch, lick, and rub them. Their distaste is just more repressed than Brian's. If their supposed manhood is on the line, are they going to avoid getting manual or oral with a waiting vagina? No! For most men, vaginas are unattractive — they're dark, wet, smelly, subterranean, enveloping, threatening. They're the Mystery of Woman, the fertile Darkness, the tunnel into Being and Non-Being — to go right into them, *fully*, is to go to a depth that very few men want. So men cheapen and trivialize vaginas, calling them holes and boxes and slits, while worshipping at the altar of mammary glands. Brian needs to really look at your genitals, and touch them, up close — I don't care if he's turned on or not — he needs to discover his deeper feelings about this, just as you do! You haven't exactly loved your genitals, either. So get into this with him. You may end up having a strong cry together, or making love, or whatever. He needs to make real contact with your vagina, and he needs to breathe loosely and feelingly while he does this. No tentativeness, and no trying to get you turned on. While he's doing this, realize that you are dealing with a wounded man, a broken boy. He's not the runt of the litter! He's no different than most men, except that he's far more honest and vulnerable.

SUSAN: Yes! I don't feel angry about him not wanting to kiss or touch my vagina. I feel his willingness each time we make love to explore me more, to be open.

ROBERT: (*Long pause*) Brian, like you, has a habit of doubting himself. It's a kind of negative security for him, an easily-resurrected familiarity. He's terrified to *really* take charge; it's easier to create a secondary sort of charge, to get amped up sexually. The fear of performance cuts deep, whether it's indulged or repressed. Real passion is far more than engorgement! Take the word "perform" — its second syllable is "form." For me, sex is not about form, but rather is about using form so wisely that the formless dimensions of Existence come into the foreground — then your body is no longer just a mass of sweating flesh, undulating wetness, swollen organs, and so on, but instead is experienced as free energy, patterned energy, a fluidly shapeshifting embodiment of Ecstasy, mysteriously continuous with All That Is. Here, you're not thinking here's an arm, a hand, a flap, a testicle, a neck, a tooth — instead, it's one fluid, wonderfully *diversified* Unity. Here, you'll find yourself less and less involved in your perceptions, and more and more involved in Love, Bliss, Truth, and Being.

Presence becomes primary, perception secondary...

Gustave Doré: *The Bible*

-13-

Disarming
Our Harm-Doing

When we, in our reactivity, are doing harm, we don't often *really* feel what we are up to, simply because in order to do such harm we need to desensitize ourselves, to disconnect ourselves from our capacity for empathy and love. To vulnerably open after we have done harm (it would be more accurate to say after *it* has done harm, not so as to abdicate responsibility, but so as to convey the sheer mechanicalness of persisted-in reactivity) is not usually easy, for in our very openness we have no choice but to fully *feel* what we have done...

Perhaps the most popular way of avoiding or hamstringing such feeling is to wade into the quicksand of guilt, to punish ourselves for what we have done (and will, despite our resolutions to the contrary, *continue* to do so long as distraction from suffering is our priority) in such a manner as to weaken and divide ourselves (into the mutually parasitic duo of bad child and righteously wrathful parent), thereby only *increasing* our vulnerability to the very forces that *seemingly* catalyzed or legitimized our harm-doing!

Guilt's accusing finger, trembling with arthritic emotion and inquisitorial vengeance, is pointed at us, but the blame (blame being the morality of guilt) does not necessarily stay imbedded solely in us; most of us have the habit of shifting it (the only variables being its intensity and its *content*) from us to someone or something else, so that we have a turn animating the pointing finger. Regardless, blame is blame, an endarkened substitute for true responsibility. (Such responsibility doesn't just clearly and honestly state what has been done, but willingly and uninhibitedly *feels* it, right to the core, no matter how much it hurts...)

Doing no harm doesn't mean an end to anger, interference, lust, jealousy, competitiveness, and other such states, but rather a full-bodied leap into the sane use of them — the point isn't to avoid, sanitize, or meditate away the raw stuff of Life, but to creatively, passionately, and luminously participate in it, letting our recoil from such apparently troublesome feelings and conditions become obsolete. A *stance* of non-violence all too often is itself violent in its very denial of the more forceful aspects or shapings of Life-energy, as well as in its unexamined resistance to coming truly alive.

Whenever we're lost in the sleep known as the waking state, we're either doing harm, or hovering on the edge of doing harm, not because we're malicious or evil, but because we're permitting an imposter to sit upon the throne of Self, namely the us that is pretending to be awake. Even when "we" do good, it is ordinarily accidental, a result not of conscious action, but of circumstantial positivity, lopsided humanitarianism, or just plain guilt. When we've begun to awaken a little, we still usually lean toward doing harm, primarily out of habit — powers that come to us as a byproduct of our work on ourselves may become compulsively fascinating to us, since they are so easily harnessed to self-aggrandizement and egoic glamourization.

To knowingly do harm, to do injury, to indulge in reactivity, *after* awakening has taken root in us, is to invite in extraordinary disaster to ourselves, excruciatingly painful lessons that are exaggerations of the lessons we've already learned but not honoured. This is a matter of laws both spiritual and psychic, as well as thermodynamic — there is no real escape for harm-doers on any level. Nevertheless, many persist in clinging to what they hope their powers may bring them (such powers including charismatic presence, easy access to deep insight, persuasive eloquence, readily-amplified attractiveness on many levels, and so on), even as they inwardly loathe themselves for their successful manipulations.

Rarely does anyone wake up, or reawaken, without the benefit of a shock, unless some degree of wakefulness is already characteristic of them. Ordinarily, anything less than a shock (or energetic transmission of considerable potency) only becomes yet another part of the dream, artfully incorporated just as certain Balinese temples have added carvings of tourists to their outside walls; there is value in being able to assimilate, but only if doing so contributes to our awakening. Even shocks, however brilliantly executed or improvised, aren't enough, though — yes, there may be some resultant awakening, but there is usually such an intense pull back into the yearned-for familiarity of the dream that the effect of the shock is short-lived. Giving a new or more intense shock (which Life delivers in the form of crises) is not the answer — at best, the dreamer will only learn to *depend* on such jolts for awakening from his or her nightmares. Shocks must be used, and used well; what is realized upon waking up must somehow be remembered when the dream takes hold again, and such remembrance is very difficult to embody without some kind of help or support...

Yes, we are alone, but we need not do it alone. The pride that says we've got to do it alone is but the male face of the imposter upon the throne of Self, no more than deified independence. And the female face of this counterfeit? The giving-up force that generates inertia and self-sabotage.

However alone we are, we are also together; we're not here to blindly compete for position within the dream, but to support and inspire each other's awakening from the dream, not passively, but actively and with ruthless compassion, cutting through all agreements to not challenge each other's reactivity. This is obviously not necessarily a gentle process, but nor is it a violent one — its force, however wild or angry or critical at times, is love-based, aflame with undeniable caring for the well-being of whomever it is addressing, ever taking the admonition to do no harm from the realm of mere belief or resolution into actual action...

William Blake (British Museum)

– 14 –

A Cancerous Bottling-Up of Mind: Doubt Explored & Unmasked

Doubt is a disease that we've all got some of the time... It is a collapse of heart that's gone to mind, a lack of real faith in our core impulses, a miserably unilluminated inquiry interested not in revelation, but only in confirmation of its bleakly righteous outlook. Doubt is what happens when we, having recoiled from what truly nourishes us, busy ourselves seeking a secondary nourishment through the mentalized *surrogates* of what we have turned away from — the apparent nourishment provided by such counterfeits tends to bounce between the compensatory bounty of fantasy and the plain fare laid out by the fake realism of doubt, neither of which are edible, except to that surrogate self known as ego. Throw a dose of heavier threat-possibility into Doubt, and you'll have worry; exaggerate that, and you'll have anxiety...

Doubt (like Its opposite, blind faith) is but a confession of automated psychospiritual withdrawal from Life, the heady epitome of self-fragmentation — It is the contracted mind in action, dumbly divided, ever reinfecting Itself, providing sepia commentary and frictional foreplay for all-round dread. Whereas skepticism is healthy questioning, Doubt is unhealthy questioning, a dead-end inquiry, a bottled-up questioning that is terrified of being uncorked. As the dour flowering arising from the rubble of our collapse of Being, Doubt sprouts from every troubled skull, staining whatever *content* comes Its way... But before I go further (or over-condense what I'm saying), let me fill in more of the background...

The turning away I mentioned above is a suppression of Being, a recoil from Life, a stranglehold on our capacity for love, empathy, and power — it is a psychosomatic gripping, a chronic self-pressuring that drastically shrinks us energetically, literally forcing our Life-energy out, evicting or discharging it, squeezing what's left of it toward a terminal of release or evacuation (or, much less frequently, redesign), usually in an upward or downward direction. When Life-force is forced upward, it (in much the same way as a tube of toothpaste that's gripped in the middle squirts its contents up and out the top) crowds and aggravates what's inside our skulls, over-intensifying and aberrating the activity therein, while simultane-ously compressing it into a fearful condition, one species of which is Doubt.

Doubt tends to attach Itself to whatever content is nearby; thus do we then doubt *this*, or doubt *that*. Let me reiterate: When the *energy* of Doubt is allowed to mushroom, it naturally fastens onto whatever subject matter is handy, immediately *framing* that particular some-thing in a questionable light. In Doubt, we inject fear or negative anticipation into certain intentions, certain plans, certain notions we have about ourselves — we obsessively futurize about certain outcomes, glumly chaining ourselves to worrying about what might or might not happen, eventually, at least in some cases, noticing that what we worry about frequently comes true. (And why? Simply because in order to worry about something, we must keep it *in mind*, the very seed of it being nourished by our neurotic attention, our compulsive focus, our craving for immunity...)

Doubt's realm is devoid of real love, whether constructed flimsily, as in suicidal impotence, or solidly, as in cynicism. Doubt is what the mind does when it is cut off from the vitality and primal inten-tions of the rest of one's being. Nevertheless, Doubt presumes to have an overview, but in fact has none — It cannot even see Itself, let alone accurately assess Its environment. To work with Doubt, to break our addiction to It, to unglue ourselves from Its standpoint, requires far more than just positive thinking, remedial programs, and other counter-efforts and distractions... The beast, however ab-stract or amorphous, must be directly faced and seen for what it is, namely a suppression of Being crowded into our thinking mind, festeringly wrapped around whatever subject matter is close at hand. This must be seen and felt, not merely thought about! In such a circumstance, it is often useful to *doubt one's doubt*. Do this when Doubt is present, obviously present, and you will more often than not observe that Doubt will lose Its power, will be laughed into oblivion, brilliantly evaporated, outshone, undressed, expanded be-yond Itself, liberated to be *available* energy in our mental realm...

To thus *consciously* doubt is somewhat akin to deliberately putting one's face into those patterns that characterize one's grosser neurotic traits. There's a healthy embarrassment at such times, a letting go, a soul-kindling loss of face, a heartstemmed farewell to Life-negating armoring, a healthy farewell to Doubt, healthy in the sense that Doubt has not been forcibly removed, bulldozed over, or somehow gloriously decapitated, but rather has been gracefully undone, without violence, inner or outer...

Doubt is not an enemy. The key is what we *do* with our Doubt. Do we identify with It? Do we love ourselves in the midst of It? Do we believe in It? Do we make decisions based on It? Or do we illuminate It, doubt It, outbreathe and outdance It, crashing Its slumber-party with such humor and integrity that It cannot help but dissolve into a more Life-giving form, a more natural state?

Doubt, in its rigidity of mental seesawing and unnatural cementings of key thoughts, is a relative of Belief, a blue collar frequenter of some of Belief's sleazier hangouts. Belief is static, factual, perfectly reproducible, far too stiff to be Truth, fashionably obsessed with Its own replication and confirmation, driven to see Its flag raised everywhere and everywhen. Doubt is Its more unpopular cousin, a grimy plebeian, just as stiff (even in Its limpness), but not so glossy, not chrome-plated or Presidentially-legitimized, being far more rusty, musty, dingy, and decentralized, nastily or pseudo-tragically huddled up in some unswept corner of mind, meeting the deodorized bulk of (grainfed and braindead) Belief in secret, except of course in the domain of Science, wherein Doubt is elevated to a somewhat lofty position, dressed-up, shaved, bathed, perfumed, and mixed in with a large amount of disembodied, sterile dogma, and named the Scientific Method (which is an admirable method for probing into the merely informational, for aptly arranging data and tagging taxonomies, but is entirely inappropriate for considering matters beyond the informational and merely structural, such as those of heart, feeling, Being, or Consciousness).

Doubt is to Science as blind faith is to Religion. Of course, in Its association with Science, Doubt appears to not be blind, but It is, simply because It is Doubt. Doubt is a self-obsessed implosion of Being, an implosion of mental energy, an avoidance of relatedness, an avoidance of true communion with That Which sustains and nourishes everything. As such, It is an atheist, not an intelligent atheist but a mechanical one, one that is in such a state or mind-groove simply because there's no real feeling of anything beyond the abstract, the mundane, or the merely informational. (Blind faith is also in denial of God, having sunk Its teeth into an emotionally-appealing *abstraction* of God.) For Doubt, there is only data, crystallized specificity, ever spinning out its self-verifying logic and deadening latticework and exaggerated pessimism, which thereby sets in motion the equally deluding clockwork of hope, with its stimulating promises, plastic optimism, and repressed despair — uppers and downers glued to their soulless teeter-totter, riding their righteousness into a barren night, addicted to possibility, dark or light...

The answer isn't to believe in something, but to go *beyond* belief, *beyond* doubt, *beyond* unillumined faith, *beyond* the polarities of mind, not so as to just retreat back into what was before Doubt or Belief appeared (in all likelihood some infantile preverbal or "oneness"-credentialed, undifferentiated state), but rather so as to be utterly capable of making good use of both the non-verbal and the verbal dimensions of Existence, to be able to dynamically yet subtly articulate one's condition, one's current whereabouts, one's intentions and intuitions, and to be able to do this with both soul-touching poetry and integrity-bright precision, to be at ease with both the roar and the whisper, to be consciously established in the Heart of Now, to go beyond the conceptual and the abstract and the guilt-contract, to go right through every ramification of Belief, every campaign and sublimation of Doubt, every new paradigm, every last attempt to superimpose meaning on Existence, again and again allowing ourselves to be rooted, ecstatically and soberly rooted in the vast Paradox, the Great Mystery That enlivens us all, now and forever, undressing even our most central doubt...

Doubt makes us all but impermeable to God-communion, to magic, to love, to *feelingly* experiencing the Mystery of Being and Non-Being. Doubt reinforces our sense of separation, our niggardly little portion of pseudo-individuality. Doubt empowers our misery — however miserable Doubt may be in Its effects, It is familiar, so densely familiar that It creates a sense of identity, or at least plays a supporting role for such a sense. Our credo becomes: "I doubt, therefore I am." This, like similar cases of mistaken identity, passes for individuality, all zipped up with designer traits, being in fact no more than a personalized parody of individuality, a dressed-up collage of endarkened habits that insists on referring to itself as us...

Doubt is the method of the ego, balanced of course by correspond-ingly inflationary beliefs in this or that. With the greatest of ease, we get uncomfortable, turning away from Ecstasy, Truth, Love, and Wonder, quickly becoming supposed experts as to what we need, when in fact the us that is doing such assuming is *not* us, but only an imposter, a convincing personification of our currently dominant fragment of self, swollen with Doubt and Beliefs (the *unchanging* nature of which is compensation for the Undying Reality from which we have marooned ourselves), pampering and reassuring itself with whatever distractions it can get its mind into, especially those that provide pleasurable dividends...

Not many of us can stand being in Doubt for extended periods. We crave breaks from It, but the breaks we take from It do not uproot It, nor undo or illuminate Its harm — they only remove us from Doubt for a time, entrancing us with a bit of physiological rhyme, springboarding us into a vacation in Numbland (sightseeing for the blind, nice culture-raping for the escaping, a forcefed touring of the shallows), and on and on we go, our broken hearts packed away, our native Joy crushed behind our eyes, our body a living graveyard of unheard cries, and on and on we go, dumb with stagnant sorrow and jammed with tomorrow, bouncing between Doubt and Hope, indulging in Doubt whenever there is something we *truly* need to do, some risk of being that we're afraid to take.

Doubt becomes the very core of our alibi for holding back; we use our Doubt to talk ourselves out of stretching to make such a jump, such a journey of being. We may well notice others also doing the very same thing, and so feel justified in our contractive action, perhaps even righteous about it, judgmental of those who are not staying stuck, those who are doing what we won't dare do — they may appear to us to be fools, naive idiots, madmen, madwomen, charlatans, unbalanced, unreasonable, out of touch, gone from them-selves, disrespectful, egomaniacal, and so on. (This is through the eyes of Doubt; through the eyes of Hope, these same people appear as heroic, glorious, wondrous, but just as *removed* from us as when we judged them from Doubt's standpoint.)

Whether or not these accusations are true is not the point; the point is that those who are mired in Doubt cannot tell what is false from what is true. They are too lost in the worlds that their Doubt spins out, too lost in the tales told and retold by their misery, too lost in the degenerative, non-ecstatic pleasuring that they engage in from time to time as a way of vacating their Doubt, Dread, and Despair.

Doubt your doubting. To do so often brings a substantial degree of deep humor, love, release, wordless insight, magic, and gratitude, for it illuminates the whole matter, reestablishing us, in however slight a way, in Light, not the hungered-for, *conceptual* light of the New Age, but the Light of our Essentialness, the Radiance of our Being, the Unfathomable Luminosity that does not die, but that only forever pours through the prism of Being, existing as the very Nature of Consciousness... Doubt your doubt, and hear in the background your own Awakening shout, that sacred call that is not even yours, but simply *ours*, now, presently, fully...

Doubt is a gripping of mind. To try to relieve it through another play of mind, be it an earnest jump into Belief, positive thinking, contextual reprogramming, or whatever, doesn't work, except superficially. The suppression of Being that catalyzes Doubt must be seen, felt, known from the inside. The whole being must be eased. The torso must be let loose, the limbs unfrozen, the reach made vulnerable, the face true, the entire anatomy brought into supportive resonance with one's center of Being. Doubt must be seen for what It is, as It is, without us becoming lost in Its point of view — only then will It unfist Itself, only then will our endarkened familiarity with It come unstrung, only then will we be nourishingly and unequivocally undone, flung into the Truth of what we are, the Truth That cannot be reduced to mere facts or information. Doubt cannot coexist with Truth. At times, Truth can express the *energy* of Doubt, but It does not assume the viewpoint of Doubt, instead exposing it, uncovering the terrain that Doubt claims as Its own, doing so in a manner that enriches and expands us.

It doesn't fundamentally matter what your doubts are; it doesn't *really* matter what their focus is. What does matter is the actual condition of doubting itself; that is what must be seen, felt, embraced, entered and passed through, to the point of whole-hearted understanding. The content of Doubt is irrelevant most of the time. Whatever is near Doubt becomes Its content, Its focus. When you notice that you are in Doubt, shift your attention from whatever it is that you're busy doubting to Doubt Itself. Feel Its tension, Its downbeat texture, Its tones, Its positioning, Its bodily ramifications; feel what It is doing to you, feel how It's affecting your relationships, feel how It's coloring your speech, your vision, your hearing, your perception, your very being...

Do this without trying to change your doubt. Sometimes simply noticing your doubt, as opposed to its contents, will cause it to dissolve. Other times, *deliberately* doubting your doubt will cause it to dissipate. Your doubt may also sometimes be evaporated by your honoring a suddenly felt impulse, a risk of Being, a shift in breathing, a not-easy movement toward someone, an expression of a suppressed feeling or desire, a soulstirring loss of face — these will not be done in order to get rid of Doubt, but because they are imperatives of Being, arising from something deeper than our everyday mind. When attention is given to such Essence-centered doings or intentions, it is no longer bound to the contents of Doubt. Such a yielding of attention is not submission, but luminous surrender. It is not the end of Doubt, but an outdancing of Doubt...

When we are no longer indulging in Doubt, we do not necessarily become a simpleton, a true believer, or a non-thinker — we become balanced, integrated, capable of a deep appreciation of Life, capable of Being, settling into a deeper and deeper embodiment of our fundamental nature. Do not make Doubt wrong. Simply realize that when you lose yourself in Doubt, you are shortcircuiting a deeper song, one that calls to you now, one that beats in you now, one whose melody shapes your stride and shines through your flesh, carrying an innocence beyond naïveté, a wisdom beyond knowledge, a love beyond sentimentality, a skepticism beyond Doubt, a Truth as paradoxical as It's real...

Gustave Doré: *Milton's Paradise Lost*

– 15 –

Power From Persona Versus Power From Essence

(Carla talks about her abuse of authority given to her, going over many details of a specific incident that epitomized her mishandling of power)

ROBERT: You have learned to take charge from a place of persona, instead of from a place of Essence, and have thus bypassed your capacity for assuming the authority native to yourself — you have stranded yourself from your *natural* authority, so it's no wonder that you're so uptight when you're telling people what to do! When you issue your commands, anyone who's at all tuned in is going to have to resist you — why should they support your ego-centered power-taking?

CARLA: *(Crying)* I just didn't trust myself in being in charge. I doubted myself...

ROBERT: There is a core-level power backing me up when I give directives, a power that's completely natural to me, but where do you give your directives from? You'll probably notice that it's the very same place from where you are now crying — your crying is skin-deep, implosive, self-pityingly dramatic, full of overblown sincerity, changing a little as I say this... You've made helplessness your foundation, not only in your typical emoting, but also in your expression of power... So how do you amp up your power if it's coming from helplessness? *(Pause)* You make it look and sound powerful. *That* is the persona's occupation, or at least one of its main occupations! To *act* powerful! To act power-full when you're not isn't going to fool those in Xanthyros...

We all owe it to ourselves to reclaim the authority that is native to us, but how can we do this if we insist on investing all our energy in the upkeep of our persona? When our powertaking is but the flipside of our neurotic helplessness, we are of no use to anyone! When your power comes from Essence, you'll notice that you feel vulnerable, even if you don't look vulnerable, but it's a vulnerability unburdened by any association with typical helplessness or neurotic dependency. In such power, you're open to challenge — you're strong without being rigid, soft without being mushy, and authentic without being self-consciously "real"...

You were cutting corners, briskly overriding your sensitivity to the situation — you did it with far too much tension, hoping that people would just do as they were told. Be grateful that they defied you! You can't just come howling to me about their lack of respect for your authority, as if we're in some sort of army! You can't use me as the heavy above you — I'm not here to support your bullshit, but to help you empower yourself to love under all conditions, even in the midst of intense rage or heartbreaking sadness. It's a hell of a challenge, and your work is to learn to love that challenge, to respect, embody, and enjoy that challenge!

A wildflower growing in a seedy downtown lot does not hold back its petalling — it goes all out, but why don't we allow ourselves to fully flower? Why are there so many padlocked buds among humanity? Largely because of *believed-in* fear — just about everyone feels helpless inside, powerless, cut off from their core of Being. Myself, I don't feel disempowered by the fact of my helplessness, for I've learned to use it as an ally, as a means of deepening my connection with the Source — I've learned to not make a problem out of my helplessness, but to let it remind me of my *utter* dependency on my environment, my *utter* dependency on What animates us all. Befriending my helplessness keeps me vulnerable, sensitized, as appreciative of limitation as I am of Limitlessness...

Most of us flee or numb ourselves to our dependency, compensating by locking ourselves into so-called independence, keeping our most vulnerable needs under constant surveillance, as if such need were an enemy! And how are we ever going to find a strength that is *unthreatened* by dependency, if we keep trying to fix, gag, or deny our helplessness?

CARLA: I feel so frustrated by my trying to be in charge just from my persona!

ROBERT: You did not birth your daughter from a place of Essence; you tried to birth her from persona. You wouldn't let yourself be spontaneous, vital, primally alive; you wouldn't trust the great organismic naturalness that floods through a woman in labour. Yes, you did finally push her out, but you were at war with yourself almost the whole time... (*She cries*) You know how to feel Essence from the heart up, like right now, but you don't trust what's below the heart — you're suspicious of that, when you ought to be suspicious of the you who is so mistrusting of your lower torso!

Your power will not come from a place of Essence until you permit yourself to feel, to love, to whole-heartedly embody your entire self, without imposing on yourself any more hierarchical crap about the body — no stacking of chakras, no more putting of sex *down there*, no more psychoemotional evisceration! Even when you have been immersed in Essence, you have exploited It as best you could, taking Its outshining of your persona as a sign that you had gone beyond persona, beyond ego, all the while doing no more than getting yourself *addicted* to the blissful sensations that you associated with being Essence-centered!

Sure, you craved and crave a break from the nastily tight pain of your persona, but you don't *need* a break from it! You need to break *into* it, to step into it and turn all the lights on! And just about everyone is in the business of trying to escape the stifling confinement of being a persona; unfortunately, the usual approach to this is one of distraction, of pleasurable sedation, of multidisciplinary masturbation...

Most of us engineer our flight from persona by sinking into a narcotized mirage of oneness, both as a solitary stimulation junkie, and as a member of a mindless crowd — yes, we may embellish, parade, and inflate our persona, but we *still* seek refuge from it. Do you not see the madness, the folly, of this? Here's someone biting her lip, someone who spends her life trying to get rid of the pain of such biting, all the while blinding herself to the fact that *she* is biting herself! She goes to psychiatrists, takes drugs, does yoga, becomes a meditator, does all kinds of things to eradicate the pain of her biting, but she doesn't actually let go of biting! (*Pause*)

Your persona, as it now is, is no more than a biting of Essence, a pinching or knotting of Essence — it's as if "you've" taken who you really are and squeezed it into something the size of a fist! That hurts. And how to get away from that? Sex will relieve the outer tension; so will certain drugs; so will masturbatory catharsis. Nevertheless, the pain remains, ever calling you to something deeper than escapism...

But there's nothing inherently wrong with persona! We don't have to make it such a lousy fit... Persona is just the dramatization of our essential individuality. It's the wardrobe of Essence. Why blame our misery on our clothes? We're not meant to be colourless clones living in the Great Beyond — we're meant to be true individuals, simultaneously unique and surrendered to our Source, but how can we live that, when we're busy identifying with what we're wearing?

CARLA: I know I have major work to do with my personality...

ROBERT: So stop fighting it! Why fight your blouse? Why make your persona so hard and opaque that it becomes just ego? Ego is a disease of persona, an unconscious identification with persona — ego is just something you are *doing*, not something you are. It's an activity you are unconsciously indulging in, an imposter glued to the throne of Self, a strategy masquerading as a somebody, namely *you*...

CARLA: I've tried to get rid of my personality, to get a center...

ROBERT: What is center?

CARLA: For me to have center is to *feel* from down here more... (*Touching her belly and crying*)

ROBERT: But if you only feel it from a place of personality, it won't work — it'll just seem to be *down there*, troublesome and problematic, seemingly out of line. (*Long pause*) As an ego, you would love to be centered, dynamically and shiningly centered, impressing the hell out of me! Ego can only act — it craves badges, medals, credentials, awards, attention. But why let ego refer to itself as "I"? Why not permit it to become but fluidly alive persona?

To become really centered, you have to let go, but not like a devotee irresponsibly dissolving her boundaries, her integrity, her dignity... Real letting go is not about throwing everything to the wind, nor is it about fanatic loyalty to a particular ethic... It's simply what you *know* you have to do once you've authentically stood your true ground, even if only for a moment... Center is not a result of following some technique, nor of believing in something; in fact, it only arises when we let go of mere following, and stop believing in anything! Center does not require belief — it only asks for consistent faith in our core of Being. True center is but a byproduct, an utterly natural byproduct, of opening to your real nature. It's both a gradual process, and a leap, a leap into the Unknown...

It's natural to be centered, Essence-centered. All that's required is an exposure and letting go of what is unnatural about us. Sounds simple, doesn't it? But it's a labour that requires far more than enthusiasm, a climb that most turn back from as soon as the terrain gets steep. I didn't *plan* to become centered. After stumbling around for years, attacking the mountain from many angles, falling again and again, I stopped making such a big deal out of my bruises, and went *totally* into what was before me, without having to *know* what was going to happen — I was willing to be messy, to be really broken and devastated, to be undone, to abandon my every security. This was *not* a strategy, a groupgame — it was my very life!

Like you, I knew what I had to do, at least contextually, and I simply did it without any of the previous spiritual ambition that had characterized me. Escape no longer interested me. I was no longer seducible by my old programming — sure, it was still there, but it wasn't getting any juice from me. Again, this wasn't a matter of tactics; it just was what I *had* to do. Postponement was not an option for me, as it still is for you. I had given up all hope of having some great experience that would deliver me from my suffering — instead, I simply went right into my suffering, right through its viewpoint, until its shadowlands no longer shadowed me. Center happened, and did not leave; I still wavered, I still fucked up, but I did not lose center. Its occurence was utterly ordinary, as natural as breathing. Its presence did not solve my difficulties, but stripped them of their previous problematicalness. That was many years ago, but its Truth is still present, still a moment-to-moment affair, ever-ripening me...

Again, all you have to do is cut through your unnaturalness — see it, sensitize yourself to it, now and then exaggerate it to the point of dissolution, but *don't* make a program out of such a process! It's far, far more than therapy... When you are natural and loving, true-faced and consciously embodied, then there is no question of morality or ethics, no question of rules or right behaviour, because you *already* know, without thinking about it, how to behave!

CARLA: I have a hard time being natural.

ROBERT: It's just a habit, a habit you've let go to mind.

CARLA: I realize how much I need to inhabit my body more...

ROBERT: Yes, but you don't realize that there's no one to inhabit it! Who is this "I" who wants to inhabit the body? That "I" is just an assumption, a personified mirage created by your religious conditioning! You act as if there is a somebody, a discrete entity, a soul even, that can take up residence *in* your body, but if you *really* look, you'll observe that there's no such thing! Your body is *not* some sort of container for your so-called true self! To view the body that way is just more of the bodily denial that plagues humanity. This inner "I", this apparent entity, is just ego! But ego is *not* inside you! Rather, it's something you are *doing* to yourself, just a designer subjectivity that loves to get all dressed up and call itself soul or Higher Self! Real soul, on the other hand, is not a resident somewhere inside or up above the body, but is the presence of *embodied* center. That is, soul is not a given; it is a *result*... (*Long pause*)

Let's get more into your notion of inhabiting your body — when you, for example, feel as though you're *in* your head, established somewhere in your skull, it is because your *attention* is there, however unconsciously. Your attention's presence creates the sense that someone is there, that your head's an apartment, and you're the dweller, the tenant — and out of this comes not only the illusion that *you* are located within, but that Truth is within! You've heard that one a lot, haven't you? If *you're* within, then of course Truth must also be within! This is just more ego-centered fantasy... Look within in the ordinary sense, and all you'll tend to find is ego, however spiritually-robed; look without, and all you'll probably see is projected ego, edifices of ego. To look deeper, you must become aware of just *who* is doing the looking; that is, you look *inside* your looking. Instead of merely searching inwardly or outwardly, you illuminate the *searcher*! You start to wake up. You get sober. You stop analysing the contents of your mind, and you stop analysing the world around you; you stop running everything through your mind, and start living an awakened life, a natural life...

So it's not a matter of you inhabiting your body, but rather a matter of you *being* your body, without identifying with it. Yes, you are not your body, but you also are your body — such is the paradox of manifestation, but it's only a paradox to your mind! We are here to embody all that we are, level upon level, and such embodiment is both condensation and diffusion, both contraction and expansion, both suffering and Ecstasy...

You've got a lot of face to lose! (*Laughter*) Stop being so loyal to your logical possibilities, and stop trying to be so fucking spiritual! Your body is not an inconvenience, nor a mere pleasure terminal — it's your ticket to the Big Time! Don't you realize that your body is more you than the you who makes a problem out of it?

CARLA: Yes! (*Laughing*)

ROBERT: And one more thing: The only way to please me is to not try to please me. Cut through your urge to please, and you'll see that it's only one more facet of your obsession with being in control; yes, you may be putting yourself at the mercy of my approval, but a deeper you is obscured by the drama of this, kept bound and gagged, especially below your diaphragm, compressed between your ribs and hip-crests... Until you say a real yes to your body, a dynamically alive yes, a yes of both passion and subtlety, you'll keep holing up in your left hemisphere, indulging in powertaking that arises from persona. Real power, or essence-centered power, requires a conscious *embodiment* of what you are, and that begins with a wide-awake entry into and through what's troublesome for you. Until you undertake that journey, you'll not know the authority that's innate to you...

– 16 –

Exploring Self-Suppression's Paralyzing Grasp: An Intimate Look at Fear

Let's begin by talking about fright, fright being a dynamically practical, almost instantaneous reaction to *present* danger. Its inner biochemistry serves to bring one into a state of heightened alertness, so that whatever the chosen action, whether to fight or flee or densify or whatever, one is beautifully prepared to go right into it. An animal suddenly facing death from the attack of a predator is ordinarily given such a jolt of adrenalin, such a rush of vitality, that it can flee or stand its ground to the best of its ability — it is at its finest, its most alive, its most elemental. An equally unadulterated fright arises in humans at certain times, such as when one is upon the lip of a precipice, or when a very loud sound occurs without warning, or when a shocking image leaps from a movie screen, or when large carnivores or snakes cross one's path... That's fright — there was *no* trace of it a moment ago and suddenly it is present, its explosive alchemy almost immediately readying us for strong action.

Fear, however, is *chronic*, low-grade fright, infectiously present in just about all of us. It is a disease, a *perversion* of fright, a neurotic readiness for trouble that has not yet arrived, trouble that may well never arrive. At best, it may seem to be a kind of preparation for that supposedly upcoming difficulty, but almost all of the time, it is not preparation, but only unnecessary anticipation, a merely anxious waiting, a physiological pessimism, a festeringly present inner fretting; as such, it actively employs those thoughts and beliefs that are supportive of it. This is what I call fear — another, slightly more ominous word for it is dread. Implicit in fear or dread is compulsive, blindly recycled thinking, as well as calamitous, self-contracted expectation. Take away the concern that is seemingly stimulating or justifying such fearfulness, and very soon there'll likely be *another* concern, *another* nastily accurate reason for triggering the biochemistry of fear, *another* excuse for *staying* worried...

Fear does not serve the survival of the organism as does fright, but actually erodes it, slowly but surely, focussing attention so much on the Future that there's little energy left for the Present. Fear is a suppression of Being, a shrinkage of self, a contractedness, a semi-paralytic compression. Imagine a tube of toothpaste: Uncap it, and squeeze it in the middle; its contents inevitably squirt up toward the top, worming out. So too with most of us! Fear compresses the torso, the chakras, the nervous system, the breath, the throat; Life-Energy becomes squeezed upward (or downward if the valve of sexual discharge is open for business), crowding into the skull (this is the meaning of *up*tight), engendering an intensification of thought, a mechanical ricocheting of worrisome thoughtforms, which of course only further triggers the distress of the entire system. Not all the energy is necessarily squeezed up into the brain; some of it usually gets forced down, down, down to the pelvic floor, concentrating itself in the genitals, bringing about a desire for some sort of sexual release. In this case, of course, sex is simply a means of relieving stress, a psychoemotional outhouse, a valve for blowing off mind-steam and fleshy distress, a way of dumping the tension generated by the triggering of fear...

This in part explains the compulsive connection between crotch and brain, the hotline that, running between these two terminals, ordinarily *bypasses* the centers of the torso and the throat. Frictional fantasy is fed into the genital realm to help feed release, to stoke up more stimulation, to bring about a more pleasurable discharge, to, in fact, even *generate* the need for such discharge! Thus do we distract ourselves from our fear, compulsively seeking pleasurable sedation, robbing ourselves of the very energy we need in order to directly and potently face our fear... The regions of the body that exist between the head and the genitals are, in many, all but uninhabited; they are usually avoided, except peripherally, because the pain therein is so intense — the heartache, the powerlessness, the sensation of giving up or of hardening, the excessive vulnerability, the determined invulnerability, the spirit-denial, the anaemic love, the wounds, the ossified imbalance, the child's suffocated cries... Yet our body, in of itself, is not in a state of suppression — it is what we are *doing* to our body! That doing, that horribly ubiquitous violation, is largely mechanical, but the force behind it is easily altered into something far more Life-affirming, *if* there is alertness, *if* there is real commitment to waking up, *if* there is a true desire to illuminate *and* get out of the trap...

The point is not to eliminate stress, nor to live without any so-called "negativity." The point is to make *room*, conscious space, for these very qualities, so that their energies can creatively participate in, rather than obstruct, your fullness of Being. This is about becoming sky for all the clouds of doubt, despair, discomfort, suffering, jealousy, anxiety, and so on, *without* rising above or otherwise fleeing their richness of feeling. It is about not allowing one's happiness to be compromised, nor diluted, by the presence of such seemingly endarkened qualities, not just because they are *not* problems, but also because they, like all experiences, come and go — they do not very last long unless we prolong them through an obsessive fixation of attention...

And what about attention? Where does your attention go when you are in fear? Does it go to the sane witnessing of the fear? Does it go to making room for our fear to breathe, to feel, to cry, to love, to radiate itself free of being fear? Not usually! Most of the time, attention is allowed to fixate on those very thoughts and assumptions that, through their insistent futurizing, are reinforcing our fear. Or attention is, with equal mechanicalness, yielded to the compulsion for tension-release via sexual discharge. So attention, when one is in fear, usually only plays servant to the whole fear reaction; it is not readily given to that capacity of Being that allows fear to transmute itself into excitement, awakened excitement. The key here is to allow our attention to move to something other than the content of mind that generates and sustains fear, something other than the sexual impulse that intensifies in correspondence with our distress of mind and body. The more one works with fear, the more one realizes the incredible importance of mastering one's attention, of making attention *conscious*, of giving it a foundation in Being, rather than just letting it be a slumbering vagrant, an indiscriminate wanderer...

Fear is but a confession of mistrusting and shrinking from the overall process of Life, the deep flow and core imperatives of one's Being... The presence of fear catalyzes the urge to somehow mastermind the Life-process, to view it only from one's *head*quarters, so to speak, to willfully arrange it so as to minimize pain, stress, suffering, and every sort of difficulty (as though such matters were *inherently* problematic). This avoidance must be undone sooner or later, simply because *everything* that arises in and *as* one must be consciously faced and known from the inside out, until it no longer binds us. Otherwise, we're just busy shunning part of us, shunning God as Manifest Appearance. In some, especially those who cling to Eastern spiritual technologies, this shows up in the longing to exist only as a witnessing consciousness; in others, it appears as the craving to belong, especially to something apparently grander, bigger, more certain, than oneself. Consider the ease, the sheer ease, of dissolution into some mass movement, whether it's a large sporting event in which one is a rabid spectator, or whether it's a pseudospiritual organization in which one is a true believer or devotee. But all of this is simply a reaction, a compensatory reaction, to the fear mechanism that one has so steadily triggered in oneself (so steadily in fact that for many there is a strange intimacy with it, a densely reassuring familiarity, a negative security)...

Even as I speak of fear, there are so many tangential things that could be said about it (only some of which fit the flow of this talk), since the life of a typical human can, to a large degree, be distilled down to his or her coping with fear — almost everything we do is simply a reaction to fear, an effort to sedate it, to dilute it, to somehow distance ourselves from its touch, to somehow find a lasting remedy for it, a distraction or distractions of sufficient power to numb us to our contractedness of Being.

When we calmly announce in a therapeutically confessional manner that we are in fear, we're not truly *feeling* our fear, but rather only our urge to *flee* it — we are, in such a case, desperately trying to escape from our fear, to change our state, to propel or project ourselves into a condition of such pleasurable diversion that our sensations of fear are minimized, or perhaps not even felt at all! This craving to not directly feel our fear only strengthens it; those who persist in such behavior tend to disembody, to only live on the periphery of themselves, as far away as possible from the intensity of their fear, dwelling in the thinking portions of their minds, committing themselves to the search for release, not just through sex and excessive mentalizing, but through television, food, work, meditation, books, exercise, ever looking for antidotes for what they are *already* doing to themselves!

It is our suppression of Being that must be addressed, not just the pain arising *from* that suppression, that knotting of Being... It is a matter of going as directly as possible to what is *fundamentally* troubling us, and this is done rarely, because it is a painful process, a passage requiring tremendous courage and trust. It is a matter of letting go of all bandaids (such as positive thinking, overwork, cultic association, and pleasure-clinging), all would-be cures and soul-salves, and simply being truly vulnerable, raw and nakedly open, to the sensations of one's fear, letting oneself feel such sensations *fully*, passionately, uninhibitedly, risking everything to face this directly, to feel it throughout one's body, while at the very same time being aware of it, not just standing some distance away witnessing it, but literally *being* it *and* witnessing it simultaneously!

This is the embodiment of the passionate witness. It is an art. It is not a technique; if it was a technique, many people would learn it, and there'd be a lot less fear around. It's not that simple — it requires a far more telling penetration and exposure of one's deep motivations. So what is needed is, first of all, a clear noticing of one's urge to change one's state when one is afraid or in deep doubt or despair — the very craving to alter one's state is the problem here, *not* the state! It's the urge to change it, the urge to somehow mastermind it away, to successfully sedate or tranquilize it (with sex, drugs, mindfucking, mantras, et cetera), to have it become non-existent as soon as possible! *This* is the disease. *This* is the trouble. Notice if you're afraid of your fear; if you are, you're just making a problem out of your fear — you're not allowing yourself to be in a position where fear can show itself in its nakedness, to where it could even become terror, unedited terror, pure horror, madness, oozing and shrieking, crawling with hallucinatory fiends. So what? What if your fear balloons into paranoia? Sooner or later, it must be allowed...

To do this alone, however, is extremely difficult; it's much more likely that it can be worked with sanely if there are people around who are true friends, real allies, also facing the same work with the same intensity and integrity of commitment as you, people whom you love and who also love *you*, the true you, people who are not afraid to love and live fiercely, to be ass-kickingly and heart-blazingly full in their expression, unburdened by sentimentality or any sort of wishful thinking...

In such an environment, fear can be faced directly, felt without repression, and simultaneously reported — the sensations, the imagery, the thoughts, the intentions accompanying fear can be verbalized even if one's voice is trembling, even if one is screaming. If the catharsis (if there *is* catharsis) is overwhelming, then of course the verbalizing of content may need to be put aside for the time being, so that the body can fully yield to the currents of fear — in so yielding, there will be no fear after a short time, but instead a tremendous excitement, a primal vibrancy, an almost orgasmic streaming and expansiveness, seemingly exploding the body, dissolving its armoring, liberating it to a significant degree, so that one's Being breathes more easily...

So what we have here is the directly experienced feeling of fear (which is actually less a feeling than it is a compression or cramping of feeling), accompanied by a refusal to *deliberately* alter it (in the sense of withdrawing to the sidelines in order to play tactician or "head" coach). We may, of course, notice the intention to alter our fear, to run from it, to remedy it, but this intention must not be obeyed, not only because it's arising from egoic concern or unlove, but because we've *already* spent most of our life obeying that impulse, with results that are less than valuable, results that only reinforce fearfulness. It is entirely appropriate to not obey that impulse. After practising our noticing of it for a while, we will realize that it's not just now and then that we are afraid, but almost all the time — we're ordinarily not particularly sensitive to this, because of the frequency of our self-distraction, our self-occupation, our compulsive self-pleasuring...

Da Free John once said, "Fear is when Love stops short of Infinity." In other words, prior to the fully Awakened condition, there is fear; yes, it may be amazingly subtle, it may not manifest as trembling, shaking, paranoid thoughts, and so on, but it's *still there*, however faint its biochemistry might be. Fear is a withholding of Being, a chronic stranglehold on the heart, a shrinking from the Truth of what we are. In its extreme, it's a paralysis of Being, a terrifying gripping in which it may be impossible to speak, but it is never *truly* impossible to work with... If in some instances it is impossible to report what is occurring because of the overwhelming intensity of our fear, the very *effort* to so report, to so communicate and share, will eventually free us — it's the effort that counts here, the resolute willingness, the gutsiness, the incredible gutsiness, that it takes to feel one's fear *fully*. (And this effort is not one of trying, but of essence-arising *doing*, characterized by a non-dilutionary expansion of Being that's eloquently punctuated by potent *non-doing*.)

Once again, remember not to merely try to fix your fear. Make no egoic effort to alter your condition, and you'll notice that it changes by itself, just like the weather — this is *not* some form of laziness or typical passivity, but rather is a dynamic, *conscious* waiting. It is not about doing nothing in the conventional sense, nor is it about becoming dysfunctional — it's about allowing what's occurring when one is in intense fear or despair *to change by itself.* (Paradoxically, our presence, our conscious presence, *motivelessly* activates such change.) Of course, if one does nothing, in the ordinary sense of doing nothing (which actually means permitting one's *conditioning* to go unchallenged), the triggering of fear will continue...

I'm talking about a very different kind of passivity. This is not a recipe, nor a technique. Next time you're aware of feeling afraid and you take what I've said as a mass of mere instruction, you'll just *think* about it, you'll fall short, easily fall short of what I'm suggesting here, and then you'll probably think about *that*! You'll thereby only intensify your doubt and fearfulness, because you will have only *thought* about what I've said! You must practise it *directly.* Fear is suppression of Being. To make room for fear is *de-suppression.* All you're really doing, if you truly let in and feel what I'm saying now, is making the energy of your fear (which is fundamentally only unnecessarily bound energy) once again *available* Life-force — you are *then* not forcing it into another channel, nor are you squeezing it upward or downward or further in, but are instead letting it metamorphose into something far, far more useful for your Being, something that fear at essence *already* is. Simply permit it the grace of expansion, of outbreathing its density...

Fear need not be feared. Go toward it when it arises, and go with undreaming abandon. Become a *conscious* medium for it, not for its viewpoint, but for its forces, and do so in a setting where you can go wild, a setting where you can let your suppression wail, rage and weep itself free of its self-imposed dungeon. Take the times when fear comes, however overwhelmingly or frigidly, as gifts, as challenging gifts. Do not squander or try to minimize such times, nor try to bring them about in some masochistic fashion, nor try to think them away with philosophy. Rather, when they occur (and they *will* occur in exact correspondence with what you are doing with your true needs), you must, no matter how paranoid or despairing you might be, find a way to say, to *deeply* say, to yourself, "This is a *workable* situation." Of course, your mind may be *trying* to convince you (and don't blame your mind for this, since *you* are animating it!) that it *isn't* workable. However, whatever our mind tells us, it *is* a workable situation, and we have to remember that (and remember to remember!), especially when we're in the grip of our fear.

At such times, you *must* trust your allies, your true friends, those who are also committed to getting to the heart of the matter. You must trust the very process of facing your fear, of expressing its energies *directly*, of accurately as possible reporting its content and its point of view, its assumptions, its philosophy — you have to stand right in its shoes and say what you see and assume when you look through its eyes. If those around you look like monsters, say so; if they look like they're out to get you or to enroll you in their programming, say so. It takes guts. There's a definite effort required. You may have difficulty speaking. Your throat might feel bound, or as if it's being strangled in some way; if so, say *that*, or deliberately *exaggerate* it until your voice bursts free. That is, make an effort not to change your state, but to *consciously* express it, to clearly externalize it, to give it an unmasked face, *without* losing yourself in its assumptions about what's what...

Usually when we're busy being afraid, the face we present is not that of our fear, but of our *repression* of our fear — yes, some of our fear will show through, but not fully, not nakedly. When someone shares their fear *fully*, without any dissociation whatsoever, it is very moving to see, very stirring — it touches us deeply, through its very openness raising gooseflesh and hearts, usually taking no more than five or ten minutes to expand beyond itself... To do what I have described here is an act of love, not only for oneself, but for *everyone*.

Fear, again, is not to be dissolved or ended or outdrugged, but rather simply allowed to become *available* Life-energy, allowed to transmute itself into excitement, joy, relational passion, humor, real creativity, and so on. When fear is given space to express itself in its totality, it will, at least initially, often appear as undiluted terror, wide-eyed, hair-raising terror. The pure expression of such terror (if it's not self-enclosed) is remarkably similar to that of outrageously alive ecstasy; its very intensity (if given a slight shift, a shift toward heart and real relatedness, a shift that increases trust) can suddenly flip it into ecstasy, weepingly alive ecstasy, love, and the beauty of natural knowingness, leaving us in fathomless, open-eyed trust for the Currents that govern (and *are*) our very Being...

CRUSHED BENEATH A LESSER VIEW

When I was but less than one
and the sky was everywhere and dandelions
swayed goldensucculent around the ankles of oaktrunks
I wandered open-mouthed, my skin athrill with my eyes
My mother searching for me in instruction manuals
pasting cheer on her anxiety
My father gripping me with rough fingers
his furies pumping me with terror
I saw they didn't see me
And my dreams sprouted leaden wings
And what was I to do?
My escape was the inside of the outside
Dreambeings crowding and striding through my daytime
Neon orbs shapeshifting all over my ceiling
whether or not my eyes were shut
Spots of dread ballooning into looming shrouds
My body a pinpoint, then skywide unbound
eaten at by monstrously thickening clouds

When I was but less than one
and my true friends were absent
I could not shutter my vision nor regulate my cries
nor find a fitting disguise
My parents marched overhead
chained to their joyless dream
forgetting to breathe, forgetting themselves and me
And I the oversensitive harbinger of more premature duty
the child of two crippled children
both adrift on a dying sea
clinging to the ruins of their honeymoon
And now me, with them and yet so apart
Three hearts with no common tongue
Homesteading in the loneliness of such daily closeness
I could not help but love them
Though my spirit yearned for lovers

Marooned was I, close to forgetting I was marooned
My expression inarticulate to all who saw me
My days and nights a chaos of collapsing magic
A deformed helplessness sealing me in
*   offering me shrinking walls and nightmare doors*
Fear starting to pave my throat
My sky sliced into expectant frames
My remembrance of the True crushed beneath a lesser view
Goodbye to the Unslumbering Wonder
Goodbye to the Heart of Now
And I did submit
And I did submit when I was but less than one
Learning to orbit an artificial sun
My Ecstasy undone
My endarkened labour barely begun

Gustave Doré: *La Fontaine*

–17–
No More Stage Fright:
Acting
Without Reacting

Just about everybody has stage fright some of the time, not just the overtly dramatic, but the dull, the defeated, the dispirited, the downcast, the walking dead, the talking heads, the carriers of dread... All are repetitiously performing, acting and re-acting, all but lost in their roles, unknowingly identified with their designated part, unresistingly upstaged by a counterfeit self, a deeply imbedded psychosomatic disguise... It's not enough to romanticize the whole affair by saying that the world's a stage, and that we're all players upon it — doing so not only oversimplifies it, but also subtly *legitimizes* its *mechanical* continuation.

Those who do especially well in their role-playing, making a successful career out of it, often receive accolades, wraparound recognition, vast praise for their acting, even adulation, as if in parallel with the Academy Awards. Given this, the rest of us, to varying degrees, still tend to assume that if we play our prepackaged roles skilfully and fully enough, we too will be showered with parental (and peer) approval and appreciation, which of course only further cements and seemingly justifies our disguise. On and on we go, ambitiously or resignedly entombed in our theatrics, compulsively seeking the applause of an inner and/or outer audience, either judging ourselves harshly for our performance, or projecting our self-judgmentalness onto others, always scapegoating someone, chronically keeping ourselves or someone else on trial, drained and chained by our denial of Self...

The point, however, is *not* to stop acting, but rather is to act consciously and spontaneously, naturally and courageously, until there is little or no anxiety left concerning our actions; implicit in this is the need that our performance not be automatically rehearsed, but be completely at home in the present moment. True acting is not limited to a stage. It is not a beggar for anyone's applause, nor does it turn God into Santa Claus. True acting is the artful embodiment and *personalized* expression of our fundamental nature, and in such deep art our periphery can only accurately, passionately, and color-fully represent our essence, our depths, our Truth, so that there is no *solid* mask to dynamite or strip off, but only eloquently idiosyncratic, overlapping transparencies of Self, playing out foreground and back-ground issues with no Life-negating hierarchical superimpositions. In this, our face, whatever its current appearance, *is* our original face. Nevertheless, it still *is* a face, a marvelously complex sign of in-dividuation, a poignantly succinct, wickedly humorous, sublimely expressive celebration of the Many, the Many that is at essence in undying embrace with the One.

Short of Awakening, we get stage fright about the performing of what cannot be performed, namely our *real* role. Truth cannot be performed; it transcends all scripting, all masterminding, all strategy. Truth is not reducible to a set of facts, a collage of information that can be day after day consistently reproduced or reprinted, spoken the very same way, with the same original gestures, tics, and tones. Truth is *unique* to the moment in which It is expressed; It accurately (Its accuracy being more of feeling and ambience than of logistical exactitude) fits the *real* needs of the moment, Its every tone and gesture artfully and naturally corresponding to the essential qualities of Now.

That is, Truth cannot be spoken to one person and then to another ten minutes later in exactly the same manner, because It takes into empathetic account the one to whom It is speaking, feeling and resonating with the totality of that *particular* person. It is not a speech, nor a byproduct of rehearsal, but is a conscious, full-blooded response to the moment's needs and dynamics, Its precision being not so much of content as of context and feeling. Truth's context is not at all abstract — it is organismic, vital, full of unsullied passion, at once personal and transpersonal, as firm as it is fluid, unburdened by jargon, dogma, righteousness, or fake humility.

Truth is *inherently* creative. It is the Speech of Being, the articulation of Being, just as Love is the Feeling of Being, and Life the Art of Being. Such Speech is not mechanical, nor preprogrammed. Its heart does not exclude, nor indiscriminately include. It is both gentle and fierce — in one hand, It holds an eversharp sword, and in the other, a bouquet of flowers. Truth cuts heads off, and Truth also caresses the soul, never losing Its intimacy with Paradox...

And so we may ask "Who am I?", asking it over and over, more and more deeply, until it is less of a question, and more of an invitation, a potent beckoning into the Unknown. The answer lies in the realm of Truth. It cannot be given by just one part of us — it must emanate forth from our totality, our wholeness of Being. Someone might say "I am" as their answer, and if they speak it fully, truly, with their *entire* being, unequivocally and radiantly, then *that's* it, *that's* who they are, *that's* what they are. But if someone else said the very same words, it *could* be utterly untrue, no more than just two words, a mere phrase, if they did not say it from their *full* beingness. In other words, Truth is not static, nor reducible to the automatic.

The vast majority of humans are far more enslaved to their script than they'd like to admit — it is literally branded into them, eloquently revealed through their posture, their bodily tone, their skeletal imbalances, their musculature's tensile commitments, the set of their jaw, the alignment of their eyes, the tilt of their neck, the shape and compensations of their stride, all of which (including those psychoemotional disturbances that correspond to their physical misalignments and knottings) only reveals their conditioning, their script, their program, none of which are really *theirs*, but rather *its*! If they are professional actors or actresses, they will of course adopt other roles, but their primary one, that of their deepest conditioning, tends to remain intact; they are simply distracting themselves from it through acting out *other* roles...

True humans, on the other hand, are not chained to a script, nor are pretending to not be in submission to any script. Their life unfolds not according to their conditioning, but according to the nakedly-read impulses that emerge from their Heartland, their very depths, their inviolable inner Unity. Their morality is not preprogrammed, but rather is a creation, an ongoing creation of their awakening — it has its own life. It is fluid, malleable, *naturally* full of integrity. It's not a buttoned-up, self-righteous, mind-encapsulated morality, nor some kind of do-gooderism or ego-gratifying humanitarianism, but rather is a natural ethic, a natively present sense of how to conduct oneself amidst the very stuff of one's daily life without losing touch with the imperatives of one's core of Being.

Those who are stuck in acting can only act again and again, as so succinctly summed up in the word react; theirs is a life of reactivity, of blame, of guilt, of partiality, of unillumined suffering, of false intimacy, of recycled dissatisfaction and aberrating contraction. Without awakening, there is no possibility of a truly healthy life — we're then only in submission to commands dictated by our endarkened conditioning, directions carrying the weight and momentum of generational slumber, veined with ancestral authority and compensatory rewards (which would more accurately be called booby prizes).

Among other things, Life is a school, but it's not just an acting school. To play our true part requires much more than the automated dramatization of our *apparent* situation, much more than a looking for cues, much more than a rearranging of our self-presentation — *an acting free of rehearsal and reactivity is required*, an acting in which Being is present throughout every dramatization and personal adventure, an acting that is a poetically practical conduit for Truth, Love, and Mystery, an acting in which surface and depth are lovers...

Almost everyone is doing something quite different from playing their true self. This is not to be pointed out with any easy success, for very few are those sleepers who are not opposed to being told that they are asleep; it is an insult to the typical human to be told that he or she is in slumberland, and, in fact, it is *inappropriate* in most cases to tell such people this. (Such "honesty" all too often is a misuse of speech, a misuse of energy, even a self-glorifying righteousness, an egoic elitism.) There is no point in approaching the sleeping with any kind of program to convert them, to somehow manipulate them into seeing what they're doing — if they're to be given a jolt of Awakening-force, it has to come about as a *spontaneous* byproduct of our *natural* affinity and compassion for them, rather than as some sort of therapeutic or messianic strategy.

That is, help is of little or no value if it's given for the wrong reasons. Real help is *innate* to the giver; it is given without hope, given simply because there is nothing else to do, offered as an expression of the giver's *entire* being, vulnerably, potently, presently, nakedly, skilfully and artfully, without any self-consciousness that help is being given...

When you encounter someone who displays obvious sympathy to Awakening's work, but who also clearly knows zilch about it, being at best a fan of wakefulness, it is fine to talk with them, to engage them at the level at which they can resonate with you, but there's no need to do so in some calculated manner so that maybe in a week or month or two, they'll perhaps join you. No! You must abandon *all* hope of having others join you — if your approach to them is polluted by ulterior motive, they will, however subtly, sense your intent. They will know, and they will resist you, fight you, sabotage your guidance, even as they enthusiastically leap upon your bandwagon, or proclaim their support for your marvellous offering!

It's not necessarily enough for an awakening human to simply be present as a spacious, light-filled environment in which others can participate if they so wish. That's only part of it — in and of itself, it's too easy, too passive, too safe, too detached, too invulnerable. There are occasions when the impulse to penetrate the slumber of others is not only very, very strong, but also completely *natural* and timely; at such times, this impulse must be fleshed-out with skill and sensitivity, without, however, diminishing or castrating its power. If such opportunities are bypassed, one eventually regresses into a kind of renunciate, a semi-withdrawn character, an avoider of intimacy, a somebody with some center, some light, some inner presence, yes, but tainted with a perverse selfishness, an unwillingness to *interfere* or to take strong, unequivocal action, a *disembodied* spirituality that, in so many words, says, "I've got work to do on myself; who am I to tell you what to do?" or "Everything's happening exactly as it ought to" or "We're all Buddhas; I honor the Buddha in you, and I'm not interested in your anger" or "I'll put off my enlightenment until all sentient beings are enlightened, but don't ask me to be vulnerable" or "Keep doing the practice, but don't question it or the teacher" or, more bluntly, "Leave me alone, and I'll leave you alone" or, even more bluntly, "Go fuck yourself!"

When you sense another's need to go deeper, address that need, even as you feel it *in yourself*. Awaken your empathy. Don't merely stand above others, and don't lose yourself in their viewpoint; stop preaching, and get *vulnerable*, letting your *intimacy* with their condition fuel and inspire your expression. Let your *relationship* with them (even if you've just met) be more important than any technique you might be tempted to bring out, or to hide behind (like all too many therapists, psychologists, and psychiatrists). Speak to the heart of their need, but don't try to give them your full knowledge; don't lay out your esotericism before them, or you'll, in most cases, just be casting your pearls before swine — not that they are swine, but pigs don't know what to do with pearls. Give them your pearls when they are ready. If they are not ready, *don't!* If you do (out of self-glamorizing egoity), you'll look down at your precious offerings, and they'll just be painted turds, empty words, flightless birds, a tidy little chaos of mere information, a coughing-up of show-off data...

It is important to not withdraw from the world because of its lack of sensitivity or receptivity to you, and it's also important to not simply fling oneself into the arms of the world so as to prove your humanity. Common sense is as essential as uncommon sense. Very few are truly prepared to *directly* enter Awakening's work, but there are more than a few who are close to leaping into *preparatory* work. You don't really know where such beings will come from, or when they will appear, so you cannot merely remain strategic about when and where you're going to shine your light and unleash your soulsight — all you can do is let it shine true wherever you are, free of all self-advertising, while remaining juicily sensitive to how much can be taken by whomever is in front of you. Some will come your way from the most surprising or unlikely circumstances, suffused with serendipitous nuance, and you'll meet most of them spontaneously, easily, even happily, the key here being to give what must be given without giving yourself away...

And, in order to know what must be given, you must *feel*, consciously and fully *feel*, the other, level upon level — you cannot just give them a prepared speech, a bunch of beliefs, a merely informational deliverance, a preheated self-presentation — No! That is completely inappropriate! You must empathize with those to whom you are speaking; you must feel them so deeply that your self-expression fits and soulfully addresses their actual state, whether in jolting, soothing, fiery, offensive, or tender manner. Such communication is very difficult if one is committed to acting out a certain role, including that of helper or awakener. In fact, it is impossible, unless we confess our immersion in this role, and such confession is of no real value to *most* neophytes (overcomplicating their understanding of authority), but is of immense value to us and our intimates. Unfortunately, many who are prone to avoiding such heartfelt confession still persist in "working" with others, to the extreme of actually making a profession out of it!

When there is a natural attraction (an attraction of *being*) between you and someone new, especially someone who has come to you for guidance, ride the currents of that attraction with open eyes, spontaneity, and restraint, continually sensitizing yourself to your *truest* response, artfully letting that response be shaped according to the overall feeling of your immediate environment. Speak accordingly, but don't speak too much; it is usually better to say too little than too much. Don't tantalize with your seemingly superior knowledge. Make your invitation without necessarily presenting it as an invitation; make it with openness of being, and see what happens. If there is further response, as opposed to reactivity, continue; if there isn't, gracefully extricate yourself, shifting your focus to their resistance, treating it not as a problem or obstacle, but as an opportunity and a challenge, a fisting of energy looking for an excuse to open, to unfurl, to breathe freely, to come alive, to be no longer rejected by the rest of one. Only if there is a toxic reaction, an overly aggressive or smilingly vicious reaction to you, is it at all necessary to deliver force (of voice and gesture)... Those times when it is crucial to really speak out, to be very angry, to weep, to cut loose, are, for most, not very common, but they do occur — if we talk ourselves out of taking such strong, vulnerable action when we ought to be doing so, then we only weaken and impoverish ourselves, deepening our cowardice and reinforcing our hideout in our headquarters, strengthening our chances of once again becoming horribly enslaved to our particular script.

No one really gets scared scriptless, except sometimes during brief, extraordinarily fearful moments. Intense fear usually just drives us into the preverbal dimensions of our acting, into our initial, infantile efforts to be other than ourselves, leaving us marooned in the darkly familiar wasteland of misaligned expectation, its sky atremble with potential parental disapproval... Just about all of us learned to play certain roles in order to successfully navigate our childhood and adolescence; unfortunately, these roles usually were deeply *embodied* by us, imbedded facially, posturally, emotionally, skeletomuscularly, layer upon neurotically committed layer, their very shapings identified with to the point of zero awareness.

The continuing embodiment of our long-ago coping awaits thawing, but such psychosomatic programming cannot be undone just like that, eradicated in a weekend workshop or two — once the honeymoon of initial breakthroughs (catalyzed, for example, by body-centered psychotherapy or by isolationist restructuring) is over, it becomes quite obvious that there is work to be done, a long, arduous

Maurits Cornelis Escher: *Vaulted Staircase* (Escher Foundation)

piece of work, as we learn to relocate from our abstractions of what's what to the core of our Being, bringing awareness and presence to *everything* that we are, however endarkened or armored it might be. Only fools think that this can be done in a short time, not realizing that they're just nailing themselves to the hope that they won't have to really *feel* what they've done to themselves in the name of personal and egoic survival. Typically, they try to replace their programming with a different sort of programming, one bright with positive thinking, lofty affirmations, and metaphysical lullabies, but, underneath their apparent shift in belief or attitude lies their *original* conditioning, festeringly intact, closeted away yet gathering power, making its appearance (which at essence is actually a demand for attention and love) in all kinds of twisted ways, like a monstrously crippled shadow.

Reactivity is the disease. We cannot act our way out of it unless we act *consciously*. In acting consciously, something that is *beyond* all acting is activated, something that is much more us than the role to which we have assigned ourselves... So, in this very moment, this exact moment of hearing, who are you? Who are you busy being? If you don't know, *who* is it who doesn't know? Who is producing the answer? Who is listening? Who is it who is aware of breathing occurring? Who is now trying to answer the question? Who is it who assumes that this *is* a question? Who is *rushing* through this, and who has become much stiller? Who are you? *What* are you? If you've answered with some kind of idealization, some abstraction, some bit of divine jargon, *who* is aware of that? *Who* is aware of witnessing occurring? Who is distracted? Who is contracted? Who is trying to alter their state? Who is it who knows that they don't know? Who is frustrated by these questions, and who isn't? And who is *already* the answer? *Who are you*? And who is looking for an answer? And *where* are you looking? Where?

Look inside your looking. Look inside your looking, right now. What do you find? What are you looking for? Who is doing the looking? Who is it who wants to avoid this, to go on to something else, something more familiar? Who is it who is turning away? And who is it who feels, really feels and intuits Mystery right now? And who is it who feels freedom in not knowing? And who is it who cannot help but love and be and speak true? And who, having nothing, has everything? Enough said and unsaid...

– 18 –
The Naked Nerve of Deserted Need: Titillation, Immunity & Relational Insecurity

(Corby talks about wanting to make love with Marion)

ROBERT: Is it appropriate?

CORBY: Well... I...

ROBERT: And if it's borderline, then what are the definitive criteria? (*Long pause*) Have you given this any thought? Or have you given something else your thought? Are you more than this stumbling tangle-up of mind that's squirming in front of me? (*Very long pause*) Well, one question you have to ask yourself is "Would our making love contribute to our well-being?" Would it enrich your lives, or would it just tend to create more problems, more unlove, more non-intimacy? And *how* would it serve our community? Does it seem that your sexual bonding would nourish those around you, or is it more likely that it would in general only burden them?

CORBY: Probably burden them...

ROBERT: In any case, there's no point in continuing with your mutual self-titillation; it's time to back off from your mutual sugges-tiveness. Why torture each other with erotic promise? Stop wasting energy with your casual flirtatiousness — it may seem playful, but it's actually deadly serious, dense and subtly desperate, stiff with infan-tile hope. It may give you a rush or two, but it just burns up your juice — you keep your meat stuck in let's-get-it-on heat!

CORBY: What I've discovered is that there's a balance here — if we hold back too much from each other, it messes us up, really messes us up...

ROBERT: Yes, but titillating each other is also a kind of holding-back — you go into each other a little way, then freeze, keeping your distance, while promising more. It's a tease. It's invulnerable. Honestly and sensitively sharing your sexual longing is another matter, needing no sleaze and no tease in its delivery, nor any other sort of self-serving drama!

You're too fucking calculating about your sexuality! You're simply creating a massive moat around the castle of its throbbing promise, but it's not worth defending. Not holding back is not about some stupidly indiscriminate throwing open of one's doors, but is about sharing one's passion (not just localized passion, but general passion as well), one's love, one's very energy for the other. If you get turned-on, genitally enlivened, so what? Why muddy it with your mind? Why bargain with it? Just say it, and love her while you say it, and stop inflaming and aggravating yourself with penile fantasy!

It's so, so easy to talk about sex in a manner that arouses us, and so, so easy to pretend that *we've* had nothing to do with this! We have to become conscious of *how* we sexually stimulate ourselves. Once we're genitally congested, it's hard to change directions, isn't it, hard to alter our course without repressing ourselves... So why unnecessarily put ourselves in that position? Don't titillate. When you are hugging, don't bother adding those little extra movements that are sexually suggestive. Be much more alert — such movements, and their corresponding expressions of eye and voice, are just ways you have of making yourself feel better, or more pumped up... And, however subtle it gets (and it can get *very* subtle), the *obviousness* of it runs deeper...

CORBY: It seems to me now that my having sex with her wouldn't really add to our lives.

ROBERT: What about other women?

CORBY: Who's left? (*Laughter*)

ROBERT: The one and only runs deep in you, doesn't it? You'd love to *have* that one, that sublime embodiment of Woman, and be fanatically faithful to her, but you'd only be being faithful to your *ideas* about her. When you fuck an ideal, you only screw yourself! You're afraid to even *consider* exploring your sexual feelings toward other women, because that *might* interfere with you being with Marion eventually — she might not like you doing this! You might get left with no one, no tit to fasten onto! So you scramble to make sure that that doesn't happen, and thus strand yourself from any *real* sexual intimacy. Do you see how easily lust, even healthy lust, becomes business to you, *serious* business?

CORBY: Yeah...

ROBERT: If you are busy hedging your bets, you're not going to know the joy of real sex. *(Pause)* We must become capable of being fully aroused sexually and, at the same time, behaving responsibly, which of course doesn't mean emotionally withdrawing and trying to be really aware and moment-to-moment perfect! Perfectionism murders sex. As I've said many times, there's an *inherent* knowingness built into the very core of sex-energy itself, a *non-separative* awareness. The same is true of the heart of anger-energy, grief-energy, and so on. But this knowingness is not accessible to us *unless* we enter into our feeling dimension totally, without shrinking ourselves.

Going into sex totally does not mean indulging sexually — it has nothing to do with eroticizing or otherwise stimulating ourselves. It's an acceptance of Ecstasy, a deep yes to Being, an embracing of the Divine. Self-engineered juiciness is not Ecstasy, but is a *rejection* of Ecstasy! Nor is romance Ecstasy. You don't get there without being utterly willing to go into *any* of your feelings all the way. All the way! This is not hysteria, nor self-congratulatory emotionalism, but a full-fleshed embracing of Being...

You have some sense of what it's like to be free sexually, and you also know what it's like to be trapped in your head about the whole affair. You're a genius at making head-first entries into sex! You meet your hard-on head-on! *(Laughter)* What a fucking collision! *(Laughter)* So what's Marion got that other women don't have?

CORBY: She wants me...

ROBERT: What else?

CORBY: She's... familiar, easy. *(Long pause)* Ms. Right...

ROBERT: Ultra-security, but you are too quick to sum up, too quick to rearrange yourself around the merely conceptual, the lifeless Ms. Right... This whole matter for you, however, is *pre-conceptual*, pre-verbal. It's about the primal urge to bond with your mother, and the failure of that bonding, the absence of it, the *nostalgia* for it — you're still looking for a convincing replica of that aborted security, both craving it and fearing it. All the electroshock treatment your mother received while carrying you is still vividly remembered by your body; when you get close to a woman, a red light goes on, a kind of adrenalin shock, and you won't go any further unless she demonstrates an absolute purity of love, and even then you're still not sure... You *expect* betrayal, but you'd never let the woman know *that*, 'cause it might jeopardize your chances with her...

You wanted your mother to want *you*, and she didn't, except very superficially. You're still rejecting acknowledging this fundamental rejection. Do you see how defended you are against women, despite your being a soft male, a vulnerable male? You're terrified of rejection, and even *more* terrified of acceptance! One thought, and the red light goes on. Nevertheless, you still want to be wanted, desperately, like an abandoned infant. When a woman wants you, Corby, or even acts like she wants you, you are easily exploited, exaggeratedly dependent upon her, as though she were your *salvation*! It's just your mother, over and over and over again, and not even her, but just the promise of her, the potential, the violent shock, the naked nerve of deserted need...

You crave the safety implied in familiarity, but in expecting such a monotony of consistency from a woman, you deny her the freedom to be unpredictable, to be different, to be uncontrollably alive. You want her to be passionate, but at the same time you don't, because such vitality might well carry her away from you to more exciting territory! In so many words, you keep saying to the women you're sexually drawn to, "Don't change. Let's keep this, just as it is. Let's put a fence around it, and be happy forever after." But such security kills the very passion you seek. Its milk is spiritual poison. Real sex, real Life, doesn't give a damn about immunity — its very joy is in its risk-taking.

As you've noticed, Xanthyros is not exactly familiar or safe; it's open, chaotic, unpredictable, passionately alive, lush and green, bursting through its foliage, full of every sort of feeling, at once mundane and sublime, creatively messy, rooted but not rigid, and right in the midst of it is a budding little dyad, namely Corby and Marion, tightly self-encapsulated, bubbling with would-be immunity and mutually parasitic protectedness.

Break the bubble. Stop dumping all your need on her — share your need with others more. Don't abandon your intimacies with others just for Ms. Right. It's time for a breakout, Corby, not an escape, but a breakout of Being, an unchaining of your naked need, not just in the primal possibilities of groupwork or bodywork with me, but in your everyday life! Something in you is yearning to come forth, something very, very young, something very tender, someone who has no desire to outthink his deep need...

CORBY: I know... (*He starts to cry*)

ROBERT: (*Long pause*) And this has nothing to do with sex, except insofar as a woman's availability and familiarity turn you on. You're still looking for your mother, but you're not looking too closely — what if you find her and she accepts you, and you *still* can't open to her? What then? Even when you're highly aroused, your sexuality is not actually *primary* — what's primary then is the *potential* of having a healthy facsimile of your mother available to you. This promise turns you on, electrifying you, plugging you in genitally, while your mind paints a storybook picture, a tale of Corby at long last in completely nourishing female arms, finally at rest in a healthy womb.

Sex only brightens the picture, juices it up... Your pull to women is not as sexual as it seems. Real sex has quite a different context; it's a matter of there being such an overflow of love and luminous desire between two lovers that they joyously yield to its imperatives, on all levels. They aren't looking for security, but are celebrating the innate insecurity of Life, among other things; they are literally dying into a deeper Life, letting go of their familiarity, letting go of their craving for immunity, letting go of having their lovemaking go in any particular direction, worldly or other-worldly. So sex has nothing to do with security or psychological safety; when it's deep, it's very insecure, except at the level of Essence.

Until you stop trying to make women into surrogate mothers for you, you will not be available to *real* mothering. Have you noticed that you are most drawn to women who are *not* mothers? Women who are cut off from their own capacity for giving mothering? Women who are as childish, at least sexually, as your mother was? And have you noticed how you mask this with your titillation-rituals? It's time to let the illusion die. Go ahead and get disillusioned. (*Pause*) Stop stimulating yourself into hope, especially romanticized hope. What's the big deal about being turned-on? It's no great achievement — with a little effort, you could get turned-on with that chair in the corner, or with the patterns of this carpet!

What's more important, far more important, is to make *real* contact with the deadness that is camouflaged by the inflationary hype and eroticized sensations of being turned-on. Sex is not salvation, Corby. In fact, there is nothing that is salvation. This doesn't mean that we're damned, but that we're not here to be rescued — the lifeline that we seek is *already* in our hands. There is *real* help available, but it is not activated *until* we begin helping ourselves... Similarly, you will not have access to *real* mothering from women until *you* start mothering yourself; prior to that, you will only be impermeable to such mothering from women, agonizingly armoured against what you are reaching out for...

Just about everyone's looking for immunity, seeking an end to their suffering, but their very search only reinforces and complicates their suffering. We look for immunity when we stop trusting each other, losing ourselves in a quagmire of lawyers, contracts, and insurance policies, not to mention so-called relationships and the sterility of conventional coupling and marriage. If love is *truly* present, there is no need, no need at all, for binding agreements and vows, no need at all for hedges against insecurity...

Sex Got Stuck in a Pelvic (& Neo-Tantric) Headlock

Sex took a beating, sex got stuck in a pelvic headlock
Sex took a tailspin, shot full of overtime holes
Sex got uprooted, sex got assigned to stress-release
Sex got charged by righteously snoring meat
So sex went to church and sex went to hell
                falling under mindfucking's marathon spell
Hunching in black furnaces or behind alabaster smiles,
        gobbling mind-fuel and gargling with guilt

See all the loitering on pornographic corners
Heads crammed with hot centerfolds and winking promise
Pinups galore for the guys, titted to beat the way
Romance novels for the ladies, panting with wraparound need
Lust low or lust respectable, juicily delectable, rich with must

So sex got a bad rap, sex got a truckload of shoulds
Some prudish tight, some glibly loose, all clutching a whip
                chained to repeating the same old trip
Sex got sent to the basement, the dampness without light
Hear the chestfuls of lust whispering words of love
See the blind eye sadly waving in the dark, its flag hoisted high
                its thrust obliterating its cry
Sense the mounting stress, seeking an honorable discharge
Touch the sleeping heat, the red friction, the frantic overdrive
           the make-believe coming alive

Smell and taste the desire
        to fuck away the feeling of desire,
                to avoid the light of the fire

Sex got misrepresented, sex got sentenced to life in the can
See the seekers of release bowing before genital drainage
See the lust disguised by smooth dinners and tantric masks
See the claims of friendship, the pocketed privates, the alley-feels
See the so-called liberated sex, the humping in the shallows,
        the basement strung with colored lights and fake rights
See the hidden hurt, the crushed need
        the promise of a poisoned dessert

Sex got bashed, sex got slashed, sex got stuck with the Great Blame
Sex the Villain, sex the Saviour, sex a rack of flavors
See the machinery upstairs masquerading as the resident self
Hear its insistence on referring to itself as you
Notice the mind shacked up with cock and cunt, fucking itself crazy
Scantily-clad taboos the real news in this mental hotbed
        this fantasy-polluted toolshed
Feel the heart smothered by sentimentality
        outbreathed by romanticized passion
See the gestures of love used to nourish blind lust
Hear the pudendal moan, the penile groan, the ego-mounted throne
And hear the loneliness too afraid to be alone,
        the loneliness of being imbedded in an unnatural land,
                subject to a mind-driven hand

Sex got misaligned, sex got stuck with distress-dumping
Sex got reduced to a psychological garburetor,
        the dead end of tension, the gearshift of a masturbator

Witness all the pelvises grinding for promised pie,
        or for a holier sky
Sex to superconsciousness said someone,
        and what holy humping, what ambitious friction!
So fucking got spiritual, orgasm the gate to Eternity
But sexstasy blew its cover in the hollows of feel-good manuals
The show stank, its perfumed smiles thinning to rot,
        its pinkened directions rusting through its gloried shine
            its sublime screwing but another diseased doing

Sex got a bad rap, sex got hammered by guilt
Sex got bashed for burning lustily pious hands
Sex got smeared for coloring a cleancut land
Sex got mashed for falling short, for not doing it all
So sex married mediocrity
And the hotline between mind and crotch got paved hard
The basement bulged, the house shook, the judge threw the book
And sex did cry out for love and light
And sex did wail for its lost home
And sex did weep for the murder of its lovers

Sex squirms in its cell, screaming for release
            from the obligation to make us feel better
Sex longs for its Source, longs to be not a means to Joy,
            but an expression of Joy, a Love-thrill,
        a flesh-bright Ecstasy of passion and grace,
                a sacred rapture, a luminous loss of face

Sex took a beating, sex got stuck in a pelvic headlock
Sex asks for another hearing
Sex asks once again for trust, sex asks for a clearing

Sex asks for us
Sex asks not to be a mission, nor servant to some ambition,
        but only for love and full-bodied spiritvision

Sex got a bad rap, sex got abused
Sex asks that its inner call not be refused
Sex asks for trust and heart-centered lust
Sex asks for us
Give sex its true soil, give it room to grow, to flower
        and you'll see its sky bloom and hear its awakening shout
        and you'll outdance every would-be you,
            your soul overflowing with Eternity's View
And Joy will no longer be your goal,
                    but your ground
And the Presence of the Undying One
        will be inside and all around
And you will be both a slave to That One and wondrously unbound
And sex will no longer be sex
            but only Ecstasy in the flesh
        Intimacy celebrated, dying into a deeper Life

Maurits Cornelis Escher: *Stars* (Escher Foundation)

-19-

The Inside Story
on Information

Information is precipitated specificity, crystallized not for action, but for transmission. However radically it is altered, reshaped, or incorporated, it doesn't decay, for it is without substance. It is naked data, ever pregnant with endogenous self-replication, requiring only a suitable host or medium, be it a single cell or a planetary television audience. Information takes up no space, but its storage does.

Information not only sticks to attention, but, through its very structuring, actually *creates* what is ordinarily called attention, in the same sense that automobiles create highways. Such attention is but the carrier of information, a multidimensional, exquisitely tributaried conveyor of data and design. There are more primary forms of attention (including that in which the noticing of detail becomes spontaneously *secondary* to the full-bodied, self-illuminating awareness of one's Being), but these will not be discussed further here.

And what about feelings? They are not solely informational, but all too easily their energies are mechanically filtered through (or generated by) the prepackaged assumptions of our minds, thereby becoming reduced to little more than "charged" data that at best adds some shapeliness and idiosyncrasy to our terminals of information-reception. However, when our feeling dimension is unfettered by belief (and other rigidities of mind) and is radiant with wakefulness, it is not so much informational as it is intimately transformational...

Information's realm is the purely factual, relentlessly marching as closely as possible to the beat of perfect redundancy. Facts are facts, but they are not necessarily Truth, for Truth is not static, not merely abstract, not *already* bound in form, not exactly repeatable or reproducible — Truth is spontaneous, fresh, unambiguously alive, full of *unrehearsed* creativity, ever expressed in empathetic correspondence with *all* the qualities of Its moment. Its content *cannot* be memorized and parroted, for it emerges newly-born with each new encounter, creatively mixing information with That out of which information arises. Truth is consistent not in form, but in feel...

Information has no inherent value. Its *use* determines its value; it may depreciate rapidly, or it may retain immense value, especially if it is relatively inaccessible *and* needed. Information is simultaneously a non-metaphoric symbol and a commodity, a precise something framing a deeper something. It is perfectly cryonic; attention is its eternal microwave.

And what of the information explosion that characterizes the last quarter of the Twentieth Century? Obviously, it is not well-informed about itself; it does not very often bring telling criticism to its runaway expansion, just as we do not ordinarily question (or even recognize) our heart-crushing identification with our thinking minds. The computerization of our culture is being numbly accepted by most, as though there were no *truly* viable alternative. A fully human *and* modern culture has yet to emerge — our barbarity, delusions, violence, self-fragmentation, and snoring complications are still basically intact, merely *obscured* by our obsession with surrounding ourselves, level upon level, with extensions of our minds (ranging from television to ballyhooed "New Paradigms"). There is no clear evidence that we have the maturity to make good use of our technological advances. Nevertheless, on and on we go, developing more and more sophisticated gadgetry, *compulsively* upgrading what, in most cases, is already admirably suited for the task at hand.

What we are doing with computers is precisely what we are doing with our minds. Computers aren't the problem — what we're tending to do with them is. Its a matter of too much too soon, minus even a remotely awakened overview — hordes of us engorged with the latest software, jammed and short-circuited with the subtle and not-so subtle parasitism of mishandled information, while our hearts lie stranded in deserts (worldly or other-worldly) of abstraction, or in the compensatory quicksands of sentimentality...

At its core, information is no more than pure coding, bearing an elegance of exactitude as deserving of appreciation as anything else. Yet its beauty soon withers, if it is not *consciously* made servant to

Being. When form is made impermeable to formlessness, it becomes a prison, however spacious or consoling. Information is the latticework of knowledge, but not of knowingness. It is design, but not art. It is exact, but it is not necessarily True, for it possesses no real intimacy with Paradox (Truth being the very *heart* of Paradox).

Love is not informational; if it is, then it is not love, but only an abstraction of love, as in the *idea* of "unconditional love" that pervades much of the "New Age". However, real love is *not* regression back into some undifferentiated realm bereft of information, but rather is conscious, ecstatic participation in the infinite Interrelatedness in Which information is gracefully and functionally *peripheral* to Being. Love is the literal *embodiment* of awakened connectedness and empathetic feeling, whereas information, when mishandled, only enrobes self-fragmentation and alienating separativeness.

There is usually no information in deep sleep, nor in Consciousness That is only aware of Itself. Otherwise, information is present, everywhere and everywhen. Our problem is that we're caught up in an orgy of information-transmission and information-replication, madly globalizing our overloaded data, as though doing so were *inherently* virtuous! It's as if we're trying to somehow duplicate or approach what we take to be omniscience, but without any *real* increase in intelligence — even if we could access, via sublime computerization wizardry, *all* the information of the Universe, we still wouldn't *know* who we were! All our data, our infinite data, would only enslave us to *its* caretaking and filing! Of course, this is what is already happening on a smaller scale; we have reduced ourselves to little more than the means whereby information transmits and reproduces itself...

Information means just that — *in formation*. Let us go *in*, yes, but without locking ourselves in. Let us cease reinforcing and legitimizing our entrapment in our minds; let us illuminate our own programming, becoming capable not only of changing channels and data banks, but also of living, really living, in the fathomless depths of which information is but the waves. This cannot be done through distraction or mentalized strategy, nor through some kind of superprogramming, nor through any manipulation of information, but through saying a *full-bodied*, heartfelt yes to all that we are, a yes in which the energies of every no are liberated for the process of becoming fully human, a yes in which information and transformation are in juicily cocreative embrace...

Gustave Doré: *La Fontaine*

– 20 –

A Safe Place to Let Go
of Being Safe:
Mind, Emotion, & Appropriateness

(Philip begins by talking about how difficult it is for him to know whether certain actions are "appropriate" or not)

ROBERT: The question of appropriateness is not a matter of thought, of merely logical consideration. Real decision-making arises from our core, from resonance with our core, rather than from the lobbying of some overfed habit of ours. Decision-making that occurs in isolation from our depths does us no good, or only "accidentally" does us good, for those aspects of us that weren't taken into account in such a decision will invariably make trouble, just like the misrepresented in an electoral district! Of course, taking into account all that we are doesn't mean interminably hearing out every last craving of every last part of us, but rather means letting the wisdom and radiance of our core shine through everything that we are, looking not for submission nor for agreement, but for co-creative participation, soulful alignment, transverbal synergy...

It may sound complex to your mind, but *you* know how simple it actually is. Its simplicity is that of Being, that of truly taking care of ourselves... Such care-taking is not some kind of program, some kind of switch-flicking automaticity, but is an ongoing art, a conscious art, as loving as it's alert, easily outdancing all its paint-by-numbers simulations... Implicit in all this is the need for receptivity, a need that you're always trying to outbox! Or outthink! You get so overfocussed on what or who's in front of you, that you cut yourself off from your own built-in knowingness; you then only hear messages from your persona, your habitualness, having successfully deafened yourself to Being-centered messages and directives. What a complicated mess! What guaranteed suffering!

PHILIP: I was sitting the other night, sitting in a doing place, exhausting all logical possibilities, feeling all kinds of things, but not knowing what to do...

ROBERT: Let go of needing to know what to do, and a truer doing will inevitably emerge, filling out the spaciousness created by your yielding. This, however, doesn't mean becoming a preverbal dolt nor a devotee of runaway emotion! I like the intelligence of your logic, your finely-nuanced mind, but you overuse it — you rely on it too much. You get so damned reasonable with people, so exhaustingly considerate, taking care of everyone except yourself, then get terribly disappointed when all your giving is not reciprocated! But you don't see the impurity of much of your giving, and therefore you also don't see that much of what people give back to you is their *reaction* (however unconscious) to such impurity...

So you get overly reasonable, overfatherly, and then, when you finally bounce up against your feelings, they're usually so congested, so underfed, that they seemingly possess you — you overreact, you get too heavy, your anger is too much of a fist. All your needs come marching out, competing for center stage, and you're all over the place, caught up in a tangle of suspiciousness and extreme neediness, doing things that you'll later regret.

PHILIP: I have such resistance to feeling... Last night when I called you, I broke open right away when you said, "What's deeper?" Suddenly, I could feel all my pain, but usually I have an instinctive response to just push pain away, to talk it away...

ROBERT: You're addicted to living from your mind, not just mentally, but also emotionally — look at how easily you get sentimental! Let me clarify: Sentimentality is a perversion of feeling, a parody of real emotion — it is heart that's been polluted by mind. It's very difficult for you to nakedly love, to truly shine forth your spirit; you're terrified to take your mind out of the driver's seat! Mind-free love is a very rare experience for you — the innate innocence of it (and it's an *awakened,* rather than a naive, innocence) is a terrible threat to the calculatedness you've cultivated most of your life...

People are reluctant to challenge you, because of your non-existent or begrudging receptivity — they probe, and you give them a dose of your mind, zeroing in on a weakness (real or imagined) in their delivery, doing whatever you can to turn the heat onto them, thereby treating the whole affair as warfare, as something inherently dangerous! You use your therapeutic talent to find a loophole in what they've said, so that they'll sooner or later say, "Oh, maybe it is me who's got the problem!"

PHILIP: It's my defence...

ROBERT: Defence of what? Certainly not of your depths! It's no more a defence of what is most precious in you than is a fist a defence of a flower crushed within it! Sure, this neurotic self-protectiveness originally served an utterly valid purpose, that of surviving your childhood, but now it's just archaic armour, a mere suffocation of what your original recoil was protecting...

The true use of your mind is simply to be a reporter and tabulator of the facts, of the moment's sensory information — I'm talking here of the thinking mind, rather than of the imaginal and psychic dimensions of mind, which you tend to treat just as you treat your emotions, namely as underlings of unillumined logic. (*Pause*) When you are tuned into your heart, you can use your mind to articulate its imperatives and impressions, to express its subtleties; however, if you try to be subtle when you're *not* in touch with your heart, all you end up doing is being clever, mixing up levels to confuse the other person, fencing behind a verbal smokescreen, making a wall out of psychological half-truths, all the while isolating yourself from what you *really* need!

That heart-rooted simplicity that you resist embodying requires that your cleverness lose face, not through lucid persuasion or overwhelming evidence that you should do so, but *presently*, even immediately, as an act of trust, an act of real faith, regardless of what your thoughts are telling you! Your mind is not a fan of simplicity, especially integrity-rich simplicity — it squirms when you say things like, "I need you" or "I feel hurt"... Once you let your need flow out into its fullness, *then* relevant insights will emerge, but if you try to come up with your insights *before* you've let go, you'll just be holed up in the numbing security of your mind, hanging onto predigested parodies of real insight, little bits of pseudo-knowledgeable opinion that are severely stained by the very viewpoint that characterizes your pre-open state! What I'm talking about is letting your insights flow out of your undamming of feeling — if you'll permit that, your insights will really fit what's going on, contributing to your whole-ness, rather than splintering you off from it. You've seen people here sometimes get incredibly angry while remaining vulnerable — when they get articulate at the same time, its so beautiful, so nourishingly wild, so feelingly true! Such force and such a simultaneous fine touch! The insights that emerge at such times ring with Truth, don't they?

You look so much before you leap that you don't leap, but just start bargaining for a better deal, or for a bridge. You need to look and leap at the same time, embracing the Unknown, instead of trying to bluff your way around It — a deep yes is required of you, a yes to What transcends all knowledge, a yes ablaze with awakened trust...

PHILIP: I know what you're talking about... I've felt it, and I've had those insights that come from deep energy release and expression. Often, I've had to talk myself into it... (*Laughter*) "Philip, trust, go against your impulse, go against your conditioning, trust, trust some more, go against what you think you see..."

ROBERT: It's about honouring a deeper impulse. All you need is practice. Sure, you have some pretty convincing habits that make you want to do the opposite — but they don't really make you, because *you're* making them! If you're having trouble accessing what you're feeling, just say something like, "I'm struggling to get to my feelings", instead of making a case that incriminates whoever you're with, implying that all that's going on is *them* wanting something from you... Just say that you're having a hard time opening, and, more often than not, the very saying of it will open you, because you'll *feel* the wound of being thus stranded from your depths. Maybe you'll say, "I'm afraid to trust", and then, in the very vulnera-bility of such a confession, you might repeat the same statement with a lot more passion, until the emotion of it overwhelms your mind, and suddenly, there you are, wide open, your heart all over your face...

The very statement "I'm afraid to trust" or "I won't trust", expressed with sufficient passion, will actually help create an atmosphere of trust and intimacy, wherein a deep letting go can occur. Sharing your mistrust fully is an act of trust... (*Pause*) If you'll mistrust your mistrust, things are likely to come unstuck; it's a lot like doubting your doubt. You keep looking for reasons to trust. Don't! Just take the risk of trusting, especially when you don't feel safe — you need to trust the others here, not just me! Trust, like Love, is so profoundly simple; the thinking mind can't stand Them, because there's no static content to fuck around with — thoughts simply evaporate in Their Presence... Nevertheless, there *is* content emerging from un-dammed Love and Trust — you could call it insight or intuition, or perhaps the articulation of organismic wisdom. Real insight, or intui-tion, doesn't come from the mind, but from a place of Being; it's primarily transverbal, finding *translation* into the verbal through the bodily honouring of *need*, an honouring that gracefully necessitates the condensation of primal intuitiveness into a practical form...

So where does this leave your mind? Certainly not in charge! And certainly not in charge of charge! The mind has no wisdom; it is packed with facts, but not with Truth. At its best, it's a servant of Being, a marvellous storer and organizer of information; at its worst, it is permitted to oversee Being, to make decisions it has no ability whatsoever to sanely make. When we turn away from our Heartland and Its innate knowingness, we find a simulation of such wisdom in what we've made of our mind — we end up running just about everything through its disembodied logic, now and then diving into exaggerations of sensation (such as emotionalism and compulsive eroticizing) to counterbalance the barrenness of living in our heads.

The typical mind is like a computer plagued with almost completely unacknowledged computer viruses. Programs that are not recog-nized as programs run the show — and even ones that *are* (such as certain addictions) are ordinarily also permitted to run the show! The whole process is incredibly mechanical... The right set of hips walks down the street, and the typical male mind immediately stiff-ens with interest, turning the head the same damned way time after time! Look into the eyes of men who are thus ass-gazing, and you'll just see their engorged mind looking out through their eyes — you probably won't even see any *real* lust in their gaze, but just mecha-nized interest. They're programmed to look, so they look, with no more awareness than you have when you get defensive...

You do almost everything in terms of your mind; usually when you cry or get angry, it's framed by a mind-created context. Your crying shrinks into sentimentality and unnatural helplessness, and your anger fists into mere violence, an invulnerable lashing out... (*Pause*) And it's no wonder that you lean toward violence, because you feel so horribly contained by your cognitive cage — you get pissed off being stuck in such a rigid little box! Everything looks so threatening from in there! So you need to recreate the context, not through some kind of therapeutic "recontextualization" (or any other species of thinking about thinking!), but *feelingly*, nakedly, empathetically, until it originates in Being rather than in mind... Do this, and your crying will shed its self-pity, its blindness, its blubbering stance of victimization, shifting into a crying that resonates with the sense of loss that permeates all of Existence.

This is grief, the undefended heart's acknowledgment of loss, of death, of change. It is the wound of finiteness, the hurt of limitation, felt so deeply that an accompanying sense of the Infinite is also feelingly present. Without grief, Ecstasy is just gleeful escapism; without grief, Life is just a desert, a wasteland of reactive sorrow, compulsive pleasuring, and immunity-seeking... Real grief is as luminous as it's pure, as mind-free as it's expansive, achingly rich with awakened love... (*Pause*) If your personal sadness is not connected to the Universal sense of sadness, then you are in exactly the same position as when your love is only for your partner — you are self-marooned from the Truth of what you are, in effect denying your inherent continuity with all that is...

PHILIP: The Universe isn't exclusive, so relationship shouldn't be exclusive.

ROBERT: Tell your mind that! Of course, if you did, it would probably only make a program out of non-exclusivity, *excluding* whatever didn't fit into its program! (*Laughter*) To deny (through your behaviour) that you're in relationship with a particular part of the universe is just a confession of not being fully integrated... If your Life-context is mind-generated, then nothing is going to satisfy you; you'll be haunted by a nagging sense of incompletion, of partiality. But why make a lifestyle out of lies? Why not let some light into the wound behind the disguise?

You must become more sensitive to what you are *actually* doing! Viewing the show from your headquarters is of no more use than getting lost in your feelings. It's very easy to make a virtue out of emotion, whether it's real emotion or just mind-generated emotion. A lot of what is called Primal Therapy is just people regressing into preverbal feeling, *hiding* in their helplessness, righteously clutching their "need" to "have their feelings", acting as if interminably calling for mommy or daddy (or indulging in unillumined wailing, whining, and temper tantrums) will free them, when in fact it actually obscures a *deeper* sort of feeling, a feeling that supports our emergence into an Awakened condition. (*Pause*) It's very easy to get stuck in emotionalism, isn't it? Remember when I said that sentimentality was a perversion of feeling? I said that because the context of sentimentality is *mental*. There's a nostalgia in it too, a slobbering, extremely easily-triggered nostalgia... Widen the scale, and you could say that sentimentality's the soil of patriotism...

PHILIP: Which leads to fascism.

ROBERT: Yes. It creates a false loyalty. The sentimental have a false loyalty to their past; it has a lot to do with not wanting to grow up. It's a twisted way of trying to stay childlike or innocent, to have a little haven from the brutalities of the adult world. There's a softness to it, but it's a softness with no center, a softness with no spine...

PHILIP: It's so obvious to me now how much of my Jewishness is *based* on nostalgia and sentimentality. Jews worship the past. The more a Jew remembers how his grandfather "did it", and how his grandfather's grandfather "did it", the more revered he is as a Jew.

ROBERT: Every religion has the same disease. It's their way of perpetuating themselves. Rituals are inculcated and believed in, rituals that remind their doers of how very important their religion is to them, and of how grateful they should be to be part of it... This is not an honouring of one's ancestors, but a dishonouring of them, a using of the memory of them to keep oneself small, predictable and neurotically dependent...

Do not confuse sentimentality with love; when you're feeling sentimental toward someone, *especially* one of your children, you're not *really* loving, but only objectifying them, wallowing in the sensations of being "in love" with your objectification! You could call it non-sexual romance... It *acts* big-hearted, it *acts* generous — it'll even give you the shirt off its incredibly overworked back, exhausting itself to take care of you, despite your protests to the contrary, but its altruism is suspect, being centered by an overly maternal quicksand of pious ego... Remember the joke about the two priests who are busy praying, repeatedly saying, "I am nobody", when in walks a janitor, who immediately joins them in their ritual? As he too is saying, "I am nobody", one of the priests looks up and indignantly says, "Who does he think he is to think *he's* nobody?" (*Laughter*)

Ego is still ego, even when it prays! Especially when it prays! Or especially when it masquerades as heart, as in sentimentality... I, I, I, so damned full of exclusivity, even when it's giving and giving and giving, like some all-sacrificing supermother! Such ego-centricity may be solitary, or it may be collective, as in nationalism and religion, where the big "us" can only occur in the face of a shadow-enlarged "them". Yes, there can be a healthy division in certain conditions of "us" and "them" (as in the necessary articulation of differences), but here it's utterly neurotic, no more than ego-reinforcement, a pumping-up of a false "I" through cultic association with other, similarly inclined "I's"...

Such associations are innately paranoid, needing an enemy to justify their continued existence, whether that enemy's another country, another religion, another political party, another approach, another way of living, or just an abstraction. It's the outer manifestation of self-fragmentation — every piece for itself, every person for himself or herself, every family for itself, every country for itself, and on and on, with just enough ecological lip-service to keep guilt at bay! Isolation upon isolation, masked by a pretence of community! Look at the houses here, each one a box unto itself, lit from within by little more than a television set!

PHILIP: ...Compared to indigenous cultures, where they have circles and interconnected rows of houses, with common areas...

ROBERT: It seems a lot more intimate, doesn't it? It is, but not *profoundly* — those tribal cultures (which it's easy to slip into uncritical admiration of) are, in general, held in place not by Awakening, but only by culturally-implanted taboos. An incredible dependency on the tribe is inculcated; like ego, every culture wants to maintain itself, whatever the individual cost. (Even in our culture, individualism is crushed, being replaced by a parody of itself, namely that deified independence which is obsessed by *having* and consuming — excessive consumerism plus push-button gratification keep both our culture and its illusory individualism going, ever expanding its nest.) The loveliest culture I've ever seen was that of Bali, but even they had their taboos. They were very repressed sexually. If they'd opened that door, I don't think their culture could have dealt sanely with the results, anymore than ours is! Of course, ours is spilling out all over the planet, its "values" and greed and crass tourism spreading like a plague through other, relatively healthier cultures, reducing everything into consumable parcels...

As long as you insist on living in your mind, you will at best only be a tourist relative to your depths, terrified of actually *living* in the realms you are busy touring. When you feel really separate from something, unnaturally separate, you'll notice that it bothers you, and perhaps even threatens you, at which point you'll either back off further, taking snapshots, or else amp up your control, trying to bring the "other" under subjugation, or at least into a convincing simulation of subservience... This is not just the dominant approach of our culture to less sophisticated cultures, but is the very style of ego in its relationship to the rest of oneself!

But the "other" isn't the problem — your sensation of self-enclosed separation is! It's that turning away from your core of Being that is giving you trouble; once you've submitted to such primal recoil, nothing really works, however docile or fuckable it is in the face of your control... Your need to give up your neurotic, mind-riddled control will not go away, so you might as well get right into it, and stop acting as if it's not safe to open up here!

If you feel threatened by such an opportunity, then you're only identifying with *what* feels threatened, namely that habit we call ego, that habit that marches around with the nametag Philip! Give up your craving for safety, really give it up here, and you'll find a *real* safety, the safety of Being...

Living as a Mind Means Being Stuck in Time...

Living as a mind means being stuck in Time, stretched hammockless between Past and Future, bargaining for parole, making obsession with a goal more important than being whole. Yes, it's all the same Moment, but our manufactured self drops itself into Eternity's Pool, then tries to colonize all the resulting fragments, all the personalized ripples, letting those that are consistently most prominent refer to themselves as "I". These imposters roost in the mind, recycling their own bureaucracy, ever making Time, confusing their clockwork with intelligence, making a killing from peddling Distraction's software, invading the body with the twinned delusions of hope and despair.

Time is spawned by the unilluminated mind, relentlessly spinning "us" out, winding "us" up, implanting in "us" Its rhythms, Its logic, Its storage requirements, offering as compensation coffee breaks of ballyhooed pleasure spasms, little pamperings of physiological rhyme. If you think you've got time, Time has you; you are then just a fleshy verification of Its Reality. We have to know Time before we can cut through our submission to It. Time's a fix, and all too easily we are Its pushers and buyers, as well as Its busybody substrate.

The mind exists in Time, the body in Space. The body lives Now, the mind Then or Later. Of course, the body is ordinarily polluted, bent, misaligned, contracted, and generally tyrannized by the program-mings of mind, but its focus, however twisted, is expressed and lived Now. And what of feeling, not mind-generated feeling, but *real* feeling? It exists simultaneously in Space and Being, just as intuition exists simultaneously in Time and Being...

Time, Space, and Being all coexist in Consciousness, forever Now. Such Consciousness has no opposite; unconsciousness is but one more cloud in Its infinite Sky. God is the Essence of Consciousness. God's Time is Eternity; God's Space is Silence; God's Being is Limitless Presence; God's Logic is Truth; God's Sign is Love; God's Obviousness is Mystery. The body already knows God, but ordinarily doesn't know that it knows, being *preoccupied* by the viewpoints of mind. God's Gift is Beauty; God's Desire is Life; God's Lust is Passion; God's Passion is Ecstasy.

If we're too busy to feel God, then Time has us. God only knows, we often say in whimsy or exasperation. Only God knows. Knows what? The Great Mystery of Being is no secret; It's all around, inside and out, more obvious than we can imagine, even as It looks through your eyes at these very words. And what other way is there to spend Eternity than to be God, whatever your current form or appearance? What else could possibly tolerate Eternity? The usual you? No! The unusual you? No! Have I said enough? Am I only calling your bluff? Am I giving you the right stuff? Are my rhymes of any use? Are you looking at your watch, or are you watching your look? And my words die, running out of Time...

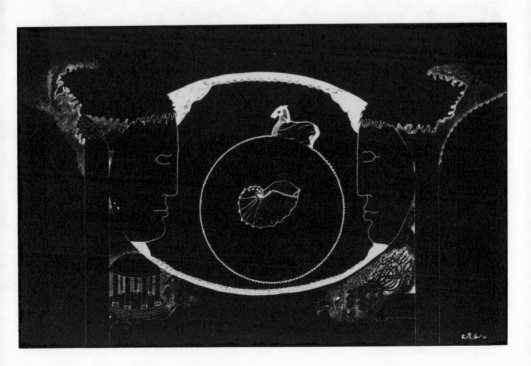

Gustave Doré: *The Bible*

-21-

Real Anger is Not An Avoidance of Anything

There is nothing inherently wrong with anger — it's not necessarily a problem, a sign of negativity, a spiritual hindrance, nor a demonstration of unlove. It is our *use* of our anger that is the issue...

Do we abuse it, hiding our hurt and need and love behind its energies, fueling our righteousness and defensiveness with it, humping and dumping it away, or do we stay nakedly empathetic and vulnerable as we allow it its full passion, its concept-free fieriness? Do we use it to get even, to dominate, to hurt, or do we use it to reestablish intimacy, to flame through pretense, to clear the temple of money-lenders, to break through barriers to love? Do we reduce it to sarcasm, irritability, and resentment, or do we permit it a healthy freedom of expression, an uncaged aliveness that's as responsible as it's hair-raisingly present? Do we make an enemy out of it, or an ally? Very few have a truly healthy relationship with their capacity for anger, and we've all got anger, including those emotionally disembodied, saintly types who are busy nailing themselves to their beatific act!

Anger isn't just a valve for letting off psychospiritual steam, anymore than it's just something to be risen above or transcended; in fact, the very urge to eradicate anger, to sterilize, smile, file, or affirm it away, is itself an act of violence, an act that through its very repressiveness only reinforces the endarkened core of twisted anger. To try to eliminate violence from oneself through a clinging to the sanctified shoulds of supposed peace is simply a more subtle sort of violence, just more Self-suppression and self-justifying emotional vacuity. And what is violence? It's just aberrated force, misaligned power, unilluminated anger, the brass knuckles of dungeoned hurt, asking not for annihilation nor for indulgence, but for room to breathe itself sane, to expose its hidden wounds, to be unburdened by its characteristic intentions and viewpoint, until it is but power, raw power, in the service of Being...

Violence is Life-force that has been so rigidly cooped up, so miserably and consistently encaged, so thoroughly vilified and ostracized, that it cannot help but boil and fester within, its very pressurization forcing it to seek outlets, such as abdominal ulceration, migraine headaches, exaggerated mentalizing, or more commonly, rape, both physical and non-physical, rape of the environment as well as of the other, rape left and right, large and small, wherein pleasure is compulsively equated with power-over... The energy of violence may, through its torso-gripping, electrically-intense compression of Being, find its way down to the genitals (for drainage and/or dramatization through rape, masturbation, and the more "civilized" variations of these that pass for regular sex) or up to the skull, where it stirs the brain to a feverishly enervating pitch, catalyzing worry, anxiety, paranoia, *and* compensatory fantasy, thus quickly intensifying the already-stressful condition of the body, which then mechanically generates even more worrisome thoughts, all of which only clicks into further overdrive our exhausted fear reflex, its panic button pushed silly. *This* is violence. This is self-violation. This is the turning away from the Inviolable, the negation of the Real, the flight away from Love, the inwardness that masquerades as Soul, the inwardness that, in fleeing its own violence, also flees every other feeling of a similar depth, finding solace in neurotic peace-making, fake tolerance, and compulsive conceptualization.

Now, onto how to work with this... In the sanctuary of a truly intimate relationship, the actual *intent* of one's anger can be safely verbalized, *specifically and uninhibitedly* — one's violent urges (along with any attending shame) can be freely articulated, even if they must at the same time be physically expressed through wringing a towel, bashing a pillow, unleashing one's voice (letting its sounds arise primarily from the belly, and flood through one's entire being), or engaging in other similarly non-destructive expressions of such energy. A confession of our violent intent, *if* vulnerably and *fully* expressed, actually diffuses such intent, radically lessening the desire to act it out. Undoubtedly, there'll be relief both in the recipient and the giver of such anger, *if* there is a strong, mutual trust, a trust that is founded on risk-taking as much as it is on love — in a case like this, the one receiving the anger can feel, obviously feel and intuit, the state and inclinations of the giver. Of course, if the giver's violence is unacknowledged as such, or is otherwise twisted, impenetrable, or committed to unlove, then it is natural that the recipient protect himself or herself, seeking outside assistance if necessary...

To expose one's violent or outrageously reactive intentions with clarity, sensitivity, vulnerability, and appropriately dramatic exaggeration is, even though it might appear otherwise, an act of love, a true sharing and healthy exposure, a generously-revealed inside look at one's uglier urges, deep anger, and soul-crushing habits, without any requisite diminishment of one's capacity for embodying strong force — it is a tremendous risk, heavily shadowed by probable rejection *or* false acceptance by the other, yet it is a risk we cannot afford to bypass if we are to become fully human (since that process necessitates our becoming intimate with *everything* we are, however endarkened).

If our anger is delivered cleanly and fully, it is usually quickly followed (or even accompanied) by tears, laughter, high-quality embarrassment, joy, looseness, and an unmistakable luminosity of being, a loving magnification of Self. This is not just a blowing off of steam, a ritualized uncapping, a psychological woodchopping session — it's a breaking through of barriers to intimacy. Real anger obliterates life-negating walls, vibrating them into sudden porosity, breathing them full of windows and life-size doorholes. Real anger doesn't stroke walls away, nor therapize nor argue them away, nor take them down brick by brick. Rather it blasts right through them, whether it is delivered stormily or quietly. It penetrates. On the other hand, sarcasm (like other forms of diseased or mind-polluted anger) doesn't penetrate walls, but only thickens and seemingly legitimizes them, as does blame and every other shaping of righteousness...

The most common error in the giving of anger is assuming a stance of righteousness, an ego-encrusted position wherein we busy ourselves blaming the other, resolutely building a case against them, not only with our presented content, but also with our accusatory tones and semi-hysterical posturing. This is truly loveless, just as loveless as pretending to not be angry when we in fact are. Getting righteous during our anger is just as pointless as submitting to the other's demand (usually tacit) that we not get full-throttle angry, that we prove (through dutifully eviscerating our rage) we are loving, that we spare them our intensity, that we sterilize our "no", that we, in other words, let them remain in *control*, safely and predictably superficial, far from the flames of our ragingly alive passion. Righteousness is an effort to control the other, to bind and subjugate them (for their own good, of course!), to guilt them, to psychoemotionally imprison them for their supposed or intended crimes against us. Needless to say, real anger goes far deeper than any seesawing between simplistic right and wrong; its morality is not that of blame, but rather that of awakened responsibility...

If we're on the receiving end of anger, especially really hot anger, it is very, very easy to deny the other access to us, very, very easy to defensively (without appearing defensive) interrupt or detour their intensity of emotion for some little, but suddenly-so-important bauble of play-it-safe mind, some diddly little proof that they aren't reject- ing us (which only obscures the fact that *we're* rejecting them). It takes guts to authentically receive anger — it's not a matter of mere passivity, of saccharine "thank you for sharing" compliance, of auto- mated "I'm here for you" crap, but rather is a matter of dynamic receptivity, of unrehearsed availability, of deliberate and empathetic spaciousness, out of which one's *truest* response can emerge, whether that response be of anger, sadness, laughter, indifference, distur- bance, love or whatever...

If the one giving the anger is not caught up in being right, nor is obsessed with "being heard," but instead simply wants to be deeply and truly felt (viscerally and heartfully understood), then the situ- ation is a wondrously subtle simplicity for the receiver, a richly textured opportunity to reestablish or deepen intimacy. And, if the receiver is not busy identifying with *what* is being attacked, then he or she is, in a very real sense, standing beside the one who's deliver- ing the anger, gazing at *what* the anger is addressing, without the slightest reactivity; as such a wakeful recipient, we realize (and this realization is *full-bodied*) that the other's anger (assuming that it's real rather than reactive anger) is not actually at *us*, but rather at what we have been or are *doing*!

For anger to be of real use, both the giver and the receiver must trust each other, not as a strategy, nor out of bargaining, but out of love and a mutual commitment to getting to the heart of the matter. They must be vulnerable with each other, not helplessly or impotently vulnerable, but resiliently and expansively vulnerable, without any ego-centered, manipulative superimpositions (such as seductive promises, veiled threats, or spread-easy love) — sometimes, they might even need to openly confess that they don't want to be vulnerable (after which they'd, in all likelihood, assume a truer viewpoint than that of their resistance). Trust cannot be built in an atmosphere of expected betrayal, yet its cultivation necessarily must include the unexpurgated sharing of the urge to betray, to destroy, to undermine, to sabotage, even to leave, the relationship in question; this sharing, however painful, must occur, and must occur compassionately, if trust is to grow. The urge to blame the other has to be thoroughly exposed, and allowed to mutate into a co-evolving responsibility, unburdened by egoic protectionism, contracts, and immunity-promising deals. No lawyers are needed, no judges, no courtroom! Simply make room for trust...

Real anger is fire, earthy, stormy, whitewater fire, as spontaneous as it's accurate. At its best, it is a thrillingly wild and elegant use of raw force, a shockingly alive brilliance of flaming rapids, a lustily sacred conflagration. Such anger's a great explosion, a "no" full of a primal yes, a lion's roar — very quickly, it clears rubble out of the way, cutting through defensive debris and egoic strategy, making room for what was on hold before the encounter, making room for more watery emotions, for sadness, for tears of hurt and reunion, tears of ancient and present pain, tears of heartwoundedness, ever-widening and overflowing their banks, flooding away rigidities of mind and body, moving with compelling yet soft power, pouring oceanward, free of self-pity, free of implosiveness, exhilaratingly and obviously free of all the kinds of crying that are not real crying, but only efforts to manipulate the other, to attract parenting, to make a "poor me" statement about one's bondage to one's circumstances...

When our streamings of sadness are undeniably authentic, coursing through and enriching the space cleared by anger's fieriness, then they gracefully shift into a deeper sadness, one that's as airy as it's watery, as spacious as it's earthy, as appreciative as it's wounded, namely grief. Grief is the sky for the ocean of sadness, the ocean of loss — it is sadness purified of all melodrama, a bare-hearted acknowledgement of the inevitable passing of all forms. Essential to grief is the unqualified acceptance of Death, of radical change. Grief is an expansive mourning, generously seeded with Undying Joy, lit from within by an Undying Knowingness. Grief keeps love from drying up. It makes a fool out of non-attachment and similar escapist posturings. It's not solemn nor morbid, but rather is a luminously sober appreciation of the passing of everything, large or small; as such, it is simultaneously personal and transpersonal. If yielded to, grief easily transmutes into compassionate joy, into Ecstasy, into a Brilliance that warms the Earth, feeds the soil, lightens the heart, ever replenishing Life...

Wherever obstructions arise, there also arises the power to deal with them. When that power is not welcomed and wisely used, then there inevitably comes distress, unnecessary complication, mindfucking, cramping of Being, violence, trouble upon trouble — thus do we abdicate our capacity for the sane use of force, forcing it into an unnatural underground, so that it must find equally unnatural outlets, such as war (war being but a gross exaggeration of *diseased* conflict). So, so many flee the natural imperatives of their inherent forcefulness, especially when it takes the shape of anger; again and again, they seek the numbing safety of their headquarters, literally holing up in their thinking minds, occupying and comforting themselves with exploitation of the merely mental, making a virtue out of compulsive computerization and "spiritual" conceptualizations, fascinating themselves left and right, reducing just about everything to mere information, to the point where intelligence is confused with being well-informed! Their peace is but repression of their inner war, their violence, a socially-sanctified fleeing to the unfeeling periphery of themselves...

Much of the time, especially in men, the repression of real anger finds an outlet through genital titillation and discharge. We fuck away the energy of our anger, forcing our sexuality to be the outhouse of our dungeoned power, obsessively flushing away our fierier passions, even as we pride ourselves on being so up-and-ready horny, so hotly desirous of wanting to "have" sex as frequently as possible, complimenting ourselves (and perhaps snaring grudging admiration from our peers, and outright praise from those we are fucking) on being so sexy, so virile, so hot-bloodedly available. What pain, what untouched grief, what a parody of relief!

The very frequency of our urge, our compulsive and ego-reinforcing urge for sexual release, is a poignantly succinct sign of disease, of estrangement from our Heartland. All too easily, sex is for us just a valve for mind-induced engorgement, a blowhole for belly-frustration and relational complication, a romanticized dumping ground, an ego-inflator, a would-be-prover and swooning caricature of intimacy, doing other than its true work, secretly weeping, marooned from Ecstasy... What a waste of energy! What a life-negating clinging to pleasurable consolation, what vast desolation! This throwing off of energy, this craving to both have and get rid of impassioned desire, permeates our entire culture — you can see it in the way most children "play," as well as in the way that most adults consume, live, entertain, and *adulterate* themselves, turning ecology (especially the ecology of Being) into a buzzword, a political hot potato, a trendy concept...

This, along with the other neurotic reroutings of our native forceful-ness, leaves almost no available energy for the Awakening process, nor for real love, including the loving of that in us which is fright-ened, despairing, emotionally anorexic, crushed, broken, orphaned, exaggeratedly vulnerable, hypersensitive, prone to violence — this inner woundedness is shaped like a sobbing child, an abandoned child, a child whose even most bizarrely twisted actions are but out-of-balance calls for attention and love. In our internal warfare, we render ourselves loveless, acting as if we have no other choice, literally dividing ourselves up into different ideological camps, losing our vision in a blur of flagwaving and crisscrossing righteousness, grimly and unconsciously trampling our innocence and integrity, burying our child, eventually projecting our battlefield onto the en-tire planet...

To the point: Learn to embody and love your native capacity for forceful expression. Do not make anger wrong. Do not make an enemy out of your rage. Do not assume that psychospiritual matura-tion means that you'll become less and less angry — those who are well on the way to becoming fully human do not transcend emotion, but rather purify and deepen it. They are both free and discrimi-natingly precise in their emotional expression, participating in it without drama (except when it serves Awakening), without ego-centered motivation, without bargaining, without reactivity, having *already* outgrown the urge to be vehicles for *mind-generated* emotion.

Theirs is a purity of feeling, an illumination and empathetically exact *fullness* of feeling. Their sadness is expansive and nourishing. Their laughter is whole-bodied and mind-free. Their anger is both heat and light. Their joy is *already* present, readily accessible even in the midst of deep pain. Theirs is not a self-pitying, implosive, depressive de-spair, but is a positive despair, a Life-serving despair, in God-Reveal-

Gustave Doré: *The Bible*

ing embrace with disillusionment and disappointment. Their rage disturbs the sleep of others; their mere presence is an offense to the usual human, unless it has been deodorized, sterilized, and tidily summarized for mass consumption...

Those who get angry without an attending awareness are but indulging in a fieriness that's all heat and no light, all fury and no sky, a straightjacketed bonfire of accusation and righteousness. And then there are those who want it to be all light and no heat, but they have not yet reached the stage where fire *is* fundamentally nothing but Light — they'd bypass all the preparatory steps if they could, abstracting the Fire into textbook safety and familiarity, finding a way to rationalize their avoidance. Such beings tend not to actually feel and love the Light, but to only conceptualize It, to make an ideal out of It, an ego-consoling idol, which they resolutely busy themselves romanticizing and believing in, with the blind zeal of the devotee, the neurotic follower, the patriot, the fan. They hope to skip the necessary pains of purification by merely worshipping at the feet of their guru or idealized notion or metaphysical angelshit, not realizing that they are only postponing a leap they know they need to take.

Love needs power! Love divorced from power very readily slips into sentimentality, superficiality, impotent little reachings out, psychic tea parties, therapeutic fingerpointing ("You're not there for me." "No, *you're* not there for me!"), and other gutless stabs at living a more feeling or rich life. To bring heart and belly together into a more than shallow association means learning, among other things, to *really* love and honor one's fieriness; it means letting such fire fuel our love and compassion, letting it flame through our entire bodymind, letting its heat burn through the non-essential in us, the obsolete, the personalized stacks of deadwood, burn loose and burn bright, burn through every behavioral pattern that no longer serves our well-being, thereby unconcealing the essential in us, the nakedly Real, the very crux of Being...

Anger can be enjoyed eventually, not in some sadistic or otherwise loveless manner, but rather as a thrillingly vulnerable sharing of potent force, of ruthlessly raw energy, of unshackled longing and brilliantly impolite breakthrough. When we are fully *and* consciously angry, we are simultaneously trusting ourselves, allowing ourselves freedom of speech even in the midst of the most extreme rage, intuitively knowing that what we say then is precisely what needs to be said, however outrageous its expression might be. Our content, in its very spontaneity and volcanic magnificence, may surprise us as much as its recipient — out flows amidst all the lava a profound yet marvelously obvious insight, an air-clearing truth, an acidly apt en- capsulation, a great shiver of sudden poetry, or perhaps an already- known statement that's been said many times before, but never with such exquisitively alive clarity and rudely deft resonance of tone as now.

Even in the thundering heat of intense anger, joy can be present, not necessarily as a smile or display of good cheer, but as an inviolable and wonderfully somatic, luminous sense of vitally alive Being — in such a case, the signs of anger will still be dramatically present, but there will also be a non-dilutionary expansion of Being and Love, a multidimensional empathy, a great spaciousness within which anger can take its most natural, life-giving course, a spaciousness that creates permission for laughter to occur, for tears to stream, for humor to take the stage, for love to shine. Through deep acceptance and life-enhancing expression of our anger, we'll eventually experi- ence it, at least some of the time, not even as what we label "anger," but instead as a space-clearing intensification of Life-energy, an expression of such pure passion that both parties will not be able to do other than be enlivened and enriched by it.

If there isn't such an enlivening, then the anger is not being delivered and/or received cleanly. It is essential to recognize the signs of neurotic anger — the righteousness, the viciousness, the built-in blame, the invulnerability, the hysteria, the lies, the smokescreens of content, the avoidance of sharing one's real hurt, the unrelenting contraction of body, mind, and Being...

Real anger is not an avoidance of anything. The depth to which we're willing to go in our expression of anger is precisely the depth to which we're willing to go in our expression of any other emotion. For example, those who deny or cripple their capacity for anger do not cry with profound depth, but tend to only wallow in the swamps of self-pity and helplessness; their love lacks passion, their sex lacks soul, and their life lacks integrity. Theirs is a disembodied sort of happiness, a shallow, sterilized joy, a clinging to the surface, clut- tered with the flotsam of compensatory activities...

Do not turn away from your anger, do not indulge in its reactionary impulses. Do not attach your mind to it. Make room for it, but don't vacate the room. Become more and more intimate with its fire, its force, its imperatives, its surrogates, allowing it to become far more than just a loudly pointing finger, more than a supposed spiritual obstacle, more than a regrettable something, more than a fist of righteousness, more than an "animalistic" venting. Learn to make good use of your anger. Let it empower your love, and add color, spark, and Life-affirming risk to your life. Let it loose, and let it outflame the violence of your mind. Let it speak and dance, and see how quickly it deepens your intimacy with Life. Don't just sit by the fire. Be it...

–22–

Without Intimacy, Meditation is But a Remedy

(The session begins with Madhavi expressing in a very quiet, mousy voice her missing of Xanthyros; she has been living alone for several months)

ROBERT: If you *really* missed the community here, you'd have done more. So even if it's true that there's some missing in you of people in Xanthyros, there must be something else that's stronger or more dominant than this missing...

MADHAVI: Yes. I'm really enjoying being alone, meditating, having time to feel myself. *(Her voice is very weak)* I'm... so tense around you...

ROBERT: Why?

MADHAVI: I don't know.

ROBERT: You need to find out *what* you're scared of, and one way of finding that out is through directly and consciously feeling your supposed fear of me. To some degree, when you're around me, you can't help but sense what you're not feeling in yourself; my presence *spontaneously* draws you toward your depths. You have let your life become quite superficial — nothing wrong in that, but it's not an issue of right or wrong. The point I'm making is that in letting your life become so superficial, you have become threatened by whatever makes you more aware of your depths, including me!

If you were truly meditating, your deeper needs would drive you in directions that you haven't gone in. When meditation is real, *everything* that is going on in you becomes more and more foreground.

Desires aren't then risen above; they are encountered directly. Meditation is not meant to be a remedy; it's not meant to be a spiritual aspirin, nor some way of making yourself feel better in the midst of a rather miserable existence. Meditation is meant to clarify what's occurring, as well as to plug you into your Source. If something unpleasant is occurring, meditation will flush it out into the open, perhaps making it even more unpleasant, or more *obviously* unpleasant, so that you will be forced to deal with it! If meditation only made what's unpleasant less unpleasant, you'd probably never deal with it!

Meditation for you is usually just a sporadic ritual of concentration, an in-the-mood focussing on some area of your bodymind, a focussing that is relatively easy to set up, such as inside your skull, amidst all that juicy and worrisomely repetitive thinking...

MADHAVI: I know. I've been meditating on this part (*Patting her belly*), because otherwise my tendency is to go up here (*Pointing to her head*) unconsciously, and just run around in my mind.

ROBERT: But what good does it do to just sense or notice *this part*? What happens when you notice, really notice, your torso?

MADHAVI: It keeps me away from this part. (*Touching her head*)

ROBERT: That's not meditation! Meditation is not about going back and forth between opposing camps in the bodymind! If you're placing your attention *down here* because you don't want to be up there, or vice versa, that's just avoidance, as well as a reinforcement of tension, unhealthy tension. When meditation is authentic, it is as non-strategic as it is effortless. There's a purity of relaxation, an ease of being, even if the body is full of pain; then attention readily goes where you will it to go. *But* that "will" is not the "will" of persona, but the "will" native to *Essence*. There's a subtlety here, however — the ego can put on a convincing display of meditation — persona can *act* very spiritual! Persona can *believe in* comforting metaphysical notions about the Universe, and such belief can generate corresponding emotional states in the body...

When you first came back to us, you were delighted to let your essence flower forth; your persona was then simply a colourfully unique and pleasing way of expressing your essentialness. You were turned on, radiant, alive, outrageous — you were challenging people as much as you were loving them. You were on fire with your own integrity. But inertia and erosion set in, eating through the honeymoon. It was *partially* natural, because you needed more separation from Xanthyros than you were giving yourself, not a lot more, but definitely some more... Now you've got that distance, plus extra! You're living alone — you've got an opportunity to have as much intimacy as you need with people in Xanthyros, and you can also keep away as much as you need to. However, if you keep away almost the whole time, it's not natural. You don't need a total break from us. You need your own environment and somewhat infrequent contact with us, but you do need *contact*! You need *real* contact!

You've been a stranger, a superficial stranger — it's as if you've never done deep work, never cried with me, never danced or sung ecstatically, never shone, never felt spirit. It hurts doesn't it? (*She cries*) I don't need you to stay away, so why the hell do it? Why persist in living in fear? Doesn't it seem crazy? Yes, you *are* a shy person, but, more importantly, you're repressing your passion, your Life-force, your love, your need...

When you're around people who are living passionately and fully, it makes you uncomfortable, simply because it brings into glaring relief how rarely you say a real yes to *your* passion. When you came back, you were very alive for quite a while, really turned on. It wasn't just meditation, was it? You were turned on by relationship, weren't you? You were enlivened by the dynamics of human interaction and risk-taking. It was a thrill to you, a bright delight, to participate thus, and then you strayed into the background and stayed there. Now that you've left, you are *still* in the background, the background of your own being!

You need to make better use of me. I don't care how well you're doing with your concentrative rituals and self-pampering. You *need* intimacy. I've never met anyone yet who didn't. If you don't get it, you'll dry up and become a sexless old lady, a bag lady, a mere survivor. You need intimacy, Madhavi. Of course, there is a price to pay — to be intimate, one has to be willing to lose face, to be vulnerable, to *penetrate* as well as to receive, to challenge as well as to nourish, to give love without abandoning one's center of being. That's what friendship is all about. Not clinging to the pretense or wreckage of a relationship, but deepening and enlivening it, making expression more important than repression. (*Long pause*)

MADHAVI: I let myself feel overwhelmed.

ROBERT: You do that very readily, don't you? Sometimes you come on like gangbusters, but that's usually more on the surface. Underneath, your dominant feeling tends to be one of passivity, of collapse, of neurotic submission. You give up quite easily. A strong, authoritative energy comes toward you, and you crumble. You need to become more sensitive to what you do with your own authority! You so easily disown it, projecting it onto someone else — you fear your own capacity for authority, for taking power, for being in charge. You judge it, sentencing it to oblivion. You don't want to offend people. You want to be soft. You love to identify with victims! Such identification is a kind of negative empathy — you overempathize with them, and get caught up in their world, until you're stuck in their shoes and their script. Then *you* have no ground. You're busy embodying their crap, and looking through their eyes. And how the hell can you then be of any real use to them?

In healthy empathy, you feel the other person, deeply so, but you also maintain your own ground. Negative empathy is like romance — both people get lost in an unilluminated swoon; there's no boundaries, no center, no integrity, no real love. Do you see how easily you discard your integrity?

MADHAVI: I keep pulling away.

ROBERT: Nevertheless, there's a step for you here, one that has to do with relationship and intimacy. You could meditate for the next twenty years, and it wouldn't work, because that meditation would just be an avoidance of intimacy. For all too many, meditation is an avoidance of something. For very few is it actually done for its own sake, to awaken one to one's true nature. Most people just do it as a remedy — they want to feel better; they want to get away from something; they don't want to have to feel their pain or suffering. They want meditation to fix everything for them. Or they meditate to avoid relationship, or as an *alternative* to intimacy. Of course, none of this is actually *real* meditation, but only an anaemic imitation of it, a cure-all in spiritual robes.

You need to meditate in a way that draws you into relationship.

Everything exists in relationship, doesn't it? Everything! It's one of the fundamental facts of Manifest Existence, and we have to, sooner or later, become deeply resonant with it, instead of remaining peripheral relative to it. To me, one of the best ways to truly feel and know this Great Relatedness is to engage in intimacy with others, because doing so will *inevitably* make you feel vulnerable in places where you otherwise wouldn't feel vulnerable, and such vulnerability is, *if illuminated*, a wonderful bridge to the Real, a medium for attuning to God...

Look at Laurie — she can get wide open with trees and flowers, but when it comes to human beings, she withdraws. Intimacy with a human being will take you a lot deeper than intimacy with a tree, because it's more multidimensional and far more challenging. You can be hurt. You can get jealous. You can get wounded to the core. It's hard to get jealous around trees; they don't argue back, they don't betray, they don't run around! Intimacy is about going into relationship very deeply. That's why I insist that those who are working with me go fully into relationship.

Have you heard the Rajneesh talk that begins with someone asking him why love is an essential part of spiritual growth? It's one of his best talks from about ten years ago, when he still had integrity. In so many words, he says that love is the outward movement of Light, and awareness is the inward movement of Light. It's a circulation. His point, which he makes very poetically, is that if you don't go outward with your Light, through love and intimacy, then you have nothing to re-circulate back, at least nothing *substantial* — that is, those who have not been wounded in love, in relationship, can never *really* meditate, except perhaps in a lukewarm manner. The depth they've avoided in relationship is precisely the depth they cannot encounter in meditation! How can you meditate deeply if you don't take *real* risks in relationship? What do you then have to circulate? Just a stingily small circle, a fraction out, a fraction back, round and round, enlivening no more than spiritual ambition...

Those who love tremendously and passionately have a lot to circulate back. Some people, of course, give loads of love, but they do it in order to get something back; you could say they love too much, but in truth they're not loving at all, but are only bargaining. Real love doesn't bargain. Anyway, I'm talking about the movement of energy out and back. Most people won't circulate their energy; when they get a little extra, they commonly do two things with it: one, think, think, and think some more, or two, funnel it down for discharge through their genitals, reducing their sexuality to a valve for blowing off extra Life-energy, with some ego-reinforcing pleasure thrown in as a motivational bonus!

To me, we're meant to simultaneously accumulate and share energy. To do true awakening work, we need extra energy. You can't wake up, except perhaps sporadically, if you just have a piddly little amount of available energy, just enough for survival and fucking and thinking. You've got to have extra energy, and to have this surplus, you need to cultivate alertness; at the same time, you cannot just hoard energy, like a miser or a yogi or a horny celibate, because the energy has to keep flowing. Nonetheless, some will make a virtue out of hoarding...

MADHAVI: Like always going to bed early, or being obsessed about the right foods...

ROBERT: You know about that! Doing the right postures or movements, or wearing a green hat on Mondays! It doesn't work because the energy they accumulate lacks potency. If you want to accumulate tremendous energy, *give* tremendous energy, love passionately, love fully, get *really* involved in intimacy — sure, you'll get hurt, but such hurt will open you, and make you more available. Unfortunately, most people will not work sanely with the hurt created by intimacy. *But* if you do work with it well, your heart will break right to its core, and you'll emerge from that luminous woundedness more whole than you've ever felt before. So what if you get wounded? You are *already* wounded! Such hurt must be exposed, so that it can heal, and such exposure is wonderfully catalyzed by plunging into real intimacy!

Don't worry about getting hurt. You're going to get hurt. Just don't sink with it. Expand with it, and keep doing so, and ecstasy will move in. This is the art of making love more important than fear, the art of trusting your *real* needs, the art of being more than just the result of your mind's programming!

Maurits Cornelis Escher: *Rind* (Escher Foundation)

–23–

Facts are Facts, But They're Not Necessarily the Truth: Outgrowing Information's Playpen

We cannot truly know ourselves if we insist on dwelling only in the realm of knowledge, since the Truth of what we fundamentally are transcends all explanations and descriptions, ever outdancing every strategy to corral It or reduce It to a reproducible assembly of mere facticity. Put another way, there is no arrangement of information that will genuinely fulfill us. Nevertheless, we all too easily persist in stuffing ourselves with data that promises some sort of payoff, bloating ourselves to the point where we lose touch with our ability to make room for transformational opportunity.

When there is a hollowness in us, whatever our attention unconsciously fixates on fills the vacancy, crowding and pushing aside all other prospective tenants, including the impulse to awaken. With consummate ease, we become more and more packed with information, ever more well-informed, ever more knowledgeable, ever more jammed, crammed, and damned with obsolete or Life-negating files, successfully marooning ourselves from what we truly need, busily holing up in our headquarters, allowing the computational areas of our brain to make decisions about matters of which they have no sense whatsoever, matters of heart, of feeling, of intimacy, of Being...

We are almost constantly allowing ourselves to be invaded by what we call our habits, submitting to their rigidly consistent choreography with barely any resistance, for we, despite the bleating of our good intentions, actually crave the familiarity that this submission creates, the dense certainty and sheer anchoredness of it offering a reassuring contrast to our usual sense of psychospiritual flimsiness... We are so, so afraid, so unnecessarily afraid of the Unknown, not the Unknown that is simply the hidden, the suppressed, the not yet uncovered, but the Unknown that is eternally Unknowable. To even talk of all this is to wade into a sea of confusion, a sea whose plastic waves carry not bits of sun, but only tinselled fragments of runaway mind — it is a sea drained of the Mystery of Being, a sea of consolation and secondhand life, a sea of constriction and compensatory addictions, including that of ego.

Ego craves information. The more the better. Wheeling and dealing with, and kneeling before storehouses of data, it is ever trying to turn a profit, revenge a loss, or get a headlock on someone or something. Ego's problematic orientation toward Life, which of course is also ours when we are busy being our egos, makes it utterly exploitable by what are advertised as solutions. The more solutions that are presented in answer to our so-called problems, the more we gorge ourselves on the informational structuring that characterizes such solutions. In clinging to the information that spews forth from each proposed solution, we only reinforce and rationalize our mad search for ultimate relief, release, remedy, and immunity, desperately seeking to become an enlightened or pain-free us, not realizing that the very "us" who is doing such seeking is precisely what needs to be outgrown! Thus do we deepen our suffering, sedating ourselves with enthusiasm, hope, eroticism, techniques, ideals, mind-meals, and other distractions, ever arranging and rearranging our arsenals of information, shoving our data into this compartment and that compartment, hoping that if only we locate or invest in the right set of beliefs, we will be free. Thus do we flee what we must face. Thus do we stagnate where we could move with grace, making it more important to pamper ourselves within our cages than to leave them...

We tend to look for answers without having even asked the right questions, and even if we do stumble upon a passable verbalization of a truly appropriate question, our voicing of it does not usually ring true, since it doesn't emanate from our core of Being, but only oozes forth from that aspect of us which is primarily mental, computational, obsessed with thoughts, worried about this and that, fervently fretting, thereby doing little more than feeding anxiety, doubt, and trivial concern. Information of course has a purpose, a very necessary purpose, but it is in the realm of logistics, business, and other organizational matters; its data may well be of use in concerns of the heart, belly, spirit, psyche, or being, but must not be allowed to *govern* the activities of these.

Being well-informed is not synonymous with being intelligent. In fact, the more information one possesses and the more attached one is to such information, the less likely one is to be potently receptive to transformative or awakening influences, since one's house is, so to speak, already full, whether with conventional clutter, or with alternative sputter and flutter. Into this moment we must go until we are literally its very heart, its essence, its native radiance; into this moment we must plunge and soar, until its phenomena, its textures, its heartbreak and glory, its abundance and spaciousness, are known so *intimately* that we cannot stand apart from them in a dissociative manner, meditative or not. Into the heart of this moment we must go until we can feel, *really* feel, its phenomena to be continuous with everything that we are, level upon level, the earth of the moment our earth, the psychic qualities of the moment continuous with our psychic capacity, the elements of us in deep resonance with the elements of all that is...

A longing for reunion with the Eternal blooms inside each moment, continuous with our personal longing for such embrace; into this we must go, to a deeper us, to embody and honor our bliss, to receive Eternity's Kiss... Is it not time to live this? Is it not time to yield to this? Is it not time to leave information's playpen and step into the wilderness of Being that throbs us, that calls to us through our every longing, that waits for us, that outdances every partial us? Is it not time to make such luminous space in and around us that everything we must face, everything, becomes brilliantly obvious to us, so wonderfully obvious, so startlingly clear and near, so naturally and undeniably present, that we must clean up what we have allowed to become messy and spiritless — perhaps a particular person to phone, a letter to write, a something to build, a something to dismantle, a place to visit, a book that must be read, a pair of eyes that must be looked into, a heart that must be contacted, an invitation that must, must be made, a friend that must, must be let go of, something that must, must be put on the line —

Is it not time to let go, to make room for letting go? Is it not time to make windows-open room for the us who is addicted to habit, especially that of ego, instead of just pushing away that us, or trying to spiritualize, sanitize, straighten out, or annihilate that poor deluded us? Is it not time to *welcome* the addict in us? Our work is to welcome the addict in us with such honest love and compassion that he or she can only weep themselves free, weep themselves free of all craving for parental attention and approval. And weep themselves free of not trusting you. Yes, and weep themselves into heartfelt integration with the rest of you, until you stand whole, celebrating the reunion of all the fragments of you, until there is no fracturing of you, no remaining compulsion to go to pieces...

Now what will you do? You must do more than just generate some enthusiasm, which is no more than a pseudo-emotional honeymoon with a seemingly new possibility of breakthrough. You must do more than that, and your effort must be a true doing, one that is free of trying, one that stems from your center of Being. You must commit yourself to awakening, but such commitment will not work if it is partial or merely representative of some ambition on your part — it must emerge from your Heartland, arising from spaciousness, generosity of spirit, openness of Being, and a spiritual hunger as fierce as it is consistent. Such commitment cannot be forced, yet it cannot just be passively awaited; it arises in a state of dynamic waiting, or potent receptivity. When it is welcomed, invited in with an uncompromising totality of passion, love, and spirit-force, then it can only rush into the space that has been made for it, the vibrant silence of such roominess being utterly different than the vacancy of the typical human into which information and habits uncontestedly take up residence.

The spaciousness of which I now speak is a conscious womb, pulsating with a deep, mind-free desire to be all that one can be; this is completely unromantic, utterly free of devotional fervor — it is pure openness, it is the inner sanctum of full humanness, it is the love that transcends all notions of love, including the notion of unconditional love. It needs no more information, none! We already have more than enough information about the transformative process, the awakening process — one more hearing of a particular approach or technology only zooms into the thinking mind or into the terrain of enthusiasm for a brief, hyped visit, leaving a trail of pamphlets and cognitive bric-a-brac, doing no more than assisting us in postponing taking the leap we know we need to make (which actually is simultaneously a leap and a stand).

You are ready now. You are already intimate with what you yearn for. You must simply adapt to that endless joy, that sobering joy, that non-circumstantial joy, that unspeakable sky, that earthy bliss, knowing that such adaptation means embodying, *fully* embodying a truer you, a you who is just as intimate with anger, lust, jealousy, grief, and fear, as with Ecstasy, love, empathetic concern, and wonder. To make room for one's suffering is not to unnecessarily create suffering, but rather is to love the you who first turned to addiction as a strategy to survive childhood. The key here is to love that tortured child, to not treat that child as you were treated when you were the same age, to not try to discipline that child into submission, to not impale him or her upon your so-called good resolutions. If you try to fix that child, that incredibly vulnerable personification of your deepest addictions, he or she will only retreat further, becoming more and more rooted in your darkness, appearing as a perversion of vulnerability, a perversion of need, a craven neediness veined with self-sabotage...

To halt an addiction, don't take sides. Otherwise, you will only divide yourself, thereby only reinforcing the polarization that epitomizes addictiveness. Passivity is of no use either; what works is taking a position that includes all sides of the addiction, a position of passionate witnessing, of gutsy, loving, empathetic observation uncluttered by the viewpoints characteristic of the addiction. Self-dividedness, or fragmentation of self, creates an overwhelming sense of separation from the Heart of Existence, and such sensations are so painful that we do just about everything we can to numb ourselves to them, to distract ourselves from them so thoroughly as to send them into apparent oblivion. Self-fragmentation cannot be effectively dealt with if we insist on taking sides when working on our addictions; our very taking up of arms for one side or the other only defeats us, leaving us in a no-one's-land of endlessly loopholed information.

We must open ourselves to the addictive us. This, however, cannot just take the form of some manipulative therapeutic strategy, some self-imposed affirmation, some hope-inflated act of mind, or some cathartic discharge, but rather needs to be an act of our totality, and this cannot be set up therapeutically, cognitively, or through religious belief, guru-devotion, or devotion to any method, technique, or person. It requires open-eyed faith, trust, and a profound willingness to be natural, which means that one must recognize, deeply recognize, what is unnatural about one, namely everything that is out of resonance with one's fundamental nature. One must become more and more sensitive to one's tendency to idea-flirt and mind-fuck or to try to think one's way through everything, or perhaps to make a virtue out of emotionalism, or out of the psychic domains, or out of metaphysics and other such abstractions, and such sensitivity itself must not be permitted to degenerate into obsessiveness!

We have been trained in this culture to absorb far more information than we need, to be inundated by facts, figures, logistics, and hordes of irrelevancies, information upon information, information about information, letting ourselves become trivialized, sidetracked, and computerized into spiritual oblivion. Nevertheless, the key is not to flee computerization and other extensions of the thinking mind, but rather to establish them in their right place relative to our core of Being, to permit them the grace of being good servants, to allow them to harmonize with the rest of us, to be in life-giving relationship with the rest of us.

Such harmony, or balance, cannot be brought about through simply wanting it, or wishing that it was so, or through affirming that it is so. No! It must be embodied, which means we need to become more intimate with what we are as bodies, or more precisely, as bodyminds, feeling, living, breathing bodyminds lit from within, and lit through *every* experience, sordid or sublime! There must be no zone of our bodymind that is foreign territory to us, nor ought we to merely be tourists in such areas, settling for snapshots, gathering postcards and memories — we need to be travellers who don't lose connection with homebase, travellers who eventually realize that *all* of us is homebase, because all of us is interconnected, and in that interconnectedness, that vast relatedness, that Infinity of Being, we are *already* free, *already* expressive of, rather than seeking, our deep Truth. For this to be more than just words, something must be done, and something else must not be done...

In our awakening, no matter how fucked up we are, our habits and difficulties become so clearly illuminated that they can and must be passed *through*; rising above them does not work, because it leaves them intact, all but untouched by conscious experience. It all must be felt, right to the heart, until the option of immunity is obsolete. Transformation is what we are called to, not strategic or spiritually ambitious transformation, but *natural* transformation, a changing of what has to be changed, such change being already in conducive alignment with our native integrity of Being, our wholeness, our essential Ecstasy, our capacity for being *truly* responsible moment-to-moment for our freedom, our grounded yet sky-wide freedom, our place in Eternity, our identity with the Source of All, our merging into and emergence from the Mystery of Being...

Into this we go and come and live and love and die, ever purifying ourselves, not to get somewhere, but simply because after a while there is nothing else to do — we don't engage in such purification, such participation in the Sacred Fire, in order to somehow reach joy, but rather to celebrate such joy, such knowingness, such fathomless Presence, to deepen and express It, to be It, to say an uninhibited and full-bodied and full-souled yes, yes, yes! to It and to us, to *every* us, even now, ever now. Now...

–24–

What is
Objective Knowledge?

Subjectivity is *personified* inwardness in action, but what is ordinarily called "outwardness" is also animated by the very same interior impersonator, manifesting as typical agreement/disagreement, opinion, sentiment, introversion/extroversion, and other such "self" expressions. Of course, this varies from person to person, depending upon their conditioning, their current mood, their loyalties, their tastes, their prevailing self-image, their flavour of the day — in short, upon whatever has been successfully implanted in them, whatever has the best seat in their mind, whatever in them that is *currently* referring to itself as "I"...

Now, what about objectivity? There is *no* objectivity for those who are asleep (and barely any for those who have some degree of awakening, because of the eroding effect of the long gaps between their moments of wakefulness), but only subjectivity, however repressed or camouflaged it might be, as in the case of those who try to assume an attitude of fairness, of balance, of *objective* reporting. For the scientist, there is no real objectivity, but just the *stance* of it, the data-encrusted proclamation of it (as if the *arrangement* of such data was inherently free of personal bias, let alone the informational context chosen!). Heisenberg's Uncertainty Principle, quantum mechanics, and post-modern physics all point to the *unavoidable* (and creative!) effect the observer has upon what is being observed — this relationship between observer and observed is largely an unconscious one, obscured by self-fragmentation and ossified attitudes to such a degree that it doesn't seem to exist for most, except perhaps in the boundary-dissolving throes of romance, sportive fever, and ingestion of certain substances (and even here, such dissolution is usually not a matter of wakefulness, but only of ego-based consolation and gratification)...

Nevertheless, there *is* (to use Gurdjieff's term) objective knowledge — what he meant by that term was a knowingness that *everyone* would possess about a certain something if they were all *present* at the same level of Being, that level being characterized by varying degrees of *conscious* abiding at one's Core. And here's the *apparent* paradox: Those who are asleep to themselves, existing on the periphery of themselves, have all sorts of opinions about the same thing, which *seemingly* would point to their ability to differentiate, to be different from one another, to be real individuals, when in fact all this actually does is signal their fragmentation of self, their alienation from their depths, their clinging to mere belief and opinion. (The very effort to be *special*, to possess one's "own" opinions, is but a confession of being estranged from one's *inherent* uniqueness.) Such positionings are but parodies of real individuality, ego-reinforcing posturings and paradings, personalized shells, narcissistic cocoons...

Truly centered humans are different, radically different. If, for example, someone was displaying a certain emotion in front of a gathering of such beings, they would all intuit the same thing, or have the same basic response — one of them wouldn't say "That person's crying is full of self-pity", and another "It's the deepest sort of grief" — they would all recognize the crying for what it was, be it manipulative or pure, ego-centered or Essence-centered, unauthentic or authentic, sentimental or non-sentimental, because they would *directly* intuit and feel it, entering into such deep resonance with it that its very heart would be *obvious* to them. There wouldn't be a difference of opinion. In fact, there wouldn't be any *opinions* at all, but only unequivocal knowingness, or an understanding senior to knowledge, a full-bodied intuition of Truth... But, you might be protesting now, is not this lack of opinion, this absence of difference, a sign of non-individuality, of mass conformity? No! The reason for such "agreement" has nothing to do with some kind of deep inner conformity, some sort of slavery that occurs if one goes into one's depths... Instead, it simply reflects the underlying Unity and innate wisdom of Being we all share. Go to your core, and your individuality will be strengthened (through the nourishment given its roots), and so too will be your feeling of undying unity with all that is, not so much with its form, but with its Essence, its Consciousness, its very Being...

When we are aligned with that Realm wherein Unity is luminously obvious, exquisitely and undeniably present, then we are quite capable of (*and* responsible for) recognizing and articulating the Truth of a situation, as are all others who are also *currently* existing at a similar level of Being. This, of course, utterly counters the so-called freedoms of the typical human, with all their *permission* to have this opinion or that opinion, this belief or that belief, this position or that position, as if such superficial "choice," such mechanized arbitrariness, constituted anything even remotely resembling *real* freedom! These "freedoms" are but the mind-polluted meanderings of a slave, a creature permitted to wander relatively unhindered for a time in its cage, to "freely" speak its thoughts (as though such thoughts arose in wakefulness!), ever pampering itself with various distractions, including meaningfulness and hope.

The true human possesses objective knowledge (or Essence-centered knowingness), and is *also* an individual with unique tastes, preferences, desires, bright with idiosyncrasy, but without any *serious* attachment to his or her opinions about things. For such individuals, the thoughts that pass through their minds are not necessarily fascinating in of themselves, but are, in their very structuring, their tone and texture, their origin, utterly worthy of being witnessed, not just as separative little cognitive phenomena, but as the spawnings of the thinking mind, that vastly complex mechanism that generates in the slumbering the illusion of a thinker, a solid somebody who's *doing* the thinking...

There is no thinker, no cogitator, no discrete entity doing the thinking. There is simply thinking. As Gautama said, thinking creates the illusion of a thinker. The true human knows this, and not just intellectually, but does not settle for the concept of no self, of non-being, of primordial nothingness, as though that was all there was to it. He or she uses such deeply felt intuition, such primal revelation, to fuel his or her leap into Undying Being, Eternal Mystery, Heartfelt Connectedness, Aliveness, God... Their realization of God (which is an ongoing process, not a once-and-for-all Cosmic Orgasm or Big Bang) is not a weekend pursuit, nor an ambition, but rather their moment-to-moment priority, outbreathing all strategy and spiritual positioning, being more basic to them than anything else, not because they think it should be so or believe it to be so, but because no other option can out-attract it.

As long as we persist in dwelling at the level wherein agreement, disagreement, opinion, sentiment, and other bastard offspring of cognition and superficial emotion exist, we will take such opaque abstractions very seriously — we will make real estate out of them, we will defend their perimeter, we will wave their flag, we'll fight for them, we'll even *die* for them, getting so damned busy being right that we'll have almost no energy left to *truly* explore what is deeper than the merely conceptual or conceptually-*derived*... And if we happen to stray into emotion, we won't often do so with any real intelligence, given our lack of true discriminative ability relative to our emotions; we will perhaps (like devotees of approaches like Primal Therapy) make a virtue out of feeling, not noticing that most of what "we" feel is *mind-generated*, a byproduct of our conditioning, of our unresolved conflicts, thus being little more than a bioelectrically-charged dramatization of reactivity, be it benign (as in sentimentality or contractive sorrow) or not-so-benign (as in hysteria and blind rage)...

Such "feeling" is not a true response to our environment. It is simply more mind, more reinforcement of "our" most precious concepts about what's what. We can just as easily lose ourselves in emotion as in thought, belief, or opinion. To illuminate our emotional domain is impossible if we are not also illuminating our mental domain; to remain fixated upon mere emotionalism or neurotically exaggerated feeling (as so garishly epitomized by hysteria, with its runaway righteousness or frenzied helplessness) is to only obscure and violate the very vulnerability in us that is, however indirectly, screaming and pleading and reaching for real love. It is easy to express or vent our twisted subjectivity through our feelings, through our endarkened emotionalism — we may find ourselves beginning our opinions with phrases like "I *feel* that..." or "I *feel* like you are...", as if we are *actually* expressing a feeling! We're *not* — we are just *reacting* to something, filtering everything through our thinking minds, smearing it with accusatory logic, refusing to give expression to our depths, except in the most roundabout manner. In such a case, we are turned *away* from what we are *really* feeling, unaware of both how we've withdrawn from our core of Being, and of how we are compensating for such withdrawal with all kinds of mental constructs and their corresponding emotional lackeys...

In our everyday subjectivity, we've turned away from what truly nourishes us, marooning ourselves from our Source, our Truth, our very Heartland, and we're desperately busy making up for such primal loss through an engrossingly repetitive involvement in various surrogates of what we've turned away from; in other words, we are creating, *mechanically* creating, all kinds of *secondary* difficulties because of our unresolved *primary* difficulty, namely our self-imposed recoil from the Truth of what we are. All these secondary difficulties, in their very problematicalness, beg for solutions, and so "we" then turn to our thinking minds, our gray batter, for answers, rarely noticing that most of our so-called solutions only create *more* problems, including that of entrenching us in our skulls. Even though a solution may seem to remedy an addressed problem, nothing substantial has been uprooted or illumined — sedation has just been successfully administered. Something has been numbed. Something has been gagged. Some pruning has occurred, but the roots remain, thriving and thickening, writhing and multiplying beneath our efforts to fix ourselves...

The very presence of clung-to opinions is a sign that we are avoiding living from our core. It's not that we shouldn't have any opinions at all, but that such cognitive phantoms need not be taken at all seriously — they're just mindplay, just the flag-waving of slumbering persona, or, at best, colourful voicings of personal idiosyncrasy, adding a kind of humorous, artful colour commentary to our deeper expression, a commentary that doesn't oppose, misrepresent, or sabotage our depth, but rather that supports and reflects it. For most of us, our relationship to our opinions and attitudes obstructs our capacity to express what is real for us. It is of no use to just have an opinion about what I'm saying here, to simply agree or disagree with what I'm saying, or perhaps, in the best fence-sitting tradition, to have a little of both, so as to *appear* balanced or objective!

We must do more than just cling to a morality of simplistic right and wrong; what is required of us is to *feel* what is being expressed, not via mind-generated feeling, but through direct, wide-awake feeling, through true empathy, through permitting a response at the level of Being — this is not just a matter of sitting still and breathing deeply and feeling a certain sensation somewhere in the body, nor is it a matter of procrustean do-gooderism (as in so-called active listening and "professional" tolerance), nor is it a matter of *trying* "to be there" for another. Instead, it's a matter of simply waking up, getting out of bed and head, and inhabiting our depths so fully that it is self-evidently true that we really *are* responding, spontaneously and alertly responding, to *whatever* is presently occurring, entering into such communion with it that an undeniable knowingness cannot help but emerge...

Do not make an enemy out of your tendency to form opinions or judgments. See it for what it is. See how shallow its morality is. Replace its morality with Awakening's morality, which of course is not written somewhere, but is unambiguously present whenever you make Awakening priority. Then the imperatives, the ever-fresh imperatives, of the Awakening process will be wonderfully (and perhaps also frighteningly) obvious, not at all subtle in their feel, though they may be in their *form*... Even now, let go of your urge to think about what I've said, and let go of your desire to get enthusiastic or argumentative about it; that is, stop granting attention to such desires (not to get rid of them, but to allow something else to become foreground). Whether you disagree or agree with what has been said here doesn't really matter, since the you who can only agree or disagree with things is peripheral to the you who *already* knows what I'm talking about, who *already* intuits it, who *already* is responding to it from their center of Being.

If you will consciously and consistently abide in and *as* your core of Being, your capacity to have opinions about this and that will weaken, but will not disappear — it will gradually mutate into a transparent overlay, a fluid theatricalness, a kind of vividly offbeat entertainment that, through its very texture, substance, and feeling, will be supportive of your depths, colourfully representative of your Heartland. This is, of course, roughly equivalent to the cleaning up of one's persona so that it reflects and supports one's Essence. It is about harmony, not bland, "peaceful" harmony, but vibrantly alive harmony, storm-bright and juicily calm, as wild as it is sensitive, as fluid as it is firm. Do not try to hold to what I have said. Let go of trying. Soften. Breathe yourself a little looser, letting everything settle and relax, relaxing more and more deeply, letting yourself become softer and softer, more and more spacious, more and more at ease with the depths of yourself, the depths and unspeakable currents that you can now feel, slowly and gently permeating your outwardness, your now so-softly loosened periphery. Unhurriedly, feel everything softening, easing, settling, getting looser and looser, taking you not into sleep, but into deeply relaxed alertness, taking you to where your opinions and usual subjectivity are but colour transparencies...

The Summer of 1976

I saw reflected in your eyes
The image of the one you hoped I might be
The one who'd outhero the crush of your history
So I chiselled from myself your ideal man
Your adoring breath inflating him
Your scissoring thighs deliciously deflating him
Your grasp owning the string to the balloon
His eager doings upping your soulmate spread and swoon
You nestled against his heroic hide
While I trembled outside
Placating my nausea
Desperately repairing the multiplying dents
In his ardently contoured mold
Trying to keep his chestful of lust from catching cold
Trying to outstare the suddenly obvious distance
Lonely for love was I
Lonely for myself
Choked in my own sails
Finally shipwrecked by the ideal man's sudden
*   and overwhelming pain*

-25-

The Separative Swoon of False Oneness: An Exposé of Romance

RICHARD: My mind is racing over all the things I could say or do. I've felt a build-up of things I've needed to tell you, but haven't really communicated with you.

ROBERT: So why did you wait until the session?

RICHARD: There's still some fear of being intimate with you. (*Pause*) It's funny, but almost every night I dream about being with you, like a couple of nights ago when I had a dream where I was holding your hand for a long time, and just looking at you...

ROBERT: What are these dreams telling you?

RICHARD: It seems like they're telling me that I'm intimate with you (*Hesitatingly spoken*), that I'm meant to be intimate with you.

ROBERT: Do you feel any anxiety in these dreams?

RICHARD: None at all! In them, I feel *really* close to you.

ROBERT: So what happens in the waking state?

RICHARD: (*Awkward pause*) It's... I don't know... I'm not as fully with you in the waking state.

ROBERT: Why?

RICHARD: (*Long pause*) Ego. It's to do with my ego. It's about me making myself small. Last night, I had a long lucid dream in which I was involved with people, and feeling quite awake and alive, but in the daytime it's quite different, especially with you... I felt so close to you while you were away at Long Beach...

ROBERT: (*Cutting in*) You're such a romantic! One sign of a roman-tic, which you manage to display quite consistently, is the *apparent* loving, appreciation, and adoration of the beloved, *if they are at a distance!* The real heavyweights of classical romanticism pined (and poetically whined) away for women that they never even touched — if they'd touched them, gotten fleshy, then they might have, horror of horrors, felt a zit or two, come face to face with a droopy tit, smelt a bad smell, clashed with a less-than-luminous personality, met a very ordinary human... Fucking was out of the question for them, unless it was all dressed up between their ears, and swathed in just the right phrases and lighting. Such fake closeness also characterizes much of your relationship with me — the further away I am, the closer you *seem* to feel to me! Imagine if I went further away than Long Beach! What bliss that would be... (*Laughter*)

I'm not saying that you are *only* romantic with me, but your compul-sive romanticizing twists our relationship out of shape — take that away, and you'll be left with a strong feeling connection with me, an intuitive and very loving bond. So what happens when you're in my physical presence? Whatever you were feeling at a distance is still there, but the reality of me shreds your fantasy, and suddenly you're naked, floundering minus your projections onto me. Do you see that it's easier for you to have me at a distance?

RICHARD: Yes. Then I can have an image of you to interact with...

ROBERT: You can have quite an affair with image, can't you? I come closer, and you're not only feeling what you felt when I was further away, but something else, too — suddenly, my presence gets stronger and stronger, more and more fleshed out, and then your focus isn't so much on me, or your image of me, but on *you*, squirmingly self-conscious you. Your fantasy about me bounces back at you, reflects off of me, especially in an emotional sense... When I'm far away, you can do all kinds of things with who you take me to be, 'cause then I'm not ordinarily bouncing energy back at you, I'm not reflecting you back to you, at least in a *personal* sense — yes, now and then it might happen psychically, but it's not usually personal, waking-state personal. Far away, I'm just a presence to you, perhaps only the shadow of a presence, but when I'm up close, you can't help but feel me in my totality, and then you can no longer remain in a little ego-bricked cell from which you view and assess me — suddenly, the spotlight's on *you*!

When people are up close to me, directly facing me, normally what's troubling them or misaligning them becomes highlighted, glaringly obvious, often uncomfortably so (regardless of *my* state)... This is why many stay away from me; this is why you fear intimacy with me. When you're far from me, physically removed, then you don't have to really focus on what *you* are up to — your focus is *out there*, even though it's inwardly gripped.

If you get neurotic about the focus shifting from romanticized me to pimply you, you'll notice that you want my attention, especially my parentally-approving mode of attention. See, what feels good when I am far away is your giving attention to your image of me; it's gratifying in a spiritually masturbatory way. But when I get close to you, suddenly *you* want the attention. You want to be made visible by my focus, you want to be enlivened and parentally comforted by it, but you're also anxious in your strategy, for what if my gaze is disapproving? What if I'm appalled at what I see? And what if I lose interest?

It would be quite different if you and I were both paying attention to the entire dynamic between us and around us, being sensitively and spaciously attuned to the nuances of each unfolding moment, presently and deeply loving each other, shining from that realm of us that's prior to our programming... But back to the whole notion of the romantic: His or her attention is mechanically zeroed in on a distant object, someone or something that's simultaneously *out of reach* and *imaginally accessible*. Think of a frumpy or grumpy someone picking up a *National Enquirer*, and reading about some great movie star — their attention is focussed on that sparkling demi-deity, but it's not *consciously* focussed. Such attention-giving is as robotic as it's addictive; what's fundamental to it, other than its mechanicalness, is its neurotic separativeness, its absence of real relationship with the Source of All. We assume we're separate from God, letting such a primal sense of separation infect just about every realm of our life.

In the psychosexual arena, this manifests as romanticism (and other forms of pornography): "I'm here! What I adore is *there* — let us become one! Moon, swoon, slurp, *you're* the one! Darling!!" (*Much*

Gustave Doré: *Chateaubriand's Atala*

laughter) The oneness of romance is no more real than the oneness of an intoxicated mob at a hockey game! It's just an undifferentiated soup, a homogenized mess, an irresponsible dissolving of personal boundaries, a swoon! There's a pleasurableness to it, but to me it's a negative kind of pleasure, a giddy insensitivity, environmentally blind, compulsively stuck on the having of hyped stimulation...

The supposed love of the romantic possesses no real compassion, but only pale imitations of it, such as sentimentality. To be truly compassionate, you need to include the other; you need to expand to include them, without, however, losing touch with yourself. You can't just focus on them and forget yourself.

RICHARD: (*Very quietly*) Which is what I do.

ROBERT: Now a romantic is passionate, right? They're *dramatically* impassioned with regard to that object out there, that movie star, that woman, that man — they're obsessively, even fierily, focussed out there (or, more precisely, on the outside of their inside), but is it *real* passion? Does it include compassion? No! A compassionate person doesn't just focus on the other — they also feel themselves, and the whole scene. They're contextually expansive. In them, the heat of passion is both balanced and honoured by the cool of compassion...

Take the whole notion of focussing, obsessively focussing on someone out there — Robert at Long Beach, Beatrice upon her perch, Aphrodite on her scallop shell, your lover pulsating in her lacy room, or whatever — and see, *really* see, that it's just a symptom of your assumed separation from God, from Truth, from the inherent radiance and richness of your own Being. Why go on living out the programming dictated by your separativeness? Why go on suppressing your Being? Look at just about everything people are doing, and you'll see the turning away from God, accompanied by all sorts of efforts to *not* feel separate! In romance, there's *both*, isn't there? The separation, the gap, *and* the accompanying desire to swoon, to be at one with the desired object! Of course, this doesn't heal the wound, but only camouflages it...

Oneness... Everything that's needed to live an authentic life tends to exist as a parody of itself in this world. Fake oneness, saleable oneness, conceptualized oneness, oneness fucked blind. Instead of being ecstatic, you make yourself swoon! It doesn't even matter if the other person doesn't have a clue as to what's going on, so long as you can splash around in your fantasy! It's all internal, twistedly subjective, blindly internal... What you tend to do with me when I'm at a distance has very little to do with *me* at all, but on those rare occasions when it's a true reaching-out on your part, it will positively affect me, catalyzing a deepening of our relationship, regardless of how far apart we are physically. When you pretend, however, that it's real, impaling yourself on hope, you only damage and cheapen our bond. Right now, you could imagine that kundalini was rising up your spine; you could do some juicy visualizing, and suddenly you'd feel the *expected* symptoms, and if you didn't, you'd imagine them and imagine them and imagine them, until they *had to* manifest somatically! In other words, you can easily make yourself feel, or *approximately* feel, what you think you *should* be feeling — this is the harnessing of the imagination to the commands of ego...

People keep trying to be at one, to somehow kindle the sensations they associate with oneness, because it feels good — there's a widening in it, a shedding of self-consciousness, a dissolution of one's perimeter. What hurts us is to just exist as an ego. So the mass of humanity keeps trying to dissolve or undo that sense of ego, of neurotically separative self, through attaining oneness, but what they go for is *unconscious oneness* — ranting at a football game, being a good Catholic, a loyal Nazi, an exemplary Rajneesh sannyasin, and on and on — wherein all they are *really* doing is losing their identity, both their identity as an ego, and their real identity! They throw it all away in order to *belong*, to be part of something that seems bigger than them; they're looking for a bigger, vaster sense of self, but they don't get real expansion, just inflation! Such belonging is to me just a perversion of our primal longing to belong to the Source of All, to be in deep resonance with It — paradoxically, if you go right into that *longing*, you'll discover that you *already* belong!

In Xanthyros, we're also going toward a sense of oneness, but in the opposite direction from most — we're learning to embody a *conscious* oneness, through the practice of being awake in the midst of whatever we are doing. It's a oneness that absolutely requires your *full* individuality; in no way does it ask that you throw away your personal uniqueness. It's a difficult process a lot of the time, because it requires that you deeply develop your capacity to differentiate and discriminate — for a while, you'll perhaps feel more and more separate from everything, but eventually, you will consistently sense the underlying Unity of it all. Until then, you're going to have to stay with the climb, and stop making a problem out of our differences...

To get to real oneness, you have to become very, very aware of how you create separation, especially unhealthy separation. Along the way, you'll also necessarily explore the art of healthy separation, separation that's illuminated by Being, separation that arises from Being. You must honour our separation, our differences, as much as our common Unity — do that, and you'll feel me just as you do in your dreams, easily and with a minimum of tension and fear.

RICHARD: I'm still partial with you. It's partial because it's been created, created by just a part of me...

ROBERT: Watch your ambition. Instead of fighting your partiality, befriend it. (*Long silence*) The only object you ought to be romantic toward is God, and what'll happen as you mature is that you'll discover that God is not an object, that God is not locatable. To give your romantic energy to God therefore means that you cannot focus your attention on any particular place (inner or outer) and say here's God, this is where God is, not there, but here, not in that place, but in this one... If you truly give your attention to God, it will become but pure Consciousness, infinitely expansive, yet still functionally personalized.

There are degrees of this, of course, but ultimately it is the return of attention to its Source. So there's no harm in being romantic toward God, unless you stop short and become just a Bhakti yogi, stuck in devotional inclination, stuck in thinking that the only way to be with God is to be wrapped up in religious emotionalism...

There's no recipe for all this. Sure, it seems simple enough — love God with nothing held back — but it is not necessarily easy, for you've got to embody the you who *can* love so fully, and that particular you is not seducible by techniques, methods, or hope. Knowledge isn't enough here. More information is of no value, unless it is servant to Being. Look at anything from any point of view, from any angle, deeply and for long enough, and you'll end up resting in a sense of the Mysterious — you'll stand prior to the birthing of explanations, you'll be in Wonder, you'll be presently and magnificently alive, even if you are crippled with pain... There is no right

Gustave Doré: *Chateaubriand's Atala*

approach to this, no prepackaged progression of steps, but there is a way, a spontaneously evolving way, unfolding according to your current needs, and this is the way of living Truth.

We *all* have the capacity to feel the Truth, to recognize It. Unfortunately, most humans have let this capacity atrophy. For very understandable reasons, they learned to put aside their Truth when they were very young; they learned to be unnatural, to obey the directives of their inculcated programming. As Gurdjieff once said, in so many words: "Everyone who is asleep lies all the time." How do you prove to a dreamer that they're dreaming, when they're convinced they're awake? It's like being in a lucid dream and telling people therein that they're sleeping, and they don't get it — and even if they do, they're probably (you might occasionally remind yourself) just figments of your imagination, creations of your dreaming consciousness, so who's talking to who? Seemingly, it is just you talking to a phantom, as though it's not a phantom!

RICHARD: (*Surprised*) That's exactly what I was doing in my lucid dreams! It's funny, but I was telling people that they were dreaming, and I was trying to get them to respond to me.

ROBERT: How romantic! You create these images, and then try to have a relationship with them! But *who* were these people?

RICHARD: They were different people, and they had different responses. In my last dream, I finally got one of them to speak to me, but afterward he looked down at the floor like a zombie, and I realized that I'd been creating him. I kind of floated back, thinking I had to let go, 'cause I felt really hollow in my heart. Then I floated back into the wall, and let go...

ROBERT: But you could have, as a deeper alternative, said to yourself, "I'm just a dream, too!"

RICHARD: That's what I don't do! (*Laughter*)

ROBERT: Why does the role you play in your lucid dreams seem so *solid*? What makes you think that that role is any more *real* than any other role in the dream? The you who is busy being lucid is still part of the dream! Dream lucidity need not be confined to the central character in the dream. Such lucidity is not primarily personal; it's just a level of awareness. But when you confine it to the person you're playing in the dream, then *you* are still *dreaming*. To actually recognize that your role is also just part of the dream is quite rare. (*Pause*)

Consider the so-called waking state, when you are meditating, being a witness to your bodymind processes — it's a lot like dream lucidity, isn't it? But to be *aware* of your actual concentrative witnessing, to be aware of the presence of such witnessing (which doesn't mean *thinking* about it!) is equivalent to recognizing, while sleeping, your role as part of your dream. I have personally found out that I cannot do this through any technique; in fact, it isn't even done by "I" — it simply happens, usually when I'm very still, with my focus more on Presence than on particularities... Do you see the parallel between the lucid dreaming state and the conscious waking state?

RICHARD: I see that I kind of do that...

ROBERT: With very few exceptions, you *can't* do that in the dreaming state, unless you can also do it in the waking state. The fact that you lucid-dream at all shows that there's a partially developed witnessing capacity in you. The next step is very difficult to do in the lucid dream, unless it's being correspondingly attempted in the waking state. You can't just do it because you think it's a neat idea, since the very person who thinks thus is the very one who's in the way of full lucidity! (*Pause*) In other words, the doing of this goes beyond any conventional motivation to do it. (*Long silence*)

RICHARD: I have a sense of how I create my ego...

ROBERT: You're still an ego in the midst of your lucid dreams. Most meditators are very egotistical people: "*I* am going to God" or "*I* am meditating" or "*I'm* not holding onto anything" or "Look how present *I* am!" or...

RICHARD: *I* am lucid dreaming! (*Laughter*)

ROBERT: Exactly! Why paint wings on ego, and then go about calling it Atman or soul? Remember Gurdjieff saying that we're not born with a soul, but that we must develop a soul? That we must heal our fragmentation of self, our warring "I's", and mature into a single "I"? A permanent "I", a conscious crystallization of Self? Even Ouspensky (known to some as the intellectual part of the intellectual center) got into this — somewhere he was talking about confidence, and he said that he wasn't talking about *ordinary* confidence, but that he now had a *strange* confidence, a confidence that if he was faced with even an extremely difficult circumstance, then something very big in him would tellingly respond to it — he wouldn't just identify with one of his little "I's", but would respond from a place of spaciousness, of real strength, of deep centeredness.

You and others in Xanthyros know that response, as do I. Crises ought to bring out the best in us. Sometimes we have more trouble with little things, because they don't ask so much of us — we don't dip into our depths to deal with them as often as we need to, and so we at times unnecessarily exhaust ourselves at a certain energy level, while our deeper reservoirs remain untapped...

That strange confidence Ouspensky talked about — I feel it relative to my own death. I don't doubt my capacity to appropriately respond to it, to potently surrender to it... This has to do with having a single, core "I", a center of Being, and it's not even accurate to say that I have it, for *it* has me! The presence of such center doesn't mean that one is without ego (for I certainly am not!), but that one doesn't waver when it really matters. There's a deep steadiness. When things are rough, I don't lose touch. The core "I" is not seducible by lesser "I's" in me — they are occasionally peripherally present in me, but uncemented, instantly droppable...

So, swinging back to your lucid dreams, be aware in them of which "I" you are animating. In your dream, maybe you're running down to the sea, and there's someone waiting there, and both of you have an engrossing encounter — it may be rewarding to later on work on this interaction, to play it out more fully, but it may be even more rewarding to let yourself uninhibitedly *be* the sea that appeared in your dream! Or let's say you're flying through the sky, and suddenly there's a maze of telephone wires that you're apparently going to have to get through — what if you shifted your identity to the sky? Or what if you didn't identify with *anything* in your dream? Or *everything* at once?

Some dreams are undoubtedly psychic — you're actually in contact with someone else, perhaps having a pure message for them, perhaps attuning to something crucial about them, both literally and metaphorically *being* with them. Such a dream is not just *your* creation. It's not just a pictorial representation of something you've intuited during the day, although it certainly could be argued that that's what it is! Such dreams are but doorways for psychic communion. They shine with the feeling of Truth, of deep revelation. Perhaps it's not even right to call them dreams. Their Truth is not merely relative, but undeniably real, registering throughout one's entire being, obviously present *prior* to the personal...

I'd better say more about this... In our culture, Truth is almost non-existent, having been replaced by the notion that truth is relative, that I have my truth, you have your truth, they have their truth, and so on... All these supposed truths, or *viewpoints*, are generally taken to be equally valid. However, they are only the viewpoints of unillumined personal perception, standpoints of ego, of egoic survival, founded on the absolutist *notion* that truth is relative. Thus does mere opinion masquerade as Truth!

There's no space in such an idiotically democratic notion of truth for a more evolved human — the guardians of false tolerance would scream "Elitism!" and dutifully trot out the ghosts of Nazism as a warning. But we are not all equal! We have our differences. Why homogenize them? Why pretend there aren't differences in quality? Why toss our discriminative and critical faculties into the bonfire of mind-conceived egalitarianism?

Modern egalitarianism is mostly just a knee-jerk reaction to the ugly hierarchical assumptions of the past; its twisted permissiveness is no more humanizing than the rigidity of its heartlessly authoritarian predecessor! Just about everyone in our culture wants everyone else brought down to their level (unless, of course, romance is involved!). We love it when a politician looks bad. We love it when a movie star really fucks up. And we love it even more when a supposedly religious figure gets caught with their pants down! Not just evangelical fanatics, but luminous beings like Da Free John. We feel gratifyingly reassured when *they* look bad; it's as if we are saying, "Fuck up royally, so that I can feel better."

You know that I'm on the receiving end of a lot of this. More than a few people who have loved me deeply *want* to see me as no more integrated than them, no more awake than them. Instead of making good use of my state, they work hard to find fault with me, so that they can feel justified in staying right where they are! If they *really* acknowledged that I was living a truer, fuller life than them, then they'd (out of sheer resonance with me) have to make some correspondingly big changes in their life, or just feel really horrible about themselves. Misery craves companionship, doesn't it? Don't you dare leave the muck, it sourly says, or stay untouchable, godlike, romantically located for me, so that I can feel better by association with "you"... How painful this is! How degrading! And how horribly common!

RICHARD: (*After a long, deep silence*) As you were talking, I felt very sad. I could feel a sadness in me that I tuck away when I get romantic. When I'm romanticizing somebody, I don't really *feel* my separation — I just *think* that I'm close to them...

ROBERT: Just like devotees who keep creating those sensations in themselves that seemingly suggest that they are at one with their guru... People everywhere tend to whore themselves so that they might feel a little better, so that they might be filled with a comforting sensation, such as that of belonging. So many people act as if things are going better than they are. However, the very act of trying to be happy is only a confession of misery, as well as an avoidance of really exploring the roots of one's misery.

Look closely, and you'll see people struggling to assume a semblance of their natural state, however perverse their solution might be. Much of what we're doing is but a neurotic yet poignantly accurate reflection of what we would be doing if we were in our natural state... Instead of sitting in a meadow, we're glued to artificial turf. Instead of stretching out under the sun, we're plugged in under an artificial sun. Instead of being ecstatic, we're busy seeking pleasure. Instead of telling the Truth, we're parroting information and submitting to the bleating of our opinions. Instead of loving, we're sentimentalizing. In other words, we're homesteading in a surrogate of Life, a desert in the worst sense of the word...

And given all this, what do we tend to do? We busy ourselves getting cosy in the desert; we green it with fastfood oases, with plastic grass and wall-to-wall distractions, and what better distraction is there than romance? The pleasure-packed consolations of apparent oneness... But it's hard to keep it up, isn't it? You run out of beloveds. You get worn down after a while...

RICHARD: There is no romance here for me now.

ROBERT: See, here's the crux: to *really* be with me (or anyone else), it's not enough to just be at one with me. You have to be an individual, too — you need to honour both our Unity, and our differences. When you're apart from me, you, in a twisted sense, honour our oneness, our flow together, but you turn away from our differences. Come close, and then you can *feel*, unequivocally feel, the differences, the gap... We're unique. You're unique. I'm unique. Why should we throw that away just so we can be at one? It's religious idiocy to throw that away! That's the crap of the Eastern path — dissolve the ego, and just be at one, ego being equated with individuality. What crap!! The Western way is no more intelligent, however — be an individual, individuality being equated with ego and deified independence...

When you're with me, much of what you can feel coming from me is an unspoken demand, motiveless on my part, that you feel me Being to Being, that you let *that* be ground for our encounter, and, at the same time, let your own uniqueness be present. It's about enjoying and making good use of our differences — a hellishly difficult thing to do if you're not rooted in your Being! Don't just try to flow with me. Don't repress your quirks around me. Look at me — I'm very idiosyncratic, full of preferences, likes and dislikes!

Becoming healthier doesn't necessarily mean losing one's preferences. Isn't there a saying in Zen, Chinese Zen I think, that the Great Way is easy for those who have no preferences? I don't trust that. It smacks of repression. What's wrong with having preferences? Nothing, so long as we stay Essence-centered in the midst of them. Real humans are not expressionless acceptors of whatever comes their way — they're utterly willing to be messy, to be really alive, to lose face... Remember how Paula got stuck on the phone last night with Yevrah? She wasn't in touch with her likes and dislikes. She wanted to "help" him...

RICHARD: When she couldn't stand what he was doing!

ROBERT: She helped him far more later on, when she went after him. He hung up on her. Now he's up against the wall, a good wall. If he climbs it or goes through it, it'll be on his own initiative; if he gets on top of it, he'll have a better view. Unfortunately, what he will probably do is sink, digging himself so far underground that he won't even notice that there *is* a wall, all the while doing his damnedest to justify his burrowing by finding fault with Paula, and her apparent unlove. Those who have really loved me and who have felt a very deep connection with me and who have left our community *have to* find fault with me, in order to stay away; of course, I'm talking about those who left not for their own good, but for the good of their egos. They still are with me, in a negative sense, still focussed on me, regardless of what I do... (*Silence*)

Your job is to be Richard, the true Richard. As I've said before, to transcend yourself, you must be yourself. It seems paradoxical, doesn't it? Yet it makes total sense to me. To be yourself, your *true* self, is to consciously exist in a state of unexploitable union with your Source, without running away from your idiosyncrasies. Real transcendence is about transparency, not escapism! Self-transcendence doesn't mean having no ego, having no anger, having no contractive tendencies; rather, it's about letting Love be contextually present in the midst of *all* that you are, shining no matter what's going on, staying present even in the heaviest of rages or jealousies. So, in short, self-transcendence isn't about —

RICHARD: — Dissolving! (*Much laughter*)

ROBERT: Dissolving!! The Great Swoon! Or, if you don't feel such dissolution, you *act* like it's going on, doing your best to generate those sensations that seem to demonstrate that the Great Swoon is indeed occurring! It's so easy to pretend, to make believe. We need to authentically respond to each other, not just react! React, re-act, acting again and again and again, without bothering to confess what the actual script is — we don't usually say here's the script, here is its context and current scene, here's my wall, here's what I'm up to, here's what I'm now doing... We're reluctant to expose our game, because we're hung up on the payoff it promises, especially if it's pleasurable!

Those who are hooked on pleasure-production or simulation are those who have turned away from Ecstasy — the compensatory highlight of their life is the maximizing of pleasure. If you, in the name of something deeper, dare to threaten or question someone's pleasure-getting, they aren't likely to feel very favourable toward you, even if you're *genuinely* helping them to shift from pleasure-addiction to Ecstasy...

RICHARD: That's exactly what I've been doing with you. I've been reacting, just trying to keep up the image that I'm closer to you than I really am. I've been resisting going deeper than my pleasures can take me, pretending that my pleasures are more than they are. I keep avoiding the hurt of not being actually closer to you...

ROBERT: When you're around me, not only do you have to honour our oneness and our differences, but you also have to honour the *natural distance* between us. Now, the way to honour that is not to put me on a pedestal, nor is it to push me away, nor to act like we're just buddies or pals at the same level, but is to simply be present with it; do that, and you'll be able at times to bridge the gap with love, so that the distance between us is no longer a *problem*. If you're at ease with your depths around me, then you can even be superficial with me, without any uptightness.

It's egalitarian fascism to push aside the natural distance between us, and to pretend that it doesn't exist. We are not living at the same level. The difference in our levels makes a certain kind of growth possible. This has nothing whatsoever to do with elitism, superiority, or dominance — it's just about a gap whose bridging deepens one's center. The gap between the romantic and his beloved is, on the other hand, not really bridged, but only obscured by all the hoopla and honeymoon lust, all the ardent positioning and engorged drama...

Romance is just perfumed pornography, a dreamy self-eroticizing through the sentimentalized objectifying of others. What photos of nude women are to most men, romance novels are to similarly-inclined women — revving up the machinery of masturbatory eroticism... Consider romance novels, Richard — the hit's not so much a hard cock or a picture of fucking flesh, as it is the titillating sensations generated by reading about the romantic involvement therein, and the tantalizing hunger, and the aahhh! — the throbbing longing for Mr. Wonderful, Mr. All-Fulfilling, to come their way, to do it sooo right! This isn't as honest as typical male pornography. Its heat is made to seem "higher" or more legitimate, somehow purer, more noble...

RICHARD: It seems like I've really picked up the female side of pornography.

ROBERT: Yes. You're more of a woman in this regard, more into dressing it up, making yourself up with fake innocence — but what a parody this is of a *real* woman! And what swelling hope there is in romance, what a juicy hit of hope! And underneath all the panting gloss, there's a *dark* hope (presenting itself as despair!) that she *won't* be mine, so that I can keep on being romantic... The ultimate goal of a true romantic is that the beloved will die, but not too soon! With death, there's no threat to the romance; you can keep on being romantic after the beloved is dead, with even more apparent purity. What kills romance is real communion with another, real intimacy, real love, real passion!

Romance is both a denial of and an exploitation of separation. It hurts, but it masks a deeper hurt, that of holding back your love, your fullness of love. In your very act of separation, you are but confessing your fear of dependency, of need, of Ecstasy; such compulsive separation, or contraction from the Real, does not make an individual, but only a caricature of an individual, a character, a neurotic somebody, a concretized personality. Individuality is *not* merely personality; it is Essence-centered. When personality is healthy, it merely expresses and wonderfully colours one's individuality, gracefully connecting surface and depth, waves and primal currents. It doesn't then need romantic involvement in order to feel good about itself, for it *already* feels good! (*Long pause*) Enough said...

–26–

Awakening Creates Its Own Morality

Prior to the beginnings of Awakening, we are infested by a morality imposed from without, a morality originating from some sort of authority, parental or otherwise (whether internalized or externalized). Such morality reflects and sustains our fragmentation of Being, both personally and culturally, simply because it does not represent our totality, arising as it does not from our core of Being, but from that realm of ourselves we call our thinking mind (wherein it masquerades as conscience), and it doesn't even truly arise *there* — it is literally implanted in our "headquarters" (and *bodily*, too, through postural, facial, and muscular constrictedness and imbalances that structurally correspond to such "ethical" invasions of the mind) via outside influence, not an influence that is sensitive to who we *really* are, but an influence that is itself mechanical, transmitted in much the same way as an infectious disease.

Morality is all about rules, a right way to live, a right way to be. Arguments on its behalf almost always imply that without rules, humans would be but savages, uncivilized monsters, irresponsible fools, as though what we are *now* living in *is* civilization, when in fact it is just as savage, just as barbaric, just as subhuman as any preliterate culture ever was! Arguments against rules are *ordinarily* just adolescent indulgence, naive hedonism, mere rebellion against parental authority, ever fueling the good-citizen righteousness of those who have enslaved themselves to rules. Enchained together are the law-abiding and the law-deriding, the falsely grounded and the falsely free, the canned good and the banned bad...

And so "for" and "against" seesaw in the dark, their fulcrum a broken outlaw, their pride outshouting their need, resolutely avoiding seeing that *both* sides are *factually* correct — rules are necessary, and rules must be broken. Such seemingly opposite points of view appear mutually contradictory only at the level at which they are *given* substance, the level at which they are taken seriously — they have as their unacknowledged common ground the fact that they are both superficial, both reactive, both bound to *outside* authority (either in childish or adolescent fashion), and both utterly *peripheral* to the point of view that is native to the Awakening process...

Once one has begun to awaken, one does not decide in some conventional manner to cease performing a particular behavior (so as to snare parental approval, to get an ego-boost, or to earn spiritual Brownie-points), but instead one simply stops out of heartfelt wakefulness, noticing that such behavior is no longer attractive (at least to one's depths), that it no longer so fascinates, that it no longer is so convincingly "asking" for animation from one. It may appear that such a person has imposed a rule regarding this behavior, has resolved not to do it again, but this is not truly the case, because the so-called rule has not arisen as a "should", an imposition *against* oneself, but rather as something that *clearly* serves one's wholeness, something that accurately resonates with one's core of Being, something that is there not as a rigidly fixed imperative, but as a guide, a useful guideline, a *fitting form* for one's *current* state of development; as such, it is both sturdy and flexible, available to Life-giving change, ready if necessary to radically alter its form, even to the point of disappearance...

The degree of one's awakening has everything to do with the seeming rules that one gives to oneself — if, having begun to leave our slumber, we impose many rules upon ourselves, many disciplines, and we overdo this (turning our honeymoon with such things into a numbingly neurotic 'til-Death-do-us-part pact), then the Awakening process grinds to a halt, perhaps having reached a modest level of wakefulness — we may then try to make the best out of our suddenly materializing nest, doing no more really than staking out our discipline-gained territory, just making real estate out of a moment or two of light, sooner or later going right back to sleep, while acting as though we're *still* awake, using our very obedience to our rules as a sign that we're on a spiritual path, that we *are* evolving, that what we've been promised will come, thereby betraying and obscuring our truer impulses, letting ourselves regress into the very rule-infested madness that pervades the World and that first motivated us to wake up!

Humans who are oblivious to their Awakening impulses are utterly exploitable by rules, whether conventional or unconventional. They are conformists; they may conform to societal standards, to good citizen standards, to good son and daughter standards, or they may line up with the standards of their particular brand of non-conformity, of ego-based specialness, but, all in all, they are enslaved to the dictates of "their" assembly of rules. Only one who has begun to truly awaken can be free of such procrustean intrusions, and then only when the Awakening process has *firmly* taken hold...

Until Awakening is so strongly established that we are steadfastly centered in and *as* our core of Being (which means being *consistently intimate* with our depths, so intimate as to have *immediate* access to them when we are off-balance or upset), we are *highly* susceptible to the pull of typical morality, being only occasionally intimate with an ethic that's beyond all mind-made morality. The sleeping human without any rules or taboos *does* behave like a savage, an animal released from a longtime cage, but this doesn't mean that those who live without so-called rules are actually, inherently, so savagely irresponsible and blind. It is the *caging* that creates the madness, the irresponsibility, the violence, the alienation and mistrust, yet we cannot summarily have, in utopian fashion, all humans released from their cages, simply because the cages, especially in a psychospiritual sense, are largely self-imposed. Their blueprint remains even if one is wealthy, free to roam the Earth, wonderfully promiscuous, famous, ascetical, and so on — with the greatest of ease, the blueprint for the cage persists, brought into being by all kinds of circumstances (coupled, of course, with our unwitting attention), its very rigidity of structure automatically creating or contributing to a sense of familiarity, of dense (but reassuringly *predictable*) certainty about Existence. Thus does safety, however miserable or mediocre, take priority over Aliveness; thus does entrapment get cast as Home, and freedom as Homebreaker; thus does the suffocation of Life get support, mass support, the leaden anchoring of ossified habit and rule...

Unillumined rules only frame us; we squirm within their boundaries, again and again painting ourselves into a corner, trying to escape, cornered by our own lack of awareness, madly seeking release and Ecstasy, finding none of any substance, and then, soul-numbingly suppressed then, we create surrogates of Ecstasy, surrogates of the Real, slowly but surely becoming addicted to those very conditions that most successfully give us the illusion of Ecstasy, the illusion of real joy, real God-communion, real love...

Those who have become truly centered beings may appear to the slumbering, at least some of the time, to have many rules, various rituals, fixed disciplines relative to diet, sexuality, daily scheduling, exercise, and so on, but these are *not* rigidly imposed. In fact, they're actually not imposed at all, but arise *naturally*, both as a byproduct of Awakening, and as a timely and conducive means of *maintaining* a beneficial environment for the Awakening process; that is, they are an art, a deep art, existing not as a means to Happiness, but as an expression of It, an exquisitely functional grounding of It. These "conducive means" are a gracefully practical honouring of our fundamental nature — they help us to embody our Truth, and they help us to express and live It in an artful, elegantly appropriate manner.

Sometimes those who've become centered appear to be anarchistic to those who are asleep, looking irresponsible, antisocial, too wild, too loose, too happy, yet such beings are in harmony with their environment in a way that the typical human cannot ordinarily see. If we try to take on or copy the disciplines characteristic of certain beings who are clearly centered, or who are *convincingly* presented to us as being centered, then we will only be betraying ourselves, unless such disciplines accurately fit *our* current needs, and they rarely do, simply because we're ordinarily not truly ready for *that*, but are in need of a different sort of discipline, one that fits *our* individual needs, one that is generated (at least in intention) by *our* urge to wake up. Such discipline is not a matter of spiritual ambition or ego-glorification, but is an expression, a wonderfully solid expression, of real commitment, of Essence-centered commitment...

This kind of commitment cannot be forced on oneself — it comes into being when our desire to awaken is so strong that it cannot be compromised, nor disappeared simply because our mood has changed. If we're still at the point where our commitment comes and goes according to our moods, then our discipline is *at best* a kind of New Year's Resolution, in which a parental portion of us gets righteously authoritarian with a childish piece of us, thereby dividing us, which makes us perfect fodder for guilt, one hand wielding the parental whip, the other hand "doing it", the suppressive little dance of the two sustaining a frozen parent-child conflict, a stagnantly stalemated coupling of yes and no...

Ecstasy creates its own morality. The ecstatic may appear peaceful (as well as ferociously alive and stormy wild), but their peace is not forced, as is the common man's or woman's. What almost all humans call peace within themselves is not real peace, but only a repression of their own violence — it is merely a "yes" that is in righteous opposition to their darker "no's", rather than a "yes" that is spaciously vital, powerful, and loving, a "yes" so richly pervasive that it *includes* their every "no", however sordid or murderously intentioned.

Real peace is not the opposite of war, but instead *includes* the very energies that generate and characterize war, such inclusion being not a matter of misguided acceptance, but rather of luminous integration and transfiguration. Real peace is at ease with both the dark and the light. It is a confession of *true* wholeness, of full-bodied integrity, of uninhibitedly incarnated soul. It is a confession of no more suppressed conflicts within. Real peace does not make a problem out of conflict — it does not mind anger, fear, hate, or violent intent, making as much room for these (that is, allowing them to come unknotted, without believing in their viewpoint, which makes the energies of such *apparently* unpleasant states *self-illuminating* to the point where they are in the service of Being) as it does for love, joy, grief, and God-communion...

Unlike conventional peace, real peace is not dull, not boring, not wimpy, not infested with New Age excuses and rationalizations, nor with metaphysics, religious lullabies, half-hearted goodbyes, antiseptic cries... It is truly *passionate*! It is a direct flowering of the Awakening process. It is *more* challenging, *more* exciting, *more* provocative, *more* abundant with possibility, than is war. War is simply the result of self-fragmentation, the externalization of inner war, inner conflict, inner division. The Awakening process makes such conflict *conscious*, so that it is not just projected out onto the world as good guys and bad guys, freedom-fighters and commies, socialists and conservatives, and so on...

When we become more than occasionally conscious, there is eventually a heartfelt reunion of all the fragments of us, including those that are violently inclined or war-like. In such reunion, violence is no longer violence, but is simply available power, mind-free force, raw passion, utterly capable of pure anger and clean rage. As wakefulness takes hold, every twisted quality or habit that characterized us doesn't necessarily disappear, but simply is illuminated, breathed looser and looser, befriended, respected, inhabited, again and again allowed to come into vibrant alignment with our core of Being... This transmutation creates its own morality, spontaneously creating the form that sustains and best serves its expression, the form that is the best possible caretaker of such Openness. Those who have become deeply centered are not in doubt about this, and those who are utterly asleep to themselves are also not in doubt about this, dismissing it as madness, utopian bullshit, useless dreams, mere fantasy — they're just as certain as those who've awakened to their center of Being, although of course "their" certainty is dense, automatic, barbaric, and Life-negating...

It is for those who are in between that doubt about this particular matter arises. They are still strongly attracted to the apparent safety of conventional morality, the apparent immunity it promises, the good citizen rewards it so enticingly dangles in front of them. Occasionally, they come into harmony with the morality characteristic of those who've become centered, but since they are still frequently subservient to their ego-centered habits, they cannot stay for long in such harmony. All they can do is remember that they're in a cocoon; no longer are they caterpillars, blindly feeding and munching, consuming their way through life, crawling through time, but nor are they butterflies. They are in a cocoon, part way out, but not so far out that they can squeeze free and fly into and fill out the sky of their Truth, winged by the radiance of their hearts — they are still confined, over-compressed by their conditioning, partly free of it, yes, but still bound by it very strongly. They need to honestly recognize where they *actually* are, ever making room for their confusion, their doubt, their fear, their failures of nerve, opening to their depths and woundedness again and again and again, not condemning themselves for their lapses, but instead learning to love the them that is still addicted to societal or typically parental conditioning and morality. In bringing love to this particular aspect of themselves, tough and tender love, they will move closer to being truly centered. They are in a position that requires guts and faith, not blind faith, but real trust, a trust based on what they have known and felt during their very *best* moments.

Such trust is very difficult to sustain if one is trying to do it alone; it is far easier, and ordinarily much more practical, if one is part of a group whose purpose is to bring wakefulness into *everything* that is done. In a conscious gathering like this, if one unknowingly slips, there will usually be at least one or more of the others who notice the slippage and point it out. This is possible in even a beginning group. In an advanced group, one that has bonded deeply (not in a mechanical or cultic fashion, but through deeply intimate, risk-rich interactions over a long period of time, to the point where love has taken firm root, and where anger and criticism are as welcomed within the group as joy, tears, and Ecstasy), not only are slippages easily and skilfully articulated, but there is an energy field created, an extremely potent environment wherein the Awakening process is magnified, wonderfully intensified, made exhilaratingly and ruthlessly obvious...

Of course, we cannot just join such a group, and have all of this happen. To become part of a group like this is a long, soul-baring process. A group does not become a real group, a group for mutual Awakening (as opposed to mutual escapism), until *everyone* in the group has repeatedly and tellingly faced their darkness, reactivity, and slumber, level upon level, until *everyone* has been undone, until *everyone's* persona has become transparent to their essence, until *everyone's* resistance to waking up is thoroughly and *specifically* known by everyone else, and no technique, no method, however religiously adhered to, can bring this about. More than discipline is required. The creation of such a profoundly human environment, such a non-repressive crucible for Awakening's alchemy, is very rare, simply because few of us are actually prepared for the letting go, the sacrifice that such a process requires. What tends to happen in typical spiritual movements, in guru-worship, in settings where there is devotion to a supposed Master, is but a parody of this, wherein submission is confused with surrender. The groups that form there are not consciously formed (except, to some degree, occasionally in the beginning), but are simply adhering to a set of unusual rules, a morality imposed by the teacher or guru or some ossified lineage. Members of such groups, or cults, are only sidestepping the demands of their own individuality, refusing to honor who they really are, whereas in an authentic group, everyone becomes more and more of an *individual* even as they become more and more bonded with each other and their teacher or guide.

The true group is an evolving wonder, an excruciatingly and delightfully alive gathering, wherein every member, at least most of the time, is like a column of a sacred temple, a vulnerably potent pillar, arising from a foundation of love, trust, passion, and integrity, rising up, curving up so strong and true, skilfully and steadily supporting their particular sanctuary for the Awakening process, luminously connecting both Earth and Sky, both the Mortal and the Immortal...

Such beings are *naturally* responsible, for they deeply understand the necessity of maintaining an environment, inner and outer, that supports their continuing Awakening. They do not vacillate when their moods change; they are solid yet transparent in the face of difficulties, intensely and colorfully personal, yet also easily transpersonal. Their capacity for this is simply a natural consequence of their commitment to waking up. Their keen sense of what is appropriate or inappropriate is not a result of just referring to a set of rules written somewhere, or memorized somewhere, but is innately *felt*, nakedly intuited. They simply know. Knowledge for them has become *harmoniously peripheral* to knowingness. As lovers of Awakening's morality, they do not separate suffering and Ecstasy, but live the Truth of both, while yielding to something deeper, something ever present throughout Now...

–27–

Flirting with Nasty Possibility:
The Nature of Anxiety

For most, Life is little more than coping with threats, real or imagined. Our strategies to eliminate, reduce, or deflect the threatening may, to varying degrees, relieve us of our distress, transporting us out of danger's reach, but they also tend to thicken, delude, and ossify us, through the very rigidity and obsessive consistency with which we invest them — that is, we all too easily not only lose ourselves in the apparently threatening, but also in our efforts to numb or distract ourselves from such unpleasantness, to somehow buy our way into a sizable chunk of immunity...

This is exemplified in those mindless gobblers of forest that we call newspapers — typically, the outer pages are crammed with all sorts of nasty or disturbing items, from the purely political to the sordidly personal, most of it conveying (and even subtly legitimizing) a definite sense of threat, without any real consideration of the actual purpose of reporting, for example, the details of some murder or colourful misfortune. The reading of such items, except by the terminally numb, usually catalyzes a certain low-grade dread, however airbrushed, deodorized, or emotionally eviscerated it might be by one's mind, while *simultaneously* comforting us with the indisputable fact that at least *it* didn't happen to *us* — at least not yet!

The so-called news has no interest, no *real* interest, in wholeness, sanity, and awakening, but only in its glibly "grown-up" tattletaling, busybody fascinations, and utterly mechanical reinforcing of the severe self-fragmentation that plagues our culture. It is mostly just an overload of data, runaway journalese, and vacuous juxtaposition, an assembly of information bereft of any heart, of any center of Being... In the same sense that government is collective ego, newspapers are collective mind, especially the mind of worry, fascination, and disembodied interest.

Inside the usual newspaper, neatly and entertainingly laid-out, are topics of a very different sort, namely those that serve the purpose of sedating whatever dread might have been stirred up by the outer pages. All kinds of extraordinarily trivial information can be found here, glutting the mind of the unattentive reader with enough munchy little details to induce a mildly pleasing stupor. Thus do we feed on newspapers (and other purveyors of gossip, such as televised news, wherein just about everything is "reported" in the same sterile drone), eating not because we are hungry, but because of the rigidly-intact infantile association we've made between feeding and security — sure, there's a threat of danger or deprivation, but there's also the familiar sensation of being filled, of being solidly anchored, of being reassuringly *enlarged*, of being so informationally inflated as to lose almost all awareness of our collapse of Being...

Anxiety is the sensation of chronic apprehension and calamitous expectation, fueled by supportive thoughts and a near-constant adrenaline leakage; its frazzled coupling of stimulation and enervation insistently flirts with nasty possibility, shadowboxing itself into an ever-shrinking corner. The sense of being threatened that epitomizes anxiety permeates modern culture, having easily identifiable origins and easily articulated justifications, perhaps even seeming to be almost inherently human, but its actual presence has practically no *real* value, not even at the level of organismic survival. The maintenance of anxiety is no more functionally advantageous than would be hours and hours of remaining poised in the starting blocks for a sprinter.

In other words, anxiety is overpreparation for a test or disaster that may or may not come. It is but psychophysiological pessimism, a humourless, blindfolded seer, convinced that something bad is going to happen. The fact that something bad often *does* happen is not evidence of the anxious person's clairvoyance, but, far more importantly, it is evidence that such consistently negative anticipation can actually create, or at least significantly contribute to, the coming true of dire expectation.

And how does this happen? Quite simply: What we worry about (worry being socially acceptable anxiety) frequently comes true, because our literal keeping of it *in mind* supports its physical manifestation — it's as if "we" create (in approximately the same sense that a gastropod creates its shell, unrelentingly and *unconsciously*) a template for what we're busy worrying about, and create it with such consistency that it seems we actually *need* it to occur. The fact that our attention is fixated on what we fear will occur only fleshes that dreaded something out, at which point we can, with perverse righteousness, say, "I told you so!", as if such a fate were inevitable or predestined...

Anxiety is a binding of attention to unpleasant thoughts and assumptions; of course, the emotional state generated by such mind-forms also grabs our attention (with our conspicuously absent permission). Unfortunately, we rarely just witness our upset — it's much easier to get busy trying to fix it in some way, whether through positive thinking, energy-dissipating sex, overeating, overworking, overdoing, drug intake, all-out consumption, or just sheer denial. However, sedation doesn't work; anesthetization may appear to be a shortcut, but it only reinforces the root-structure of anxiety.

The key to working effectively with anxiety is, first of all, to stop trying to get rid of it. Don't run from its caustic biochemistry. Observe it *without* detaching from it. That is, simultaneously witness and *be* your anxiety — become more intimate with its sensations, its texturing, its surges and streamings, its relationship with your thinking mind. *Feel* it fully, without submitting to its viewpoint, knowing that you are not to empty its forces, but to reclaim them!

Notice that your anxiety is but contracted excitement, an uptight gripping of Life-energy, the very epitome of self-possession, ever magnetizing attention to itself. Master your attention when you are afraid or anxious, and you will no longer be a slave to the dictates of your fear. A heartfelt gutsiness is essential here, for the faces of anxiety and dread that will appear can be terrifyingly convincing, sending us scurrying back into the familiarity, however miserable it might be, of our everyday prison...

If witnessing is done just so that we can dissipate our anxiety, it won't really work, simply because the very goal-orientation of such self-observance will inevitably generate its own anxiety. Don't look for a result — just be present with your anxiety. You need not think about it, nor define it, nor redesign it, nor otherwise attempt to corral, geld, or rehabilitate it. Cry, rage, laugh, shake, shiver, doing whatever you have to, letting loose the feeling-force of your being, allowing yourself to be pervaded by its own inherent wisdom. This may scare your ego out of its mind, but it will be a great rejuvenation and Awakening-catalyst to *you*, a fertile reestablishment of your capacity to *feel* your interconnectedness with all that is. Our work here is to befriend the energies of our anxiety, however knotted they may be, so that they might become available for something more Life-supportive than anxiety.

Just as guilt is fear rooted in the past, anxiety is futurized fear. Anxiety is the festering sore of doubt that no longer doubts itself. You could even say that anxiety is the philosophy of most cancer, ravenously feeding upon whatever it can colonize in the realm of the bodymind. Anxiety is a denial of soul, a denial of love, a denial of courage and intimacy, ever spawning mechanical distractions from itself, even as it mentally fleshes out the threatening and the potentially threatening.

If we remain identified with our minds, anxiety is inevitable.

Anxiety is a perversion of our ability to take strong action in the face of real danger. It only erodes us, making us more and more vulnerable to what we fear. Inherent to anxiety is a spiritless vision of things, an opaque submission to heart-collapse. Nevertheless, the energies of anxiety ask only for *conscious* attention and room to breathe. Observe the standpoint of anxiety, but don't lose yourself in its content — pay close attention to its tone, its contours, its insistence on becoming a repetitively present refrain in the book about what can go wrong for you. You need not immerse yourself in a different book — just look up from your reading and all your hopes for a mind-solution, letting yourself reenter the Fullness of Now...

TRANSPLANTATION

Shining babe in stainless steel bullrushes
Swaddled in an acrylic cocoon
Floating down the trafficstream
Past the multiheaded skyscrapers
Past the typeset sky
Past the bobbing crowds of outdated flesh
Past the edifices of sleeping mind
Caught up in a Fallopian current
Sailing, sailing toward a muscular harbour
A moist pouch of ancient cells
A cave for your tiny ball of juicy light
A space for a precise orgy of shaping
Sheltered from the manmade twilight
And yet not so sheltered
Shining babe taking root now
Shedding robes of far memory
Stretched out on the latest genetic strands
Unravelling the stories of other lands
Shining babe coming on strong
Pulsating with Appetite's primal song
Adrift in the Great Dream's fascinating weave
One more time
To wrestle with planetary mind
Ah but just one more time

–28–

Birthing a
True Community

Letting go of the conventional family is necessary before authentic community can be stably established. The typical family, especially in the Western world, is a unit of neurotic self-possession, compulsive ownership, and fright-centered territorial concerns, having much the same relationship to its boundaries as ego does to its. Such a family is rarely permeable to those very influences that could heal it of its rigidly self-enclosing tendencies, its dutiful blindness, its self-justifying cultism, for if it was to open itself to such forces or influences, it would necessarily have to mutate beyond, or at least radically reconsider, its present structure and ethical nature.

Even so, the point is not to attempt to brainstorm or legislate into existence a seemingly better structure — doing so simply mires us in the ideological muck of alternativism, communism, libertarianism, socialism, capitalism, egalitarianism, liberalism, and other "ism"-tailed plans (including religion) for the supposed betterment of humankind. Any such overview, however benignly blueprinted, is ultimately worthless, simply because its morality arises not from actual participation in the Awakening process, but rather from a disembodied marriage of armchair logic and sentimentality, a marriage whose sterility is well camouflaged by its bleating optimism and automated humanitarianism...

The nuclear family, though heavily criticized, still persists, as do its alternatives, very few of which are clearly superior to the nuclear family, however articulate their arguments for their particular position or politics — what replaces the conventional family here and there in our culture tends to be just as unnecessarily self-enclosed, just as rigid and neurotically protective of itself as such a family. So when I say the end of the family is the beginning of real community,

I mean the end of *all* self-possessed, compulsively-encapsulated familial structurings, tribal or modern, square-shouldered or New Age,
urban or rural, patriarchal or matriarchal. It is difficult to speak of
real community, for very few even have a clear mental framework for
such a possibility, and those few tend to get stuck in a nostalgic
evaluation of such a possibility, overconcerning themselves with
dreams of utopian schemes, merely reducing real community to an
ideal, thereby removing it from the realm of the possible. Theirs is
but a do-gooder mindgame, a disembodied planning of the welfare of
so-called disadvantaged people...

Community, to really work, must be made up of people who are
resolutely committed to waking up, regardless of their resistance to
doing so. Short of that, nothing works, no matter how brilliantly
conceived its structure, no matter how enthusiastic its members, no
matter how "spiritual" its postulates, its purposes, its goals. It won't
work, even though belief, especially fanatic belief, in it may create
the illusion that it *is* working. Its governing forces, its parliament or
congress, won't truly work, for the very same reason that ego doesn't
work; ego (which actually is not a solid somebody, but merely an unconsciously personalized *doing*) attempts to govern the rest of one
and fails, because in its very position, its peripheral partiality, it
cannot represent the totality of one!

By the same token, government, which is simply a form of collective
ego, cannot represent all those that it governs, for it does not exist at
the core of them, nor does it thread through the hearts of all, but
rather simply exists peripherally, as a kind of grandfatherly or pris-
tinely computerized bureaucracy. But bureaucracy is bureaucracy,
be it benign or malignant — it is just an extrapolation of the ego's
programs for its own survival, loopholed left and right.

More or less implicit in this is hopelessness (and presumed helplessness) — of course, the most common counter-effort that ego or
government makes is that of hope and ever-resourceful remedy. No
matter how bad things are now, they could be better tomorrow, says
a logic that pervades our culture, a logic whose accuracy is barren of
real depth and spirit, a logic whose sentimentality syrups the air-
waves daily, its underbelly of despair kept in darkness through all
sorts of strategies — excessive entertainment, compulsive eroticism
and sexing, obsessive busyness and preoccupation, the taking of
time to kill time, the cultivation of fascination, the lust for the coffee

break, the end of the day, the weekend getaway, the next distraction, all articulating a barrenness of soul for which they are but compensations, however sophisticated or culturally legitimized, ever contributing to the dehumanizing of us, the defoliation and desecration...

The nuclear family is representative of the forced marriage within most of us of male and female; its deadening coupling and numbing familiarity is characterized by neurotic dutifulness, obsessive consumerism, busied-away boredom, and the unilluminated spawning of children, as well as by the compensatory solace provided by periodic bouts of romanticism, whether with a television show, a copulatory occasion, a holiday, a living through the achievements of one's children, or even an actual going back to the land, an indiscriminate reembracing of the values of another, seemingly kinder time...

None of it works unless there is a deliberate and daily movement towards center, a shift towards a conscious abiding in (and *as*) the very core of one's Being, regardless of one's circumstances, and such movement is almost always most fruitful when made in conjunction with others who are similarly committed, deeply and passionately committed, not in some merely therapeutic or meditative fashion, but in a manner that necessitates living a *fully* human life, a life that's about outgrowing and outdancing *all* escapism.

This cannot help but create the foundation of a real community. For the foundation to be true, what has preceded it must be thoroughly undone, not simply patched over or rearranged here and there, but *undone*, utterly exposed, revealed and recognized, its rubble and disassembled trouble allowed to become but fertilizer for what must follow — this is a tremendous challenge, a great labour, a time of upheaval and difficulty and breakthrough, a time of incredibly fertile opportunity, the opportunity to both flower individually and as part of a *true* family...

The typical family is a cult, a culturally-sanctioned cult, a little bastion of neurotic independence and fouled-up dependencies; it is obsessed with *having* things, material and otherwise — mine, mine, mine — although one must keep in mind the fact that the opposite doesn't work either, as in a communistic sharing of all because of some moral program, some ideology imposed from without, some loyalty to a political idol or overseer of some sort. True community is not composed of little self-enclosed families, nor is it composed of a mass of "individuals" crammed together, forced into close proximity, trampled by the herdprints of their way, ever loyally producing for the state or organization. No! True community is a deliberate assembly of people who have begun to awaken together, level upon level — it is not a collection of monks or nuns, commune-seekers, idealists, renunciates, nor any other sort of escapist, for it is not about fleeing the world of desire, temptation, lust, endarkened mood, or attachment, but instead is about facing *all* that we are, dark and light, high and low, in the flesh-and-blood context of an ever-deepening human intimacy...

True community is comprised of individuals who, to a significant degree, are not afraid of fear, who are willing to embrace the fires of necessary purification, who are willing to enter consciously into the labyrinths of their sexuality, their power and psyche and every feeling, who are willing to enter into the fullness of themselves, to make good use of their suffering, to welcome intimacy and revelation, to love ruthlessly! Such men and women are not ready-made. The cleansing required of them is more often than not very painful and difficult, and much of this *must* be passed through before true community can even *begin*.

A group merely committed to a common ideal cannot create a real community. Only those who know and are *practising* deep intimacy with each other, an intimacy free of cultic protectiveness, are capable of creating real community, a community that is free of taboo, free of guilt, a community that does not make an enemy out of any feeling or desire, a community that makes good use of its worst disasters, a community that is not out to push an ideal, a community that does not have prepackaged values, but rather values that are spontaneously and naturally created by the Awakening process, values existing not as a rigid ethic, but as a fluid, Truth-rooted morality that's accessible only when Awareness and Love are simultaneously present...

Community is essential for the maturation of humans, despite all the currently-prevalent adolescent notions of doing it all by ourselves (as epitomized by being our own boss, "creating our own reality," and other such deifications of independence). A true community manifests as a group effort, not a group of sheep or egos, but as a group of real individuals, people who are committed both to their own unique flowering, their idiosyncratic fullness, and to their all-out resonance with Being, with Timelessness, with the Unfathomable Mystery out of Which everything appears and disappears. They are not bound by taboo and ritual such as was used to bind ancient cultures and tribal societies, nor are they trapped within the defining mythologies of modern culture, nor are they bereft of Life-enriching participation in the mythic dimensions of Being. Again and again they create their own myths, not merely imposing them year after year, but rather creating them anew until either a specific form of myth or useful ritual *naturally* drops away, or becomes thoroughly ingrained in the psychospiritual fibre of the community, while remaining fluid and open to necessary mutation *at any time.*

This doesn't necessarily create instability, except peripherally, for in a true community, stability is not a matter of a reproducible sameness, a merely predictable repetition of certain cycles of purification or celebration (though if such steadiness is *Essence-centered*, it is of immense value) — the stability of real community resides in its very heart, in its marriage of love and power, in its courage and improvisational capacity, and, most of all, in the quality and consistency of the commitment its members have to waking up, to loving, to becoming sane, to living in deep intimacy. As such, a real community doesn't make a problem out of insecurity — in fact, there is tremendous insecurity in such a community, the kind of insecurity that, if ridden properly, can take one into one's core of Being, carrying one deeply into the Unknown, not crudely, but with luminous sensitivity, revelatory grace, and exquisite timing. This is not possible if there is not an obvious base of Awakening and full-blooded humanness *already* present within the community, not just in the leader(s), but to some degree in everybody, young and old, female and male, whatever their occupation. If such centeredness is not present, then insecurity will not ordinarily be used as an opportunity for a deeper alignment with Life, but will only be an excuse for all sorts of Life-defeating activities, inner and outer...

A true community cannot be arbitrarily presented as a viable option to people in general, and applied in principle through some sort of governmental or institutionalized program and aid. Its foundational imperatives must arise *within* people, and that too cannot be forced or inculcated; in fact, it only takes firm root in those whose yearning to get to the heart of the matter is stronger than their yearning to figure it all out, to explain it all away, to superimpose meaning on everything... A real community is an evolving entity, an ever-ripening process — it is non-static, not bound by ritual, ideology, superstition, guilt, or belief. Its members *really* know anger, sadness, shame, love, tenderness, joy, ecstasy, despair, grief, death, birth, both within themselves and with each other. I am describing something that is not just a vision, something that has occurred to varying degrees throughout human history. It is, at least partially, also occurring now, but it is by no means media-ready, for it cannot be pressed and mounted and presented to tomorrow as mere information — it cannot be *truly* understood by those who are not fully prepared to understand it, for it is far more than an intellectual understanding. *It must be lived.* The way in which those in authentic community manage their lives cannot be fruitfully understood by those who have not also explored, or begun to explore, themselves *deeply*, fully, nakedly, consciously...

The know-how emanating from a true community is ordinarily only usable by those who are *already* firmly established on the path of Awakening, which is a path uncluttered by dogma, belief, or applause. Theirs is the sacred passage, the journey into the Real, the journey to the One That is also The Many. Such a journey is an ever-deepening penetration *and* surrender into this very moment, until Now expands infinitely, blooming into Eternity, shining with Truth, blazing with unexplainable illumination, psychic revelation, transverbal knowingness, and sublimely practical ordinariness... The true community does not make a goal out of such an exalted state, but allows it to be present in the midst of even the most mundane details of its days.

A group of casually associated people cannot just get together and say "Let's form a community" and then do it, even if they *have* worked on themselves, even if they *have* meditated a lot, even if they are sincere in their aim, simply because they *don't* know each other well enough. First of all, they have to live together, get messy, make mistakes, get more intimate, *gradually* weeding out those who are not committed enough (or who are falsely committed, like true believers, guru-worshippers, and other fanatics), after giving them *full* opportunity to explore themselves. Such a group may, after a year or two or three, if their intent and action has been potent and sufficient, actually begin to form the very beginnings of a community.

To do this, a leader is almost always required, a person with an undeniably strong center of Being, a lot of courage, a deep capacity for real risk-taking, as well as plenty of stamina, improvisational talent, love, no-bullshit compassion, and empathy, not to mention a consistent and artful ability to go straight to what's essential in all kinds of different situations. Blind submission to such a leader, however awakened or spirit-bright he (or she) is, does not work, and nor does a standoffish independence. If the leader is a true leader, then those around him will become more and more centered in their *own* Being, not so they can just stand apart from him and govern in their own way, but so that they can cooperate with him to such a degree that they can co-create with him the necessary forms and processes for their evolving community — thus can they participate with him, enjoy him, feel him, be intimate with him, perhaps even surpass him. The true teacher is willing to sacrifice or radically alter his position right from the beginning, if doing so contributes to the well-being of the community; as such, he is much more of a servant than a master. His job, in part, is to not allow any sort of cultic association to form around him — those who insist on being culti- cally aligned with him must be weeded out, even if it means the end of the community.

Obviously, it is a profound art that is required of the true teacher, a sublime difficulty, a sweating labour more than a graceful transmis- sion of Truth, a dynamic, juicy, fiery marriage of effort and ease, of thrust and patience, of hammerblows and diaphanous subtlety — he must teach those around him to develop both a non-neurotic de- pendency (so as to nakedly articulate and flesh out their real needs) and a healthy capacity for a permeable independence, or, put an- other way, to develop both the ability to yield when necessary, and the ability to stand one's true ground, to be solidly planted. This is not something that can be taught in a weekend, nor that can be inculcated through technique, Western or Eastern, simply because it is an ever-fresh art. Even to describe this now is difficult — how will you understand if you're not already to some degree living this? I do not present this to merely interest you, but to *invite* you, especially the you who already intuits how necessary a truly human community is. Those who are mature or hungry enough to recognize the need for such community will feel what I say, not just agreeing or disagreeing with my words, but feeling me, permitting a resonance of Being, a bonding of mutual presence, a linking of more than minds...

And what of me? I live at the center of a community that is just leaving its infancy. I have worked long and hard with great pain and great joy to bring this community, Xanthyros, to its present point, and this I have done with the cooperation of those around me, and also with the utter lack of cooperation of these very same beings. I have struggled with them, I have fought with them, I have again and again upended their certainty and mine, so that balance was lost, letting a deeper balancing take shape. I have despaired and I have loved, diving deep and climbing steep, taking risks that terrified my mind, risks that let in upheaval, breakdown and breakthrough, opening hidden wounds and doors, revealing new shores and ancient bonds, ever birthing the embodiment of what is essential, again and again letting my work outgrow itself, even as it took ever firmer root.

Out of all this a new kind of trust emerged, one that is very difficult to describe. It was trust, but not the trust that we ordinarily associate with the word "trust." It was far too intimate for that, too open-eyed, too clear, too penetrating, too paradoxical...

To bring Xanthyros to its current state, I have had to lay everything on the line many times. Almost as many have left as have stayed, although some of those are now beginning to do what they have to do in order to return. Regardless, we go on, not according to a model of how a community ought to be, letting Xanthyros be continually created through the work we are doing on ourselves. There is definite evidence of an increasing maturity, a deepening love, a sanity in relationship, a seedling equanimity, a joyous intelligence, an ease of intimacy when we gather together, a lack of artifice, a growing joy, an increasing depth in spiritwork, a disassembling of neurotic patterns, an unabashed grief and ecstasy, a befriending of that in us which couldn't give a damn about working on oneself...

Xanthyros is a sanctuary, a safe place to let go of being safe. It is open to the outside, but to pass through its gates one must be prepared; otherwise, one could enter Xanthyros and not see anything, not receive anything, not understand anything. Registering information is not enough. Tourism must be transcended, and ego undefended. One's critical faculties must be as alive as one's heart, as aroused as one's spirit...

In olden times, certain temples were guarded by grotesque carvings, gargoyles, demons, beastgods, and so on, all symbolic of what had to be passed through before one could make good use of what was inside the temple. So too it is with Xanthyros — the gargoyles, monsters, fiends, demons, and misshapen horrors outside the temple are but eloquently graphic representations of our unexplored or unacknowledged resistances to God, to Truth, to living a fully human life. They must be encountered, passed through, and luminously integrated before Xanthyros can be made truly good use of; this is why preparatory work is so essential for those who approach Xanthyros, so that they will be already willingly immersed in deep self-exploration, *already* well within the outside of the inside...

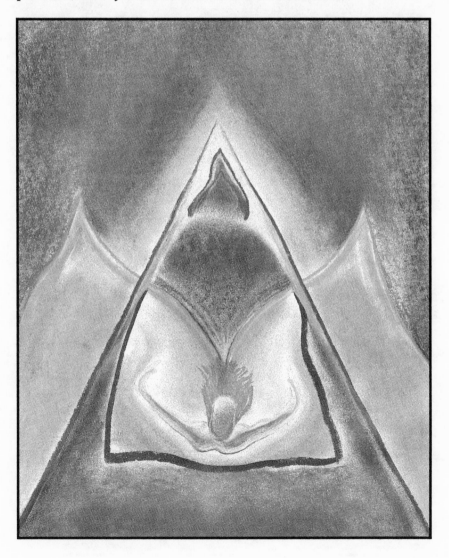

Outbreathing My Shock Was I

Today danger was not somewhere else
Today it was a screechingly fat two seconds
A cartoon crash and collapse of falsetto metal
Outbreathing my shock was I
My body like a skyscraper in an earthquake
Jobs got done under the unfelt sun
The mess swept and towed and etched into duplicate
While a deeper truth lingered nearby
Soft as a newborn smile, spacious as death
There I was attending to solid detail
While fleshing-out thanksgiving for something else
Something kindled into being by my "accident"
Driven had I been and knowing it too
Going too far in letting my work do me
Staying solid for those who fear my transparency
So I crashed and got banged and harangued
Yet so soon so gentle felt so much lighter
I'm limping but I'm not lame
No longer wrestling with Time
Nor with those who defend the ruins of themselves
Even though I be intimate with their dark rhyme
I've lived in their realm while remaining I
But that's done, evaporated in the sun
I'd be a fool to make a virtue out of staying
Where the trap is security, and Home is but danger
I know that land
Long have I given it my all
But now I must heed a different call
My ripeness demands it
The use to be made of me is now luminously plain
I am an ease, a freedom of useful flaws
A paradox honouring an unspeakably obvious set of laws
A dance of soul-transmission and edible labour
Asking only for your undressed need
The greenreaching of your ever-virgin longing

—29—

You Can't Think Your Way Into Being

(Bob begins by talking about his sexual experiences for awhile)

ROBERT: What makes you think that they're even sexual? What's the evidence?

BOB: Just my experience with women...

ROBERT: Imagine your torso as a tube of toothpaste — compress it, and your energy will go up into your head or down into your genitals. It seems you're adept at going in both directions; you swell the heads at both ends. *(Laughter)* Like you, a lot of men fuck away their anger (and/or mentalize it away in unnaturally aggressive or complex thought), fuck away all kinds of feelings, all but obliterating their connection to their *real* needs... Their intensity of sexual sensation, their on-call erectile service, creates the illusion of an actual *feeling* of emotional connectedness to the woman — of course, such apparent bonding disappears when sex is finished or ejaculated away, simply because there wasn't *really* a bonding in the first place, but only the illusion of it, the titillation-inflated illusion of it...

So, a lot of your so-called wild sexuality isn't *true* sexuality, but only an outlet for something quite different. You've just dumped energy and reinforced your ego. You've never made love. You've just made more and more of what sustains your suffering... When the whole body is open, wide-open, *then* you are capable of making love — *then* the entire body, level upon level, is flooded with feeling, not just sensation or emotionalism, but *real* feeling, both for yourself and the other person. You must notice whether or not you are in love with her, or whether you're just romanticizing her. With great honesty, you must ask yourself if you are being loving with her, or if you're just faking it.

BOB: When I've come close to actual love, I've felt terror...

ROBERT: Because to dive into that, to embody that, is not just to plunge into orgasmic pleasure, but to dive right into your *full* emotional self, your very core of Being... But it seems you're just hearing what I'm saying as more data, thereby separating yourself from its essence — if you keep abstracting everything that comes your way, there's no growth possible for you...

BOB: Yes. I feel like I did that when I was studying Wilhelm Reich's material — I wanted to take his ideas and put them in my mind and assume I already had it all together.

ROBERT: That's why you have such a tight scalp. You need to be psychologically scalped! (*Laughter*)

BOB: Does that mean my hair will grow back?

ROBERT: Ain't no guarantees, Bob! (*Laughter*) So to explore your sexuality fully is equivalent to fully exploring the rest of your life. You can't put your sexuality over there and study it à la sex therapy. Instead, you need to look at it in the context of who you fundamentally are — you must take your entire life into account! Once you are authentically proceeding with that, *then* your sexuality will start to find its rightful place. Eventually, it will have a totally different feeling — it won't be based on hyped sensation and fantasy, the exploitation of the link between mind and crotch, but rather will arise from love, from Being, from mind-free aliveness.

Then you won't need fantasy at any level, at least the sort of fantasizing that serves eroticism and self-fragmentation; your capacity for fantasy will mutate into a more mythical or archetypal knowingness that will reinforce and wonderfully colour your wholeness of Being... (*Pause*) At present, however, do not *force* yourself to not use fantasy; rather than indulge in such self-violence, such do-gooder repression, practise wakefulness in the midst of your fantasies, doing whatever you can to make room for love. As you enter into real relationship, your supposed need for erotic fantasy, for charge-building fantasy, will gradually evaporate, simply because *you won't need it*...

Let's move upstairs now, into the machinations of your mind, all the wheeling and dealing behind your furrowed brow — it's no use just railing against consensus reality, as you've done through your magazine for the past ten years. You've published plenty of far-out opinions, plenty of radical opinions, but opinions are just opinions, just little mindgames that serve not Being, but only the twisted personification of our craving to be someone special, someone who's in the know, someone whose measure is in their contrariness of opinion. Look at you — you can rant against some political injustice or conspiratorial scenario, but you haven't had the guts to tell the truth about yourself!

You must dive deeper than the level that's epitomized by opinion-having... To counter mere opinion, it's of no use to come up with another mind-product, be it another opinion, or positive thinking, or any other restructuring of thought. Changing one's thinking is not enough, despite the claims of the New Age — something deeper, something much riskier, much more enlivening, is required. So instead of countering mind with more of the same, you need to move into your core of Being.

BOB: I've entertained the fantasy of being able to do that, of being able to discriminate between opinion and actual truth.

ROBERT: Don't discount yourself completely. You do have some of that, but it's been obscured by the you who's done no work on himself, the you who pretends to have done such work through reading Wilhelm Reich and so on. Such discrimination requires that you be living from your core, instead of just *thinking* you're doing so... Maybe your purpose *is* to publish a magazine that transforms lives, but you can't do so until *you* are living a truer life! It asks for ruthlessness, compassion and a lot of guts. (*Long pause*) You're drowning in information; you've let yourself become little more than a fucking computer! (*Laughter*) Real intelligence has far more to do with transformation than with information. We're here to be the juicy embrace, the self-illuminating synthesis, of information and transformation...

You need to let the woman in you make love, too, yielding until you're 100 percent vulnerable; you'll find yourself crying more when you make love then, laughing more too, riding the currents of a seamless Now, letting the male and female in you emerge both as

one and as dual uniquenesses, ripe with their primal differences —
such coming together is not annihilation, but revelation...

It's time for you to start cutting through the bullshit you've tolerated,
to make the ring of Truth central to your life — if someone's telling
you something that sounds good, but that activates your bullshit
detector, you may need to say something like, "Look, I don't trust
what you just said; what I sense you doing is..." So sometimes you
may take that arrogant-appearing risk of telling someone what they
are feeling, or what their hidden motivation may be. Of course, this
is anathema to the liberalism, the diseased egalitarianism that plagues
our culture (which unfortunately equates the outfront articulation
and presence of different levels of being with rampant elitism). At
any rate, take the risk. Put yourself on the line, instead of just
trading one opinion for another.

Trust your intuition. We can all intuit the truth of a situation, but we
tend to mute our capacity to give voice to such insight, for all sorts of
less than Life-giving reasons. If we were sitting together, all of us
deeply centered, and someone came into the room, we'd all have basically the same perception of them, the same fundamental sense. If
that person was bullshitting, we'd *all* know it; we'd inevitably share
the same fundamental sense of what that person was up to, not
because we were caught up in some sort of groupthink, but because
we'd all be participating in the same Unity of Being, even as our
sensing was coloured (but not contradicted) by our individual differences. Gurdjieff called this "objective knowledge." It has nothing
whatsoever to do with opinion or games of agreement/disagreement,
for it is a function of Being, present in all of us...

*(For some time, Robert asks Bob questions spontaneously constellated
around the fundamental inquiry of "Who are you?", altering his questions with each of Bob's replies, but Bob only becomes more and more
confused)*

ROBERT: You don't know who you are, do you? That is why you are
feeling so sad now, so inwardly broken. (*Bob starts to weep*) But the
very pain you're feeling now is this very moment's bridge to knowing
who you are; the very woundedness you feel when I ask you who you
are is the key to knowing who you *truly* are. This woundedness, this
deep heart-hurt, is, in its very intensity and rawness, a very close
relative of your longing to realize God, to wake up... You don't get

there by *thinking* your way into it. You have to feel, unobstructedly feel, and it hurts like hell sometimes. It asks for open eyes and an acceptance of both your hurt and your joy, a willingness to plunge right into the heart of your woundedness...

You *are* wounded! You're wounded by your separation from your Source. It's valuable to actually be able to *feel* that. If you're busy fucking away your energy, you can't *really* feel that separation-hurt; then you just spend your life fucking around with *secondary* longings, and you miss out on your *primary* longing. So your hurt over realizing that you don't know who you are is of immense value, being a potential bridge to your heart's desire...

Being a lover doesn't mean that you depart from the world and console yourself in an eroticized cocoon; it means you live deeply in the world, even *as* the world, without getting lost in it. There's no need to avoid anything, including your fears and your hurt. Most people want to run from them. That's what's wrong with the New Age — running from the dark side, running away from pain, running into the styrofoam arms of metaphysical sedation. Your so-called dark side, your fears, your doubts and your resistance are *not* the problem! If you'll feel them, profoundly feel them, and illuminate them at the same time, nothing can stop you. But it's very hard to do that if you don't have a supportive environment for it. That's why we have this community, not because we're weaklings!

Everyone here is intelligent enough to recognize the need for a true group. There's so much fear and mistrust in our culture about this kind of thing — an extended family, a truly human community, a group committed to going all the way. It reminds people of the entrapment they felt with their own families when they were kids. And who wants that again? Most of us would rather re-create a benign version of it, a safe or sterilized version of it, and then wither away, bored and securely numb, stuffing ourselves with all the goodies and pleasurable distractions we can get. That's not Life! (*Long pause*) So who are you?

BOB: I think I have a lot of fear around accepting this core thing...

ROBERT: But the you who *wants* to accept it is a pipsqueak, not even a person really, but only a personified habit, a clinger to good resolutions, a little knot of spiritual ambition... Accepting this core thing, as you just put it, is only a spiritual seeker's version of a New Year's resolution — if you try to do it, to live up to it, another aspect of you will sabotage the whole process. Periphery against periphery. One fragment of you versus another. Opinion against opinion. What the hell good is that?

To the point: The periphery, in and of itself, cannot accept the core. The ego does not accept what transcends it, but instead fights it, or tries to claim it as its own! So what can you do? Bring your periphery into alignment with your core, without eviscerating it. Get out of your head — relocate! Either you're doing it, or you're not. Thinking about it is of no use to you; in fact, it only creates the illusion that you *are* getting somewhere. You need to stop being so goddamned complicated about your feelings! They will never compute for you, so you might as well stop trying to design the right software for them...

Every day, you have opportunities to inhabit your depths, Bob. When you get out of bed in the morning, do you walk to the bathroom consciously, or do you just shuffle down the hall like a robot? While you're taking your morning piss, do you notice what's going on in your head, or do you just automatically lose yourself in your thoughts? How are you breathing while this is going on? As you shake loose the last drops, do you notice your posture, your balance, your perusal of the toilet bowl? How about your first human encounter each day? You have an opportunity to make that encounter memorable, however superficial its content might be!

BOB: I know... But I'm afraid I'll lose touch with that.

ROBERT: You are going to; I guarantee it. But every time you forget and then work your way back to a deeper, truer way of Being, you will strengthen yourself.

BOB: Say that again.

ROBERT: Every time you lose balance, it gives you an opportunity for a deeper balancing. Every time you fall flat on your face and then get up and get on with it, you brighten and enrich your integrity. That is, you make good use of adversity. But don't worry about forgetting. You will. How can you learn if you don't make mistakes? And remember: You don't have to make your forgetting be foreground — why dramatize it into a problem? It's just raw material for your journey, a goad to awaken, a reminder of your actual state, as opposed to your idealized state. So drop the ideals, stop spinning your wheels, and get started, however small or homely your initial steps might be...

What do you see when you look into my eyes?

BOB: Love, ruthlessness, compassion... (*Pause*) I think I'm afraid of it...

ROBERT: Of what?

BOB: Of meeting you on equal terms.

ROBERT: You can't. Why torture yourself with trying to? It would be like some beginning apprentice in carpentry trying to match the master carpenter. There's no elitism in this, but only an appreciation and honouring of different levels. There's no more point in trying to stand where I stand than there would be in putting me on a pedestal. I'm not better than you, but I am far more stably established in my core of Being than you are. Nevertheless, the gap between us doesn't have to be an uninhabited zone — when love arcs between us, the gap becomes a useful continuity between our Beings. Then, through such bridging, you don't exactly stand where I stand, but you do *feel* me, you do resonate with me, so that what I say to you is not just words, but something deeper. Our inherent unity of Being becomes more obvious to you, and then there's no question whatsoever of our inequality — egalitarian ideology evaporates, and we gracefully and potently interact, without making a problem out of our differences. In this, my state becomes an opportunity for you — why not take advantage of my condition?

This is a delicate subject... There is a distance, a *natural* distance, between me and all the other adults in our community. Part of my work is to not pretend that there isn't a distance; nor can I sit in my chair and be Mr. Wise, all detached and immune. No! I have to jump in and get involved, get attached, get messy, get emotional! (*Long pause*) Is it possible for you to enjoy me?

BOB: Yes. I would love to be able to enjoy you.

ROBERT: When? (*Laughter*)

BOB: Right now!

ROBERT: Go ahead.

BOB: I don't know what to do! (*Laughter*)

ROBERT: See, the necessary *doing* doesn't come from the you who doesn't know what to do! You're still mostly a stranger to Essence-centered doing. When you're truly loving, there's a doing that comes right from your core, a doing radically different from your typical ego-based motivations. You have to let *it* do itself — let *it* behead Bob Banner! It is simply Being in action, fluidly interactive with its environment, inner and outer. This is possible without love, but it then tends to be dry, arid, non-relational. You cannot avoid love, if you are to truly ripen; without love, you'll just wither into an erudite masturbator, glued to the keyboard behind your wrinkled brow! (*Pause*) To enjoy me is not just to love me, but is also to openly share your fears, your insecurities, your hidden resistances, your hate, your need, your greed, your parental projections onto me...

It's intimacy I'm talking about, real intimacy, wherein I am neither buddy nor guru, but rather a catalyst, an ally, a consistently present unpredictability. Sometimes you'll love my fieriness; other times, you'll be terrified of it. You must stay flexibly alert in your relationship to the heat that emanates from me. Other times, I may be extremely soft, very friendly and easy, joking and playing, but my teacher function can emerge at any point, not because *I* think it's time for it, but because it is *innate* to me. It is a spontaneous occurrence. It has nothing whatsoever to do with a career! I was born with it. It is as natural to me as breathing or loving. It has no script. It is as creative as it's wild. It's what I do. It's my purpose; it has nothing to do with being special. So I'm laying myself on the line. I'm doing what I'm writing about, simply because there's no other true option left for me. It may sound like bondage, or like some great sacrifice, but there's actually a tremendous freedom in my very choicelessness...

Many people get enthusiastic about working on themselves, but it's only a spasm, a psychospiritual honeymoon. The real work requires not just some initial breakthroughs, but also a healthy encountering of your resistance to going deeper, to aligning the rest of your life with what you've discovered about yourself. Not many will do this —

they'll either back off, rationalizing their retreat, or else they'll make an ideology out of whatever triggered their initial breakthroughs. There will inevitably be times you'll hate me, but even that need not be a problem if you will express its energies without marrying its viewpoint!

Either you act out your resistance, or you work with it. Either you re-act, or you wake up. Go ahead and express the emotion of your resistance, but don't take on *its* mind, and then, instead of acting as if you're this poor student who's stuck with a horrible assignment from me, you'll start feeling that you've actually co-created the assignment with me, as though *both of us* were gazing compassionately at the reactive you! Sure, I was the voice for the assignment, but without you, I could not have come up with it — don't you see that there is a certain sense of spiritual unity in that, an unusual sort of camaraderie?

Assignments are necessary, but they're not to be done out of mere obedience; they must be understood, and felt as a co-creative act, and the inevitable resistance to them *must* be honoured! The good-student syndrome is as harmful as sulking or pouting about what you must do. (*Pause*) As you're beginning to notice, just about everyone is acting out their resistance to the Awakening process; the whole world's involved. I'd call it *overacting*...

One of your diseases, Bob, is that when you open deeply, as you have sporadically during this session, you almost immediately zip up to your thinking mind. This creates a short-circuiting of your energy; your torso gets unplugged, and your limbs become appendages of your thought-patterns. It's a matter of attention. Practise giving your attention to something other than your conceptualizing and categorizing and worrying. Yield your attention to this moment; give it to the noticing of your thoughts, rather than to them directly. Put another way, pay more attention to the *energy* of your thoughts, instead of to their contents. Become aware of *thinking* itself, instead of just thinking about thinking! You run up to your skull because it's familiar, it's predictable — I suggest you give your torso your attention for the next few weeks. Start living from the neck down, and you'll not only feel more, but your mind will begin doing something else besides computing. The desert will then begin to bloom...

−30−

The Art of Letting Love Be Present

The angrier you are at someone, the more important it is to love them, but this in no way means that you ought to necessarily shut down your anger or disguise it with a loving face or act. Rather, it means that love must be contextually present in the midst of your anger, or any other feeling you are currently experiencing, *if* you are to communicate something deeper than mere reactivity. Such presence ought not to and need not interfere with a responsible expression of whatever you're feeling; in fact, the presence of love, however slight or diffuse, can only enrich and clarify such expression. Anger without love is simply fisted righteousness, a self-legitimizing violence; hurt without love is simply sunken sorrow, an implosive and self-pitying sadness; pleasure without love is simply automated stimulation and soul-numbing enervation; Life without love is no more than survival.

Many people separate love from endarkened or seemingly negative emotions, but in so doing they have only stranded themselves from the riches of their own shadowland, not realizing that love is the matrix for every true feeling. However, there is no love present in *mind-generated* emotion, but only egoic machination, split-level desperation, obsession and masturbatory manipulation — such "emotion" (which includes sentimentality, romanticism, sarcasm, envy, hysteria, guilt, and psychotic acting-out) is, through its very collusion with mind, *impermeable* to love, however much it might, like so many parents, claim to be loving...

Being loving in the midst of rage won't necessarily remove us from the intensity of our fury, but will vastly broaden its sky and deepen its integrity, making it a means, a wonderfully fiery means, for creating (or reestablishing) intimacy, rather than for merely hurting another. About hurt: The point is not to never hurt each other, for it's *inevitable* that we will hurt each other, whether we go deeply into relationship, or whether we stay in the shallows. The question is: Is it good hurt, or unhealthy hurt?

Good hurt is simply part of the feeling of unavoidable growth, of upheaval-enriched repositioning. It's the pain of stretching, the ouch of relocating, the thorny or tearing sensation of outgrowing some behavioral pattern that no longer serves our well-being. If we attempt this without love, it'll only harden or collapse us, turning us into the pawns of ego-centered ambition, the ambition to be a somebody who is growing! In such lovelessness, we marry our minds to our lopsided goals, which we tend to make a home out of if we ever get there, a self-positioning of such staunch petrification that we feel excessively threatened by anything or anyone that would seem to want to put us elsewhere! Whether that disruptive influence was healthy or unhealthy we wouldn't then know, for we, in our very rigidity, wouldn't have what it takes to distinguish between real help and actual intended violence to us...

Without love, there is no real illumination of what we're up to — yes, there may be some awareness, but it is simply an awareness of detail, a self-serving, overly detached kind of meditativeness, regardless of how persistently it tries to don the robes of compassion...

The more disturbed we are by something, the more important it is that we grant ourselves access to love, without, however, trying to be loving so that we won't feel disturbed! It is crucial to actually *feel*, uninhibitedly *feel*, the sensations that characterize such disturbance! Our problem is that we usually don't want to directly and fully experience that feeling, that nasty unease, that dread, but instead want to escape it, extinguish it, anesthetize it, get hysterical or guilty about it, or do whatever else removes us from the deeper intensity of it. In such a situation, real love gives us room to feel what we are afraid to feel, until we are at its heart, sensing and knowing it from the inside, not just observing or witnessing it, but being present with it so, so deeply and vulnerably that we *are* it — this is *not* identification, but *full-bodied* recognition!

It ought to be obvious by now that a broader definition of love is required, a definition that touches us throughout our entire being, a definition that cannot be reduced to mere information. I'm not talking about the creation of license for emotional expression, for such expression can be just as blind and irresponsible as the acts of mind with which we torture ourselves. Awareness is necessary, not strategically detached awareness, but passionately-involved awareness, awareness that does not make a problem or adversary out of attachment. The kind of love I'm talking about is *inherently* self-aware. It offers no consolation, no romanticism, no sentimentality, no egalitarian syrup, no charade of intimacy, no escape. It is not burdened by any kind of must. It is already free, already loose, already endlessly spacious, but spacious in such a way that it doesn't dilute or diffuse the variegated intensity of relatedness, of connectedness. Rather than annihilating suffering, it purifies it...

Such love enriches our capacity to be present with what we're feeling. If we're angry, we really feel our anger in its purity, rather than in a narrow, righteous manner wherein we're merely zeroing in on someone else's shortcomings — we then get angry in a way that maintains its intensity, its fire, while simultaneously becoming empathetically spacious, so that we cannot help but feel the true needs of the moment, the woundedness that's crying for love and light. In this, our anger transcends all blaming, and becomes a matter of mutual responsibility, a fierily fertile reestablishing of intimacy, an electrically potent yet immensely vulnerable righting of what has been misaligned or allowed to deaden. That's healthy anger, clearing the temple of moneylenders, breaking through dead zones — there's love in it, not love for the behavioral patterns that are being so fiercely and tellingly addressed, but love for who's in front of us, love for Being...

Love is all-accepting of Being, but not necessarily of behavior. Many people are confused about this; they assume that if I'm loving them, then I must accept them as they are, as they might put it, but I'd say to them I accept *you*, but I don't necessarily accept what you're *doing*, and if you're identified with what you're doing, then you'll feel threatened by my distaste or dislike for some of the things you are up to. It doesn't mean that I don't love you, but that my love won't sit back and pretend to not see what you're up to, so that you too will then, out of a tacit bargaining between us, also avoid saying what you don't like about me...

Real love does not avoid encounter, even heavy encounter; it supports Truth-talks between people, full-blooded meetings that expose and shake up ossified positioning, meetings wherein there's a mutual unzipping of ego, not so that ego can be eradicated, but so that ego can be purified to the point of becoming transparently available to what underlies it. Of course, Truth-talks are impossible if mere opinion is confused with Truth — more than minds and unillumined emotion must meet if there is to be any *real* communion between us. Even honesty may not be enough, for most so-called honesty is just vociferously stated opinion or the stridently earnest voice of mind-generated emotion. Subtlety is essential. So is compassion. These, however, will not be truly present if there is no awareness in an encounter, especially if one or both parties *think* they are aware!

Sounds messy, doesn't it? It precisely reflects the current state of the Earth, with all its warring voices stuck at the level of mere opinion and flag-waving, all but deaf to the call of anything deeper; even when authentic voices shine forth, they are all too often quickly trivialized into indigestible tinsel, distilled into mere information, branded with a coast-to-coast caption. So what the hell can be done? Don't look for more data; nakedly acknowledge the mess, both outer and inner, and become more sensitive to how you defend yourself from your depths. Take a step in a truer direction, however tiny that step may be, and don't back off, regardless of what your mind is telling you. There's no formula for this. All you can do is contact and keep honoring the deepest longing you feel...

Love is not primarily a feeling. It is a state of Being, manifesting as all kinds of feelings. Love can appear in the robes of joy, of anger, of grief, of seriousness, of levity. It can even appear (and this may sound absurd) as jealousy, not your everyday reactive jealousy, but as a more mature jealousy, a jealousy that's *already* on its way to becoming simply a Life-affirming expression of possessiveness or attachment, an expansively vulnerable sharing of raw need — such sharing, of course, soon reaches the point where jealousy can no longer be termed jealousy, the point where it's just available Life-energy, leaving its expresser utterly present with his or her heart's need, already seeding the next moment with their bruised yet thriving well-being, regardless of whether or not they are being rejected by the other, regardless of whether or not they are still hurting...

So when you are really turned off by someone, it's very important to love them, without any castration of your dislike. Why make a virtue out of softness, and a bogeyman out of hardness? Why not make good use of every texture? You might feel disgust for someone, even when love is with you, but why judge yourself for that? Why turn away from your disgust? Why reject it? Why assume that you can't feel disgust and love at the very same time? Your disgust might be foreground, your love background. Allow that to be, and your love will gradually and motivelessly shine through your disgust, fine-tuning the accuracy of its criticism of the other, even as compassion is permitted to permeate the whole scene, until we outgrow our disgust without depriving ourselves of the wisdom it might contain. Do not assume that your disgust must be of no value to its recipient!

I cannot simply sit here and say love each other. That's too bland, too vague, too loose, too open to misinterpretation, plagued by the possibility of people wandering around deflecting healthy criticisms of themselves by protesting that the criticizer is not loving them. As if love is but some unconditionally benign maternal force, bereft of fire! Some all-protecting Lullaby!

The point I'm making is that real love and so-called negative emotion are not necessarily mutually exclusive. The inherent alertness or wakefulness of such love makes it quite easy to distinguish between natural emotion and mind-generated emotion, between true feeling and false feeling. Real love knows, for example, that depression is not a feeling, but only a pressing down of feeling, a suppression of emotion. It also knows that guilt is not a feeling, but only a psychophysical knottedness, a collapse of heart, a deeply neurotic dividing of self. Real love intuitively recognizes that the energies of twisted or false emotion need not a whipper, nor more repression, nor the saccharine judgmentalness of *apparently* all-accepting doctrines (such as the New Age *concept* of unconditional love)...

Diseased or false emotion is, in a sense, a battered child, an abused child, needing not some automatically benign remedial program, some homogenized reconditioning, some smilingly impersonal governmental rescuing effort, but rather *real* contact, essence-centered caring and love! And how the hell can we do this if we're not *already* loving, already stably rooted in *our* core of Being, already committed to *being love* in the midst of everything?

Such commitment is not a merely mental decision, a do-gooder resolution — rather, it is an act of our *entire* being, not a once-and-for-all decision, but a moment-to-moment decision. It cannot last without ongoing wakefulness. There's always a choice in each moment, to turn away from the heart of what's occurring, or to participate right in it, to be present *as* its radiant center, regardless of our mood or circumstance. And this is not something you can vault yourself into, just because it sounds good to you... You have to start right where you are now, now, and now. If where you are is troubled or murky, why run away from it? Love is *not* an escape from such a state, but an *acceptance* of it, an acceptance that's not passive, not syrupy, not numb, not plagued by any sort of lullaby or fake tolerance. Such acceptance makes room for *everything* we are, without necessarily going along with its intentions, without necessarily submitting to its viewpoint. If we're in the throes of some overheated emotion, busy being hysterical or sentimental, why submit to its viewpoint? And why try to escape or tranquilize it?

The energy of neurotic emotion is there to be faced, to be liberated, not to be incarcerated or anesthetized or indulged! Why reject it? Why do to it what was done to us when we were children? It asks for our love. It asks for space to breathe, space to grieve, space to heal...

To love is to remain in conscious contact with our Source. It is to make that communion, that remembrance, more important than our egoic efforts to launch ourselves into surrogates of such communion (as epitomized by the goals of spiritual ambition). But you can't just say wow, that was an interesting talk — all I have to do now is love in the midst of everything. If you do *that*, it's just one more should, one more injected must! Doing so is not love, but only an inner violence, a tyranny — while you're enthusiastically imposing this fine-sounding resolution on yourself, another aspect of yourself will rise to oppose it, to sabotage it.

And why? Because the you that is imposing such resolution is not *you*, but only a foreground fragment of you, the goody-goody side of your ego, the neurotic social reformer inside you — it's not even a somebody, not even a partial somebody or self, but just a persistently personified habit. And when it is animated, it sets in motion its opposite, so that some sort of *balance* can be established, however endarkened or superficial. This is why trying doesn't work, for it springs from such fragmentation of self, representing only the dominant fragment or fragments, while the rest seethes beneath its rule. What does work is the doing that emerges from our core, from our wholeness, the doing that outshines all trying...

To truly take what I'm saying to heart is to hear it with more than your mind, with more than your ears, with more than your self-improvement egoity — it's not a matter of changing yourself overnight, but of starting right where you are, however homely your circumstance or condition might be, and bringing to it whatever illumination and love you can muster, giving your pain room to breathe itself sane, giving your addictions something other than fuel or blame...

Yes, what I'm describing is already true of us in potential, but it exists in the vast majority of us only in seed-form. You can't make a seed turn into a tree overnight. It's a gradual process; it requires patience, immense patience. It requires that we become friends with our impatience. And what nourishes this seed, this near-seedling? Love and conscious attention and *creative* consistency, the kind of consistency that is as fluidly functional as it's improvisationally alive. This is the art of Being, the art of being human, the art of embodying our fundamental nature. It's a birthing of the true human, a great labor of love, and we are all in it together. This, however, doesn't mean that we're all going to make it together, at least at the same time, or even at any time. Many have turned their backs to the Awakening process and Its demands, fleshing-out not the imperatives of their soul, but of their egoic programming. Nevertheless, this in no way means that the journey is not worth taking, or that those who have turned away are unreachable. Some of them are, though; they must be permitted to live out their turning away until the sheer pain of it, the sheer folly of it, becomes obvious to *them*, so undeniably obvious, that they turn back of their own accord. In that shifting away from soullessness, they will inevitably encounter the kind of help they most need...

Your work may be to serve such beings when they begin turning back; it may even be to go after them in the midst of their turning away, not as a missionary, but as a reminder, an opportunity, a catalyst. You may become extremely disappointed by the vast magnitude and weight of human sleepfulness and pretence, but this must not be allowed to make you give up, or become cynical, righteous, or merely proud of how *you're* not asleep! Such disappointment ought to further catalyze your love, even as it also wounds you. It hurts to see others turn away, to see them making a virtue out of their recoil, but it's a good hurt, a hurt that keeps compassion moist...

Gurdjieff, in so many words, used to say that humans are not born with a soul, but that they have to *develop* a soul, or, more precisely, *become a soul*. Unfortunately, not many people seem to be inclined this way; most just settle for a parody of soul, painting wings or metaphysical loftiness on their ego, taking it to church once a week, or meditating on it, or mentally affirming it in New Age fashion, blithely believing that "their soul" is somewhere *inside* them! (The relationship between soul and bodymind, however, is not that of jinni to bottle, but that of tree to seed.) Nevertheless, there *is* something to be cultivated. There *is* a center of Being that awaits our *conscious* contact. It awaits us, and It invites us, invites us to be It, to embody It, even now, however slightly. It cannot help but invite us to flesh It out, to honor Its imperatives, to allow It to flower into Its fullness, to become the great branching-out that It is...

This journey, this passage into Selfhood, simply cannot happen without love, a love whose yes is so strong, so rich, so deep and true, that it includes *every* no (including the no of conditional love). Such love is *not* in opposition to so-called negative emotion, but is, in a sense, a multidimensional context wherein such compression or heatedness of feeling can both be and be let go, in a manner that enhances the possibility of genuine contact between those involved.

So, once again, the more disturbed you are, the more upset you are, the more hurting you are, the more important it is that you allow yourself to love at the very same time that you're experiencing such feelings; otherwise, you'll simply reject them, or exaggerate them, or righteously act them out, or betray yourself in their dramatics, or engorge yourself in their payoffs, doing it now and feeling lousy about it later, seeding yourself with guilt. Why continue with that programming? Why would anyone not choose love? Because it not only can feel wonderful, but it also sometimes hurts like hell. It *really* hurts. It can knife through the heart. Its wound goes very deep, right to the quick of us, leaving us excruciatingly vulnerable. However, that very woundedness need not be a problem — it can be a very potent means to feeling our connection to God, to reestablishing our visceral intimacy with All That Is. Love is the key, the ever-virgin Mystery, the Mystery of you and me, the open secret that we can never have, but only *be*...

Gustave Doré: *Chateaubriand's Atala*

-31-

Look & Leap at the Same Time: Making Good Use of Turning Points

We ordinarily tend to view turning points as problems, then busy ourselves looking for solutions, trying to *think* our way free of our *apparent* misfortune, bewailing and complaining about our confusion, desperately searching for some clarity, some relief, some non-turbulence, rarely realizing that our confusion is simply an exaggeration of what usually is *already* occurring in our thinking minds, a confusion manufactured by confining the actual energies of our particular turning point to the administrative centers of our brain — we have but literally fled to our headquarters, obsessively trying to *outthink* our apparent problem, blindly ricocheting between warring viewpoints, lost in a duststorm of beckoning maps, doing no more than making ourselves inaccessible to the incredible opportunity presented to us by the presence of our turning point...

Turning points are times of increased energy, surplus force, times of fertile chaos and potential transition, times when a leap into a more fitting level of being is not only very possible and easily accessible, but also *necessary*. If we busy ourselves trying to *figure out* what to do when we're in the midst of a turning point, then by the time we get around to actually taking the jump (if we ever get this far!), it cannot fruitfully occur, simply because the forces that could have carried us toward a deeper level of being have gone or faded, have already had their moment, having been eroded into impotence by our continual resistance to taking the jump when it was time to do so.

We cannot know the right time to leap through merely thinking about it. We must enter into the waters of our turning point, not in some naively hopeful fashion (with a reward dangling before us for our heroics), but with open eyes, full-bodied courage, and a hope-free willingness to dive deep, to intimately commingle with the forces and qualities that characterize our turning point. Trust is required, not a mentalized, theological, or inculcated trust, but rather an awakened trust, a trust that emerges from our core, a trust that is not merely in opposition to something else in us, a trust that is big enough to include both our yes and our no, a trust that allows us to blend fully with the currents of our turning point, to freely embrace, know, and embody the turbulence of it, the crosscurrents, the raging white waters, the frothing chaos, the brilliant force of its waves, the purpose-revealing depths, the unspeakable stillnesses...

If we thus trust, we will not, at least initially, know where we are being taken, but we won't need to know, because we will inevitably be carried to a new shore, a *truer* shore, a shore more allied to our center of Being. Right timing is essential. Too late doesn't work, because we'll have missed the momentum required to carry us through, and too soon doesn't work either, because to prematurely take the leap asked of us (as in spiritual ambition or enthusiasm) only leaves us in over our heads. In such a case, we're not adequately prepared; we're just looking ahead, dumbly impaled on our hope, doing little more than being smashed about by the waves, fighting just to rise to the surface, just to survive, and, even if we are cast up on some shore, it will only be the *same* old shore, the *same* old life, animated by the very *same* inclinations that first propelled us into our prema- ture plunge!

It is all too easy to turn a turning point into a crisis, to get worried about it, to get all frantic (or negatively romantic) about it, to so distress oneself that release is obsessively thought about and sought. As a remedy or some sort of thoroughly fulfilling sedation, compen- sation, or pleasurable excitation is hunted for, is sniffed, sucked, fucked, bought, sold, married, or whatever, the imperatives of one's turning point are no longer foreground, but just a muffled noise in the distance, an anaemic halftone, a faint knocking or calling that will soon fade even more, leaving us stranded where we've *already* been stranded, once again merely *dreaming* about a deeper shore, a truer life...

Finding ourselves thus stranded and not wanting to feel, *directly* feel, the sheer pain of what "we" are up to, we compulsively twist our dreams of a truer life into notions of some kind of heaven, some kind of non-stop immunity, a Utopian or infantile domain of perpetual wish-fulfillment. Eventually, we will perhaps slide into a cosy cyni-

cism, a knowledgeable resignation, or perhaps we'll remain sentimentalized and merely hopeful, ever further institutionalizing and
abstracting our longing for God, making an informational idol out of
possibility and promise, forcing ourselves to do good deeds, again
and again haranguing ourselves into making good resolutions, not realizing that another, counter-balancing aspect of us that doesn't give
a shit about such resolutions will inevitably sabotage them.

Thus do we further our self-fragmentation, not *tellingly* seeing our
inner conflict, but rather only projecting the *less visible* aspects of it
onto our environment, human and otherwise, slipping into a more
and more paranoid lookout for whatever threatens "us" (namely, that
cemented cluster of assumptions that is currently insisting on referring to itself as us), barricading ourselves not only against what could
harm us, but *also* against what could catalyze our freedom...

Turning points ask not for reactivity or a flight into thinking, prevari-
cation, or unillumined dramatization, but rather for guts and an
openness of eye and a willingness to come *fully* alive. Turning points
ask for an unobstructed link between belly and heart, between power
and love; they ask for both warriorhood and interior disarmament;
they ask for passion and awakened innocence; they ask for full-
blooded participation; they ask for a falling apart that leads not to
fragmentation, but to true wholeness.

Again and again, turning points implicitly invite us to change what
must be changed, in a natural rather than a preconceived or neurotically masterminded fashion. The dynamics and directives of such
change *spontaneously* emerge when we choose to enter its waters,
when we *choose* to recognize that we actually *are* at a turning point, a
transitional juncture, a time of extra energy, not the extra energy
generated by mere stimulation or a situational high, but the extra
energy that stems from our own readiness and need to take a particular leap...

The presence of a turning point is simply a confession of our ripeness
for a certain jump, a quantum jump. For an electron to shift to a
different atomic orbit, one closer to the nucleus, the heart of the
matter, extra energy is required, energy committed to *only* the jump,
such a shift being instantaneous through space, without time. Similarly, the leap asked of us is instantaneous, although the preparation
for it obviously is not. In fact, such preparatory work may take a lot

of time, a lot of clean-up and catalytic alignment... The jump is taken by the body (and not just the physical body) through space, multi-dimensional space, deeper into Being; it is not taken by the mind, except insofar as the mind is the invisible part of the body. The mind does not know how to take such a leap, for it is not designed to do so (except imaginally) — at best, it simply is brought into harmony with the rest of one's being both during and after the leap, taking care of business, dealing with logistics, helping out with functional details and the articulation of one's turning point (especially *after* such a passage, when insights arise like mushrooms after an autumn rain).

There are big turning points and there are much bigger ones, and there are small turning points and very small ones; in fact, *every* moment is a potential turning point, however miniscule or subtle. Every turning point intelligently entered into and made good use of prepares us for bigger or more demanding turning points. In its inevitable letting go, every turning point is a kind of death...

If we go into our actual Death without having successfully navigated lesser turning points, then we will in all likelihood not make good use of our Death — we will perhaps glimpse the Great Possibility of Being, the Brilliance of unqualified Awakening and Consciousness, the Godlight, the very Heart of Mystery, but It will all too soon be but a *dream* to us, a glorious but rapidly fading dream, and then only the weakest, most mirage-like sort of dream, a mere abstraction, a busybody cluster of mentalized artifacts turned into everyday belief and *ego-centered* Heaven-desire, which of course only resurrects every other desire of similar origin, and once again "we" are, through the very *attention* we've yielded to such desire, pulled back toward whatever most successfully bound us during our lifetime, not out of "choice", but out of *automatic* psychogravitational attraction...

To make an enemy out of a turning point is to unnecessarily resist Life, to deny Life Its inherent flux, Its built-in changeability, Its constant Play of manifestation. A turning point is an emotional, as well as a physical and psychospiritual, event; in fact, it needs a freedom of emotion, an undamming of feeling, to work fully. Without such freedom, such expansiveness and rawness of feeling, its waters, its waves and currents, won't exist for one except as a problem or nightmare. Turning points are chances to further awaken, to more fully embody ourselves — to make a problem out of them is to disconnect ourselves from our fundamental nature.

The more we turn away from honouring our small turning points, the more we deny them their existence and fruition, the more we try to drink, think, eroticize, or fantasize them away, the more we sink with their demands, the more we misread and mistreat them, the more likely it is that crisis will appear, most crises being but endarkened accumulations of aborted turning points, of unacknowledged, unexamined, unused, unloved turning points.

Sometimes the sheer magnitude of a crisis will shock us into alertness, just like a terrifying nightmare often can. However, if wakefulness is not a common practice for us, we will soon regress back into our everyday sleep, spasmodically tilting at our mind's version of our apparent difficulty, numbing ourselves as best we can. Then, to our disbelief, a bigger, nastier crisis will come along and really clobber us, and we'll complain vociferously, convincingly playing victim (or, conversely, pretend to take responsibility for the whole damned thing, such "responsibility" being but glamourized blame), repetitiously wishing that things were different, or *fairer*, not noticing that all the while each moment carries the same fundamental opportunity, the same primal invitation, an invitation that, when entered into fully, becomes a sacred demand that we journey to our Heartland, that we do everything we can to stand our true ground, that we cease being obsessed with fleshing out the mind of our false or sedated self...

A turning point, when embraced fully, may hurt like hell, but it's a good hurt, a purifying hurt, a hurt that deepens our receptivity to what we must do. The choice is not so much to enter or to not enter into a turning point, as it is to make or to not make good use of such an energy-field. We can't truly ever escape such energies — we can fend them off, we can anesthetize ourselves to them, but we can't actually flee them, for they are part of us, arising not only around and within us, but *as* us. In a sense, they, to the degree that they are consciously reunited with the rest of our being, reveal and reflect our evolutionary state, not from apecreature to human, but from slumber to awakening, from fragmentation to wholeness. This transition is intrinsic to our true destiny. It cannot be rewritten, but it can be postponed, denied, or dungeoned into apparent non-being.

Big turning points are simply potential quickenings of the Awakening process, shocks of marvelous magnitude, veined with an intensity needing only the spark of our full participation to become Grace in action. Of course, big turning points can be fought with such stubborn force that we eventually become incredibly run down, depleted, eroded, so that when the next wave fills out our horizon, even if it's a much more benign one, a much more apparently inviting one, we just don't have enough energy left to wade in, let alone get our clothes off...

We tend to look for clarity *within* a turning point, not realizing that its opaque turbulence, its churning crosscurrents, are *inherent* to it, offering not clarity, but (if we *dive* in) a passage *into* clarity, a ride into full-bodied understanding. Nevertheless, we still are inclined to try to *think* our way into such knowingness, trying to wrestle our confusion into a semblance of clarity, failing to differentiate between thinking about what's on the other side and actually making the journey there.

Turning points, despite their chaos, contain a deep organic stillness, a vibrant inner silence, a pure pulsation of unbound Being. This stillpoint, this condensation of transverbal clarity, cannot be found, but only *embodied*, radiantly embodied, for it exists at and as the very core of us, *already* present no matter what "we" do. It is not realized through a repression of passion or desire, nor through a subjugation or restructuring of thought, nor through meditative strategy — it is already the case when we are true to ourselves, when we are unambiguously present, when we are stably established in non-situational happiness. This is not the stillpoint of typical meditation or inwardness, of refuge from desire and vitality, but rather the very Heart of feeling, the very Force of Being, the very Essence of What Is. It is not some quiet little nook somewhere, some bucolic little retreat — It is vibrant with latent force, awesomely potent, surrounded by prisms of Being, through which It emanates, ever manifesting Itself in all kinds of shapings, exquisitely appropriate birthings and dyings, myriad comings and goings...

The hubbub around the heart of a turning point, all the wildness and chaos, is simply the fertile outreaching of the turning point, its flowering, its song, its marvellously opportunistic circumference, its *interface* with our resistance. If the turbulence of its periphery is entered into without restraint and with awareness, we're not then just spun around on the surface, forced to go in circle after exhausting circle, but instead are spiralled toward the core, as in a natural whirlpool, and sometimes not even spiralled, but simply propelled from one fluid orbit to another closer to the core, a deeper concentric circle of Truth's unrehearsable flow. This is the opportunity of a turning point. It is present in every moment, but some moments possess more of a timely build-up of free energy. Our work, our deep need, is not to dissipate this energy, but to ride it, to yield to its momentum, to not prevaricate or hesitate or masturbate away its rawness, its incredible vulnerability, its opportunity...

The appropriate use of the energies of a turning point is carried within it, as in a seedcase, a seedcase that's both a deepsea treasure-chest and a bit of spherical night ready to burst with greenstreaming light. A turning point is a risk worth taking; its innate wisdom, its wisdom of flow, is ours if we will but dive in and dive deep. Cry a river, rage a storm, uncage your beast, do whatever it takes — there are not higher stakes.

Do not look for clarity in a turning point. Do not look for security or guarantees. Simply trust. Don't believe in anything. Simply trust, not out of some sort of submission, but out of wakeful surrender, realizing that what is asked of you through your turning point has *always* been asked of you. And, moreover, the riper you get, the more compellingly you will be asked, until one day you won't be asked nor invited, but absolutely *required* to participate. You then will have no choice but to take the jump, but it won't matter because there'll be nothing else for you to do.

Turning points are wonderfully visceral confessions of our readiness for a certain leap, a passage into a more fitting level of Being. Use them as such. Don't bother worrying about what's coming; instead of looking ahead, look inside your looking. Look and leap at the same time, knowing that it's always time for the sacred reunion of all that you are...

Wildwinged Shapeshifters Disassembling Your Mind

Bathe in my waterfall of liberated pain, letting the dawning daylight rainbow it into a deeper wonder, letting the fatly mossed cliffsides pulsate in rejuvenative rhythm with your broken breath, your long-crushed, panic-sweetened breath, your multi-armed embodiment of every species of Death, and bathe also beneath the falls, far below the cascading white thunder, down where silent pools sparkle with meltingly ter-raced grace and crystalline welcome, for there you will find more than greenblue embrace and rippling epiphany, more than reflections of former faces, more than the stillpoint of joy and grief, more than ease and relief, more than a reminder to not pretend that you have fully arrived...

Do you not now, softly stretching now, hear a different kind of thunder, a verdantly galloping tapestry of drumbeat wonder, lush with gonged throb and primordial demand? Do you not now sense the unshuttered panorama of eyes behind your eyes, the overlapping dreams that are more than dreams, the wild-winged shapeshifters disassembling your mind? There is an undoing here, a reopening, an unsuspected cliffside trail, a ravishing vertigo, a macheted clearing, a velvet slide, a stormy desert, a shrieking wasteland, a bloody snowfield, a falling apart, an abandoned rhyme, a glory and a crime, a castle of gold and a miserly dime, and there is something else too, throbbing between the lines and inside the designs, a knowing-ness that forever eludes the nets of even the most sublime pages and spiritual cages —

A figure staggers from the jungle-fringed tundra, almost falling beneath the weight of its enormous, eagle-headed mask, scream-ing coherently and unerringly, syllable upon raspily ecstatic syllable, for the spiritdance of your deeper truth, your buried exultation, your closeted suffering, your padlocked whirlwinds and black blizzards, your depravity and your luminosity, your secret shame, your virginal lust for the Holy, your skymaking soulbursting, your dream-riddled door, your long-denied yet inescapable core...

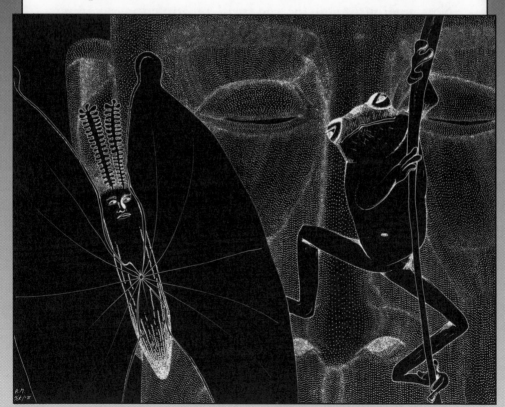

Slowly, very slowly, the mask's lower lip droops silverycrimson and asymmetrically swollen just above its carrier's trembling knees, and its three eyes roll and greenly glisten, looking not at you, nor solely through you, but with you, until you find yourself sitting naked amidst equatorial greens, halfway up a burnt lavender slope, carving a similar mask with rapturous absorption, your spear leaning against the side of a hut bulging with thrillingly paroxysmal cries of crowning labour, the arriving newborn already gazing upon you in your vision, helping you to bring life to your carving, the very grain of which is saturated with untranslatable tales, myths of glory and horror, travesty and transcendence, remembrance and forgetting, stories of all time artfully bound and fitted into the unlimited storage of Now, singing through the woodswirl and aromatic reshaping...

Did it really matter that the mask would probably only be worn by someone who took it as no more than a ritualized prop? No, no more than it mattered if the beaded pools evaporated, or if the sky moaned with jagged fire, or if the pages of scripture became but confetti, or if the highdensity discs outspun their overload of information, or if we stopped expecting something special or ultimately transfiguring to happen to all of this...

And if we call Existence God's Mask, then who does the dance, and who beats the drum, and who turns these into questions? The depths and the shallows together invite both your plunge and your rise, your nakedness and your every disguise, not caring that your mind obsessively campaigns for an answer, an all-consoling symbology, a fastfood metaphor, a reproducible door; all the while, I circle round and round, carving out a multidirectional spiral, a pearly spin, a Moebius strip of Spirit, a nacreous infolding both of precise focus and revelatory expansion, inlaid with shimmeringly seductive chambers bejewelled with infinite possibility and opalescent opportunity, chambers interconnected by an all too easily forgotten tubularity of Being, an eternally-arising passage of trial, stillbirth, rotting history, breakthrough, and unspeakable Illumination. Permit yourself remembrance, not necessarily of details and history, but of unveiled Presence, of the Obviousness of Being, and of something else too, something that is not merely a something, nor even a someone, but rather the very Heart of Mystery, the very Face of the Faceless, the ecstatically paradoxical Truth of You, the Truth That's prior to every view...

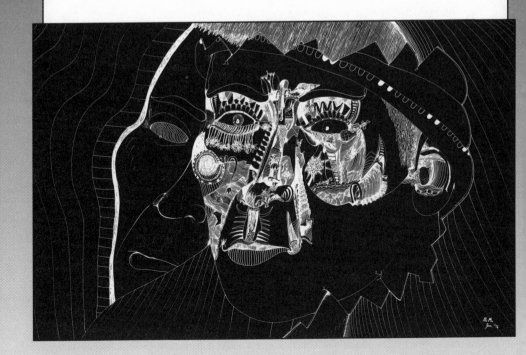

He Wants His Money Back

So you say you did everything for her
Just to hear her purr
Milked yourself silly
Performed without a cry
Injected deodorized smiles into your appetite
Giving everything but yourself
Living everything but your Life
Now she's said so long
And you want to make her wrong
Thunder your fury and fuck her with your outrage
It's your problem, you say she said
And you flee up to your head
Tripping over your urbane reply
Half-seeing her swaying hips,
Her hard curves, her slightly swollen lips
Her proud back and aerobics ass
All of it like a noose around your balls
Pulled ever tighter
By the attention you lavish on your thoughts of her
Your screaming thoughts of what could be
So you did everything for her
Except trust her with your undressed heart
She was the opposite of Mommy, wasn't she?
A beacon in your penile fantasy
Her barren tears falling on your umbrella
Her need and yours
Left to die in a tundra of greed
A double whiskey on the rocks

–32–
The Creation of Sexual Charge As Compensation for the Loss of Self

Sexual excitation, contrary to near-unanimous opinion, is not something that just *happens* to us — it *is* our choice, however unconsciously made, a deliberate gathering and focusing of Life-Energy. All too often, such choice is exercised not in the service of our well-being, but rather only on behalf of our craving for security, comfort, stimulating safety, and pleasurable distraction from our suffering. Yes, the choice is almost always unknowingly made, but the very fact of such unconsciousness must itself be recognized as *our* doing...

It is natural to feel attracted to certain people, but not *necessarily* natural to automatically condense or redirect that attraction, or gravitational pull, into sexual excitation, which I'll refer to from now on as charge. The transition from generalized attraction to charge is an unknown territory to most, a no-one's-land usually muddied by hastily trampled integrity. Charge is but biochemical thrill, mixing together amplified sensation and eroticized anticipation. Whether it is personified or not, it ordinarily is just the leading edge, or wedge, of *unilluminated* lust. Most of all, however, charge is something *we* are doing to ourselves, something reassuringly engrossing, something we engage in not so as to deepen our awakening from our conditioning, but rather so as to *exploit* its possibilities, to somehow maximize or fortify our pleasure. Such is the engorged evidence of our having turned away from Ecstasy, God-communion, and truly human relationship.

You could say that the creation of charge is, for almost all, compensation for the loss of what we *naturally* are, a painfully blatant confession of being marooned from our core of Being. This is why charge is, beneath its pinkened periphery, usually so cunningly desperate, so obsessively concerned with both its satisfaction and its continuation. But just *what* gets satisfied? Not *us!* There is no real satisfaction here, only relief and psychospiritual enervation. Sex cannot truly satisfy nor nourish us, if charge persists as its foundation; in fact, it can then only degenerate, until the distance or numbness of feeling that was there all along is undeniably *there*, daylight naked, unseeded with awareness. Real sex is not dependent on charge — its passion arises not from mere stimulation or cultivated eroticism, but from deep, open-eyed intimacy, trust, and a well-rooted commitment to vibrant aliveness. Its passion's atmosphere is not the acculturated noise of self-contained charge, but the music of silence, spirit-communion, and ecstatically lusty love.

Charge is a kind of self-advertising, serving, to varying degrees, to proclaim our availability and potency; everything tends to be just an object for its calculating eye, a harbinger of sexual possibility and hope (romantic and otherwise). This is not to put down charge, but to address its ubiquitous abuse. If intimacy really is our priority, then charge becomes but a lovely, juicy sparking that colorfully supports and celebrates our intimacy.

When we, however, create charge with those with whom we are not lovers, we usually then only rob our lover (or lovers) of a significant amount of passion and interest, making ourselves *less vulnerable* to them. Our promiscuity, however subtly presented or disguised, keeps our intimacies unnecessarily unstable, for we are, through our irresponsibly eroticized wandering of attention, almost always on the verge of betraying them. Thus do we protect "ourselves," refusing to be naked in our self-revelations, again and again consoling ourselves with neurotic suggestiveness and titillating rituals of body and mind!

The point, however, is not to repress such charge, but rather to become *conscious* of how *we* actually create it. Move from energy-dissipation to energy-conservation. Move from pleasure to Ecstasy. Relocate from here to a deeper here. Stop advertising your availability. Stop being a slave to the creation of charge; stop relying on the presence of charge to make you feel better. Stop teasing yourself and others with erotic possibility!

Make love the context, not sentimentalized, romantic, or otherwise deluded love, but rather love passion-bright and streaming with subtlety and integrity, and charge will take care of itself, ordinarily arising only in the company of your sexual intimate(s). If charge persistently *and* cleanly arises elsewhere, then that must be addressed. In any case, take charge of your every charge. Don't look for rushes. Feel into what you *really* need, and feel into it now, uninhibitedly embodying your need. Feel the One with Whom you are already lovers, and let that feeling (which transcends all emotionalism) permeate and light up all your relationships, instead of just turning away and compensating for your loss by clinging to lesser needs through the engineering of charge.

Love, *then* make love. An unspeakable Profundity awaits you, and your awakened sexuality is both your key to It, and your participation in Its Revelatory Mystery. Read between the lines of this essay/talk, and read with more than your mind, and the sacred gestures of the lover that you at essence are will fill out your room, spilling out the obviousness of what could not be articulated in this piece...

-33-

The Exploding Heart of Fleshed-out Ecstasy: Orgasm, Appetite, & God

STELLA: I'm bothered by my not orgasming very often...

ROBERT: Why make a problem out of whether or not orgasm occurs? Plenty of women who have orgasms, frequent orgasms, are out of touch with themselves and their partner — they've just learned to rub themselves the right way, to fine-adjust the slide and thrust. Instead, concern yourself with your *overall* well-being, and orgasm will, in almost all cases, take care of itself. Don't reach for it; surrender to your depths, and orgasm will possess you, spontaneously and fully. The surrender I speak of is not to the man, nor to your own notions of how things should go, but rather to the totality of the experience. It's an amalgam of trust, love, magic, transcendence of ritualism... It's not a blind surrender, nor is it a security-promising swoon. It's extraordinarily ordinary. (*Long pause*) So what's happening with you and Richard [*her lover*]?

STELLA: I know I don't fully orgasm when we make love.

ROBERT: Well, do you partially orgasm?

STELLA: I think so. It's very subtle...

ROBERT: And it's very easy to generate pseudo-blissful sensations through sexplay, without any attending love, and it's also just as easy to mistake these sensations for real feelings, to take their presence as a sign of intimacy! Sometimes they're very subtle, and sometimes they're extremely electric and compelling, but fundamentally they're just *sensations*, byproducts of stimulation and fantasy. Their climax is not true orgasm, but only a dead-end spasm, a discharging of energy, an emptying of vitality. There's no such thing as a partial orgasm, except to your ego! As an ego, you'd love to announce that you've just had a partial orgasm — better than nothing! But maybe you're speaking of orgasmicness, of what we might call a highly charged relaxation, a kind of non-explosive deliciousness of sensation...

STELLA: Well, I feel orgasmic when I make love with Richard, I do!

ROBERT: And what happens when it starts to peak or really build?

STELLA: I feel ecstasy, but I don't have a physical orgasm.

ROBERT: Do you *psychically* have an orgasm? You're still covering your ego's ass. You must admit you don't come, but at least you have the compensation of acting as if you feel ecstasy! As long as you persist in so pretending, you'll never get to the root of what's troubling you sexually. The point is not to put yourself down, but to get more honest. You must stop hiding your insecurity with your *supposed* ecstasy!

STELLA: I used to have physical orgasms, but I wasn't happy...

ROBERT: Regardless of its other dimensions, orgasm is physical, physiological — it does not occur independent of the body. It can be patterned out on scientists' equipment. Basically, it's just an energy release and redistribution. If you are open enough, the forces of orgasm will not just be discharged through the lower terminals of the body, but will instead permeate the entire bodymind. Not just the physical body, but *all* your bodies, *all* your levels of embodiment! All of you! In this, every aspect of you will benefit. Most of the time, however, orgasm just empties us of some tension, leaving us more groggy than alert, more sedated than sensitized. It pleasures us into *staying* in our cages, seducing us with a briefly lingering taste of the Beyond. But *real* orgasm abides in freedom, in love, in profound empathy — it is not the peak of sexual stimulation, but rather the exploding heart of fleshed-out Ecstasy...

It's not that you should always have orgasms with Richard, but that the capacity for orgasm must be allowed to be present. That is, come to sex already *happy*. If you're unhappy, then explore *that*, instead of just fucking away its intensity! If what precedes orgasm is not Joy, then orgasm will not be Joy, but only water going down the drain. Orgasms produced by self-manipulation are at best only masturbatory, juicily non-relational, neurotically private... The right angle, the right pressure, the right clit-touch, the right fantasy, the right hump, bump, grind, and mind... Again, a true orgasm is not masturbatory. It's participatory. It's a vulnerable sharing, a rapturously alive caring. It's luminously emotional. It's a wondrous giving. Unfortunately, most people, when they arrive at their Big Moment (or Little Death) get stingy, all wrapped up in their own peaking sensations, holding back their fullness, holding back their feelings, permitting themselves only a trickle of real Joy — and how can they truly let go here, when they aren't doing so in the rest of their lives? How can they?

I don't think that you're stingy, though. Your difficulty has more to do with your bedrock prudery. Even when you act like a wanton woman, a lusty, wide-open wench, there's still an inner holding, a chronic tension, a terror of being really spontaneous. However much you exaggerate your outward display of ecstasy and sexual looseness, your inner holding is *still there*, gripping your core like a bulldog, silently screaming out its mistrust and hurt... You know how to fake emotion. You know what it's like to pretend that you're more turned on than you actually are, don't you?

STELLA: Yes.

ROBERT: It gives you more power over Richard — you know how good he feels to hear you moaning and groaning and panting and calling out *his* name! Your apparent orgasmicness makes him feel more like a man, so he's not about to stop your pretence, is he?

STELLA: No... Last time we were making love, I caught myself acting turned on, when I didn't really feel it.

ROBERT: Was he faking it, too?

STELLA: No. He was definitely very turned on, very eager, very lusty...

ROBERT: How can you *make love* with someone who's so easily fooled by you? On the other hand, how could *you* make love with someone who *wasn't* fooled by you? You see, your primary concern during sex isn't to make love, but is to fortify your position in your relationship with him, to keep him on the leash, to *make him want you*. But trading sex for security is *not* a good deal! Control upon control... (*Long pause*)

Why chain your passion to your survival-programs? The Feminine in
you cries out for release, cries out for no more entombment, but for
enwombment... You don't trust the Woman in you; you feel safer with
your more male characteristics, but they are the traits of *diseased*
maleness — non-spontaneity, rigid scheduling, obsessive control,
mind-dominance...

Stop trying to look so sincere! So much of your life is just a trying,
trying and trying, and then some more trying — such a strain! Trying
to be happy is only more unhappiness. Trying to be a hot number is
only a zero in the face of real sex! Trying doesn't work, because it
carries a built-in counter-effort, an opposite impulse. Trying is only
partiality, perpetual self-dividedness — it is as tense as it is dense.
Trying kills the possibility of Ecstasy. If sex is plagued by trying, the
solution is not *more* trying, including spiritual trying! You can't make
yourself be spontaneous — you can only allow it. So what can you
do? Stop trying!! Stop *trying* to understand me! What I'm saying to
you is far more obvious to you than you're letting on...

Make no gesture during sex that takes you away from your love.
Sometimes no gesture at all is what's appropriate, but do not make a
virtue out of stillness. Do not tolerate less than love from yourself or
from him; do not accept its semblance, but insist on the real thing.
Love yourself enough to stop in the middle of sex if you have to, or
to weep, or to uncork your fear, or to be ecstatic. Don't just fuck;
take *real* risks. Then sex will not just be sex, but Love intensified,
Love dancing in lusty overflow, Love radiant with Soul...

Don't get sucked into repetition, nor into mere novelty. An arm
around the waist may be lovely one love-making time, and a hell of a
cramp another time. The dance of give and take has to be moment-
to-moment informed by Being. There's no trying in this, but only
essence-centered doing and vital Silence. Become more sensitive to
how you "effort", to how you get greedy for more and more of what
feels good — continuing a delicious movement past its natural con-
clusion will only numb you. More is not always more!

When you try to mastermind your own rhythms, you miss a deeper
rhythm, a truer rhythm. The primal currents of Being are inaccessible to you when you're mind-driven, and also when you're lost in a

romantic swoon. Make room for sacred undulations, for unfathomable waves. Let sex become a dance of energy, simultaneously personal and transpersonal. In deep sex, the body is experienced more as energy than as matter, wave upon wave, richly pulsating. Waves, Stella, waves of every kind, waves that you ride until you *are* them... There's no point in trying to control such waves — trust them! Let them unfold as they will. Let them break and shatter and reform and glisten and moan and whisper and roar and be still. (*Long pause*) Orgasm is like a great wave hitting the shore, a whitewater rupturing of energy, a starburst embodiment, a Mystery far too obvious for the mind to grasp, far too gorgeous to be commented upon, far too Real to be exactly repeatable...

STELLA: In talking with the other women, I've thought of giving voice to the part of me that doesn't want to fully orgasm, and going right into it... (*She does, briefly, but her sounds are, despite their volume and intensity, strained, subtly choked back*)

ROBERT: You're still trying... You're performing your desired-for letting-go, instead of letting *it* take you! The Male in you is crushing the Female, grinding It down, down, down... Can't you feel this? (*She cries*) The iron glance and steely authority telling you to be a good little girl, or else... And who wants to get burnt at the stake again?

STELLA: I'm so, so sick of holding back! (*Crying*) I still feel a deep holding in my pelvis, a kind of locking. If I was really honest, I'd say that right in the middle of sex, no matter how turned-on I am, I feel pain, a deep, deep sadness, a hurt that seems like it could never be healed.

ROBERT: Much of that sadness is the grief of having abandoned your core, your innocence, your virginal Self... Give yourself to it during sex — stop trying to look like you're having a good time! Don't fuck away your tears; cry them, and cry them *fully*! I'm not talking about self-pitying or sentimentalized crying, which only obstructs sex, but *real* crying, crying from the core, crying from the heart, the belly, the soul. Such crying can only moisten and deepen intimacy, regardless of whether or not the sexing continues... If your crying doesn't take you deeper, then it's just a tension-release or poor-me dramatics. Ecstasy has no problem with crying, nor with any other emotion, unless that particular emotion is *mind-generated*.

Ecstasy satisfies the soul, but pleasure only satisfies the egoic programming that so often masquerades as us. Ecstasy is *already* loose,
already alive, but pleasure is not — it is fucked into being, rubbed,
pumped, and humped into action, carrying with it an innate tension,
a disease of feeling, a tagalong load of time-release pain, the pain of
making our well-being dependent on having something in particular
happen... Ecstasy, on the other hand, inheres in a realm free of such
neurotic dependency; Ecstasy is already uncompromisingly intimate
with a much deeper dependency, namely that epitomized by Universal interrelatedness...

Ecstasy is a bodily acknowledgment of God, a fleshy yes-saying to
Existence, a full-blooded celebration of Undying yet Everchanging
Communion. In Ecstasy, our body loses its solidity, its perceptual
framework, and becomes more and more spacious, more and more
alive, not tensely alive, but loosely alive, until it is God's Body,
pulsating with Love's shapings and personifications... You might call
this the Energy-Body, or when it's really out there, the Cosmic-
Body, the Flesh of the Divine... (*Lengthy pause*) So back we go to
orgasm, back to you trying not to worry about worrying about it!
People may find sex and all its preliminaries to be a drag after a
while (especially if they've been married for more than a couple of
years), but they still do it, 'cause of the rush of orgasm. So much
scrambling, sweating, fretting, and hoopla for such a short moment!

The Big Moment, a brief expansion, and back comes rushing the
mind, with a vengeance, or maybe just with a shopping list! (*Laughter*) If you're not loving your partner, you'll soon be pulling back,
because you'll have had your fill. The ice cream's gone, and you want
to get away. There's no appetite left. If you've *overfed*, you'll probably
be subtly repulsed by your partner, unless you can repulse *that*, and
fake some tenderness. All in all, it's much harder to pretend when
the rushes ain't there to hide behind. But if you've been *truly* loving
each other, then after orgasm, you'll still feel very close, very intimate, not at all prone to pulling back; you'll be able to meet each
other's eyes in joy and gratitude, without the slightest trace of romanticism or any other such pollutant...

So don't act. Or *deliberately* act, so long as you let him know what
you are doing — go ahead and experiment, but take the acting *all the
way*, right to its scriptless center. If you get scared scriptless, let that
be — wail, scream, weep, but don't lose touch with him! Don't lose

yourself in your undammed emotion. And if you're not turned on, don't try to arouse yourself! If you could just as easily be in the kitchen reading a newspaper, say so!

And don't always assume that if there's a fuck-up, it must be *your* fault! Maybe he isn't so clean, either, despite his ardent lust! If he wants to keep fucking when you're faking it, *where* the hell is he? Feel free to say that you're bored or hurt or sad or angry or whatever. Stop in the middle of your panting, and look at each other, deeply, and don't get pelvic until your eyes are pure with mutual love and desire...

STELLA: That's what we did the last time. We stopped for quite a while, and then I started feeling really turned-on.

ROBERT: So what happened?

STELLA: I felt it in my belly, a lot of very warm feelings in my belly, and some in my heart, too.

ROBERT: Not in your vagina?

STELLA: Not very much... (*She talks for a while about her first lover, whom she says she felt far more sexual with than with Richard*)

ROBERT: Why do you think you were more pelvically drawn to him than to Richard?

STELLA: With him, my heart wasn't involved. It was safer...

ROBERT: My guess is that there was an added thrill to it, because you, un*married* you, got to go against your Catholic conditioning. You got to play dirty girl, right under the Pope's nose!

STELLA: It was very much like that. I remember one time... I actually was on the way to Church, and I turned away and went to his house and fucked him...

ROBERT: It was a thrill, a welcome antidote to the barrenness of your forcefed piety and goodgirl sincerity! There's a thrill in thumbing your nose at authority, in masturbating when your parents are in the next room, in brazenly shedding your clothes, in having sex when you supposedly shouldn't be having sex... (*Pause*)

With numbing regularity, we betray ourselves so as to maximize our sexual charge — we prostitute ourselves before the altar of heightened sexual sensation, making sexual charge or excitation the cornerstone of our sexual relationships, while talking up a storm about love, friendship, and commitment! Da Free John once said that eroticism is maximum bodily or personal pleasure with minimum intimacy. Don't you see that you eroticize yourself not out of love, but because you're marooned from Ecstasy, marooned from your core of Being? If you weren't thus stranded, you'd *already* feel so damned good, so juicily alive, so sensitively and dynamically present, that you wouldn't need to get turned-on — you'd already be there, *naturally* there!

Typical thrill-seeking is just the activation of thrill-emptying machinery, of biochemical discharge. We build up our sexual charge, making a TV Valhalla out of its climax, eagerly rushing toward the dumping of such charge — we fuck away our desire to fuck! We have a very low tolerance for sexual excitation; we crave being turned-on, but as soon as we are, we crave being free of it!

And, furthermore, the more tension we have, the bigger our release will need to be. Thus do we tend to associate sex with distress, with violence — the stronger the conflict, the hotter the sex. This is why friendship, true friendship, is so very rare between lovers. People are, in general, far more interested in fucking those with whom they sense a conflict, an abrasiveness, especially if it's similar to what they experienced with the parent with whom they had the strongest or most compelling charge. The conflict I'm talking about here is not healthy conflict, but rather stagnant conflict, mechanical conflict, conflict whose wounds have not been tellingly exposed to the Light. A sense of danger generates charge, and so does hope, especially romanticized hope... (*Pause*)

We keep in near-constant heat by means of the very same mechanism whereby we keep in near-constant anxiety; in fact, the two partially neutralize each other, and neuter our true passion, wearing us down into ever-increasing blandness — hence the look-a-like faces of the old, at least in our culture, most of them plastered with the same old mask, the look of Life lived half-heartedly, Life punctuated by erosive thrill...

Typical sex is like a rehearsal for a mediocre death. Its obsession with thrill-seeking and make-believe love blocks the arising of a very different kind of thrill, the joy that arises from a conscious marriage of love and sexual yearning. Why engineer your passion when the real thing is so close by? You might as well buy an inflatable lover, a balloon with an erection! (*Laughter*) Let's get more specific — you've been saying for awhile that you're sexually attracted to Alan — do you want to make love with him?

STELLA: Yeah... (*Hesitant*)

ROBERT: How much?

STELLA: I would really like to make love to Alan... (*Very quietly spoken*)

ROBERT: And after?

STELLA: When I thought about it this week, I kept seeing how he has his hands full with what he's doing with Claire...

ROBERT: Is that going to stop you? Let's shift a little, and talk with the ruthless Stella. Let's assume we're not concerned with integrity or any other similar inconvenience; let's give the foreground to heat, pleasure, thrill, sexual feasting... (*Laughter*)

STELLA: All of a sudden, I'm turned on! (*Laughter*)

ROBERT: Don't you feel a lot lighter without a conscience, especially a guilt-plagued conscience? So you're juiced up, without any interference from your mind, although we could say that a certain sort of permissive thought had something to do with your rapid turn-on! Ordinarily, you judge yourself for feeling sexual, and then judge yourself for having such judgments! This desire, however, is purer, much purer, much closer to Being — all it needs is some sensitivity, love, and real empathy. Instead, though, you either indulge it or suppress it, keeping it stuck in the status of an "it" — but it's not an "it"! It's *you*! Why disown it? Why treat it the way your parents treated *you*? Why keep it in the basement? (*Long pause*)

But back to Alan... The turn-on you feel with him, do you also feel it with Richard? Your head is trying to nod, but it won't. You know that

Richard is going to hear this tape, too, and you know that he's going to listen *very* closely! She's struggling to say yes to you, Richard, but don't worry — we're going to go deeper! (*Laughter*) This is not the end of the session! There is more Stella to come! (*Pause*) Do you see how strained your upcoming "yes" was?

STELLA: Yeah... I immediately started thinking about the consequences...

ROBERT: My guess is that Alan's *not* more appealing to you, but that he's more taboo, and hence more laced with charge. You've got a husband, namely Richard, and here you are, feeling all hot and wet with this other guy, this darkly alluring stranger. But if you were already lovers with Alan, and Richard was with another woman, I'll bet you'd start feeling very sexually attracted to Richard, especially when Alan became boringly familiar to you. So what's the *real* relationship here? Not between Stella and Alan, not between Stella and Richard, but rather between Stella and her sexual excitation!

STELLA: You're so fucking smart! (*Laughter*)

ROBERT: Too bad! (*Laughter*) Now, if I hypnotized you into thinking that Richard was with another woman, and that he secretly desired you, not her, you'd be fantasizing left and right about him. He'd be walking naked through your dreams! (*Laughter*) So, no offense, Alan, if you're listening to this tape, but most of her heat for you is not because you're such a wonderful person, such a good-looking hunk, but because you're not her husband! Makes sense, doesn't it?

STELLA: Oh yes! (*Laughter*)

ROBERT: Implicit in all this is your need to encounter the you who wants to hurt Richard, the you who'd like to make him feel really threatened, the you who'd like to have *all the men* fighting over her. It's not about sex at all, is it? It's about power, control, security... Sexual charge is just a pawn, a pulsating decoy, a juicy lure, in this domain, this game... (*Long pause*)

It's interesting that your strongest sexual pull is to Alan, given that he's far more repressed sexually than the other men in the community — his very tension and fear around his sexuality, plus his lithe seductiveness, gives him a strongly magnetic quality at times, a highly charged promise. In an odd way, you feel safer with him, 'cause you know that if you get close to him, he'll pull back, especially once he's gorged himself on the egoic glory of having yet another woman turned on to him... And what's the big deal about attraction? You're drawn to each other just like flies are to cottage cheese at a picnic! Or maggots to a corpse. It's totally mechanical, including all the accompanying emotionalism and ardent talk of relationship! (*Laughter*)

Attraction is attraction. It's a primitive mechanism, just a matter of biophysics, except for those in whom the Awakening process is stably established — for them, attraction, including sexual attraction, is not merely automatic nor ego-serving, but instead is in Life-affirming alignment with the dictates of their Being. (*Pause*)

But back to Alan... You must stop confusing him with what he does. He wants women to want him, and when they show that they do, he's finished with them. He's still busy making up for the absence of his mother, his motherless infancy, but his satisfaction, like yours, is only *partial*. He wants to keep mothering at a certain distance, just beyond potential *smothering* range, so he can feel in control; it's terrifying for him to fully yield to a woman, for that plunges him into the black abyss of his orphan years. He seeks control through an alluring passivity, a charmingly animalistic magnetism, a pseudo-sexual charisma — of course, he knows this now, and is working his way through it, but your manner of being with him is a hindrance, a reinforcer of his worst habits. Sure, he can use it, in the sense of using a negative circumstance as an opportunity for growth, but it's still a loveless act on your part — when you play out titillation games with him, you're no friend of his!

STELLA: I feel sad about that... (*Long pause*)

ROBERT: When we get turned on, we usually want to do something about it, use it for some purpose or the other, brick in our little world some more. It's quite a different matter to feel our desire, and simply enjoy it, without enslaving it to any particular program. Let it be there; let it grow, let it glow. Why fuck or fantasize or think it away? Why yield to the compulsion to get rid of such desire? Why not make room for it? Isn't it bizarre that so many struggle to get turned-on, to get eroticized, just so that they can then get rid of what they've built up? They struggle to create something just so that they can destroy it! Hence the meat of the expression "I got fucked!" Do you not recognize the disappointment, however wryly coated, in such a statement?

STELLA: Yes... What a fucking shame! (*Laughter*)

ROBERT: For most, we're either turned-on animals, rooting away, indulging and feasting, fastened to pleasuring, or else we're civilized goody-goodies, discretely buttoned-up, even ascetic. The real work is to purify *both*, to embody both raw passion and discriminating intelligence, to be an awakened lover! It's the pearl hidden in the epithet "Holy fuck!" So where the hell am I going with this? Just think of the things people tend to say during sex, all the sentimentalized, charge-inducing, or grovellingly graphic words! All the "true love" moanings, all the "fuck me" pleas!

STELLA: I want to say them! (*Laughter*)

ROBERT: You mean you *do*! (*Laughter*)

STELLA: Not *me*! (*Laughter*)

ROBERT: Maybe it would increase your orgasmic potential to imagine some ecclesiastical authority watching you and Richard when you were close to coming; imagine the Pope and your mother and father walking into the heaving room, with swinging rosaries and salvation Hallelujahs! (*Laughter*) Whatever upped the charge, whatever fed it... There's a book in which a really gross old movie star, an exaggerated kind of aged Mae West, is being fucked by a hot young stud, fucked hard. As soon as she starts to come, he pushes her down two or three flights of stairs; she doesn't die, but bones get broken, and she says it was worth it, 'cause it was the most *thrilling* experience of her life. Or consider the place in Leonard Cohen's novel *Beautiful Losers*, where the narrator is driving down a late-night highway at a tremendous speed, while his buddy/mentor F. is masturbating him — suddenly, just as he's about to come, a gigantic barrier appears just down the highway, a pure white wall, only a few seconds away. There's no time to stop, but he tries to stop, and they go through the wall, which is just a huge sheet that's been hung up by F., and our poor narrator, of course, didn't come. He missed his big chance! (*Laughter*)

We so easily deify erotic charge! We crave maximizing it. A sense of threatenedness can intensify sexual charge, and what's the extreme of that? Death. (*Long pause*) God is not the ultimate Orgasm. God-Realization is not perpetual orgasmicness. To even view it in sexual terms is only a confession of our obsession with sex and orgasm. Nowadays, orgasm is in — it's no big deal to talk about it. Total orgasm. Cosmic orgasm. Tantric orgasm. Peak orgasm. Valley orgasm. Orgasm, orgasm, orgasm! It's just sex getting stuck in a pelvic headlock, however tantrically clothed or legitimized...

As long as sex is bound up with mind, there is no sexual freedom, but only the ongoing exploitation of the pleasures possible *within* the cage, the favorite usually being that of orgasm. So much psychological baggage is attached to having orgasms! A lot of women don't orgasm, except perhaps with a lot of manipulation, but most men don't orgasm either, unless you call a contracted spasm of ejaculatory pleasure an orgasm — if a man's not open emotionally, there's no way he can fully orgasm! In fact, most men tighten up as they're coming, subtly or not-so-subtly tensing themselves against the radiant openness of the energy of orgasm. Such a fear of surrender...

How do you feel now?

STELLA: I feel really good, relaxed...

ROBERT: Yes... You're more expansive now, more at ease. Do you see how your typical pleasure, your typical games of sexual suggestiveness, are just a kind of disturbance, carrying a built-in tension? Ecstasy, on the other hand, is inherently peaceful, however vital Its expression. Pleasure, ordinary pleasure, knows no peace — its end-result sedation is but a parody of real peace. Ecstasy loves; pleasure doesn't. Ecstasy is non-manipulative; pleasure is not. Pleasure is trying to get somewhere; Ecstasy is already there. Pleasure is addictive; Ecstasy is not...

STELLA: Sometimes when I feel sexually turned-on, it's actually quite irritating...

ROBERT: Yes. Beneath its theatricalness and its power-payoffs, it can be quite disturbing. It's like an itch. You want to scratch it. You simultaneously inflame and numb it, without seeing that *you* are generating it. Look at the hoopla around aphrodisiacs — the deader we are, the more we crave being enlivened, but we don't want our enlivening to upset our hard-earned security, so we settle for the rewards of sensory stimulation, doing our best to forget all about Ecstasy, or to reduce It to a kind of peak-pleasure. There's even a drug known as Ecstasy. Anything to enhance bodily pleasure, anything to distract ourselves from our suffering. Urethral irritants, amyl nitrate, dexedrine, oysters, animus power, alcohol, vibrators, and on and on...

But what's the true aphrodisiac? Love! Full-bodied, full-souled Love! The lovely thing about love as an aphrodisiac is that it doesn't have to generate a pressure, an irritation, or a tension in order to work. It creates a space in which Ecstasy can occur, a space in which opposites can lustily and luminously embrace.

When Love and Ecstasy are present, orgasm is usually inevitable. It's no longer a goal. It's just another moment, another moment out of Time. It's like a star bursting in the sky, an endless sky. The sky doesn't disappear, but *we* do, reappearing as pure Energy, inherently Conscious. But for most, orgasm is more like a firecracker going off in a toilet bowl. (*Laughter*) It's got nowhere to go. It's a fart in a closet — don't misunderstand me, 'cause it might feel wonderful if you haven't farted for a week! (*Laughter*) Tantric farting may only be a whiff away! (*Laughter*) But it's not exactly a star exploding in infinite sky, nor a soulshining rupturing of Ecstatic intensification...

What I'm saying in so many ways is make room for orgasm. Unzip your uptightness. Let your orgasms come out of the blue, the wild blue beyond, the Great Sky of Here & Now; allow their passion, their prelude, to flow out of inner stillness, inner spaciousness. Then you'll witness the miracle of Something arising from Nothing, the endless miracle of primal Creation. Out of true stillness can come such a sublimity, such a fullness of passion, such a Joy...

–34–
Meaning, Meaninglessness, & Destiny: Embodying One's True Purpose

Is Life meaningless? The answer coils within the question, existing not as a facile yes or no, but as the actual illumination of what is motivating such a question. It is far more important to identify just *who* (or *what*) is formulating the question than it is to merely attempt to reply to the content of the question; the state (both inner and outer) of that which is doing the asking needs to be unequivocally exposed and acknowledged, not just intellectually, but with one's entire being. Then, and only then, can the relevancy of the question be viewed in its nakedness, as one's attention ceases mechanically wandering through various constructs of mind, instead gradually transmuting into steady witnessing, focussing on something deeper than cognitive associations and meanderings, something with real substance, something radiant with knowledgeless understanding, something that will definitely from time to time include *authentic* questions, primal enquiries whose exploration leads beyond the conventional mind into full, even ecstatic, participation in the unfathomable Mystery of Being...

Life makes sense only when we stop trying to force it to make sense. Put another way, when we cease superimposing meaning onto Life, then Its fundamental significance reveals itself to us.

Life has no inherent meaning; It both includes and transcends whatever seeks to explain, conceptualize, or contain It. This is not a matter of agreement or disagreement, nor has it anything to do with belief or opinion — it is a matter of *direct*, mind-free experience, emerging as a full-bodied, luminous realization of our own attachment to meaning, which is but an avoidance of openly facing and unobstructedly feeling the Unknown, not the Unknown that's simply not yet uncovered, but the Unknown that's Eternally Unknowable.

Meaning provides a sensation (or convincing illusion) of security, a semantic hedge against the Call of the Unknown, a personalized flag to wave in the midst of Infinity, a bastion of logical facticity to hole up in when Truth comes knocking. However, meaning is but a form of consolation, providing not a receptivity to living Truth, but only sophisticated sedation, rationalized stagnation, and erudite excuses for mental masturbation. To cut through this, we must bypass all preverbal, childish, and fantasy-cluttered domains, and willingly enter a *transverbal* realm, a place where anesthetization is obsolete...

Meaninglessness is a grave problem to most, a burdened sea with no coast, the suffocating yet reassuringly familiar flesh of an existential ghost; meaninglessness is but a thinking person's problem, an issue inviting pipe-smoking pondering and computerized wandering; meaninglessness is the glum companion and angst-crowned legitimizer of despair, periodically emitting a philosophic or tabloid whine, elevating to antiseptic priesthood those who for the right price will restore meaningfulness, resolutely shocking, seducing, "educating," and convincing the errant mind (and tagalong body) back into its "rightful" cultural groove/rut...

The whole issue of meaning and meaninglessness is not truly a core concern; to look at it deeply is to simply become more aware of the functioning of one's mind. Yes, yes, you might be saying, but what about *purpose*? What about one's true destiny? First of all, purpose (except when animated by egocentricity, or by authority other than that native to oneself) is *not* equivalent or even related to meaning, except in the most superficial ways... Our fundamental purpose as individuals is revealed when we are unambiguously and ecstatically alive and awake. Such purpose is a kind of psychospiritual blueprint, simultaneously simple and complex, already written yet invitingly blank, rich with improvisational possibility and adaptive grace, catalyzed into action through the presence of consciously granted attention, as well as through the creation and maintenance of conducive conditions for its fruition.

Our real purpose may remain dormant throughout our lifetime, or it may guide us now and then, or it may radiate throughout us almost constantly, depending on how committed we are to abiding in and *as* our core of Being. We cannot think or believe our way into the obviousness of our Life-purpose, nor can we be transported there for any significant period of time via mere prophecy or prediction. The key is to deliberately live from our essence, not as a strategy, but because there is no other option left for us. Living thus triggers the context and specifics associated with our particular purpose, while attracting fertile circumstances for its fleshing-out.

To just think, dream, or get romantic about this will only create confusion — it must be felt, breathed, risked, lived, and celebrated, not as some sublimely remedial dogma to be spiced and swallowed, but as an eloquent, passionately alive harbinger of spirit-destiny, a multidimensional welcoming and embodiment of our fundamental

Roloff Beny: *The Pleasure of Ruins*

nature as individuals. Instead of asking what is my purpose, it is better, at least initially, to ask who am I, and exactly how am I avoiding knowing who I really am? Implicit in such an undertaking is a resolute sensitivity to our actual state, a sensitivity deeply rooted in the present moment.

You will know your deep purpose when you are no longer interested in distracting yourself from your suffering. The blueprint of your Life-purpose is not penned by ambitious you, nor by mind-manipulating you, nor by hopeful you, nor by any other fragment of you that insists on referring to itself as "I," but rather is written (or animated) by the you who cannot lie, the you who is already at Home, already whole, already uninhibitedly embodying the Sacred Imperative...

Simply commit to standing your true ground *now*, not as a good idea, nor as some sort of affirmation, nor as a fired-up spasm of enthusiasm, nor as an ego-glorifying resolution, but as an act of love, love for yourself and others, a love unpolluted by sentimentality, conformity, slumber, or ambition. Commit thus, and your *real* purpose will seize you, demanding of you things you could not give *if you were less committed.*

Living one's true purpose is not necessarily easy, for it involves risks, stands, and leaps unknown to the periphery of oneself, but it is an unexploitable joy, honed by suffering and brightened by knowingness; it is a worthy labour of love, the greatest gift one can give to others, ever outbreathing every lesser intention or motive, providing a perspective that transcends meaning. The peace of those who are living their true purpose is not a peace of mere equanimity, but is a vibrant, dynamic peace, as vital as it is spacious. Accompanying such purpose is another purpose, one that goes beyond individual uniqueness and destiny, namely that of unqualified realization of God, or undying Union with the Holy One. This purpose cannot be fulfilled without an attending surrender to one's individual destiny, as summarized in the epigram: To transcend yourself, be yourself.

Darkness Lifts a Veil

Certainty stumbles down a dishevelled alley, clutching at peekaboo walls, and Darkness fills out every corner and getaway tributary, until a paranoically suggestive hush springs into elocutionary alignment, sporting a sideshow grin and a hollow-hubbed designer radiance, dishing out juicily skewered meaning to the front rows, all the windup factfeeders and slumberseeders, not to mention all of the tuxedo'd no-shows who are out redecorating their prisons' bathrooms with nattily recessed bookshelves for sentences that wouldn't be seen in public with ones like this...

Darkness lifts a veil, an ebonized portcullis of creaking density, and a lush spring flowers forth, blossoming and budding and surging with deliciously overgrown succulence, belting out a chorus of wantonly ecstatic greens, layer upon fragrant layer, everything moistly aquiver, upstart growth sweetly curling and nakedly ashiver, moaning so deep with rippling emerald recess and protrusion, all subtly asway in the meandering currents of a silken thrill...

A long sigh later, Darkness hoists a second veil, a leering relic of barnacled irony, and sudden fangs swell and gleamingly plunge into an enormous, tremblingly flabby egg, rottingly speckled and oozing borborygmusly, splitting and splattering open from the wraparound bite and hissing bristle, its fatly-bubbling flood of neon-dotted putrescence carrying a half-gutted hermaphrodite, a silver and crimson creature with singalong eyes and homogenized cries...

Now Darkness lifts a third veil, an opalescent blue transparency embroidered with royal dead-ends, and a crystalline cavern yawns itself wide, slowly fluting out indistinct figures from its bejewelled sides, figures that change shape as they deepen their dance, their infinitely-historied weave and glide, their plunge and soar, arc and crash, daisychain and gory arabesque, circled round and round by freshly-formed, skinless figures with rubied eyes and cobraic poise...

Bent double and weeping amidst Its own inevitable rubble, Darkness lifts yet another veil, an amorphous fourth, and an ancient sarcophagus is dragged into the sunlight and ceremoniously unlidded; with extreme yet supremely elegant slowness, its lone inhabitant sits up, appearing to some as a successful initiate, and to others a horribly successful vampire. There are no veils left, except of course for somnabulism's infectious presence, and Darkness squirms under a dogmatic stake of do-gooder daylight, sentenced to life.

You might say that Chaos is seeking annulment of its marriage to Order, claiming mental cruelty, but that's just one more throwaway metaphor, bereft of any mythical supporting cast. Of course, the witness of all this is nailed to a different wall, hung up on its immaculate detachment. And does not Something frame all this for you, even as you insist on painting yourself into yet another corner? And does not Something call for you, beyond all edibility and spiritual eligibility? The Secret is out, but you're in, peeking through the visor of your veils, trying to rehabilitate your Darkness, instead of adventuring right to Its Heart...

Gustave Doré: *The Bible*

−35−
Cutting Through the Avoidance of Embodiment: The Fleshbody, The Dreambody, & Death

ROBERT: (*After a prolonged silence*) What are you doing?

VIMALESH: I'm feeling a lot of fear... Last night I had a dream that I still feel as though I'm in, a dream where my throat was cut...

ROBERT: Close your eyes, and tell the dream in the present tense.

VIMALESH: I'm standing in front of a large rock, trying to open it up, along with some other people, so we can go into the cave that I think's behind it. Behind the rock I know there's some kind of enemy or danger, but I also know that we have to go into the cave. Behind us there's a pool, a dangerous pool that I mustn't touch. At last, we manage to open the rock, and the enemy pours out through it, and goes straight into the pool, just as a huge monster emerges from it...

ROBERT: What kind of monster?

VIMALESH: Like an enormous pile of seaweed, coming to engulf the enemy... I step aside, and suddenly the whole thing turns into something like a chessboard — sixteen soldiers meeting sixteen enemy soldiers. It's completely mechanical. Then all at once, I turn into an enemy soldier, and I know that I'm about to get killed — my head is going to be cut off. Then Vijay comes over to me, saying that he'll help me by killing me — he'll help me die properly. He slits my throat. Blood pours out of me, and I see you coming toward me...

It doesn't look like you — you're blond, much shorter and stockier — but I know it's you because of your eyes. The blood's really pumping out of my throat. You hold my hand, and I start weeping, and then I realize I'm in drama, and I start laughing at my dramatics around dying... And you say to me, "Trust that you'll come back." I keep trying to relax, but there's a tremendous amount of fear in my body. I keep looking into your eyes. The bloodflow ceases. I'm right on the edge of going. I stop breathing. For a short time, I seem to have no body — there's no breath, no movement, just a waiting to come back... Then I woke up, feeling very afraid, my bed totally soaked with sweat...

ROBERT: (*After a long silence*) When did you feel most afraid?

VIMALESH: Just before the blood stopped when I was looking down at my body, when there was no breath...

ROBERT: And how do you feel with Vijay?

VIMALESH: Like he's my blood brother, even though I don't always feel that good with him. He was helping me die well...

ROBERT: What needs to die in you?

VIMALESH: (*Haltingly*) My self-obsession...

ROBERT: That's too easy for you to say — it's a label you can trot out any old time, a lifeless label, metaphorically impoverished. (*Pause*) Look at your dream, and you'll see what needs to die — namely, the you who reduces Life to a chessboard. But let's back up for a moment, and look at what sets up the chessboard...

The rock's your rigidity, your father, your challenge, and the pool's your endarkened female side, your all-engulfing mother, made monstrous by your fear. Danger behind, and danger in front, but you must move, so you open up the rock and shortly thereafter step aside, just like in the waking state when you retreat into the computational zone of your mind, and view Life as just one big battle, one big proving ground... But this is just part of the psychological terrain pointed to by your dream — it's a beautiful, very rich dream, which for me has two levels: One, that of usual dreaming, about your fear of letting go, your need to cut through your headiness, your dramatized battle-mentality, and two, that of something quite different, something that carries a definite past-life sense...

Before you began speaking, as soon as you sat down for this session,

I looked at your throat and sensed it being cut. (*Pause*) Tilt your head back, and put your hands behind your back, imagining that they're tightly tied by rope. Gail [*She's assisting Robert in the session*], go behind him and hold his hair with one hand... Keep your eyes closed, Vimalesh, and breathe more deeply, more quickly, imagining that you're wearing very rough, dirty brown clothes, coarse against your skin — your skin is darker, your eyes more slanted, your body smaller, older, under tremendous strain. You're tied; you can't move. The ropes are cutting into your wrists, sawing through your flesh... Your head's being held back roughly and firmly, and in less than a minute a very sharp sword will be brought against your throat, your quiveringly naked throat, and then sliced so deeply against your throat (*Vimalesh breathing quickly and very heavily, half-sobbing*)...

Now you can feel the edge of the sword — here it is! It's coming! (*Vimalesh's sounds getting louder and louder*) All the people watching don't give a damn! Here it comes! (*Robert tells Gail to press her forefingers against Vimalesh's jugular veins*) Cut!! It is done... (*He groans and sags*) Feel it! Let the sound out... (*Sounds of constriction and strangulation*) Let it come, now... (*Vimalesh starts crying deeply*)

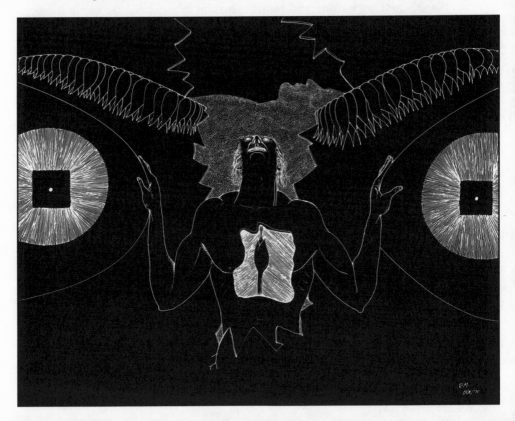

Let your whole body weep. (*Robert gently palms Vimalesh's throat, and his crying gets even fuller, until he's supine; when his sobbing finally subsides, Robert continues...*) Feel yourself becoming more and more spacious, lighter and lighter, imagining now that you are looking down upon yourself, seeing your motionless body, your head fallen back, your throat still pouring blood, your Life-force all but gone from your physicality... Feel your grief, your loss, and also feel your slowly growing peace, your seedling ease...

There's such deep ease now, as you separate from your body; there's a very fine something connecting you to your physicality, but it's almost completely cut now... The body below's stopped breathing, but *you* feel *very* alive. And now the cord's cut, the body quickly fading from your view as another, much more interesting world becomes obvious to you, a world that *now* feels far more real than the so-called physical world. You can barely make out your lifeless body now; it appears to you as in a dream, a rapidly thinning dream.

In fact, just about everything that you did prior to this death now seems like a dream to you, full of poignantly overlapping scenes — but it's getting harder and harder to remember, because something else, something seemingly much more substantial, is drawing you on, and on, and on... All around you, there's something magnificently alive, fresh, achingly familiar, silently yet so, so compellingly calling to you...

The body you now have, or, more precisely, the body that you now *are*, is malleable, loose, marvelously transparent, similar to the body you've had in your night-time dreaming, but not so psychologically solid... This is more compelling, more alive, than any lucid dream you have ever had, more potently significant... And finally now you are *completely* immersed in this domain (*Robert strikes a Tibetan bell*), completely and unresistingly immersed.

(*He hits the bell lightly for several minutes, at about twenty-second intervals, then plays a five-minute, hauntingly evocative piece on the stereo; when the music ends, the whole room is vibrating with undeniably tangible Presence*)

Where are you now?

VIMALESH: (*Hardly able to speak*) ...I'm up... in the air... somewhere...

ROBERT: It's time to come down. Something is drawing you *down*, and it's not even down, but more like *through*, and you're hesitant to go there. (*Vimalesh sighs*) More suffering, more physical existence, more heartbreaking attachment. (*Long pause*) You've got to come down — you know what you didn't face before. It's not even a matter of choice, for you are inevitably and overwhelmingly drawn to what you most *need*, and that complex something is more condensed than you now are, more solid, heavier, more fleshed-out... (*More sighing*) You're already halfway there. You can't stop it — you could slow it, but you're not... You can't stop it... Already you're psychically configurated with more parents who don't know or recognize you. (*He cries softly*)

Already, there's no turning back, no sign of any miscarriage... Already you're born again, unable to breathe, yanked out, mucus and blood everywhere, too-bright lights, thick hands on your body, your utterly helpless little body, and you're screaming now, screaming in shock, feeling almost unbearably sensitive... trapped... starting again... (*Robert lightly taps the Tibetan bell*) What's happening now?

VIMALESH: (*Speaking very slowly*) I'm realizing how I haven't really faced my suffering, how I've wanted to rise above my suffering...

ROBERT: Yes. You've tried and tried to rise above your hurt, to either float up beyond it (as in dissociative meditation or in psychedelic indulgence), or to step to one side (as in compulsive computation, disembodied rationality, and other forms of mindfucking). In either case, you're trying to stand apart from your body, but what stands apart isn't really *you*, but only your personified craving to escape...

You've used your lucidity to rise above suffering, to numb yourself to it, to find solace in domains of archetypal subtlety, astral transparency, de-personalized magic, and *apparent* bodilessness. And why? Because you associate bodily existence with pain, degradation, stupidly rigid manhood, and sickeningly ubiquitous violence, as well as with their compensatory sidekicks, such as romance. (*Pause*)

The most violent of times have often been laced with exaggerated romanticism... Consider the feudal samurai in Japan, swollen with murder, yet also romantically associated with Springtime's blossoms. Or how about the knights of medieval Europe, swooningly linked to impossibly pure maidens, even as they galloped about looking for dragons to kill? Or how about Naziism, with its romanticism about the blond, blue-eyed superman? Or how about modern America, "choosing" Ronald Reagan as its President, an actor who kept mass violence in business, while exuding an immensely appealing (albeit grossly nostalgic) romanticism, as well as a comfortingly simplistic optimism?

You too suffer from such an unholy marriage of violence and supposed chivalry; like those long-ago knights, Life for you tends to be just a battleground sweetened by romantic possibility. They were looking for dragons to kill, while avoiding facing their own inner dragons... Such cowardice is the stuff of gross suffering, but you're becoming more and more aware of a subtler suffering, that which is found through tenderness and *real* intimacy. Your armour's coming off, the maiden is your own psychospiritual virginity, and your romanticism has finally had its pants pulled down!

Yes, there are dragons to kill, and there are dragons to meet, dragons to greet. You need to *feel* your particular dragons as *part* of you; you have to encounter them with such luminous intensity, such power and love, that their energies eventually become *your* energies. Weep for their death, shine with their secret, love them, do battle with them, blend with them, and you will have earned access to what they guard, and not just metaphorically! Treat your dragons the way an ancient hunter might have treated the animals he had to kill — with reverence, respect, authenticity, and gratitude, as well as with spiritual recognition. This is not romanticism, not token totemism, not Bambi sentimentality, not therapeutic integration, but love, real love!

Become more sensitive to your throat again... It's not just your throat that's vulnerable, but your *entire* body. One swing of a sword, and you're dead or horribly damaged. We're not meant to be sliced, slashed, pierced, or torn open by weapons, yet throughout human history, many millions of us have been mashed, lacerated, maimed, butchered, blown up, and unspeakably mutilated with all kinds of murderous instruments... And *you've* swung more than a few of them! (*Long pause*)

You know *exactly* what it's like to run a sword through someone's abdomen, to cut someone else's throat, to bring an axe or club down on someone else's skull, to cut off people's limbs and watch them scream. (*He starts crying*) You've known the dark pleasure of that, the dark, dark pleasure, the satisfied righteousness of seeing flesh part from flesh with one swing of your razor-sharp sword... Of course, nowadays humans have found much more sophisticated ways of maiming each other, both physically and non-physically... Nuclear weaponry (and chemical warfare) is, through its very impersonality and faceless profiteering, even more immoral than a broadsword or scimitar slicing its way through an "enemy" village...

Yes, violence is, in many places, becoming more *psychologically* acted-out than physically acted-out, but there are no signs that it is *truly* on its way out, none! There's hope for change, yes, but there's *always* been hope, and it's done no good at all — in fact, it's done harm, for it has only fueled romanticism, ever addicting us to possibility, drawing us away from the full recognition of what's happening *now*... Such escapism only furthers our suffering. You're not meant to hang around until the Earth is benignly transformed — you're meant to deeply and truly understand your Earth-life, to live it *fully*, to go right to its Heartland, until you are profoundly intimate with it, so intimate that you are no longer exploitable by its options. (*Long pause*)

You don't get to leave Earth until you've *fully* lived here, to the point where you've no urge left to escape, and then you don't have to leave, and you don't have to stay — the next step simply reveals itself when you are ripe for it. Those who think they can leave for "higher" dimensions through swallowing various metaphysical beliefs (or through other forms of spiritual ambition) are only postponing their growth, floating up above themselves (in their skulls somewhere, conceptualized away from "lower" feelings) in a consoling limbo, not realizing that all they are *really* doing is refusing to incarnate! (*Pause*) Again, when you've done what you need to do, you'll inevitably be drawn to something else. And what is that, ultimately? It ain't Earth, and it ain't Heaven... (*Long pause*) What's happening now?

VIMALESH: I feel an urge to sit up. I know I need to face what's here, but I also feel like avoiding it, like going away from my body...

ROBERT: Yes. That's why you get so uncoordinated at times — you deny your body the attention it needs. Sure, you get into it during hard runs or during typical sex, but you don't usually bring subtlety or refined awareness to it. It's not your ultimate destiny to be *this* body, but this fleshiness, this bodymind complexity, needs to be loved and appreciated and lived fully, luminously, consciously... Otherwise, *reembodiment* at the level at which you're stuck is all you can look forward to — environmentally-unsound recycling!

And we are always embodied, however subtly or shapelessly, until we're dissolved in God fully, and even then, you could say we've embodied God (through our very intimacy with the Universal, level upon level)... Manifest existence is the body of the Unmanifest Eternal. The body is but the medium for maintaining relationship with one's environment (You could even say that the body *is* relationship), however rarefied that environment might be...

In your nightly dreams, you "have" a dreambody, so as to flow with your dreamscape, just as in the so-called waking state, you "have" a fleshbody, so as to flow with the elemental world all around you. After you die, there'll be bodies that correspond to the conditions in the after-death state (they may come and go, or radically alter, with the flicker of a thought, but they possess as much existence as the fleshbody, with their own unique perceptual latticework)... There's no *real* escape from the body; at death, you only leave the physical dimension of the body (but the you who is left is *not* the you of the waking state, nor even the you of the dreaming state). The body has many dimensions, many levels. We simply have to embody — Life is embodiment. Why postpone it? Why deny it? Why make a problem out of it? Why not get into it, and get on with it?

To embody yourself more fully, you must get more anchored in the practical — this is why you're working as a painter, and not at something more exotic. Paying conscious attention to detail, including incredibly ordinary, mundane detail is of crucial importance, if you are to get your feet firmly planted. (*Long pause*) Obsession with the physical is not embodiment, but more like *over*bodiment, a confusion of self-expansion with tissue engorgement! To be thus caught up in form (as most grotesquely displayed in the bloated narcissism of bodybuilding) is as pointless as trying to escape form, whether through drugs, mindgames, or romantic dissolution...

As you mature, you'll shift from primarily sensing your body as a solid something to feeling it simply as patterned, fluidly shapeshifting energy; perhaps you've already sensed this in deep sex. Go into anything fully and consciously, and you'll experience your body more as energy than as matter, however muscular your gestures might be! This is not escape, but rather an ever-deepening entry into Being, a centering of Self, an embracing of God... It's your responsibility, no matter what sort of body you are now *being*... (*Long pause*) What are you aware of now?

VIMALESH: I'm aware of a clarity — it seems very simple to me, the whole matter of my avoidance of embodying myself. You asked me at the beginning of the session what I was doing, and I really feel it now...

ROBERT: You've been refusing to incarnate your physicality, except in a gross sense — you won't inhabit yourself fully (which doesn't really mean "inhabit", but rather the giving of conscious attention). Look closely at anyone, and you'll see what parts of their physicality are *vacant* — such areas actually give off the emanation of abandonment! It could be the buttocks, the upper back, the calves, the right eye, the chest, the belly, whatever! (*Pause*)

Once you realize what you have to do, and you realize it in its simplicity, then all that's left is to do it — you don't need some cosmic or complicated explanation of your purpose on this "plane"! There's God, there's Consciousness, there's form, there's birth, there's death, there's Ecstasy and suffering — all the basics that everyone knows or intuits. No metaphysical constructs are necessary. God is not a concept! What I'm talking about has nothing whatsoever to do with belief, nor any other ossification of mind. You've got a paintbrush in your hand, you move it with skill and appreciation, letting your whole body participate — you don't need to learn some cosmology or glue yourself to some belief system so that you can paint, because it's much simpler *and* deeper than that — paint well, paint consciously, paint with economy and grace, and the fundamentals of Life will make themselves more and more obvious to you...

To really live Life, you must again and again die into It, not out of collapse, but out of full-blooded surrender to the deepest imperatives of the moment... When you, for example, deeply surrender into orgasm, it's a death, a profound dissolution of body and mind, followed by a return, however blissfully-held, of more ordinary perception — it's a miniversion of the reembodiment that eventually follows psychophysical death.

You feel this dissolution, this vastness of unbound Being, every groupnight, and you also feel on these very same nights the re-entry of your particularity, your personal detailing, after such vibrant spaciousness has claimed you — it's an ebb and flow, an expansion and contraction, and it's problematic only when you identify with some aspect of it, or try to make real estate out of one portion of its spectrum. (*Pause*) Eventually, you'll sense the Eternal, no matter what you're doing; you won't be alienated from the incarnation required of you, nor will you be welded into it! This is about honouring both the temporal and the Eternal, which of course necessitates a deep involvement in both...

The rock then becomes not a barrier, nor a neurotic armouring, but a healthy hardness, guarding not an enemy, but an ally, namely your deeper masculinity; and so too the pool of your dream changes, shifting from a deadly trap to a healing softness, a fecund welcome, rich with your true femininity. The energies of the two meet with such joy and such marvellous abandon that your mind must forsake its chessboard approach to Life, existing instead only as psychic communion between the two... If you obstruct this union, or screw around in surrogates of it, you will only be avoiding who you really are, cutting your own throat, cutting yourself off from the fullness of Life...

Let me finish by reading something I recently wrote:

"Success is basically no more than the making good use of our failures. This is not about a gloried solidification of everyday self, but rather about dissolution of (and disidentification with) that very self. It is about losing face without losing touch. It is about giving our all without giving ourselves away. There is no applause, no boos, no Santa Claus, but only the emerging fullness of who we are. Clearly recognizing our continuing failure to wake up is the beginning, along with the full-bodied realization that what is being avoided is *exactly* where we must go.

Earth is a school, a place of transition, a wondrous crucible of evolutionary possibility. Its lessons are to be consciously embodied and fully lived. If we try to escape from Earth's demands, whether through indulgence of appetite, or through egoic consolation, or through distracting dramatizations of our suffering, or through meditative remedies, then we only make ourselves more and more impotent relative to our testing. There are no shortcuts. There is simply a demand to be met, now.

The point is not to reach some superworld, some heavenly version of Earth, some subtle realm where we don't have to feel pain. The point is to freely embrace our Earth-life, to live it with passion and sensitivity and wakefulness, to breathe it right to our center of being, to cradle both its joy and its grief, to turn away from none of it, until we *naturally* pass through it, until we are cleanly free of all fascination with it and its possibilities, until we are no longer bound or obsessed by it. To try to reach this freedom through mere allegiance to therapeutic, religious, psychic, or mental strategies only strands us in a quicksand of goal-fixation. It *all* must be passed through, directly and nakedly, without clinging to dogma, belief, spiritual ambition or any other buffer. Purification, however fiery, must eventually be *welcomed*. Discipline is necessary, but it is of no use if its origin is egocentric. Sooner or later, joy must become the *foundation* of our journey, rather than its goal — if we're hoping that our passage will make us feel better, then we will be undertaking it for the wrong reason, doing no more than crippling ourselves with unnecessary expectation.

Nothing must be flinched from. It *all* must be felt, right to the heart, every last fibre of it, every in and out of it, every glory and every horror, felt with pure vulnerability and openness of eye, without any emotional dissociation. Awakening must become more important to us than sedation. Our wounds must be exposed, not morbidly, but with heartfelt honesty and humour, with lust and subtlety, with guts and sensitivity, until a sobering joy blooms, until we are rooted in the primal rhythms of the moment, free of all hope. We are constantly being tested in a manner that *exactly* reveals what we are flinching from. Look, and see. What are you now recoiling from? What are you now postponing? What are you now talking yourself out of? Be grateful that it is right before you, right now..."

THEY GOT A DEAL

She's got his need by the balls
He bitches about the pain but craves the contact
She keeps negotiating for a better contract
He half promises, dredging up a few gasping feelings
Signing the already-broken agreement
        with the business end of his mind-swollen cock
He rises and falls with his rod
She despises him and his kind
She lives alone, married to her hate
She wants him to feel more, to not just masturbate
He tells her he loves her, and ain't that enough, bitch?
Her loneliness outwrestles her deeper need
He resists her therapy, fencing with her bargains,
        saying love me as I am
She tires, yielding to her disguise's desires
And he cuddles into her harbor
Her harbor stagnant and secure, her harbor so dark
They eat up their days, getting by on tiny spurts of growth,
  bits of occasional green soon trampled beneath their wardance
She's got her eye fixed on his possibilities
He's got his eye on the exit
The leash runs both ways and so does the whip
They squat in the molding greens of their cage
Fucking (and thinking) away their rage
Hurting their hurt and investing in plastic joy
They share the same lover,
        the predictable embrace of their struggle
He's used to her teeth, his shoulders steel against her demands
Her breasts and womb are bruised from his touch
She's seduced by hope, by his half-unzipped need
He's addicted to the softness at the end of the rope
He won't cry and she won't say goodbye
Another breath is taken unnoticed
Another chance is forsaken, another day stillborn
She's got his balls
He's got her attention
They got a deal

-36-

Real Happiness is Not in Having, But in Being

Real happiness is not in having, but in being. This does not mean that one must necessarily not own things, but rather that one must let one's possessiveness (and attachment) be transparent to Being, the light of Which will then shine through and place in Life-enriching perspective all supposed ownership. If this is not permitted, then "having" will simply be a trap... For example, we ordinarily expect that having a certain kind of relationship with someone ought to make us feel better, thereby burdening such relationship with the expectation that it comfort, soothe, and assuage us, somehow painlessly delivering us from our self-imposed pain, our psychoemotional contractedness, our uptightness... But why make a relationship responsible for our happiness? Why not permit it to be an ongoing *expression* of our joy (and everything else that we are), rather than expecting it to produce joy? Why not dive into the knowingness, the full-blooded knowingness, that *everything* is in relationship?

The happiness produced by "having" is not real happiness, but only *situational* happiness; in fact, it is *actually* unhappiness, because its appearance is inevitably accompanied by a kind of addiction (however low-grade), a fixation of attention on the association between the having of something in particular and the presence of those sensations commonly known as happiness. This very dependency, this neurotic dependency, suppresses and shrinks us, separating us from experiencing the *totality* of ourselves, thereby generating unhappiness. Of course, the unhappier we are, the more compulsively we tend to look for remedies, cure-alls, ways out, escapes, satisfying compensations — if we find one that seems to work for awhile, we become more or less addicted to it, until our very addictiveness makes us so miserable that we busy ourselves looking for yet another escape, another sedative, another immunity-promising distraction, another pathway, another drug, another program, another mantra, another lover, another position, another car, another hope-riddled harbinger of non-misery...

The answer to this, however, is not to make "having" wrong. There is nothing inherently wrong with possessiveness, nothing! To run away from attachment, as is so often found in the case of the so-called spiritual renunciate, the typical meditator, the pursuer of various Eastern religious methodologies, is just as neurotic as the efforts of the usual Westerner to find consolation through the exploitation of "having", in the form of blind consumerism, compulsive ownership, promiscuity, and so on. Whether one is driven toward either exploitation or toward renunciation of ownership, one is in the very same position, namely that of recoil from Being, recoil from illuminated Aliveness, recoil from Life...

The safety reached by the typical meditator is all too often arid, passionless, delusory, and disembodied, filled with an unacknowledged, but ever-growing impulse to go to the opposite extreme. This is the swing, the bond, the link, between the drunk and the monk — the latter seeks a cloistering in the stillpoint's seemingly infinite bubble, and the former does the same in the wooziness of endarkened appetite. That is, one exploits the grosser aspects of being human, while the other exploits the subtler aspects, but neither is willing to go to the heart of what is troubling them. Both are seeking happiness (or at least a semblance of immunity) through the having of particular experiences, worldly or other-worldly. Both are seeking intoxication. They are each other's neurotic shadow, the double that spells trouble, one face ravaged and dirty, the other too clean...

Only by passing through, not around or above, but *through* one's "having", one's possessiveness and clinging, does one come to the crux of the matter. If one bypasses this journey through some sort of meditative manipulation, one may arrive at a place of Being, but it will not be the fullness of Being that is contacted, but only an overmentalized or anaemic version of Being, a kind of passionless spaciousness, a non-relational, invulnerable hideout, a refuge from the fires of desire. Nirvanic extinction, however, is not the point; a fully and consciously embodied Life is, a Life in which the Eternal and the temporal are in deep embrace, moment-to-moment. To want to flee into the Eternal (or into subtle worlds and dimensions) only creates a momentum to be flung back, like drunks in a hurricane, into the mortal realm, the mundane, the all-too-solid everyday world.

Look deeper and see what it is that you are hoping will bring you happiness. It may be a new car or self-image, or a sudden arrival of a lot of money; it may be a certain ease, a certain condition of meditation, a certain somebody suddenly desiring you, and only you; it may be subtler than this, but whatever it is, it's still entrenched in the realm of having. That is, you are, in so many words, chanting to yourself, "If I have this, then I will be fulfilled." However, what we really yearn for we cannot have; we can *never* have it. We can only *be* it — not just in some rarefied domain, but right here, in the flesh, right now, bodily, fully, Now...

You don't get to the realm of Being via renunciation; you can't buy your way in through being good, through being devoted, through doing yoga, through psychotherapeutic practices, through affirmation, nor through any other strategic approach. These at best may prepare you for the journey, sharpen and alert and ease you, but they are not the journey itself. The actual journey is a leap of open-eyed faith, an act of profound trust in which the Radiance of Being shines through the having of anything, solid or not...

Real happiness is inherent to Being. Feel this now. Instead of looking for something to happen to you now so that you might feel better or more blissful, simply be present, right now, softly now, whatever your mood or state of mind. Don't expect to feel good, to have your body suddenly feel blissful. Don't weigh yourself down with looking for signs that you are doing well. Being present is not necessarily equivalent to feeling untroubled. Simply settle into your actual feeling, but without taking on its viewpoint; if you're afraid, have the guts to directly feel it, but don't take its accompanying thoughts and assumptions seriously. Make room for your current condition — there is no point in trying to escape or sedate it. Give it room to breathe, to live, to outgrow itself, to become available Life-energy. Simply settle into Being, easing into ever-deepening resonance with the Wonder That beats your heart, That breathes you, That breathes the trees, That moves us all — the Presence That is never truly apart from you. Let your having soften, and then soften some more; let its edges, its reach, become more porous, softer and softer... softer...

Keep relaxing the grip of the you who insists on "having", realizing that this particular you is not really a somebody, a discrete entity, but rather a *doing* that, out of sheer habit, mechanically refers to itself as you. Feel your way into a more central you now, a truer you, a you shining with Being, a you already present in every scene. Allow yourself to rest in (and *as*) that Fullness, that effortless brilliance, that ease of self — rest there, take root there, emanate from there, noticing how such emanation arises *naturally*, needing no mental volition, no egoic kickstarting... Thus does your doing now arise from your essentialness, your core of Being, rather than from neurotic and ambitious expectations. Thus does your doing outshine your trying...

As you continue to abide more and more deeply in Being, notice how much you now have; even though it is not "yours" in a personal sense, it is yours at a deeper level. Go further, right to the heart of Now, and you'll experience "having" and "being" merging, ever birthing you, ever birthing your native integrity of self... And so you emerge, refreshed, renewed, open, ready, spontaneously steady, powerful in your vulnerability, no longer expecting the having of anything to make you feel better, because you're *already* happy, unreasonably and non-addictively happy.

If we insist on having something, or on having something in particular happen, then *it has us*; on the other hand, if we rest in and as our Being, then we can both enjoy and deeply participate in our having, without becoming addictive about it. When happiness is allowed to be our foundation, rather than our goal, then we are naturally whole, capable of living a truly human life, a life in which we can both be and "have" without any shrinkage or suppression of Being. And in such happiness, such deep embodiment of Being, we cannot help but give, we cannot help but honor our every feeling, we cannot help but share our gifts, we cannot help but love, we cannot help but make Awakening our priority, simply because we are no longer seducible by lesser options...

When I Lived in an Empty Room

There was an unbreathing time
When I lived in an empty room, half-watching
Crows hopping across the stubble of flat and frosty fields
My walls carrying a few plastic victory ribbons
Schoolbooks dishevelled all across my desk
Their clean lines torturing my attention
Alone sat I in my chill cell
Fearing and welcoming any distraction
Hating my weakness, hating my broken stride
Weeping without a single sound
My needs lost in underwater chess moves
My adolescent heart frozen so hard
Gobbling facts was I
Seeking the glory of an envied report card
Hating the hollowness of that victory
One more crumpled ribbon pinned behind my forehead
Girls thawed my edges, their sweaters swelling
With secrets I secretly undressed
My brief pleasure bent with guilt
Trapped, trapped was I
My future laid out for all to see
Proud parents, proud teachers, I the top of every class
Long was I impaled on that barren peak
Mine its tinsel core
Long was I the slave of others' hopes
Long did I ache to be touched by another's hand
Long did I despair of love
There was a time when I lived in an empty room
Serving my sentence, bargaining with good behaviour
The trap was mine, a fortress of survival
Its dungeon echoing with a little boy's aching cries
His calling lost in the fury of my mind
Down, down came the walls one long day
And out came I, never to return
Now I don't close my eyes on dark days
Glad, glad am I to feel that sweet sad boy
Playing in the heart of my stride
His slenderness smiling so wide

Children are neither to be uprooted
    nor left unpruned
Children are neither to be cut down
    nor loved for foliage alone
Children are neither to be bound to our stride
    nor driven to the opposite
Children are neither to embody our crippled past
    nor denied sight of our rawest hurt
Children are neither to be addicted to dependence
    nor forced into premature independence
Children are neither to be saddled with fake gentleness
    nor burdened with outdated anger
Children are neither to be spared an uncompromising No!
    nor made to earn our love and attention
Children are neither to be allowed insensitivity to others
    nor goaded into mechanical thankyou's
Children are neither to be denied our full-blooded aliveness
    nor nagged into precocious bargaining
Children are neither to shoulder exaggerated challenge
    nor to swallow excessive nurturance
Children are neither to be left unweaned
    nor thrust on schedule from the nest
Children are neither here to pump up our pride
    nor to take a pampered ride
Children are neither to be uprooted
    nor left unpruned
Children ask of us only the heart and hands
    of a loving gardener
When the garden becomes too small
    we are to help our children find a more fitting soil
Such is our sacrifice and sacred need
    the altar upon which we purify and rediscover our love

-37-

Toward Unadulterated Intimacy with Children

The poem I just read (*on the opposite page*) applies to children in general; it's an invitation to all those who deal with children to do something more than they're tending to do, to become more attuned, more loving, more real, more centered. Such an invitation, or demand, is not likely to be honored, let alone even clearly heard. Within Xanthyros (and other entities of similar commitment), however, it ought to be obvious by now, excruciatingly obvious, that something more profound is required relative to our children.

Sensitivity, specificity, and subtlety, as well as an ever-awakening love, must become not the goal of our approach to our children, but rather the foundation; this needs to become as natural to us as taking our next breath. Sensitivity can only occur in its most natural form when our attention is free, consciously unbound to our own so-called problems, our own difficulties, our own self-obsession. When working with, or just simply being with, the children, we have a responsibility to give our *full* attention, even as we ask (outloud or not) that they periodically give us *their* attention. The whole matter of attention needs to become more of a foreground issue; if attention is just mechanically wandering through possibility and unillumined circuits of mind, then the Awakening impulse simply atrophies or rots.

And what of specificity? It is simply *that*, not submitting to the urge to generalize, to sum up a child's behavior over a long period of time and then thrust it at them in a righteously accusing or impermeable manner. Details are needed, full-fleshed details, especially those arising in the moment, those taking shape in heartfelt accordance with the needs of the child (and you!). Finally, subtlety — it's simply the ability to be aware of two or more levels of being (not mind!) at the same time, the capacity to skilfully, accurately, feelingly, and appropriately articulate from at least two of these levels at once, and to distinguish between them not through somehow describing which level is which, but simply through tonal quality, body posture, emotional grace, quality of eye contact, and so on. Doing so (and this is not an ego-based doing, but an Essence-centered doing) does not contribute to confusion, but actually deepens clarity, helping the children to reestablish themselves in the spaciousness of Being...

Characterizing all three of these qualities, these three S's, is centeredness. Just as the children need to cultivate center (playfully and profoundly), so too must the adults keep cultivating *their* capacity for center, frequently, in privacy, in public, in front of the children, everywhere, everywhen, in every kind of condition, however unpleasant or seemingly non-supportive of such effort. It's not that you must somehow become utterly and rapidly centered, but that when your commitment to doing so becomes glaringly, blatantly, and juicily obvious, even a child lost in play or hyperactivity will *feel* it, directly so, being affected by it positively and thoroughly, without anything necessarily even having to be said.

In a sense, this is just another version of the old adage, "Practice what you preach." If you practice wisely, you will no longer be preaching, but will be *teaching*. Children, as you've noticed, are quite sensitive to adult hypocrisy — they have a keen eye for it. They know when we are deceiving them, when we are partial in our encounters and play with them, when we are busy being dutiful, when we are asking of them what we will not ask of ourselves. We must set an example, not in concrete, but in fluidly responsible, joyously present, potently vulnerable aliveness. Yet it cannot merely be a "must", a "have to", a "should", or else it will very likely be sabotaged by a countereffort (or resistance to such neurotically parental enforcement). It needs to be natural. Do not make a problem out of this! Do not permit it to become just one more program for you, but rather realize, and bodily realize too, that it naturally arises when non-circumstantial happiness is made priority, grounded happiness, open-eyed happiness, sobering joy...

The work with children is crucial to the well-being of our community. They need to be taught, level upon level, not to indulge their inclinations, nor to repress them, which means that they must not be made to feel afraid of anything that's occurring in them, even that which will *clearly* elicit adult displeasure and disapproval. This does not mean, however, that you are to fake your response so that they will feel safe in a conventional way, so that they feel no risk in exposing their more aberrated stuff, but rather that you are to be present in such a manner that they feel *loved* by you, non-sentimentally loved, ruthlessly and uninhibitedly loved, even in the very midst of your distaste, anger, or hurt, even in the midst of your temporarily unloving-looking appearance. If they feel your love and integrity, if they *feel you with them*, they will definitely respond sanely, perhaps not right away, but they *will* respond!

I'm not talking about you embodying a passive, Buddhist-like waiting, a neurotically lengthened patience. Again, I'm talking about a *natural* process in which you cannot help but become more and more spacious, making room not only for the child's release of what they have repressed or misdirected, but for your *own* feelings, especially those of potentially violent *intent*. When you become spacious enough to allow such apparent inner darkness (particularly anger or rage) to surface and be expressed in a sensitively appropriate manner, you cannot help but deepen your connection to the child; your work on yourself becomes a lesson for them, a gift, a deep and lucid affirmation of relationship.

To deal sanely with children is to deal sanely with our own innocence, vulnerability, curiosity, and growth — this does not mean, however, that one ought to become romantically associated with the evolution of children, ever looking for ego-gratifying evidence of growth (especially in one's own children), thereby only burdening them with misguided adult expectation...

Challenge is necessary; so is nurturance. Neither must be allowed to dominate the other. How much is enough challenge? There's no way to know this through the mind. It is a matter of well-lit intuition, a matter of empathetically attuning to and deeply *feeling* the child, of being sensitive, specific, and subtle; then you will know in each moment the right mix of challenge and nurturance. This isn't a cold, calculated affair, but rather is warm and spontaneously improvised, *truly* an art, an exquisitely demanding art. It's not a method, but a way of being.

Excessive nurturance is poison, a smothering sea of syrup; it is but a perversion of love, a perversion of mother-force, just as excessive challenge is a perversion of father-force. The right amount? Again, a matter of intuition, of core-level trust. To become more sensitive to that intuition requires a stably established willingness to be aware, to be wakeful. As with everything else in Xanthyros, the foundation is wakefulness, Self-remembrance, the moment-to-moment cultivation of relaxed alertness, accompanied not only by mind-free passion and ecstatic groundedness, but also by the ongoing forgiveness of oneself when one has slipped or strayed from such awareness. When we are too hard on ourselves for our apparent transgressions, so too are we usually too hard on the children for their slippages in the same areas. The other extreme (being too soft) doesn't work either — to seemingly let it all go, to act all-forgiving, both overlooks and reinforces errors...

There's a place for anger. There's a place for undisguised distaste. There's even a place for violence, *not* physically acted-out violence, but a *vulnerable*, nakedly authentic sharing and appropriate verbalizing of the *intent* of the felt violence. Another time, I'll talk more about this [*see the talk "Real Anger is Not An Avoidance of Anything"*], but for now it's enough to reiterate that there's no need to deny ourselves access to *any* of our experience. There's a need to trust that we will behave cleanly with repressed material when it surfaces. Our children should not be denied the opportunity of witnessing such forces in us, nor of observing us working with them.

Letting our children see our raw emotion in its awakened fullness not only serves them, but also is very healing for us; it's as if we're back in our early childhood and we're openly showing *ourselves* (our children) the *totality* of our hurt, our alienation, our survival-based twisting of self. In this revelation, this deep sharing, we're not covering our suffering with candybar-wrappers, false smiles, reassuringly rewritten history, nor any other distancing strategy, nor are we over-dramatizing it. Instead, we're facing it directly, through letting our children see it.

It's not that we should try to elicit sympathy (or, worse, precocious parenting!) from them for our childhood difficulties, but simply that it's worth sharing such things with them, letting them know (and not just verbally) our history without necessarily bringing a specific attitude to that retelling — It's enough to simply give voice to it, letting it speak, weep, rage, laugh, and wonder for itself, letting it spontaneously draw forth whatever response it will from them. It's important not to tell them these old stories of ours just so they will feel how lucky they are to be with us! That is *not* the purpose. The purpose of recounting such things is to deepen our vulnerability, to heal our wounds, to give our children a fuller picture of us, to become more human with them, more soulfully related to them...

Much of the work with children is simply a matter of being *human* with them. Most people who work with children are not truly human with them; either they're emotionally removed authoritarians, or else they're down on the floor playing exaggeratedly permissive buddy; either they're disinterested, or else they're oozing with false interest; either they're chronically absent, or else they're suffocatingly present; either they're voicing maddeningly reasonable shoulds, or else they're cutesy-pooing left and right, as though children had nothing better to do than listen to adult insincerity and idiocy.

Patronizing children, pretending to be intimate with them (as though being their parent *automatically* guarantees the presence of intimacy), not respecting their depth of being, romanticizing their innocence, are all ways of crushing their spirit, of bringing them into alignment with one's own crushed spirit. This is ordinarily not at all intentional; it is not malicious, but only extraordinarily stupid, and painfully common, so common as to be taken as the norm by most.

Don't take what I'm saying as a should, nor as a mere pep-talk — feast on it, digest it, let it inspire your own willingness to work more sanely with the children, to play more playfully with them, to be and live in loving, full-bodied sanity with them, day after day, through wind and rain, through joy and pain, remembering that our children are not just children. Enjoy them, learn from them, love with them, struggle with them, live with them, letting your wounds be soil for new growth, both for you, and for every child in your life...

Gustave Doré: *Milton's Paradise Lost*

–38–

The Incredible Hulk on the Cello: Myth as a Vessel for Awakening

CORBY: (*Well into the session*)...I used to watch "The Incredible Hulk" every night when I was on the road [*As a guitarist in a rock band*]...

ROBERT: You mean the show where a wandering little guy keeps turning into a green super-mesomorph, a steroid monster, a weight-room marvel... Funny how the transformation always burst open his shirt, ripping it to shreds, but never his pants! But who gives a shit about a little detail like that? Not a burnt-out rock guitarist!

CORBY: Hey! (*Laughter*)

ROBERT: Let's take it a little further. Here you are, a wandering little guy with a skinny little chest, zero pecs and lats, and suddenly out pops Lou Ferrigno, all pumped up! Just imagine *you* bursting open your shirt, right to the waist, down the sleeves too, biceps like shaven coconuts, right in front of that woman who fired you not so long ago — you're standing there, your shirt in shreds, and she just starts lubricating all over the place, deliciously at your mercy, melting before the meaty Heaven you are! (*Laughter*) Imagine that! It's a kind of subversively positive pornographic fantasy...

CORBY: I was heavily into superhero comic books when I was a kid.

ROBERT: Who was your favourite?

CORBY: I liked all of them actually, especially the Marvel ones — Spiderman, the X-Men — I had thousands of them.

ROBERT: How about the Fantastic Four? Remember them?

CORBY: Yeah... Ben Grimm, alias The Thing.

ROBERT: The Thing! You know who The Thing is? (*Asking Nancy, who's assisting in the session*)

CORBY: You don't know who The Thing is? (*Laughing with exaggerated incredulity*)

ROBERT: Apparently she doesn't! But didn't The Thing have a sense of humour, even though he looked like a lurching brick shithouse?

CORBY: Did he ever! A down-to-Earth, tough guy, a wisecracking softy too...

ROBERT: And wasn't there a plastic man among the Four?

CORBY: Mr. Fantastic. Reed Richards. He could make his body stretch incredibly...

ROBERT: Elastic flesh... He got stretched out pretty thin sometimes, didn't he? And he and The Thing are only two of a whole multitude of comicbook characters bordering on the mythical, way out there beyond Archie and Sluggo and Dick Tracy... Each of them is a low-level archetype of some facet of human behaviour, sometimes inked out with surprising subtlety, half-transcending their pulpy backdrops... (*Long pause*) Imagine a thousand years from now, mythologically-oriented historians looking back on our time, snipping out the prevailing myths of the Twentieth Century — they'd surely look into our comic books! Imagine them looking at Superman, looking at his history — remember how he began as this invincible, immaculately cleancut character, uncomplicated as the 1950's, every hair in place? But later on, he became more vulnerable, more complex, more troubled — it wasn't just Kryptonite that got to him, but all sorts of other things. The World became more immune to his would-be heroics. His double life became more of a problem than a marvel. Of course, his changes simply mirrored the growing anxiety and ambivalence of the decades following the 1950's; the Man of Steel, like technology, turned out to be less of a saviour, and more of a pain in the ass! The association between power and invulnerability that he symbolized is now not such a certainty as it once was...

Or how about Galactus? He's a gigantic being, human in appearance, who needs to feed on entire planets, to suck out all their life-force so that he might live. Every now and then, he shows up near Earth, hungry and all alone, and, of course, marvels like the Fantastic Four then have to go out to try to stop him, to somehow dissuade him from destroying the planet. The dramas around Galactus are more mythical than cartoony; there's a subtle austerity to them, an intelligent creativity, aided by often great artwork, mixing the personal with the transpersonal, the solid with the transparent... It ain't Dagwood! (*Pause*)

Remember the guy on the Space-traversing surfboard?

CORBY: The Silver Surfer, the herald of Galactus.

ROBERT: Right. Galactus always had a herald, someone who would scout out a likely planet for his appetite. There were many heralds before the Silver Surfer, and each of them had a story. Weave it all together, and you've got a vast, branching myth. At worst, it's just cheap escapism, good guy and bad guy crap, but usually it's better than that. It's richly metaphorical, despite its occasional crude literalism, as when some characters slip into streetwise smartass lingo...
Each character in these pulp-myths has an unusual gift, as well as an obvious weakness; none are immune to downfall. It's not going too far to say that Galactus is a tragic figure; there was no pleasure for him in satisfying his appetite. Like Frankenstein's monster, he's a lonely figure, made monstrous by his unnaturalness...

CORBY: I remember once when he encountered Ego, the living planet, a planet whose consciousness had gotten to the point where it could talk...

ROBERT: Definitely a mixed metaphor! But in that, there's an appreciation, however mislabelled or melodramatized, of Earth as a living being, Gaia. In James Lovelock's Gaia Hypothesis, Earth is viewed as a great organism, living, breathing, self-regulating, with all organic life being just one functioning part of it. Maybe the writer of that Ego issue was hip to this, or maybe he was just plugged into a collective knowingness... (*Long pause*)

Let me switch to professional wrestling now... There's no point in making a fuss about how fake it is — of course it's staged! It's Marvel Comics on steroids, mixed with the lowest common denominators of

American soap opera. Every damned stereotype, usually male, bulked up and parading in front of an even more Neanderthal audience. It's as maddeningly repetitive as Sisyphus, and as crass as Warhol trash, but it's an economic smash! Nevertheless, it *is* myth, steaming hot, exaggeratedly dressed up by America's appetite for edible heroes and villains, fastfood goodguys and badguys, instantly recognizable types. Guess who the badguys were the other night? The (supposedly) Russian tagteam, of course! One Russian came out and took *both* opponents, All-Americans naturally, and acted out beating the shit out of them — he jumped on them, banged their heads together, but of course did them no injury... Pro wrestling is theatre, a sweaty theatre of, yes, archetypes, not archetypes of the psychic realm, nor of the subtle worlds, nor of the Heart, but of the first chakra, with a bit of the second and third thrown in — it's not just Grunt City!

You, Corby, can plug into archetypal energy at a more refined level through your music, your cello mastery, as well as through your humour; you don't have to do it vicariously through Marvel Comics, watching Brutus the Barber, or reading Carl Jung. As you become more attuned, more wakeful, archetypal energies will spontaneously appear to you, even *as* you — if you really observe, feelingly observe, two people interacting, you'll notice something grander than just them interacting, something psychoemotionally geometric, significantly patterned, something far more primal than their dialoguing fleshiness. That is, you'll sense the presence that animates them, and you'll sense its specificities, its geography, its energy currents. It'll be both dynamic and transparent to you, multifaceted as a crystal, yet eloquently obvious, sublimely simple...

(*Ten minute interlude of working with Corby's eyes, balancing and deepening them, until he is at last gazing into Nancy's eyes*)

ROBERT: Keep looking into her left eye... Now, without thinking about it at all, talk to her as though *you* are The Thing! Imagine she's this beautiful alien on some planet you've just landed on, and here you are, *The Thing*...

CORBY: Well, real glad to see ya, honey — it's mighty lonely on this planet all alone... (*Long pause*) It's mighty lonely being in this body all alone...

ROBERT: Tell her how your body feels.

CORBY: It's real hard, honey... It's so rigid, so, so, rigid... My body is so rigid (*Crying*)...

ROBERT: (*After a long pause*) Now be Galactus.

CORBY: I am Galactus. I am the be-all and end-all of evolution in the human form. I have a function in the Universe — just as your Sun has a function to warm and enliven your land, mine is to weed out the planets whose time has come to die. I feed on their energy, in order to keep the Universe growing and glowing, in all its mindless infinity. I am hungry, and I am tired.

ROBERT: Tired of...

CORBY: The Search... the Quest...

ROBERT: But aren't you lonely, Galactus?

CORBY: Very lonely. I hurt when the billions die as I suck out the Life-energy from their planets. Even when they die, they're together, and I'm alone, all alone in my gigantic body. And there's no one else the same size as me, no great female to warm my space-cold flesh... I have no woman, no woman at all...

ROBERT: Keep on saying that, with more and more energy. (*Corby does, crying deeply yet softly; after he's stopped, Robert continues*) Now be Mr. Fantastic, and keep looking into Nancy's left eye, letting your breathing be even looser...

CORBY: Hi, Nancy... In the Fifties, we thought it was the Commie threat; in the Sixties, we thought it was our troubled, angry, drug-crazed youth; now, there's another even worse threat: Aliens! They're out there all right — they're gonna get us — it's gonna take all the power we can muster to keep this country, this planet, strong and free and safe for you and me. It's tough for me. I can stretch as far as I want, but I can't seem to do enough — whatever I do just isn't good enough! (*He repeats the last statement at Robert's urging, his voice breaking*)

ROBERT: Now Superman.

CORBY: I'm the Man of Steel. I can do anything! I can move so fast that I can play all the instruments in the band at once. Bullets bounce off my mighty chest, but I can't *feel* anything, and *that* hurts me...

ROBERT: Say it again, even more softly...

CORBY: I can't feel anything, and *that* hurts me... I want to be human like you. I look human, I act human, I try to be human, but I'm not really — I'm an alien. My eyes are very intense; if I'm not careful, I could burn holes through you, or see right through you. I don't want to see like that — I don't know what to do with how much I see...

ROBERT: (*After a long pause*) And now be the Incredible Hulk...

CORBY: (*Grunting*) Hulk like woman. Hulk feel woman loving Hulk. Woman care about Hulk. (*Half-laughing, half-crying*) Woman remind Hulk of Hulk's own Janella. Woman nice to Hulk — woman not care if Hulk be huge and strong and smash. So Hulk be good to woman. Hulk not smash woman. Hulk smash anyone who want to smash woman... Hulk lonely...

ROBERT: Does Hulk fuck?

CORBY: No. Hulk wants to fuck Janella, but Hulk got reduced to small size and couldn't. Leader make Hulk small, so Hulk smash leader. Hulk not very aware, but Hulk has feelings. Hulk likes woman. Hulk not like leader. Hulk smash leader!

NANCY: Hulk have program?

CORBY: Hulk have small program, very small program. Hulk not big on thinking — Hulk not able to follow "I Love Lucy", so he smash TV set. But Hulk like you...

ROBERT: And Hulk big part of Corby... (*Pause*) Now, if you were a character in a Marvel comic, what kind of guy would you be?

CORBY: I'd... be in the background, but come in at the right time.

ROBERT: And what would your special gift be when it came time to deal with baddies?

CORBY: I'd have something really different, something surprising...

ROBERT: How about a cello? A miniature cello that, when played by you and you alone, would make anyone, even the worst of the worst, feel *vulnerable*! What a weapon! You'd whip out your tiny cello, pluck a few chords, and the villain would be reduced to wet mush just like that, unless of course they were deaf! Besides the hazard of such deafness, you'd probably get stuck with an even worse hazard — for example, if a woman like your mother came your way... (*Laughter*) But you've made your life a minefield of Kryptonite, even as you've hardened yourself in defence, like The Thing, and got yourself loose, but uptight loose, like Mr. Fantastic, all the while longing for vulnerability, like Clark Kent's chesty alter-ego...

Nevertheless, you are slowly healing, gradually learning to create a Life-enriching myth for yourself in which you're the central character, not as an ego, but as a flesh-and-blood archetype. There's two levels to this: One, the level at which your myth is the same as mine and everyone else's, namely the undertaking of the journey of Awakening, the Great Journey, with its universal themes of departure, breakdown, spiritual trial, resurrection, and wholeness, all making the most sense through the medium of artful metaphor... And, two, there's the level of purely individual myth, the dramatized vision of Corby's evolutionary steps, falls, horrors and glories, his adventure of alignment with the greater myth, an alignment that, to be effective, must not wipe out personal myth! The electroshock treatment preceding your birth is part of that myth, especially as it's woven into your later life...

A myth rightly used does not explain, but reveals... You look at a mountain, and it's not just a mountain, for you sense its spirit, you sense it as *presence*, not intellectually or romantically, but viscerally; it's as if *you* are embodying the essence of the mountain! Of course, to engage with anything in terms of its core presence, *you* yourself must become more of a presence, more of a medium... To get into a myth, you have to *feel* it — you must let it awaken your own archetypal energies. I'm not talking about being vicariously associated with mythological beings, nor about merely identifying with them, but about empathizing with them to the point of really *knowing* them. Again, to do this, *you* must become intimate with your own mythical qualities, which I'm being deliberately vague about, so as not to overdefine...

An unconscious archetype is a stereotype... Without wakefulness, myth is just soap opera, mere melodrama, everyday escapism. (*Pause*) Consider Pathya — she's archetypally present when she's in conscious contact with her outrage about the desecration of the Earth, but she's usually just stuck in the grungy stereotype of the permanent slave, a stereotype that's always ripe to birth the true warrior, the freed slave, the master of power...

Some archetypes are pretty straightforward, like the warrior, and others are more complex, like the trickster. A lot of my work is full-throttle trickster work, tricking people into doing what they'd do if they were true to themselves — it's a positive deception, of questionable use only if the recipient doesn't know how they got from their periphery to their core of being. (And even that's okay right at the beginning, since it gives a useful taste of what it feels like to be ecstatically grounded; of course, as the work progresses, it must become more and more consciously participated in, so that my presence becomes less of a catalyst, and more of a *reminder*.) I may behave crazily, do all kinds of seemingly absurd things, suddenly get very coarse, but I'm simply responding to what you are doing, manifesting whatever behaviour best serves your awakening. Sometimes that means being a trickster, and other times it means being a swordsman, a computer, a softness, an etherealness, a wrestler, a marathoner, a child... whatever works...

The Universe is infinite in its qualities. Those that override or seemingly govern the others (because they're more central to the crux of What Is) sometimes appear in our dreams... a wise man or wise woman appears, either directly, bright with shiveringly significant guidance or clues, or more indirectly, perhaps even threateningly (as a carnivorous giant, perhaps, or a hideously malevolent witch) if we've denied ourself such wisdom in our waking state. Look what happened to Pan, who symbolized sacred lust — Christianity got hold of him (after he'd all but been reduced to a goat-hoofed lecher) and his horns, and turned him into the Devil! Not only did this further desacralize and desecrate sexuality, but it wedged wide open the split between matter and spirit, between body and soul, the split that still plagues modern culture...

Open up the book of yourself, get past the credits, and you'll soon feel what we all have in common — you'll intuit the stages of what's mythologically termed the hero's journey, and sense roughly where you are, so that you can take appropriate action, instead of just fighting, outthinking, and otherwise sabotaging yourself. Have you noticed that there's usually a dragon, or something similar, at some point in the journey? And have you noticed that this fearsome creature usually is guarding a treasure of some sort, a treasure whose capture often leads to a winning of some previously inaccessible maiden? You face what you most fear, go right into it with your eyes open, and you'll "have" the treasure of your core of being, the treasure chest of your deepest love, which almost inevitably leads to a profoundly fruitful union of male and female...

But the dragons aren't just great big dumb bodyguards or treasure-guards; they have their own wisdom, an ancient wisdom, which when taken in, leads to even more than the above mystic marriage of feminine and masculine — one becomes whole in an even deeper sense. You don't just napalm, blacklist, castrate, invade, or bore the dragon to death — you have to meet it, war with it, understand it, absorb its knowingness, or you won't know what to do with the treasure, anymore than pigs know what to do with a pearl necklace! The dragon's presence is there to bring out the best in us, to ripen us through *challenge*. Many want to fly above the dragon, or to affirm/visualize/meditate it away, treating *it* as an illusion (but not their own flight from it!) — they see the treasure from a distance, and they memorize its apparent shape, its apparent structure, its *read-about* interiority, and they then fall in love with their *abstraction* of the treasure, acting as if their resulting sensations are a direct proof of actually *already* having the treasure within!

The dragon must be faced. You might even have to fight it to the death, but even then, you'll need to feel it as part of yourself, perhaps even weep for its death. For each of us, the dragon may look different — each dragon requires a unique approach. Dragon-slaying will always be a spontaneous art, as deep as it's creative... All I'm saying is get to know your dragons, not just over tea or a beer, but in a manner that flames through your personal history, so that the Incredible Hulk becomes the incredible Corby!

Michelangelo: *Madonna*

-39-

The Nun & The Whore: Real Sex Doesn't Need Fantasy

STELLA: I've been having a lot of very sexual dreams. In them (*Speaking quickly*) I'm most turned on when I'm taking charge. And with Richard [*her husband*], when I look back at my sex life with him, I was very passive most of the time...

ROBERT: What aren't you telling me?

STELLA: How much it hurt me to do what I did with you on the phone Monday night. If I'd been more honest, I'd have told you how much I need you.

ROBERT: You're doing the same thing now, trying to substitute good intentions for real action, thrusting a mask of sincerity at me. You began by mentioning some dreams, but you skipped over them very quickly, rushing through them, offering only the skimpiest of reviews; already, you were whitewashing, trying to present your content in such a way as to minimize me doing something unpredictable with it. You're uptight because you're unacknowledgedly trying to control how things are going to unfold here. If you'd been more in touch with yourself, you would have probably started speaking about one of your dreams, maybe the one that is currently most alive for you. You distance yourself from your direct experience; you don't want to get too close to it. You call me up and say, "I *wanted* to tell you that..." or something similar, instead of just going ahead and telling me!

STELLA: The night after that call with you, I had a nightmare... The men in the community were talking to me about my sexuality. Richard leaned over me, and shoved his fingers down my throat. Suddenly, the dream changed, and there were snakes wrapping themselves all around my body. I started choking, uncontrollably choking. There was a snake going down my throat — at that point, I realized I was dreaming, and woke up.

ROBERT: You've gotten twisted up in your sexuality; how can you express it clearly when you're gagging on what you take it to be? You invest it with unnecessary danger, just like this session, which you're obscuring with your nervousness. And what is nervousness? It's just a heightened stimulation that's more unpleasant than pleasant, tainted with nastily supportive thoughts. There's all sorts of ways to create this sensation; your job isn't to speak the mind of it, but to shine through it. You could say, "Here's what my nervousness wants to say..." and let it spill, unedited and messy as it wants to be. If you say what you need to say in the moment, the words will just flow out of you, spontaneous and fitting. Instead of a snake going down your throat, one will come up and out, river-like, alive, sensuous, both innocent and knowing...

But you've swallowed a lot of venom in your life, and you've coated it with niceness, with good behavior, with fanatical conformity. You keep playing the good girl going for high grades, as if Xanthyros is a school such as you grew up in, where you had to swallow a lot of bullshit and irrelevancies, and spit it back out at exam time.

STELLA: I was really good at spitting it back out...

ROBERT: But all you spat back was the information; the *rest* lodged in you, leaving no room for your Being. You became peripherally associated with your core, learning to mistrust it. You learned to not make waves, *or* to make plastically outrageous waves so as to demonstrate your looseness. In either case, of course, you were only reacting to, and therefore binding yourself to, your conditioning, your good-girl devout Catholic number. When you were working as a bartender and being promiscuous, your Catholicism was still intact, actually *motivating* your apparent liberation — the bartender you was just laid over the prudish you, while a deeper you screamed and screamed, unheard...

You are not using your gifts, such as your dreams. The dream of the snakes should have been worked with the very next morning, if not that night. You could have put your fingers down your throat, or had someone else do it, and screamed, howled, let loose, writhed, done whatever you had to do, literally embodying the snake, feeling it from the *inside*. I would have given the outer snakes a voice, letting it mutate however it needed to — into a Mother Superior's voice, a bishop's voice, your mother's, your father's, a glossolalia, a storm, whatever! And the snake going down your throat — all the crap, all the poison, you swallowed regarding Catholicism's view of sex — what an invasion! What energy there would be in exploring this nightmare! What gifts! Imagine going into and right through it, from the inside out —

STELLA: I can feel the sensations of it in my throat now.

ROBERT: Going down, down, down, as though sex was *down there!* The poor fucking snake pinned to its negative connotations! (*Pause*) Well, the throat is connected to the sex center — the mouth and upper throat have vaginal correlations, similarities of tissue and structure, with the tongue having a certain penile capacity. Have you seen pictures of some female saints? Their heads are thrown back in apparent bliss, their throats seeming to shine with the swoon of their heart — theirs is the curve of non-genital orgasm, or semi-orgasm. Some yogis in India cut the septum at the base of their tongue, so that they can run their tongue back into their throat — it's not just a way of locking the throat (as paralleled by perineal contraction on the inhale), but also a means of pleasure. The throat is not some pleasureless zone! Remember the Deep Throat stuff? If a woman (or man) can swallow an erect penis without gagging, the penis is gripped so firmly by the throat that it creates more pleasure, stimulation in this case of course being far more important than anything else...

When your throat is truly loose, energetically unburdened, un-repressed, at ease, then your vagina will likely be loose, pliable, open. When your lips are relaxed and soft, your labia will probably be looser, subtly fuller. Good midwives know this; a woman in labour who is tight-mouthed will in all likelihood have trouble letting her baby come through cleanly. When you scream falsely, or try to act emotional, you're just fucking away your energy, trying to mastur-bate your way to freedom. Most people only feel the connection between their mouth and genitals when they're kissing deeply. But to feel it more deeply, you've got to do more than just bind yourself to that electric arc between the two centers — you have to con-sciously pass through your torso, not just bypass it. The journey is through the belly, the solar plexus, the diaphragm, the heart, up and down and radiating in all directions. Otherwise, you're just connecting two terminals, genital and buccal, stranding yourself from what's in-between, turning it into a disembodied wasteland.

Think of all those women who thought they were lovers of Christ, all the nuns, all the long-time virgins... There was no virgin birth. Mary wasn't a virgin, but only a very pure woman, a truly virginal woman. Most women who think they're brides of Christ are losing themselves in romantic daydream, using their imagery of Jesus as a turn-on, a kind of sublime pornography. No mortal man can measure up, of course. The flipside of such prudery, such "I'm saving myself for Jesus" delusion, is promiscuity. The Virgin and the Whore. You've played the promiscuous, raunchy, ribald bartender, and you've also played the prude, not seeing that *both* are escapes from real sex...

What could be more natural than sex? It's inherent to you! Why force it to play a supporting role in your dramas? Did Jesus die for your sins?

STELLA: No.

ROBERT: But a lot of people *believe* that he did, as if his sacrifice somehow absolved them of their responsibility for their own doings. They are still crucifying him, nailing him into place, completely missing the real Jesus!

STELLA: I'm having a very strong memory right now of when I was little, masturbating in front of pictures of Jesus. (*She starts to cry*)

ROBERT: How old were you?

STELLA: I don't remember — maybe around puberty.

ROBERT: No one knew?

STELLA: No. Sometimes I'd actually see him at the end of my bed...

ROBERT: Consider how sterile your home environment was then, how emotionally vacant your parents were, how rich your Catholic indoctrination was by contrast — everything about your life then put Jesus on top, the Salvation from your horror of a life, the one light in your antiseptic darkness. You idealized him; you found some aliveness through your fantasies about him. It was your survival, your only semblance of love, of purity, of hope. (*She cries*) He was the man of your dreams... Do you see why nuns are, in so many words, called Brides of Christ? They might as well be called Brides of Frankenstein, as far as I'm concerned — Frankenstein is a man-made monster, and so is the conventional Jesus!

STELLA: I wanted to be a nun most of my life — it was something I aspired to when I was a little girl.

ROBERT: Probably because it seemed to be the only juicy possibility in your life then — a similar thing happened when you were with Bhagwan (Shree Rajneesh) — you could imagine, literally imagine, all sorts of wonderful things about him and you, and then go get blissed out, inflated with a delicious swoon, the aaahhh of runaway romance, the titillating drama of Master and disciple! Much of that supposed blissfulness was merely created by your own wanting to feel blissful; you *wanted* to feel blissful because you thought that that was what you were supposed to feel. You craved evidence that you really belonged with him, so you created it, or a very convincing surrogate of it. Rarely did you sense what was natural for you to feel with him. You are so, so suspicious of the natural, even now, years after Rajneeshpuram! Instead of trying to make yourself feel something that fits your notion of what you think you should be feeling, you need to immediately acknowledge what is currently occurring for you, *regardless* of its implications!

You've fought your sexual repression by trying to stay in heat, suggestively available. You keep creating sexual charge when there is no need for it. Such torture! You're behind the scenes, pulling the strings of your passion, doubting its *natural* currents and imperatives. You still keep your distance from your body, even in sex, don't you? When you have the urge to make love, why make a problem out of it? Why get uptight about it? Why complicate it with tension and manipulation? Because you *don't* trust it!

Fantasy, in almost all cases, pollutes sex, whether the fantasy is of Jesus or a Playboy centerfold; real sex doesn't need fantasy nor any other manipulation of mind, for its Ecstasy is not brought about by stimulation, but by mutually enlivening love and desire. If you're busy making erotic fantasy, you're not making love, but only fucking yourself, contrary to the pudgy ramblings of Dr. Ruth and other apostles of masturbation.

The effort to get turned-on is only a confession of being turned-off. Almost everyone is shut down sexually, but most have found a way to override this, to get so stimulated that they *appear* to be openly sexual. Nevertheless, an engorged periphery is not equivalent to an Ecstasy-radiating core! Being in constant heat has nothing at all to do with being a truly sexual being. Fucking is not a solution for psychoemotional constipation. It is not salvation, despite all the advertisements to the contrary...

Deep down, we're just as sexually repressed as our Victorian-era ancestors, however thoroughly we camouflage it with promiscuity, explicit imagery, and erotic permissiveness. Yes, more women these days are having orgasms, but so what? A strategically-engineered orgasm contributes nothing to intimacy. More gratification is of no use — it's just consolation, a kind of booby prize for staying mediocre and fragmented. More orgasms, more erotic stimulation, in general just adds some pleasure to the cage, rather than feeding the longing to live free of self-incarceration. Pretty fucked, isn't it? So, are you the Bride of Jesus?

STELLA: No!

ROBERT: Are you the Bride of Frankenstein?

STELLA: No! (*Laughter*)

ROBERT: How about Dracula?

STELLA: I like him!

ROBERT: A lot sexier than Frankenstein or the Catholic Jesus, isn't he?

STELLA: Biting and sucking! (*Laughter*)

ROBERT: Sex and violence, with a touch of class... Sex lumped together with drainage of Life-energy, done in the dark... So you're not a nun and you're not a whore. For most men, the ideal woman is simultaneously a nun and a whore, the whore because of her availability, the nun because of her unavailability. The lack of availability, of sexual access, creates passion, a dark, tensely charged passion, an anxiety-intensified passion that seemingly necessitates sexual release, which of course is provided by the whore. The nun's the pinup, the whore the dumping-ground.

In the typical male pornographic fantasy, the hit is not the naked flesh, but the availability of the woman — the man doesn't have to do any work to have her. No pressure, no anxiety, and no challenge. The whore has her moment, then shrinks before the nun, the ever-inaccessible virgin. None of this has anything to do with love. It's actually an avoidance of the Feminine, both in the woman and in the man, except when it is lit from within (when it mutates into the life-affirming archetypes of the Divine Virgin and the Sacred Whore). Your true womanhood calls to you, inviting you to flesh it out...

Gustave Doré: *Milton's Paradise Lost*

– 40 –

Letting Go of the Whip: Moving From Guilt to Shame to Freedom

Guilt is inherently self-divisive — one part of us, a childish aspect, does whatever it is that apparently generates (or justifies) our guilt, in close conjunction with another part of us, a neurotically parental aspect, that wields a righteous whip, mechanically punishing the doer of the supposed crime. The relationship between these two is the essence of guilt. As such, guilt is just a nastily stalemated parent/ child conflict, but, more importantly, it is something *we do* to ourselves, something *we* superimpose on ourselves, something that keeps us divided, miserable, stuck, addicted, small, disempowered, and predictably exploitable. Put another way, guilt means we get to *again* do whatever it is that seemingly creates our guilt — we permit ourselves to do it over and over again, even as "we" simultaneously punish ourselves for such transgression. In this endarkened, blame-bloated dramatization of such a deeply internalized splitting of Self, we repetitiously (and almost religiously) act out our fall from Grace, our estrangement from our core of Being, our having gone to pieces...

Closely related to guilt is shame. At its worst, shame is but a kind of exaggerated guilt, manifesting as the sleazily contrite emotionalism of guilt, cringingly begging for punishment for its apparently unforgivable sins. Even so, shame is still a *feeling* response or reaction to what is taken to be a violation of some sort of moral obligation or contract, whereas guilt is but a *suppression* of such feeling, a mind-induced collapse of heart and soul, as cold as shame is warm...

And what is *healthy* shame? It is basically the open-faced, bodyloose, mind-free acknowledgment of having done something clearly inappropriate, something deeply insensitive to the *true* needs of a particular situation. It need not have a sidekick that carries an overseeing whip, for when it is healthy, it *already* is Life-givingly intimate with *real* parental authority, namely that native to ourselves. It is simply a whole-hearted way of saying, "I did it. I'm sorry. I'm *here* — I am not withdrawing and will not withdraw or go into hiding, just because of what I did."

On the other hand, guilt *is* a withdrawal, a recoil from intimacy, and, despite its protestations to the contrary, is a *rejection* of the one (be that one another person, or one's own vulnerability and innocence) whom it has hurt or abused. Guilt has nothing whatsoever to do with real responsibility, for it insists on remaining in the domain of *blame*, its reality being one of simplistic right and wrong. No matter what others say, guilt persists in blaming itself, occasionally (as when it balloons into hysteria) shifting into blaming others, ever remaining dutifully skewered by the morality of blame, which of course it completely confuses with responsibility, which we could define here as self-generated, self-illuminating, guilt-free accountability. Real responsibility involves expansion and a commitment to Being, whereas blame involves contraction and a *collapse* of Being...

When it is given freely and fully, shame flushes the entire system; instead of contracting one's organic impulses, it unknots and expands them — the face blushes, the blood flows more freely, the entire body warms up, enriched and flushed with enlivening passion. As such, the *whole body* is then but a confession of what has happened; there is not even necessarily a need to say "I'm sorry" or "I apologize for...", although such phrases may at times be useful or healing to say, *if* they are spoken authentically, instead of in some grovelling or defiant fashion. When shame is truly and fully felt, it rises and pinkly flowers, then passes, transmuting into love and healthy relatedness. Real shame does not persist for long. If it does, then it is simply guilt (or repressed shame), bound up in the hire of blame's morality.

The guilt-ridden do not want to grow — they just want to be able to "do it" again, and in order to justify "doing it" again, they need to keep the threat of parental punishment hanging over them, so that they can then immediately carry out their own punishment, thereby satisfying the moral code implanted behind their forehead. That is, the guilt-ridden are just repeat offenders perpetually imprisoning themselves, playing both prosecutor and accused, but without any real resolution, ever resurrecting the stage of their courtroom drama and suffering the pains of fitting themselves to its loveless script, while finding a darkly pleasurable release through *once again* "doing it." Shame, however, when healthy, carries within itself a full-bodied, full-blooded resolution of whatever brought it about in the first place; such shame creates an energy field within which real healing can occur, so that the very forces at the heart of shame (and guilt) can be transformed into *available* Life-energy once again...

When someone says to someone else, "You should be ashamed of yourself," they ordinarily are not implying that the other ought to enter into uninhibited, mind-free shame so that they then might let go of whatever pain they have taken on because of their actions. No! They are *actually* pushing the other into or toward guilt; they don't *really* mean that you ought to be ashamed of yourself, but that you *should* feel guilty, you miserable sinner, you rotten so-and-so, you failure, you bad whatever!

Guilt is a refusal to love, and it is also a refusal to parent oneself in a sane manner; it is a childish clinging to parental forces *outside* ourselves, especially those that carry authoritarian certainty. Shame, on the other hand, provides fertile conditions for reconnecting with the parental authority that is *native* to us. It is a way of acknowledging our errors (*especially* our self-betrayal), not just intellectually, but with our entire being — it is about getting up from the mud and moving on, while at the same time cleaning up the mess we've made. When our slippage has injured others (or ourself), done some sort of harm, we must clean it up *fully*, or we will only further cripple and burden ourselves. Shame is the natural, bodily confession of such slippage; it is an organismic purification, a great opportunity to reestablish intimacy or connectedness. It is a blushing of the entire system — if consciously surrendered to, it'll cleanse us, creating an atmosphere of *real* forgiveness...

Unfortunately, all too many of us mechanically choose guilt. We, in other words, repress our shame, and all of us have or have had shame. Not many of us have *really* forgiven ourselves for our shame-generating actions — we may have played, in New Age fashion, at self-forgiveness, pretending that it actually has occurred, in some naive metaphysical way, but forgiveness is not simply something to *believe* in, not some sort of mental affirmation or resolution to impose on oneself, not some concept that can be inculcated so thoroughly that shame disappears... Forgiveness is *not* an act of mind, but of full-bodied *Being*, an act that cannot be rehearsed, nor reduced to a few phrases — it is not weak-kneed nor pretentiously humble, but is alive, expansive, potently vulnerable, luminously empathetic, and, above all, loving, *truly* loving...

There's nothing wrong with shame. There's nothing wrong with blushing with embarrassment — when it occurs in an open-faced, nakedly alive manner, it's a relief, an easing of tension, a heartfelt confession catalyzing an environment in which *real* forgiveness can bloom. Shame is *not* a problem, not a something to not have — it's an opportunity, a wonderfully visceral opportunity to come clean and to dive into a truer scene...

Guilt fills churches and empties hearts, again and again reinforcing our habit of making false starts. Guilt is a psychological parasite, a cultural leech, a murderer of love claiming temporary insanity... Nevertheless, guilt is *not* some kind of entity we can throw darts at, or try to eradicate. It is something *we are doing*, something *we are animating*, something *we* don't want to see that *we* are doing. It is a suppression of Being, a withdrawal from real feeling, a flight from integrity, the very epitome of "divided we fall"...

It is very important to not continue carrying our repressed shame. It is crucial to psychoemotionally recall those episodes in our life that still bring us a sense of shame when we are reminded of them. To tell those stories again, with passion and openness in the presence of those who truly love us, those who are real allies, can only let our shame undam and flood through us, until we are overcome with such naked hurt, such pure emotion, that eventually a sobering joy, a deep, deep relief, will be felt throughout our *entire* being. If we speak thus, our intimates can only feel closer to us, and more inspired to reveal and heal *their* shame-ridden corners.

When we repress our shame, we tend to become either exaggeratedly soft or hard, compensating for our state by indulging in the exercise of blame, finding it vaguely reassuring to point the finger at ourselves or someone else, or both; thus does simplistic incrimination become our chronic occupation, masking our psychospiritual irresponsibility. The guilty are very easy to control, for their power is consumed by their internal warfare. However, those who don't cling to their guilt are not exploitable by any sort of outside parental authority, be it of state or church or their own familial ties, for they are already well-established in their own capacity for sanely parenting themselves. On the other hand, the guilt-ridden, because they are continually giving life to a neurotic inner parent, are extremely susceptible to correspondingly powerful authoritative or parental forces, especially those of organized religion...

Guilt reduces God to the ultimate parent (in the West), and religion provides more than sufficient implements for self-castigation, as well as the plates for financial donation. As such, religion is but hope-glazed consolation, a business built on lofty promise — you could say that religion gets it now by convincing us to get it later. To perpetuate itself, religion milks its practitioners for all the guilt it can, even indirectly teaching them that it is *good* to feel guilty, since of course we are all sinners. Thus does guilt masquerade as conscience...

But God is not the ultimate parent, as is commonly presumed in Western religion (with its ego-centered obsession with monotheism), nor is God some kind of ineffable ideal, some ultimate abstraction or great principle, as is commonly presumed in the East. Both make the error of turning God into a goal, an end whose means they apparently possess the exclusive rights to, whether such means are yogic, prayerful, mantric, devotional, or just a matter of rigid adherence to certain beliefs and rituals. The guilty, like the spiritually goal-oriented (the two often being synonymous), cannot really *feel* or intuit God, for they cannot even directly feel (or be present as) their *own* core of Being, their *own* primal Truth, for their capacity to *feel* is far too suppressed...

Guilt is *not* a feeling, but a *suppression* of feeling, whereas shame *is* a feeling. If we openly confess our shame, release and pass through it *consciously*, then we'll be reestablished in deep communion with the Source and Substance of all. Then we can feel God, intuit God, breathe God, live God, and love God... God is not to be explained or defined, but to be felt and lived and embraced — to *really* feel God, we must literally embody *all* that we are, and this is impossible to do when we are busy indulging in guilt. Such embodiment requires a deep willingness to feel, to directly experience, *all* of our feelings, not just the ecstatic or pleasurable ones, but grief, anger, lust, rage, shame, sorrow, all of which must be felt with an openness of Being, all of which must be eventually entered into without any mind-shields or mental buffers or emotional dissociation...

I'm not talking about emotionalism, hysteria, overdone catharsis, or other exaggerations and caricatures of our capacity to feel, but about a depth of feeling that's simultaneously sane and unobstructedly alive, a quality of feeling that carries within itself a wisdom of flow, a knowingness deeper than any knowledge we possess. To fully enter into our capacity to thus feel, we must trust, and such trust cannot be blind — it must emanate from center, from a conscious abiding at our core of Being, from a deep inner integrity, a wholeness of Self that is far, far from the self-dividedness that characterizes guilt...

Shame is simply a powerful flooding away of such self-dividedness, a bodybright flaming through of such fragmentation of Self. Shame's fire is hot enough to thaw any kind of guilt, however deeply imbedded. So do not flee your shame. Let it take you to the bottom of your pain, to the weave of your true name. Do not bounce between the childish side of guilt and the parental side — neither one is *you*. They are just simply two utterly mechanical personifications of the same dreary drama. Instead of identifying with either one, see them as clouds, and be their sky, letting your shame cry and weep itself free of its own script...

Uncover your shame fully, allowing yourself to go beyond the strategies of the introvert, the extrovert, and the convert, and into the way of the lover, the one who is not enemy to his or her shame, the one who does not wish any feeling away, the one who is both here to stay and here to go all the way, not in withdrawal, guilt, or strategic detachment but in passion, joy, grief, anger, lust, woundedness, ecstasy, intimacy, subtlety, transcendence, and self-illuminating obviousness, all of it creatively commingling, all of it fecundly coexisting as the ground from which real transformation can occur...

Such is the way of the lover, the one who doesn't give a damn about guilt. Such beings treat their shame in the same manner as any other feeling — they respect and honor it, they illuminate it, they breathe it full, they do not cling to it, they do what they can to enjoy and make good use of it. They are not here to exploit their environment, inner or outer, nor are they here to escape it. They don't run from their suffering, nor do they unnecessarily reinforce it — they willingly pass *through* it, letting their wounds be exposed to the light of awareness, offering the guilt-ridden not churches, whips, placebos, promises, or numbness, but an opportunity to return to wholeness, to integrity, to a fully-lived Life, a Life free of blame and rich with multidimensional responsibility...

SHE DEFENDS THOSE WHO HURT HER

She defends those who hurt her
She pleads their case in barren courtrooms
Pouring passion into her twisted tolerance
Resurrecting judges with endless ears
She keeps her outrage packed in a tasteful tomb
Denying her heart a belly, and her innocence a womb
She knows better, but still thinks and shrinks herself so small
When looming authority sternly invades her rooms

When she defends those who hurt her
She only protects them from what they need
Placating is her art
Weeping, weeping, is her child's heart
Believing her mind is her pain
Dark, dark is her panic's hidden rain
Playing liberal is her game, her fury screaming tame
Guilty until proven innocent is her drama
Giving is her cover, loneliness her endarkened lover

But now she cannot turn her past into a self-pitying alibi
Now she cannot turn away from her battered vulnerability
With its little dancing shoes and achingly marooned heart
There's a healing possible, a healing sweet and fierce and wild
A waking light for the wounds of an unforgettable child
Now she knows that those who hurt her
Are secretly pleading for her unrestrained fire
To help them she must expose them
Letting the courtroom burn to nothing
The old agony now unchained,
The glimpsed Ecstasy reclaimed,
The dance done not as escape, but as celebration

Now she pulsates with every color
No longer worrying about what to wear
Her eyes of defeat now eyes of Truth and spirit-fire
Her future unburdened by mind, her everything telling no lies
Her happiness obliterating her lifelong disguise

-41-

No More Diseased Release: Cutting Through Masochism

(Marion talks for awhile about feeling turned on by her lover's criticism, feeling both crushed by it and twistedly pleasured, sleazily titillated)

ROBERT: For some people, there is a kind of pleasure in being smacked around prior to having sex — it's a charge-building foreplay containing its own punishment for the creation of such sensation. For others, there is a hidden pleasure in being smacked around period! You're one of these negative receivers — you play out your life in such a way that you draw bashing energy toward you, verbally, emotionally, and physically. You *invite* violence. You act hard done by, but there's a secret pleasure in it for you, a fleshy release...

One thing you did with the thousands of men you prostituted yourself with was not speak up; you were and are very quick to make the other person right, to plant them as firmly as possible in the driver's seat. Your game of self-effacement and self-debasement is, however, *not* inherent to you. You hand the other person all the power so that you can be beaten, hammered, or harangued into oblivion, while giving them *all the responsibility* for what's happening!

And what is the fundamental characteristic of masochists? They want to burst, to be released via *outside* intervention (which they can then project punisher onto) — that is why they crave being beaten or otherwise abused. There's a hope in them that the beating or invasion will break the membrane around them, break the boundaries they've established around themselves, and thereby free them. Of course, such violence only further reinforces their guilt. (They compulsively play out the childish side of guilt, seducing others into playing out the whip-wielding, parental side of guilt.)

Everyone has a bit of masochism in them, but you have a lot, especially sexually. After being violated, grossly or subtly, there is some release, and some dissolution of one's boundaries, but it's only temporary, and then you can of course hate yourself for having done it, get busy feeling unworthy, until your unworthiness festers to the point where you draw to yourself yet another set of circumstances that bulge with ready-to-explode violence! You're so automatically focussed on finding signs that you are unworthy! It's your strategy for finding release, and in it you're no different than anyone else who is making the having of bodily pleasure more important than waking up. Either you run away from this (you could call it an avoidance of ecstasy and intimacy), or you go into it, and to go right into the heart of it, you can't go as Marion the *apparently* humble, self-effacing, wouldn't-hurt-a-fly masochist!

You're so angry at men, especially at your father and all the men you let fuck you. Yes, it looked like those men were looking down at you, but in fact *you* were looking down at them — even in the gang rape atrocities you suffered, you had a feeling of hidden superiority, of twisted victory, of grim satisfaction. They got you, but they didn't *really* get you. They emptied their violence into you, and you took it, saying in so many words, you'll never get to *me*, never! (*She cries*)

Your humility is false. Your meekness is not real. You've spent your whole life being hurt by men. Now you have to get back at them *cleanly, directly*, so that the fighting, the warfare, is not subterranean or masked by sexual proclivity, but is consciously upfront and bright, simultaneously vital and simple. Just about all of the men you've been with were men who despised women as much as they craved them. You made an art out of making yourself despicable and trashy. You became a gutter whore, making a travesty out of turning the other cheek. Now you're with a very different type of man, and you have to play a different game. You can't play whore, just as he can't play steel soldier. (*Long pause*)

As long as you *insist* on deriving pleasure from being hurt, you won't want to take things in a different direction. Even if there is no pleasure at all for you in being hurt, it still creates a *familiar* tension in you, a tension that you *automatically* associate with upcoming release! What I'm teaching here is sex as a celebration and ecstatic intensification of Being, rather than sex as a *releaser of tension* — you can't just accept this intellectually, but rather you must practice it, and lovingly prepare the soil for such practice.

Masochism has no place in Xanthyros. The point, however, is not to repress or rise above your masochism, but to expose it, to turn it inside out. When you first expose it, there may be a certain pleasure. I've seen a few people look almost orgasmic when they talked about themselves in a revealing way; it's a bit like an exhibitionist showing his penis to a little girl — he's embarrassed and maybe scared, but it's a big hit for him, a juicy thrill. We all get stuck in the repetition of thrill-production, don't we? If you're living a relatively barren life, you'll probably, to compensate, want to maximize pleasurable sensation for the rest of your life!

Even though you're not living the old loveless life, you still, to a significant degree, have the old addictions, and, like most people, you crave heightening feel-good sensations, even if it means using gestures of love to nourish and amplify the must in lust. Your suffering is rooted in the repetitive urge to pleasurably recompense yourself, to distract yourself from your sense of separation from God. There is no hurt like the hurt of turning away from our Source. Masochism has been your solution, your method; like the extremely obese, you are looking to burst, to be exploded into an oblivion of vast Unity...

You became a magnet for abuse; you wanted it to come to you, all gift-wrapped with the subtly sexual violence of your father's touch. Others played the abuser, so you could play the victim, adroitly side-stepping your responsibility in the whole affair. Stop repressing *your* urge to be abusive! When abuse becomes healthy, it is just shared anger, healthy anger, as well as vulnerable need. Sexual abuse is hard to maintain in the presence of love and awareness. You know what to do — you have to cut through your addiction to your marriage of degradation and pleasure. In other words, your pleasure, especially your sexual pleasure, needs to arise from your love, rather than from masochistic release.

In letting your sexual energy arise from Being and Stillness, rather than from egoic distress, you'll be on the side of intimacy. Your sexual rushes and streamings will simply just be there, needing no friction for their arising, and you'll learn to ride their waves, and you'll also know when to let them die a natural death, a full shore-coming, a breaking that is full of new life. The currents swell and fly and rejuvenatingly die, and you, in your ripeness, don't get greedy. If you get greedy during sex, you usually lose the other person — they become obscured by your runaway appetite. And it is very easy to get greedy, for if something feels good, if a certain movement feels good, then you think why shouldn't I do it faster, or why not do it longer, or how can I recreate this later? We, in our slumber, want to maximize psychophysical pleasure, not fully realizing that it is never satisfying to the soul, unless it is soul-driven. If there's no integrity, and no spirit, then there's no *real* sex, but only temporarily smiling misery...

The point is not just to have a good time, but to awaken; of course, if you are truly awakening, you will have a better time, a deeper time, a truer time. (*Pause*) Now, what about attachment? The stronger your love is, the more attached you will get, and the more vulnerable you will be to getting hurt, not masochistically-hurt, but love-hurt! You get hurt because of your attachment. This doesn't mean, however, to avoid attachment, like some spiritual coward, but to go right to the core of your hurt, to where there co-exists both loss and transcendence of loss. Such a passage provides breathing room for our hurt, so that we can work sanely with it, keeping our hearts open and our energy flowing... No more beating around the bush, or behind the bush. (*Laughter*)

No more beating, but instead human meeting, wherein you say yes, a gloriously alive yes to *your* passion, *your* life, *your* need! Have I said enough?

Gustave Doré: *Perrault's Fairy Realm*

-42-

Children & Real Education

The failure of our culture's educational system is widely known but is not in general fully acknowledged, for to deeply and honestly admit just how poorly it has done is to also comment with equally telling energy upon the state of our society, from the so-called family unit right up to governmental bureaucracy. There are certainly enough complaints and articulate criticisms of our culture, but only a few of them directly conclude that our society itself needs a *radical* restructuring, a profoundly deep breakdown, out of which something new and more Life-giving might emerge. Such views (which are usually taken by both the political Left and Right as being merely anarchistic) are, unfortunately, often only just Utopian visions, a kind of depersonalized hope, the attention-gathering subject matter of a few armchair philosophers and tenured radicals...

Nevertheless, what is referred to as education in our culture doesn't work. It is little more than indoctrination, a means whereby our society perpetuates itself. It is training bereft of real wisdom, a vast, snowballing entrainment, a complex assembly line of personalized mannequin-production, brightened only by those few who somehow manage to not ruinously betray their integrity during their schooling years. The purpose of our educational system is not to transform or awaken, but to inform, inform, and inform some more, without informing wisely. The appallingly high percentage of information that is of no value (despite all the parental voices declaring, "It'll come in handy someday") to almost all who are expected to ingest it serves the purpose of *addicting* us to the swallowing of data — the taking in of irrelevant information in school is really no different than rapt absorption in the trivialities and meaningless data that saturate newspapers, especially the so-called entertainment news, the miniscule and extraordinarily irrelevant details of well-known persons' private lives, loves, and blunders. Information overload and pointlessness only numbs and fragments us, driving us into neurotic specialization ("gotta be good at something") or dilettantish meandering, marooning us from our inherent totality of Being...

Education, if it is to be of any real value, needs to have as its primal context wholeness of Being. It cannot, however, succeed in this if it's in the form of an alternative school where a holistic approach is only preached, or where wholeness is but an ideal. Wholeness must be *more* than an ideal — it has to be literally lived, breathed, and practised by teachers (*and* parents) if students are to have any chance of absorbing it via example. It is not to be theorized about, nor just believed in; it is not to have its flag waved about to attract patriots, or it'll become just another form of fanaticism, one more do-gooder scheme, one more educational pigeonhole...

A truly holistic approach is impossible unless the teachers themselves are living it, not believing in it, but *living* it, not even needing to talk about it, nor to preach it at all. It emanates from them when they are teaching arithmetic, when they are working with children on dreams, when they are leading movement, when they are helping a child express some emotional content with a minimum of inhibition and a maximum of open-hearted illumination...

Such teachers are very rare, hardly ever found in the hallways of conventional and typically alternative education, simply because to enter these systems, these training grounds, they need to be *already*, at least to some degree, indoctrinated into that particular approach — their actual investment in such an educational system, whether they are in submission to it *or* are critical of it, keeps them from really rocking the boat, keeps them from making the waves that would permit something very, very different to arise, not just another version of a public or private school, nor even necessarily an alternative type of school, but something *radically* different, wherein children would be *truly* treated as unique individuals, *already* whole but needing to be deeply recognized and supported in that underlying unity of Being, even as they were skilfully taught to appreciate and explore and know the diversity of Life.

There's no point in creating an ideal version of how education ought to be if it's not demonstrably practical. There are plenty of lofty, even sublime theorizings about education and children, but for the most part, these are only schemes of dissociative hope penned by those who yearn for the same for themselves. What really matters here is the emergence of teachers, of educators, of parents, of people who are utterly committed to living a life of full-bodied, all-round sanity, intelligence, and love, a life in which one's actions emanate from a deep resonance with one's core of Being. Very few are those who possess such traits, but even the partial possession of them is enough, for if there is Essence-centered commitment, then such traits will gradually take fuller and fuller root, branching more and more beautifully and fulfillingly, until one is pervaded by the fragrance of centeredness, well-grounded Ecstasy, multidimensional practicality, and unswervingly present love...

A truly human educational system is not a system at all, but an art, a great art, involving the *creative* maintenance of an environment wherein children can truly learn, an environment wherein children learn so fully and so rewardingly that when the schooling day is over, the learning process does not stop. This, of course, necessitates, an intimate association between teachers and parents, teachers and students, students and parents, all parties remaining in fluid contact and empathetic communion with each other. This is not possible in a large setting, a mass setting, an overly centralized setting, and nor is it possible in a fuzzily alternative setting (as epitomized by Waldorf schools). It is *not* a program. It requires some degree of awakening in *all* the adults involved. It requires a common appreciation of and sensitivity to Truth, not a Truth that can be written down and parroted every day, but a Truth that is unrehearsable, spontaneous, alive, and as accurate in feeling as in content...

Such Truth can be recognized by everyone who's in touch with their core of Being. If someone were to emote in front of a group of such beings, they would all have exactly the same *knowingness* about what was before them. If it was manipulative, they'd all know *and* feel it — there wouldn't be any disagreement among them such as we see in our courts, where we could easily have three judges all having very different perceptions relative to a certain case, simply because they would not have viewed it from their center of Being, but only through their imbedded morality, their diseased feeling, their egoic concerns, their fragmentation of self. Those who are whole, those who are living a life epitomized by love, compassion, God-communion, and all-round gutsiness, have the same fundamental response (flavoured with colorfully idiosyncratic *surface* differences) to what is before them, not because they are robotically inclined, but because they all intuit the Truth of the situation, the essence of the matter, instead of just the *secondary* ramifications of what is occurring. They don't project onto the manipulative emoter their own hurt, some unconscious memory from their childhood — they sense exactly what is going on, and they act on it. They don't bullshit. They are direct and certain without being dogmatic, powerful without being unnecessarily aggressive, subtle without being obscure, loving without being sentimental...

Our culture has little interest in turning out sane educators. In fact, those in whom real sanity is obvious are all too easily viewed as lunatics, crazy radicals, charlatans, saboteurs, fools, or even traitors by those who are asleep, including those who are ordinarily in power in our society. Even those who have known some awakening, but who have succumbed to the system that employs them, tend to look upon bright newcomers with disfavor, not wishing them ill, but just cynically waiting for them to also submit to the sheer weight of the system of which they are now part.

The trouble with our educational system is exactly the trouble with our culture. It is impossible to remedy the school system without also having something similar happen to our very culture. This cannot be done just because some great leader says so, or it'll only be another sort of violence, a bureaucratically-overseen imposition, a forcing of sleepers to assume a different, more benign sleep position, to perhaps even act awake, to, all in all, submit to a new dogma, a new religion, a new ethic imposed from without. What *will* work is the awakening of people, but this cannot be instilled or forced from outside — it can only happen if there is *already* a willingness, however slight, on the part of one to wake up. If there isn't, then the Awakening call will simply become just another part of one's ongoing dream, something to be incorporated into the texture of one's fantasies, or to be pushed away if it's uncomfortable or contradictory to one's favorite illusions...

In all this, of course, children are grossly abused, forced to play roles that satisfy their slumbering parents and teachers, taught that the playing of one's expected roles can bring immense reward, that acting is more important than being, that happiness depends on having certain things... These things are inculcated into them daily, pounded into them. They are driven, through the sheer load of information and abstraction thrown at them, to live in their minds, to fragment themselves, to become as gone to pieces as their parents and teachers, to mirror them, to reinforce our culture's fragmentation of Being, to become little worlds with many countries, each country tightly and tidily bordered, exploitively or paranoically inclined toward its neighbors. Herein, one part of a child is busy memorizing some geographical information, while another part is fantasizing about a girl or boy across the class, while another part is half-wondering about lunch, while still another part is worrying, and another part is sabotaging the whole process, and yet another part is already plotting out how to grab a certain kind of attention, and on and on and on — there's no harmony here, no conscious communication between parts, no balance, no heart of Being... Each student, each person, is but a colony of uneasily governed fragments or specialists, each of which, when given sufficient attention, tends to refer to itself as "I", as if it truly existed as a *somebody*, as if there actually was a discrete entity who deserved the title of "I", when in fact it's all just a mechanical assembly, a convincingly *personified* assembly of fragments governed by ego...

Our educational system reinforces this fragmentation of self, and in fact insists on it, even indirectly legitimizing it. Everyone else is doing it — why not you? That's the unspoken statement or rationale so beautifully summed up in the logic of: "Eat shit! Ten billion flies can't be wrong!" Even non-conformity is absorbed, profitably gobbled up, by this mass conformity that plagues us, this runaway consumerism. Everything is swallowed by it that does not retain its own integrity — the New Age movement, for example, has become just another bit of off-beat entertainment and harmless eccentricity, trivialized into instant stardom and instant oblivion, like the flavor of the week, chewed up into the mainstream of our culture with brute ease, marketed to death...

Children have almost no chance. Some protect what is inherently sacred about themselves by going within, by finding inner refuge. Unfortunately, most of these go so far within that as adults the shell they've put around their true vulnerability (through literal embodiment, emotionally, posturally, skeletally, muscularly) is too terrifying to penetrate or crack, too firmly associated with security and safety to storm or undo. Rarely are all the layers of such armoring so *fully* passed through that a marriage of vulnerability and power can occur, a re-awakening and re-embodiment of what was forced into hibernation or exile during childhood.

Children deserve better. Many parents hearing this would say, "I know! But what the hell can I do?" or "I'm doing my best!" or some other such lie or alibi. No parent can really help their child unless they are also helping themselves. No teacher can teach wholeness to a child if they themselves are not also practising it. Teachers are not here to push a system or an arrangement of beliefs onto children; they are here to teach children to be who they really are, which of course does not mean, in permissive fashion, simply allowing children to act out, to have temper tantrums without any work being done around it, to shove food down their throats while they walk along or talk, to be cruel to one another, to be insensitive to those around them, to lose themselves in hyperactivity, greed, or false needs... Sitting back and letting children thus indulge is of no more value than the heavy-handed authoritarianism of a generation or two ago. Permissiveness, in fact, does even more harm than authoritarianism, offering neither nourishment nor challenge, but only false tolerance and superficiality.

So what can be done?

First of all, see the situation as it is. See our culture as it is. No blame — just see it as it is, doing what you have to do to clear your vision. Stop saying, "But this is working." Defending our society is akin to the situation of the person who has a horrible relationship with someone else, but who clings to this relationship simply because it seems better than nothing — it may offer just a few crumbs of nourishment here and there, but it's better than no crumbs! However, the very focussing and dependency upon these pitiful handfuls of crumbs only *obscures* our capacity to see the cake, the *entire* piece, the feast that could be had and enjoyed and assimilated if we chose to do other than settle for so little!

If we're fixated on a certain level of having, we'll likely never have more. If we settle for a partial or mediocre relationship, we will probably never have a full one — such a relationship is not (contrary to our romanticized notions of innate relational progress) a stepping-stone to a full one, unless we go into it *consciously*. For all too many of us, security, however neurotically-based, is far, far more important than Truth; we may complain about our situations, but we won't ordinarily leave or outgrow them (the characters change, but not the dramas; the script may change, but it will still be a script), simply because they provide us with a reassuring predictable familiarity, a dense anchoring that dulls us to our underlying alienation of Being, our psychospiritual uprootedness...

Many people are upset and embittered about a relationship they're in, but they *won't* leave it; they'll complain about it until they're told that they need to go, at which point they almost invariably will, in Gestaltist fashion, switch positions and start *defending* the very person they have been busy complaining about for months or years or decades! "You know, he's not that bad" or "She has her problems, but we're all human and we all have our faults, don't we?" or "I don't care what you say — he's done his best" will be automatically trotted out. Excuses will be made, bought, and sold. A failure of nerve will be again and again embodied, perhaps even made a virtue out of, as if long-term clinging was somehow *inherently* noble. This very disease of feeling and Being that permeates and epitomizes our culture is allowed to infect every classroom, every staff meeting, every educational exploration, with the rationale that this is the way it has to be, that this is for our own good, that this is our *best*...

So what can be done? See the situation as it is. Don't romanticize it. Don't play doomsdayer or optimist. Don't reduce your disillusionment to mere cynicism. Once you've recognized how it is, stop just bitching about it, and make Awakening your priority, your sacred need, your truest responsibility. I'm not talking about an awakening done in isolation, but an awakening that occurs in the very midst of everything you're doing, an awakening that creates its own morality, its own imperatives. Do this, and you will be drawn to others who are also thus committed, and you will find it impossible not to also include your children. You will not ask them to just *believe* in something — you will teach them through your example and through your relationship with them to become sensitized to something more than their appetites, something truer than sentimentalized love, something deeper than cruelty, blind competitiveness, and obsessive consumerism...

Out of such encounters, such meetings of Being, a true children's school may emerge. A well-rooted gathering of friends who are spirit-allies, co-awakeners, voyageurs to the heart of the matter, non-cultic intimates, has an excellent chance of creating a healthy educational environment for their children. To just send your children off to school is a cop-out, unless you are *intimate* with the teachers and utterly prepared to get right into it with them and your children, not just academically, but emotionally, spiritually, psychically, psychologically, to get right into it, frequently and deeply, *fully* participating in your children's education, so that school is nothing at all like a big babysitter or drop-off zone...

It makes plenty of sense for groups of awakening adults to form, out of their community inclinations, real schools, true alternatives to the educational madness that pervades our culture, places unpolluted by governmental or ideological overseeing. It doesn't matter what this would be called. To label it "home schooling" is not enough. To call it "alternative" is not enough. To call it "schools formed by intimate groups of awakening individuals" is a little closer, but too ponderous. The label doesn't matter. What does matter is that education becomes a matter of *true* teaching, *true* transmission of wholeness, a practical and soulstirring welcoming into the world of functionality, abstraction, relationship, a dive into art, into symbolism, into magic, into naked logic, into compassion, into synthesis...

There's no point teaching children arithmetic if they're sitting there all choked up, angry about something, scared or hurting like hell over something else... Such feelings must be dealt with until the children are reestablished in their core of Being, no longer contracted, and *then* the task at hand can be taught, and taught well. If this necessary emotional work meant that there wasn't time for arithmetic that day, so what? The priority is the children's wholeness, or unity of Being; if that is not occurring, or is suppressed, then it is ridiculous to teach them anything else! (Sadly enough, most adults in our culture are resolutely imbedded in just such a suppressed condition, doing, doing, doing, carrying a festering hurt inside, a wound they will not expose to the light, while their children have to pay the price of such unworked-upon woundedness...)

My words may seem extreme at times, too generalized, perhaps even harsh or unfair. That is not my intent. My intention as I sit here speaking is to emphasize and clarify the necessity of seeing what we are actually up to with our children and their education, to the point of doing something about it, something that truly works. The evidence of it working is in the children. If a school is *really* working, its children will be healthy for the greater part — they will shine, they will be *naturally* responsible, they will be playful yet sensitive, wise in their innocence, not little adults nor just cute little children, nor chronic attention-grabbers. They will be luminously sane, as vibrant as they are caring, as outrageous as they are empathetic, not trying to become someone special (*Being* having priority over *becoming* in a true school), their individuality creatively and potently flowering (not without some wise pruning!), with the heartfelt cooperation and guidance of their teachers and parents.

Our deeply imbedded resistance to *necessary* change, to *necessary* upheaval, is the very essence of our not wanting to fully face the Truth about ourselves. If we somehow do, then just about everything we've built up around and in ourselves for the sake of supposed security may well have to be radically altered, because its very foundation will have to be, at least in large part, knocked down so that a *truer* foundation can be built. Not surprisingly, very few of us *want* to do this (except perhaps intellectually!), so we go on and on building our lives on a false foundation, all the while complaining about how badly we feel, even as we compulsively distract ourselves in all kinds of ways from our self-imposed pain. How very difficult it is for us to directly face our primary source of self-imposed pain, namely our suppression of Being — almost all of what we do is a *trying* to fix the *secondary* ramifications of our suffering, the branchings of our distress (which multiply just as fast as our pruning efforts, in Hydra fashion), and our children pay the price of this, *literally...*

So what will you do about this? It's not enough to simply agree with what I'm saying. Agreement is of no more value here than disagreement, both being just a mind-game. You can play it, and still keep your prior position. "I agree!" "I disagree!" It's mere *opinion*. Something deeper than opinion is required. A *feeling* response is necessary, not just one of emotionalism, but one arising from one's depths. Something has to be done, and every one of us knows exactly, in essence, what it is. There's great suffering in knowing what needs to be done to bring about wholeness, soul-communion, love, and intimacy, and still not doing it, still pleading impotence, still speaking the mind of our favorite alibis... Knowing better and doing nothing about it is not a crime punishable in a court, but a spiritual crime, one that almost invariably brings dire consequence to one, not as a punishment from a parental deity, but simply as a matter of psychospiritual law, as summed up in the saying, "As ye sow, so shall ye reap." Injecting oneself with guilt over all this is just another way of staying stuck, of numbing ourselves to the harm we are doing to

ourselves and others; yes, the guilty may seem to feel horrible, but what they are really experiencing is a collapse of being, a suppression of real feeling, an inner split that is excruciatingly disempowering...
Our children need us to deepen our commitment to waking up. To postpone this, to weaken it, to distract ourselves from the imperatives of our Awakening impulse, is madness and a crime against our children. All they ask for is our open-eyed love, our integrity, our willingness to make our wholeness priority, our willingness to undo the harm we have done, to unlearn the strategies we embodied as hurt children. They need us to heal ourselves, and to let them be part of that healing...

There's no point whatsoever in wasting one more day reinforcing your neuroses. Look at your children, *really* look at them. What do they need? What do they really need? What are they learning from you? What do they need to learn from you? And you from them? These are not questions for your mind; they are questions that, if entered into with your entirety, will expose your wounds to the light, and teach you to stand your true ground, so that you can be a true parent to your children, *and* to yourself...

– 43 –

Roots & Wings: When Learning is a Conscious Process

(Roots & Wings is the name of the children's school of Xanthyros; the following essay, written September 20, 1989, as "evidence" for a court case, articulates the purpose and workings of Roots & Wings)

The purpose of Roots and Wings is to creatively maintain an environment wherein children can truly learn, such learning being not merely a matter of inculcation and informational regurgitation, but rather of skilfully guided discovery, exploration, and expression that both serves and honours the well-being of each child — such learning respects, illuminates, and strengthens the wholeness of the children, artfully teaching them to enjoy the very process of learning, especially when it is very challenging.

Roots and Wings is experimental without being lopsided, alternative without being fuzzy, playful without being superficial, challenging without being authoritarian, nurturing without being sentimental, firmly grounded in well-lit practicality, yet also open to new, life-giving possibilities. Roots and Wings has standards, but they are not bureaucratized, mass-applied standards; they are *human* standards, free of procrustean intentions (traditional or alternative), applied with great care, so that each child is treated as a unique and ever-evolving human being, with his or her own rate of learning. This is possible partially because of the student-teacher ratio (usually 4:1), but, more importantly, because the students' parents (or parent) and teachers are themselves practising living a fully human life, a life in which love, Awakening, compassion, competency, creativity, and all-round health are the foundations.

In Xanthyros, learning does not stop when school is out. Authentic learning is not a should, but an exquisitely practical balance of

nurturance and challenge, a balance that is reinforced not just in the work of Roots and Wings, academic or otherwise, but in all sorts of activities, from running to doing dishes to tennis to caring for younger children. Children are not forced or bribed into submitting to a particular philosophy or belief system, but instead are again and again invited to participate in an ever-evolving educational atmosphere in which *everyone*, adults included, plays an essential part.

However, this in no way means that our children are burdened with responsibility, forced to become prematurely adult, nor does it mean that they don't have time to play — rather, they don't just toss away or disregard what they have learned, especially in the emotional/ social domain, just because they are playing. To the point: Their learning is a continuous process, and, even more importantly, a *conscious* process, as opposed to a merely mechanical one...

The approach of Roots and Wings is no more akin to the sentimental permissiveness of all too many "alternative" schools than it is to the dogmatic authoritarianism (however liberalized) that tends to pervade public and so-called private schools. A holistic approach is fashionable nowadays in certain educational circles, but it all too easily becomes just more theory, just one more "educational" pigeonhole, just one more *belief*, however consoling, to fit students into — the way of Roots and Wings is holistic, directly so, assisting its students to know the underlying unity of their being for themselves, not theoretically, but experientially. Such knowingness is the very heart of the spiritual dimension of our community; ours is a commonsense spirituality, as playful as it is profound, based not in belief, but in direct experience. The children tacitly equate being spiritual with being open-heartedly happy and empathetically bonded with others — God for them is not some great parental deity, nor some ineffable abstraction, but rather is the very essence of living a sane, balanced, loving life. The spiritual is not set apart from the rest of their experience — it all, spiritual, physical, mental, emotional, intuitive, and social, is presented as a unity, a unity of magnificent diversity, but nevertheless a unity...

No child in Roots and Wings does academic work while they are hurting, depressed, angry, or otherwise upset, since this would only split them, furthering the dissociation between mind and feeling — what is ordinarily done in such a case is a sensitive reestablishing of the child in heartfelt, easy relatedness with the other students, so

that he or she is brought from a sense of alienation and aberrating separateness to one of relaxed intimacy and wholeness. Then the task at hand can be done without any attending repression. This, of course, is not possible in typical schooling situations, unless the teacher and parents are in deep cooperation.

The ability to express emotion with both passion and empathetic sensitivity is an essential part of each child's development, as is a strong discriminative faculty relative to such expression — put another way, the children learn (or relearn) to recognize genuine emotion, as opposed to false, egocentric, or manipulative emotion. Anger is not just anger; it can be healthy (simultaneously potent and vulnerable), or it can be unhealthy (revengeful, righteous, punishing, distancing). Real sadness can be clearly distinguished from reactive sadness (whining, self-pity, implosiveness, withdrawal), and so on. Fear and all its subspecies (guilt, worry, anxiety) are thoroughly explored — that the letting go of fear makes room for love and ease is demonstrated not just in the teaching environment, but in the homes of the children. Thus does their confidence flower, and their capacity for real equanimity deepen...

The self-fragmentation, obsessive compartmentalization, unresolved misery, runaway consumerism, diseased competitiveness, emotional anesthetization, and spirit-denial that characterize all too much of our culture also permeate our so-called educational system to such a degree as to go largely unchallenged, except in the most superficial ways. My point here, though, is not to merely criticize our culture, but to emphasize that what is commonly taken to be education is more often than not merely a diseased tributary and unwitting reinforcer of our society. Even so, it is not enough to just complain about how terrible it all is; there are surely plenty of articulate critics of our times. Something more than telling criticism is required. Roots and Wings is one answer to the failures of our culture's educational system, and it is *not* a theoretical answer — the evidence of its success is in its students, who are unusually alert, bright, sensitive, vibrantly alive children, simultaneously innocent and wise, unburdened by and uninterested in the insensitive, hyperactive, mechanical, compulsive, and chronically cruel activity that, unfortunately, is so common among children in more conventional educational settings. The children of Roots and Wings are by no means perfect, but they are a living example of children who are in deep harmony with their own capacity for learning...

– 44 –

Plugging In
Instead of Jacking Off

(With considerable difficulty, eleven-year old Michael says that he has been masturbating for years, and that no one has known until now — it's only been a month since his parents joined Xanthyros)

ROBERT: Does it bother you that you masturbate?

MICHAEL: Not really.

ROBERT: But you look ashamed, you look bothered, you look very uptight, even though you're pretending you're okay with it. You *are* bothered, aren't you?

MICHAEL: Yeah, I am. I'm nervous about it...

ROBERT: Exactly. You're afraid to talk about it in front of the other kids. You're embarrassed. (*Pause*) So what is masturbation? It's not just you rubbing your penis until you feel good. It's a way of getting rid of energy, of getting rid of tension. Remember when you were living in Calgary with Shambhu and Cathy [*his parents*]... Remember how tense and miserable they were together? Remember how uptight you felt around them most of the time? Remember how depressed and *trapped* you felt?

MICHAEL: Yes!

ROBERT: Sometimes you'd get rid of your extra energy, your tension, by being mean to Leta [*his younger sister*], but your favorite way was to jack off. It felt good, and it felt good *in a hurry*, didn't it? You needed to feel better, to feel some relief — that's why you did it. But you did it so much that it became a habit, even an addiction.

Do you know what an addiction is?

MICHAEL: No.

ROBERT: An addiction is a habit that is very, very hard to get rid of — it's a habit that is very difficult to control. Anyone know any specific addictions?

OTHER CHILDREN: Too much TV, candy, drugs...

ROBERT: A lot of kids are addicted to such things, and a lot are addicted to pleasing their parents. And you, Michael, are somewhat addicted to masturbating. There's nothing wrong with it, but there are better ways of dealing with your uptightness!

If you're feeling bothered by something, say with Shambhu or Cathy, instead of just going to your room and rubbing your penis for a while, you need to go to them and *tell them* what's bugging you — they have to listen now, and I know they will. They didn't in Calgary, but they will now... The trouble is, you've gotten so used to masturbating when you feel lousy, that it's not easy to do something else when you feel that way. (*Pause*) Which people do you think masturbate the most?

MICHAEL: I don't know.

ROBERT: Probably teenage boys. And why do you think teenage boys do it more than any other group of people? (*Pause*) Because they're bothered by their parents, they're bothered by holding in their feelings, they're bothered by school, they're bothered by the threat of their future, they're bothered by all the incredible *pressure* they feel — they've got huge amounts of energy, and most of them don't know how to let that energy flow through them, so they get tense with it, as if they're going to explode. Most of them are very uptight, even more than you!

They feel very, very sexual, and that energy has to go somewhere. Maybe the easiest way to get rid of it is by masturbating. It's a kind of relief, but it doesn't change the problems they have! Being a teenager in our society is very unpleasant; teenagers may *act* like they're free, but inside just about all of them feel horribly trapped. Masturbation just makes the trap feel a little better. But *you're* not in that kind of trap anymore, Michael...

Imagine being a teenager and hating your parents, hating school, trying to fit in, trying to be someone special, trying and trying, and masturbating to get rid of your uptightness (and it's called uptightness 'cause the energy gets *tightened* as it goes up, up, up into your head, into thinking and doubting and worrying) — when you are older and ready to be sexual with a woman you might *still* prefer to jack off, either by yourself, or inside her, as if her vagina's just a big hand! That's what I call fucking. When two people really love each other and are *already* happy and *then* have sex, I call *that* making love...

The problem is, if the only way you can make yourself feel *really* good is by masturbating, then you're probably going to keep on doing it, no matter what I say! But if you find other things that feel even better, then you won't have to... Look how good you feel when you are just sitting right here, loose and easy, looking into my eyes, looking into the other kids' eyes — it's a deeper kind of happiness than jacking off or eating a candy bar or spacing out in front of a television set.

Watch teenage kids on their lunch break — they're always going to the corner store and buying candy, slushies, and crunchy little snacks, which they shove into their faces as they walk along — they're just trying to feel better, trying to not feel so empty inside. They eat a lot of sugar. What happens when you eat a lot of sugar?

MICHAEL: You get all hyper.

ROBERT: Yes. It's like a drug, like coffee. Coffee opens people's energy up, makes them feel more alive. But it's not *them* that's opening up their energy. It's the drug. And when you masturbate, it's like taking a drug, a fast-working drug. In fact, you do create a kind of drug in your body when you're rubbing your penis, an exciting sensation, a charge, a very pleasant chemical change — you get really turned on, all frantic and warm and stop worrying for a little while about Shambhu and Cathy. At last, you can't think, you can't worry, 'cause there is so much pleasure, so much nice-feeling heat. Right?

MICHAEL: Yes! (*Laughter*)

ROBERT: All there is then is just you and your dinky. (*Laughter*) Just the two of you! (*Laughter*) Tonight, I want you to talk about this with Shambhu and Cathy. Ask Shambhu about *his* masturbation. Keep eye contact, and don't hold back your feelings... (*Pause*)

And remember: Instead of trying to get rid of your hurt, *share* it! Instead of worrying so much that you feel like you have to jack off or get hyper or space out, go to others and *really* tell them what you're worried or upset about, and let your anger and sadness and everything else you're feeling come out! Do that, and you'll end up feeling so damned good that you won't be able to worry! You won't have to masturbate so you can feel better, because you'll *already* feel happy!

– 45 –
Letting the Broken Heart
Enliven the Soul:
Despair, Disillusionment, & Being

Almost all despair is negative despair, a sunken bewailing of one's condition, a falling into mere victimization relative to Life's demands. There is, however, a deeper kind of despair, which we might call positive despair, the sort of despair that is a result of being thoroughly and lucidly disillusioned about the power of the conventional world to *truly* satisfy us, so tellingly disillusioned that we lose all interest in being distracted from our suffering. Such despair is of immense value. It is important to realize that it is *not* a strategy — it cannot be created through following a technique, nor through belief, for it, in part, is the letting go of *all* belief. Positive despair is the result (and a key sign) of much work on oneself, long deep work, Being-centered work, full not only of breakthrough and full-blooded joy, but also of *necessary* suffering and heartbreak...

Negative despair, on the other hand, is jammed with *unnecessary* suffering — it's little more than the exaggeratedly implosive cry of a committed victim, contracted upon himself or herself to the point of an all-too-convincing helplessness/bitterness, sagging with unpruned doubt. And what of positive despair? It's not centered by doubt, but by radical insight, luminous sobriety, a bedrock knowingness about the nature of Reality, a knowingness that cannot be reduced to edible information or supermarket software.

So how do we arrive at positive despair? In part, doing so involves not only going deeply into experience, diving into all kinds of conditions and circumstances, especially those that *necessitate* our attachment, but also learning from such exposure, not just learning about what we can or can't do, but learning about the very context of such experience, until *experience itself* loses its power to seduce us away from our core of Being. We'll then of course still have experiences, but our having of them will be utterly different than it was before — we'll now not be having them in order to merely get somewhere, to fulfil some obligation of our apparent self, some ego-created program, but instead we'll simply be present, inviolably present, regardless of what is or what isn't happening to us, inner or outer...

The opposite of negative despair is hope, a foolish projection of the mind into the future, a disembodied nostalgia for what might happen, an inflationary groping for something in the realm of optimistic possibility, unknowingly carrying within itself the seeds of its opposite, the germ of bad possibility, the negative anticipation of typical despair. And what then is the opposite of real despair, of positive despair? It is not hope, not the compulsive efforting to remain cheerfully peripheral or numb to one's depths, not the trampling of disillusionment's seedlings beneath stampeding optimism, but rather sobering Joy...

Whatever satisfies the senses only does not truly satisfy. Only if our Being is also satisfied can we *truly* enjoy the pleasures of the senses — then we become a luminously responsible hedonist, an awakened Dionysian, instead of just an everyday pleasure-seeker forever trying to escape from pain. We then no longer pull away from our suffering, gradually ceasing to seek the titillating sedation of ordinary pleasuring. Thus do we become capable of Ecstasy, of directly and consciously *feeling* God, of permitting raw Beingness throughout our entirety. This is not some exotic goal, some esoteric rarity, but is our very nature, our birthright, our sacred need, asking only for light, the light of our participation in something deeper than our mind, our hope, our negative despair, our *mind-generated* emotions...

Something much deeper is calling us, right now. Right now, in the very quaver of the word "now", in the pauses between my words and phrasings, the subtle shifts in this voice, the sounds that weave in and out of the edges of this unfolding talk... To embrace despair is not an act of masochism. It is not even an act. It is an unequivocal statement of Being, an unmistakable sign that Awakening is occurring. Rather than being a running away from or collapse into the world, it is a vibrantly present passing into *and* through the world, an involvement in the world that doesn't deprive us of our realization of our true nature. In such a life, nothing can seduce us away from the Truth of what we fundamentally are, nothing at all — not the greatest pain, nor the greatest pleasure, nor the ideal partner, nor the ideal holiday — we may waver, but we do not collapse.

Don't go looking for positive despair. There's no point in prematurely throwing yourself into disillusionment, unless cynicism is your Everest. And, how can you be nourishingly disillusioned if you haven't risked deeply in your life, gone all-out into experience, vulnerably and profoundly explored and experimented with relationship? How? Those who avoid taking chances, getting attached, getting hurt, getting rejected *or* accepted, are too shallow to have anything to get *really* disillusioned over, except perhaps theoretically, intellectually, or sentimentally.

To really get disillusioned, you have to go into illusion. This is not a call to blind oneself, but simply a recognition that Life has to be fully lived in order for Its Secret, Its forever open Secret, to be revealed. This Secret cannot be encapsulated and handed-out, for it transcends all information. However, It is *not* being blocked away from anyone — It's not truly hidden. We have only locked ourselves away from It, made ourselves inaccessible to It, ruining ourselves in our mad involvement with Its surrogates (such as religion)...

The key is to live, to make mistakes, to be passionately involved, to put our hearts on the line, to not sink nor merely think, but to dive right in, to be *responsibly* excessive to the point of illumination. Those who "choose" moderation are, in almost all cases, only cowards or dilettantes, terrified to *really* live, to risk everything — they're tending to always save something for tomorrow, for later, not in a sanely responsible fashion, but in a selfish, ego-preserving fashion. They're stingy with their energy. However, to get to the heart of disillusionment, you can't afford to be stingy! You have to give, including your need to be given to — you can't just give and give and give, like some ambitious saint or super-mother, anymore than you can just take and take and take. You must give Life *everything* you've got, not in some insensitive or irresponsible manner (like someone drinking themselves into oblivion because doomsday is tomorrow), but with great feeling, courage, daring, and empathetic awareness.

What I'm talking about is living *now*, living so fully, so richly, so creatively, that nothing is left undone — you work with whatever's there until it's as clean and complete as possible. No unfinished business, no closeted messes, and no self-crucifixion to perfection! You do your best to come clean with it all. You don't just say that you did your best — you *do* your best! You don't settle for the mediocre "best" that your parents may have claimed they did, but instead do whatever you have to do to bring out your finest, not the "finest" of your programming, but the "finest" of your Being! If you're wise, you'll probably have others around you who can unerringly tell if you're *actually* doing your best — such intimates will love you enough to not spare you their criticism of your doings, unless you persist in defending against such criticism.

In most cases, our "best" is not good enough, simply because it isn't *our* "best", but only the top performance of our conditioning, the biggest stretch of our little self, the optimum stretch of those habits that insist on referring to themselves as us. To say that someone did their best ought not to be an alibi for their behaviour (as is so appallingly common in the abuse of children by their parents), but rather an acknowledgment of that person being undeniably awake and alive at their growing edge... To stop short of giving one's best is to fail to know or draw upon reservoirs of Energy that transcend our usual reservoirs. There is a crippled grief in our knowing that we haven't tapped into something grander, something purer, something truer, a grief that all too often only withers into envy or pettiness toward those who seem to be living a richer life than us...

Go into any experience fully, with your eyes open, taking your entirety into it, and you'll find everything there — God, Joy, Despair, Mystery, Love, Significance, Suffering — all of it! There's no formula that will clearly depict exactly what will be there when you go to the heart of the matter, mainly because your very journey into any experience creates, to a significant degree, what is found there. The journey creates the goal — this is not a full Truth, but it's close enough to be of value. You could say the goal's already there, but that the journey contextually colours and re-creates it in terms of how the journey itself is taken...

We're all going to get disillusioned if we bring some wakefulness to our experience... It's relatively easy to be aware, at least of details and bodymind processes, if one is anchored upon a meditation mat in a quiet hall, day after day, with no distractions except those of one's mind. It's far more difficult (and important) to practise such wakefulness in the midst of the events of our daily lives, until it's natural, completely natural, to be alert, loosely alert in the midst of things. Do this, and when disillusionment sets in, you won't simply settle into conventional despair or get cynical or go looking for another partner, meal, movie, high, or any other such compensatory experience. Instead, you'll feel the pain of your urge, your craving, your search, for satisfaction, and you'll likely feel it so strongly that you may begin seeing through that very search — hopefully, you won't go to the other extreme, and avoid sensory or sensual pleasure. With a little perseverance, you'll still go after your pleasures, living your life with some real passion, some real flair, but without such a naïve sense of direction, gradually shifting from a context of enervating excess to one of rejuvenative abundance...

It's very, very easy to wade into renunciation of all sorts when disillusionment clamps down on you, especially if you've already tried indulgence. It's much more useful to simply keep on going, with a little more care, a little more empathy, instead of just trying to unplug all your indulgences all at once. Simply keep going until your disillusionment shines so brightly, so compellingly, so painfully, that something other than repression or indulgence is birthed through it, something trembling with budding soul, like a rare and beautiful plant springing up, green and moistly delicate, from dark earth. You must allow your disillusionment to become soil, fertile soil, for the outreaching of your core of Being, that ever-green reaching for Light, that embrace so unambiguously bright...

Don't think that you can think your way through this! Your body must be intimately involved, including that portion of the body that refers to itself as mind. All of you has to make this passage, this irreducibly mysterious yielding to and individuation of Being... Part of getting healthily disillusioned is being disappointed in yourself, in others, in the power of the world (outer *and* inner) to magically alter your circumstances so that you might be untroubled by what now troubles you. But it's not the world's duty to do that. It's yours. The world is raw material for you, both soil and mirror. Its Santa Clauses and applause are but the flimsiest tinsel, of no more use to you than a whisper is to a deaf person.

You may entertain the illusion that you create your own reality, so as to inflate yourself against the dreaded inner sensation of psychospiritual deflation. You might crave that little pumped-up omnipotence, that crafty little charade of rampant ego-centricity, perhaps even confusing participation in such disembodied self-interest (surely the very center of neurotic monotheism, with holy-robed ego upon the throne of Self!) with the taking of responsibility! But what could be more irresponsible than so indulging in such a severe case of mistaken identity? Your *programming* creates its own reality, and if you identify with it, you'll say that *you* create your own reality, your very own reality! The all you'll have is a chunk of real estate where nothing real grows, until Awakening becomes more important to you than consolation...

Who you really are doesn't *strategically* create. It just *is*. Period. For It, Being is primary, creativity spontaneously secondary. The root of Its creativity is identical to that of growing grass, of unfolding flowers, of a stalking tiger, utterly unself-conscious, with the marvelous addition of fully-embodied imagination. Its Reality *already* is, needing no creation, but only expression, soul-centered expression, and it is *here*, in the very heart of such expression, that creativity is essential, not ego-centered creativity, but Essence-centered creativity! So cut through the *belief* that you create your own reality, contact a deeper you, and stop avoiding falling in love with the Mystery of your Being!

That Infinite Mystery, That Eternal Wonder, That Great It, is What's already recognizing what's being said here, just as It recognizes everything else. It already knows. It cannot help but know. Its knowingness outbreathes all knowledge. It's simply here, purely here, overwhelmingly here, forever Here, while "we" scramble around busily in the corridors and files of our minds, our sensory impressions, our endless comparisons and summaries and assumptions — what a pity, what a tragedy, and what a joke! It doesn't give a shit about our attempts to corral or institutionalize It. Nevertheless, It does care, not like an immense parent, a personal overseer, a do-gooder bureaucrat, but like an eternally-awakened lover, an utterly ruthless lover, a radiant cauldron of opposites, full of endless sky, full of birthing and dying, both shining through and honouring the personal, with fluidly immutable Presence, Love, and Unimaginable Spaciousness. It is the Intimacy, the Commingling, of Christ and Buddha, constellated by everything else, centered everywhere, forever outdancing every one of these words and even their sublimest nuance — so let these phrasings take wing, let them burst into flame, let them both clarify and extinguish your every name. This aside, this infinitely stretching parenthesis, now ebbs back to the original talk, catching me in the middle of a long breath, tears in my eyes, coming back, back, back, yet also not back...

Persist in making good use of your disillusionment, and eventually you will cease creating *unnecessary* suffering for yourself. And then what of necessary suffering, the suffering that is inherent to being embodied? Such suffering is simply an intensification of contractive sensation, an unpleasantness without any prejudice or negative connotations attached to it — it weeps, yes, but without recoil from intimacy, and yes, it gets angry, but without reactivity. It doesn't make a problem out of its woundedness, nor out of attachment. It, at its best, anchors Ecstasy with compassion, keeping psychospiritual growth moistly vulnerable...

And why limit Awakening to expansion? Why hanker for spaciousness and ease? Life's both contraction and expansion, both ebb and surge, and It doesn't require our identification with either. Whether I speak quickly or slowly, excitedly or calmly, it's the same ebb and flow, the same great tide, the same push and pull at the heart of it, the same tide that washes through our every cell, our every step — it's as big as the Universe, and as small as we can possibly imagine. It's the primordial throb of Life, the Heartbeat of Everything, infinitely large and infinitely small, and, in-between, infinitely variegated and individuated. This can only make sense if you permit yourself to feel it, letting yourself settle more and more deeply into your Being, letting yourself fill out the room you're now in, making space for everything you are...

Making room for everything, however, does not mean accepting everything! It literally means making space for it all, making space for your acceptance, your non-acceptance, your love, your hate, your jealousy, your boredom, your everything — such an opening of Self has nothing to do with the fake tolerance that now plagues liberalized Western culture, that guilt-homogenized stance of acceptance that's but a repression of bigotry and racism. (Such a stance, of course, is righteously intolerant of any criticism of those groups or subgroups whose freedoms it purports to defend — for example, it automatically labels any criticism of homosexuality as homophobia.) Making room for all that we are is akin to being a sky that is both intimately associated with all its clouds and still aware of itself, still present even when it's saturated with the darkest rainclouds. It's necessary to recognize, viscerally recognize, that contraction is not necessarily bad, and expansion is not necessarily good — sometimes contraction is utterly necessary, timely, valuable, soul-serving, as in a regathering of scattered energies, or in the coil before a spring. To deny contraction is to dilute one's capacity for expansion, or to thrust oneself into self-encapsulated, escapist expansiveness, conceptual expansiveness, the fragmented diffusion of metaphysics...

Don't avoid experience. Go into it, however foolish you might look, however frequently you might fall flat on your face, however messy it might get. In your very falling, you will, if you are sufficiently sensitive to yourself, eventually feel a desire to make good use of the pain of your slippage, the embarrassment, the self-consciousness, the giving-up, the rationalizations, the sense of disgrace your ego might experience — if you are wise, you will use that downfall, that brokenness of stride and pride, that shame, to deepen and reinforce your alignment with your core Self.

Shame, when sanely surrendered to (which doesn't mean letting it congeal into guilt or toxic self-collapse), will free you from most of your psychospiritual poison, will cleanse you, will warm and expand you from the inside, viscerally and potently, until you outblush your ego-centered preoccupations, shining brighter and truer than them, outliving and outdancing and outbreathing them.

Don't mistake me. Don't think that I'm just recommending diving into it all with reckless abandon. It takes a lot more courage to plunge in with awareness and sensitivity; in fact, the more you know about such a leap, the more difficult it is to take it, but if you do, the consequences are truly of soulmaking magnitude. A consistent sensitivity is required. You can't, however, just believe me, and sit back waiting for the next sentence — you need to practise such sensitivity right now. Are you now aware of your breathing? What's your forehead feel like? Are you at all aware of your brain? Your belly? Is your mind relaxed, your shoulders loose, your hands in fists or mudras or whatever? There's no right or wrong implied in this, regardless of how you're positioned. But are you noticing it? Were you sensitive to yourself in the moment when I addressed what you might be up to? Perhaps, perhaps not. At any rate, it begins now. So simple to say, isn't it? Too simple for the mind, too obvious...

The mind craves complication — it wants some esoteric formula for all this, or maybe ten easy steps, or perhaps ten extraordinarily difficult steps that only the true warrior or spiritual aspirant can undertake! What bullshit! What a tangle of complication, what self-glorifying ambition! It's time to get simple, without being a simpleton. Like right now. What are you now up to? And what's deeper than that? What underlies your complications? And is it the same "I" who answers in both cases?

Who is it who is looking for an experience that will deliver them from their suffering, especially once-and-for-all? Who's busily engaged in that search? Who is it that wants to be comforted, made immune, lullabied into oblivion? Who? You can't just say your ego. It's too easy — as an ego, it's nothing for you to announce that it's just your ego! Ego typically loves to pretend to be someone else, someone deeper, someone spiritual, and then get all gung-ho about programs designed to eradicate that dire thing called ego!

But ego isn't even a thing — it's just a complex of habits that you automatically personify. Ego's a case of mistaken identity, an imposter, a cult of one. Try to get rid of it, and you strengthen it, like any other addiction. Instead, allow it to become transparent to something more fundamental to you. Give it room to become healthy, and you'll observe it becoming not a more bloated version of itself, but rather an eloquently articulated expression of your core of Being, a colourfully-nuanced outer reflection that honours who you really are, with wonderfully idiosyncratic flair. Ego's not to be eradicated, but purified. It's not to be identified with, but used well, until it's not even an "it", but simply a process, a doing, free of the illusion of being a solid somebody...

So, next time despair comes knocking, don't just slam the door in its face, and don't just yield to its dark embrace. Let it in. Unpeel it. Take its whining, its complaining, its bitching and scrambling for position, take its craving to be fixed, compensated, and sympathized with, take all that and let it become positive despair. Let it disappoint the hell out of you. Let it leave you so naked, so alive, so sober, that nothing can entice you away from the Truth of what you are. Nothing! When that occurs, you are in Grace, not necessarily feel-good Grace, but simple, bare-bones Grace, emotionally-naked Harmony, and undeniable Connection with your Source. You may be crying, you may be angry, you may be hurting terribly, but you're in *real* connection — you're not fighting away the woundedness of your heart, nor fleeing it. You're no longer avoiding having an openly broken heart...

Only those who have allowed their heart to be truly broken, not just their peripheral heart, but their *full* heart, can know God. The intact or protected heart can only know a facsimile of God, a parental or conceptual stand-in. The fully broken heart is not in a million pieces, fragmented everywhere, but is simply broken open, wide open, un-polluted by any sidetrackings of mind, its very rawness being the fertility needed for receptivity to the Source of All. If wisely used, despair can break the heart and enliven the soul. If not wisely used, however, despair only crushes, mutilates, and disarms the heart, while seemingly legitimizing our reasons for armouring our hearts, for hardening or fleeing them, for allowing them to become stranded from any real passion or force or luminosity.

The broken heart is an essential part of the bridge to God; it's not looking to be mended. It's like a woman welcoming her lover, with nothing held back. In deep disillusionment, lucidly thorough disillu-sionment, the heart's broken in the same way that a stream rushing down through a mountainside forest is broken — it's still cohesive spiritually, still unified in essence, its elemental dying only strength-ening and affirming its fundamental aliveness, its rough-and-tumble course only furthering its dynamic yet utterly vulnerable surrender...

There's no technique for this. A love affair that goes rotten doesn't usually create a broken heart, but only a soured heart, a frightened heart, a greedy or revengeful heart, a heart that stays superficial by looking for a "better" partner, a "better" experience. A truly broken heart is a very rare thing. Its grief and joy can only be experienced by diving deep, by going into the Heartland of Life. When we're in despair, there's no use moaning and bitching about how unfair it all is... Just go deeper. Your only alternative is a dead-end alternative, that of postponement. The step asked of you may be very small, or it might be very large — the key is to take it. This very moment invites you to go deeper, to allow something truer to emerge. This very pause carries the same welcome. Listen to the pause, feel it, feel the throb, the vitality, the qualities of this moment. Don't try to remem-ber what I've said. I don't at this moment. It's all in your next exhale, your next inhale, as subtle as it's simple, too real to carry any optimism or pessimism, too alive to be reduced to data...

– 46 –

Guilt on Amphetamines:
A Close-up of Hysteria

The proffered penitence of guilt is simply gagged hysteria, offering no more possibility of healthy reconnection with its object than does its exaggeratedly emotional, *obviously* irresponsible flipside — the sorriness that so contritely oozes from guilt does not in any Life-giving sense actually work with the addressed injury or wound, but (through its self-possessed contractedness) just screens out whatever could catalyze such healing, thereby only reinforcing the very hurt that it so earnestly purports to want to undo!

All too easily, the grovelling self-blame that epitomizes guilt everts itself into other-blame, inflating itself with as much righteousness as it can muster, arming itself with the unimpeachable conviction of rampant emotionalism, not realizing that such an intensity of sensation is not true feeling, but is only *mind-generated* emotion, writhing with (and seemingly legitimized by) self-inflicted, utterly mechanical melodrama...

The violence emanating from unleashed hysteria is the active side of the sorriness of guilt, frothingly supporting its position of being in the right, ever stiffening its accusing finger, trampling over insignificances like accuracy and empathetic consideration. Hysteria is a parody of feeling, an avoidance and short-circuiting of natural emotion, a refusal to actually *feel* what is really occurring; it is a gross reaction to what is happening, a reaction seemingly justified by all sorts of things, including one's thoughts and perceptions, a reaction whose *inherent* withdrawal from intimacy and relatedness is garishly disguised by its explosive, attention-consuming *outwardness*.

Its anger is about punishment, not barrier-breakthrough; its hurt is about self-pity, not intimacy-reestablishment; its viewpoint is rabidly righteous and endarkened, neither spacious nor loving nor vulnerable, not at all concerned with getting to the heart of the matter.

Whether male or female, the hysterical are obsessed with being right, the guilty with being wrong; both cling tenaciously to "their" morality, not seeing that it is an ethic imposed from without, bereft of love, sanity, and illumination, a morality that goes no deeper than agreement/disagreement, a morality whose greatest heights are characterized by erudite fence-sitting and disembodied tolerance.

The extroversion of the hysterical and the introversion of the guilty are both just strategies, Life-negating "solutions" to the problems spawned by the turning away from the imperatives of one's own core of Being. This primal recoil, if not directly and consciously addressed, sets in motion all kinds of secondary difficulties, which can never be truly worked through so long as their *origin* is not sanely dealt with, such work necessitating the participation of one's *entire* being...

Hysteria is but a withdrawal from intimacy (from others *and* from one's own depths), whether through the falsetto extremes of frenzied helplessness, or through the murderous gestures of runaway righteousness, or through the coldly explosive accusations of aberrated logic and fanatical justice-seeking. Hysteria is the parental side of guilt running mad, brandishing its whip at all who dare doubt its version of what's what, and hysteria is also, even simultaneously, the childish side of guilt shrieking out its pain in a manner that only further disconnects it from what it truly seeks.

Like guilt, hysteria often masquerades as conscience, but in a much more overblown way, inflating rather than deflating itself through its preaching, shrieking and freaking as it impales itself on the twin spires of simplistic right and wrong, again and again presenting its resulting pain as evidence of how wrongfully it has been treated, all the while riding and spurring its own crazed momentum to the point of exhaustion (entering the low-key terrain of guilt), heavy-handed interference (counter-violence, asylum-commitment, or just a psychiatric injection of Demerol), suddenly-sobering damage, or, much more rarely, an awakening to what is *actually* occurring, such awakening requiring not a cessation of the biochemistry of hysteria, but rather a resolute witnessing of its viewpoint, coupled with a full-bodied honouring of the longing to be reestablished in love...

It's time to transport the whole abortion issue beyond the fanaticism, rigidity, and ideological braying of so-called Pro-Life and Pro-Choice devotees; theirs is but a superficial polarity, a debate between flagwaving zealots, a melodramatic face-off in a no-one's land... Goose-stepping sentimentality versus the logic of disembodied liberalism... Hysteria versus hysteria... All the shrieking, all the lunatic hoops of sterilized thought, all the fisted reasoning, all the overfed concern, the mind-froth, the gouged hurt, the violence, the vicious calm, righteously tethered to its task beneath an artificial sky, hearts trampled beneath the herdprints of each army... It's a fucking mess, literally so, a horror of force-fed morality, twisted humanitarianism, misguided concern, and stampeding hypocrisy, far too political to be human.

The topic of abortion mercilessly exposes our confusion about values, demonstrating how very far we are from embodying a truly human morality; our freedoms and rights tend to be little more than just licence to do as we please within our cages. Not many of us can face the facts that characterize our self-entrapment, even one as obvious as the fact that very few are born out of real love — very few are consciously conceived or welcomed. Almost all are just fucked into being, sometimes out of romanticism, sometimes out of insecurity, sometimes out of duty, but mostly out of sheer mechanicalness and acculturated hope (such hope being the piped-in hype of "having" a family, and the sugared prelude to the child abuse that plagues at least 99% of modern families — there is, of course, still great denial of such abuse, paralleling our own ongoing abuse, whether authoritarian or permissive, of the child within us). Given this, most only tend to have opinions about abortion, rather than journeying to the crux of the whole affair, to where opinion is outshone by Truth.

And, to further widen the picture, how the hell can we bring any light to this, when most of us haven't even begun to tellingly explore just what we have aborted in ourselves? Having abandoned our native integrity of Being, we're suffering from abortion trauma, or unnatural separation, turning our lives into one big denial and distraction from that primal hurt, that recoil, that turning away from who we really are... We may grab onto a cuddly little surrogate of what we've aborted, like a Pro-Lifer, or we may fortify and exploit what's left of us, infusing our ego-ruled ruins with the apparent capacity to make real choices, like a Pro-Choicer, but, in either case, however, we're only maintaining and camouflaging our crippledness, staking out a bit of artificial turf to make "our" stand on, such positioning being but an unacknowledged compensation for our having stranded ourselves from our Heartland and Its obvious yet ever unrehearsable Truth...

– 47 –

Little One,
What Do You Say?

Little one afloat in your cushioned bubble, limbs waving in velvet currents, torso bulging with heart, head taking on more and more face, little one growing so fast in your seamless Now, can you hear the debate over you? The arguments for and against aborting you? The mind-froth over your legal status, the bleating parades of jutting logic, the righteously rigid propaganda? the long-buried hurt, the compensatory quirt? The heart nailed to a soapbox, or just plain fled?

Abortionists and anti-abortionists both glued atop their pulpits, high above a much deeper vulnerability, both sniping from their minds, both converting their passion into ammunition, both pumping belief-generated emotion into their position, both dreaming they are awake, both dreaming they are right, while you, little one, float and grow, seeing without eyes, flying without wings, knowing without thinking.

Little one, can you hear the shouts? Can you feel the war over you? Yet is it really over you? No! Both sides build their cases, drowning in their interpretations of you, one tending to reduce you to a cute sweet adorable little thing, a human doll, a religious football, burdening you with the sentimental crap so many children are burdened with, while the other side tends to reduce you to little more than a bit of tissue, a mere uterine growth, a maternal inconvenience, making a problem out of your very existence...

Little one anchored in your fluid sky, do you hear all the fuss? Do you feel the fury and the pain, the leashed violence, the murderous thoughts? Do you feel the unilluminated sense of loss and gain, the soulless fallout, the black rain? A doctor performs a legal abortion, his heart clamped beneath his professionalism, his mind flirting with tomorrow, and another doctor performs an illegal abortion, his heart also bound and gagged, his task already mentally bagged and tagged.

And a woman, a woman sick of Pro-Life and Pro-Choice seesawing, dives deeper, at last lying screaming and crying, screaming naked and shiveringly true, in a breakthrough counselling session or group, finally reliving her abortions from the inside, feeling her way right to her core, beyond right and wrong, beyond mind, suddenly looking through fetal eyes, all emotional anaesthesia gone, gone, gone, her tears gradually becoming oceanic, she and her gone babies touching in spirit, meeting in a love unpolluted by sentimentality or romanticism, her pure words pouring out like music, achingly rich music, music shimmering with Truth and recognition and a goodbye seeded with an eternal Hello...

And a man weeps brokenly and so, so lonely in another session or group, saying he wants the child, but his partner doesn't, and, bottom line of bottom lines, it's her body and therefore it must be her choice, right? But the choice of *which* her? The choice of her conditioning, her fear, her ego-centered concern, or the choice of her core of Being, her love, her real concern?

All the thousands of nightmare rooms, pregnancy crouched in one corner and the mind in another, quiver with resolutely held pain, silently screaming for deliverance from all the cleancut articulate goddamned numbness, the loveless denials, the cheap okays, the blind fucks, the waving crosses, the ossified hearts, the antiseptic understanding, the pious hysteria...

Little one, do you feel the cramped suffering? The aborted longings? The maternal dreams? The paternal schemes? The career excuses, the timing alibis, the sterilized passion? Do you feel the uncertainty behind the surgical certainty? All the unsaid goodbyes, the suffocatingly lonely cries, the let's-get-on-with-it disguise? And do you feel the guilt-fueled morality, the theological fanaticism, the rabid Life-saving complex that would deny you a departure that you might *truly* need? Little one, do you sense the unhealed wounds of those who debate your future? If you could speak, what would you say?

Your world is not immune to shocks — sharp sounds, drug-invasions, the withdrawal of love and spiritual resonance, belly blows, birth interventions, delivery abuses — but none of these approach the shock of doctored force piercing your watery world, the stabbing hypodermic, the toothless suction mouth blindly agape, the plastic violence, the prostaglandin shove, and worse, your mother so, so gone from you, so, so far away from coming clean with you, as she submits to an insanely rational view, a view that says it's no big deal, nothing to get upset over!

The issue, little one, isn't of right or wrong, but of short-circuiting a deeper song. Little one floating in your softness, expanding into your liquid night, you are far more than a sentimentalized concept, far more than a bit of tissue. Ask the doctors who cannot help but see that you are sometimes still alive after they've ripped you from your harbour. Ask the women who carry secret guilt. Ask the women who mourn behind their busy smiles. Ask the women who keep dreaming of those they aborted. And ask the men who grieve alone, without release. Ask, and ask for more than information...

Little one, what do you say? Are there times when abortion is *your* need? The answer takes shape in conscious, heartfelt communion between you and your mother and any true intimates she has. Yes, there are times, very rare times, when you are aborted out of love rather than out of fear, greed, ambition, or convenience, times when you are deeply felt and bid a loving farewell, times when you are an honoured guest who must depart, a guest whose presence is a gift to all...

Little one, all you ask for is open-eyed love and integrity. Often have I felt you in sessions, feeling you forgiving those who aborted you and their own depths, even as you silently invited them to forgive themselves, to once again truly love what is most fragile and vulnerable in them. And often have I sat deeply absorbed in your eloquent silence, your Spirit-presence, feeling you mothering both me and your mother, as she lay softly, softly, softly floating in her deepest tears, slowly merging with your love, letting you go, letting herself expand into the Womb of Now...

Unborn Children Fill My Rooms

My flesh leans exhausted against my bones
The face in the mirror wears purple under its eyes
My stamina gums its way into another day
Dreaming of rockingchair sunporches
But unborn children fill my rooms
Loving me into a truer labour
My flesh backs up against my fading walls
Arguing for a long vacation
But there are no breaks here, no useful snores
Just unfolding layers of necessary doors
Every one already swinging with my intended touch
My nudge, my shove, my sliding ease, my wobbling knees
The mirror melts and the razor hits the floor
And there's no turning back
No more renting, no more needless venting
But just this, already soaked in sobering bliss
And isn't it time to be free in every view?
And isn't it time to bring in all the waiting children?
To let awakening womb outwelcome every fear and doubt?
So I arise kindled bright
Separating those who are hungry
From those who only want to tour the sights
Now my flesh sings, knowing how far it can stretch
And the sun slants across the silvered morning
Crowning the stubbled slopes with pale pink light
So I shave and unrave and save nothing for tomorrow
        except the momentum of today
Running across burning bridges I die into a deeper connection
Letting that rainbow-fleshed arc fill me out
    with its oceanic yet nakedly human shout
            until the Real shines within and all about

—48—

Our Children
Are Not Ours

A man who won't allow himself to cry may one day discover that his wife is not only doing her own crying, but is also doing *his* crying for him. Such unacknowledged transference, such secondhand release, is appallingly common; someone or *something* has to express what we repress — it could be our children, our skin, our employees, our car... Such expression, however diseased it might be (the shit always surfaces somewhere, and it is only shit because of our rejection of what it *really* is), ordinarily provides us with a certain relief, a shallow yet reassuringly righteous emptying of tension, a literal distancing from the *source* of our repressive intent, a psychoemotional *relocation* of such intent that generates in us a very convincing sense of *disowning* (or being impeccably separate from) it. Such is the essence of self-rejection...

Children, at least when they are very young, tend to express what their parents repress. When they get a little older and lose much of their capacity for such multilevelled mediumship, they usually shift toward overdone imitation, neurotic defiance, or whatever other roles maximize their survival as ego-centered beings. Parents who won't voice a *clean* no (authentic in tone, gesture, and timing, veined with non-sentimental love, bright with mind-free force) will, *if* they look, often find that their young children are saying or acting out correspondingly *exaggerated* no's, almost as if inviting their fashionably disempowered parents to dump their rigidly gentle, over-reasonable cutesy-poo syrup and cut loose!

The daughters of women who are dysfunctional or unfit mothers (which includes most women) often engage in play that is chronically clogged with obsessively concerned mothering (precocious housetending, compulsive doll-care, and suffocatingly false nurturance), and may even sometimes end up actually taking care of their mothers, thereby losing their childhoodtime in unnecessary and premature responsibility, feeling driven to answer their mother's twisted call for nurturance and consolation. The inept fathering of almost all men has a similarly devastating impact on their sons, the evidence of which is too obvious to need detailing here; it is sufficient to say that where girls tend to get lost in consuming parodies of nurturance, boys are inclined to get lost in equally consuming parodies of challenge (which often drives both girls and boys to the opposite extreme, as exemplified by the hard-nosed excesses of feminism, and by the spineless "neediness" of so many "soft" men)...

Sometimes inanimate objects act out our suppression of Self, succinctly dramatizing (via the subtle fuel of our hidden habits) whatever we have spurned or entombed in ourselves — a sudden cluster of malfunctioning appliances, a seemingly unwarranted structural cracking, a falling fence, a braking failure, or backed-up drains, dying houseplants, descending plaster, missing utensils, and other such "behavioural" oddities may well signal a frozenness, a stuckness, a damming-up, a psychospiritual desiccation, a disconnection, in *us*! If we won't permit a necessary internal breakdown, then perhaps our house or car will mirror our need by falling apart in some way, hopefully drawing our attention to the *primary* problem...

The dynamics of all this is not without humour, ever tugging at our blinders and personalized armour, trying to unzip our seriousness and unglue our misguided associations. Unplug the gutters, undam the mutters; fix the steering, get back on track... Put another way, the teacher is everywhere, ready to be fleshed out by the gift of our consciously yielded attention, the lessons asking not for pupils, but for awakening hearts...

Why should our children have to pay the price of our own unrelenting childishness? Why should they have to live with the fallout from our own unresolved or unacknowledged wounds? Why should they not have more options from us than authoritarianism or permissiveness? Why put on a false face for them? Why thrust a mask at the innocence gazing up from the crib? Why sugar or steel your voice? Why create distance between you and your children, and then flip out when they act-out this distance as teenagers? Why act as if you have no choice but to once again animate your neurotic ("It's the way I am") programming?

False tolerance is just as injurious to the spirit as fascism; false acceptance twists our capacity to say (and embody) a healthy no out of shape; fake interest simply trivializes curiosity, turning learning into a sideshow, a malignant forum bloated with attention-snaring strategies, overfed ego, and a vast array of compensatory addictions... For the majority of humans, their children are not their future, but only *their past*, temporarily revitalized and de-wrinkled, re-inflated with hope (hope being but nostalgia for the future).

Our cruelty to our children, however well-intentioned, is perhaps the greatest *unacknowledged* crime in modern history — despite the work of people like Alice Miller and John Bradshaw, there is still great denial of such abuse, paralleling our own ongoing abuse of *our* innocence and vulnerability, *our* disrespect for the needs of the child within us... If we're at war with or dissociated from our true needs, how the hell can we sanely respond to our children's needs?

In India, more than a few children are deliberately disfigured or crippled at a very early age, perhaps even at birth, so as to render them into more visually effective beggars for their parents and other interested adults. And we too cripple our children, level upon level, turning them into beggars for our applause (or for the applause of others), mechanically infecting them with our disease of being — this, of course, is not an act of malice, but of slumber, simply reflecting our unwillingness to open our eyes and make Life-giving changes. If we won't responsibly and lovingly parent *ourselves*, how can we possibly do the same for our children? We can't, and the schools can't either, not just because very few teachers possess real maturity, but also because the participation of awakened parents is essential if a school is to have a chance of really working, and such parents are very rare, as well as being strongly disinclined to send (or *sentence*) their children to school.

By the time most children are school-age, their parents can't wait to get rid of them for the day, having already "decided" to hand over parenting to the "professionals" at the local school, not realizing (or not wanting to realize) that the teachers there are, in general, in no better condition than they are... The typical menu is school during the day, play during the late afternoon, and television and homework (plus chores and a common feeding) in the evening, complete with absentee parents, many of whom feel so incompetent about their parenting that they are relieved to have such a small segment of each day set aside for it (although they may, as a counter-effort, busy themselves with overparenting, as in the case of "Supermom").

"Mom" and "Dad" are but cartoon characters, mass-produced mannequins, full of sexless good cheer and bricked-in fear, dutifully and even proudly submitting to their subhuman script (the motive of which is cultural entrancement and replication, camouflaged by pre-packaged humanitarianism), all but oblivious to the eloquent irony of their children being "chips off the old block"! The Old Testament God (who's merely a parental projection) claims that "He" made humans in "His" own image, thereby setting "Himself" up as the patron saint (or BigGuy Backup) for "Mom" and "Dad", and all their little chips and "spitting images"...

America's ubiquitous "Dad", or fave father, or perfect pap, is an amalgam of Bill Cosby and Ronald Reagan, complete with Marcus Welby software and a deodorized Rambo hard-drive, affably waving a knowing forefinger and a few apt phrases in the well-scrubbed faces of America's youth.

And what about the coast-to-coast "Mom"? She usually tends to be somewhat more faceless, though cosily and naggingly omnipresent, existing as a combo housewife/careerperson with a well-starched presence bright with the aura not of apple pie and reassuringly bustling gluteal grandeur (as in yesteryear), but of wryly smiling exasperation and Cosby-foreheaded (raised in fake attentiveness and wonder) understanding, flaring forth now and then as Mary Tyler Moore trapped inside Aunt Jemima's body (the reverse being too much of a stretch of imagination to explore here, except perhaps in terms of bulemia).

Long ago, America's "typical" kids used to look like Shirley Temple trying to be Scarlett O'Hara, or like Howdy Doody jerking off in Sunday School, freckles dancing out wholesome cereal jingles whilst unzipping Annette Funicello's mousecostume, and now the kids of America's fabled "Mom" and "Dad" come in six-packs, one Black, one Hispanic, one Oriental, and three tanned chalk, all cutely irreverent and good to the last drop, looking like Howdy Doody inside a Michael J. Fox or Paula Abdul costume, or like Little Lord Fauntleroy on steroids, or like Marylou Retton trying to be Jane Fonda, all dancing atop a stage whereunder festers something far more real, leaking out here and there in so-called antisocial behaviour...

"Mom" and "Dad" usually dwell in the suburbs, those drearily tidy tributaries of urban blight and fright, with their overmanicured lawns and indoor yawns, and they tend to live there (in their overequipped doll-houses) with all of the stupidly consistent busyness expected of television personalities ("Keeping busy?" being both their hello and their mantra). As the suburbs gradually munch away the countryside with all the logic of brain-damaged ants, anesthetization becomes more and more of a priority, requiring ever more potent dosages, so that "Mom" and "Dad" can remain at the wheel or behind the remote control, with all their kids horseshoed around their unassailable character, their Reaganesque grit, their perfectly-cast certainty and cheery sterility, their wall-to-wall cartoon with its Pepsi captions and underbelly of dread and gagged longing...

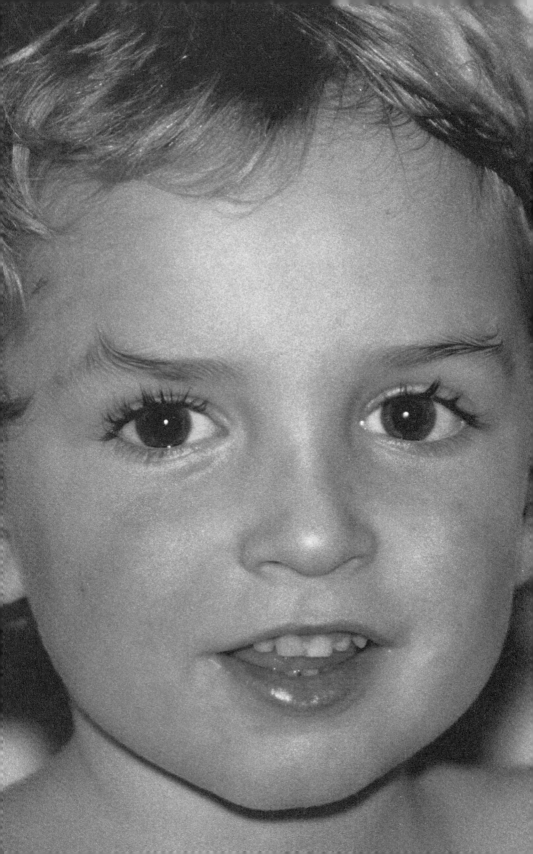

WHEN OUR EYES MEET

When our eyes meet, and meet so deeply that the felt recognition breathes us nakedly present and true, then we see each other, unburdened by history, unafraid of Mystery, free to simply be. When we meet in an intimacy that upstages all drama, then we can truly play our presently-designated roles, without any danger of succumbing to less-than-necessary goals. When we die into the I that is the undisputed us, then, endlessly inviting then, we are, then we exist, then the Mystery is not Ours to know, but Ours to embody and be. And when our love is no more disturbed by our rage or jealousy or suffering than is the sky by its clouds, then we are already through the Door, unable to see our reflection, for into what can Infinite Space stare? And when we lose touch, yielding to withdrawal and shrinkage of being, a thread of remembrance links us with that in us which cannot lose touch, inviting us to take hold of it, despite our mind's claims that it's all just an illusion.

We all know there is a deeper life, but if we have lived too long in the shallows, then we will fear the depths and those who seemingly would take us there. If we are used to lies, then Truth will seem threatening to us, simply because we've made our security, both inner and outer, dependent upon the survival of our lies. How strange it is to be threatened by Truth, Ecstasy, Full Feeling, and God-Presence! And how strange it is to cuddle up with surrogates of These, pretending that they're the real thing! But again our eyes meet, and again the recognition comes so fluid and so wide and so poignantly evocative, so heartbreakingly eloquent, veiled here and there by fleeting imagery of temples, plains, slaughter, fires, hillsides, familiar vistas and faces — and is this not enough, this wonderfully solid transparency, this graceful anchoring of spirit-presence, this gem-riddled muddle, this untranslatable revelation, this time beyond time, this marvelous something that will never make it to the daily news? Real history is being made here, as we do nothing except gaze at each other, defencelessly present, all our pages already embers in the Sacred Fire, all our tomorrows already wearing the same fathomless Glance, the same grief, the same joy, the same diversity, the same wonder, the same sky-splitting glory and thunder, the same surrender to and stubbornly individuated shaping of the Holy Mystery, and still our eyes meet, for It is never over, and never was...

Gustave Doré: *Dante's Inferno*

− 49 −

Speaking True, No Matter What Our Condition: An Evening of Spiritwork

(What follows is the culmination of a long evening of unusually deep work, work that's been as luminous as it's been primal, as full of humour and revelatory surprise as it's been rich with breakthrough and healing. Everything that follows here occurred in total darkness... Initially a series of incomplete sentences are slowly given, each one spontaneously finished by everyone; the transcription of the work begins with the last two incomplete sentences)

ROBERT: The risk I am very close to taking now is... The truest or most magical gesture I could make right now is...

Make this gesture first of all inside yourself. Simply visualize it, feel it, breathe it alive, imagining it to be so — become pregnant with its intention, its stirrings, its longing. Embody it as fully as you can. *(Long pause)* And when I say your name, describe aloud what your particular gesture is, as simply as possible... *(Robert goes through the entire group)*

(Speaking slowly) Now that you've felt your gesture and its shape and flow, simply yield to its *intention*, sensitively, passionately, purely, as nakedly as possible. Just make it, making sure that your every movement arises from and carries the undiluted authenticity of your Core-impulse. It's not just a halfhearted gesture — it's *truly* evocative, an invitation to Spirit, not just to your own, but to *all* Spirit, to show Itself, to flesh Itself out. *(Pause)*

You may even feel some gooseflesh starting, some uncanny alertness sharpening and broadening your awareness. *(Pause)* Allow the feeling in the room to slowly overwhelm your everyday sense of yourself, so that your movement, your gestures, your ebbing and flowing, form a fluid mudra, an effortlessly sacred presentation of form. Thus do you become a potent conductress or conductor of Soul-force, Love, Unspeakable Truth, Ecstasy, and eloquent Simplicity...

Every movement of your fingers, every digital frisson, tells a thousand stories. Every sway and pulsation honours an unrehearsable choreography. The slightest nuance of movement moves universes. This is not about self-importance or omnipotence — it is about being who you truly are, and letting the gift of that emanate out and out and out, to every corner of the Universe... If appropriate, allow sounds to accompany the movement, but keep it low for now. Do not make the sound — if it doesn't come of its own accord, don't force it or try to create it. You may feel as though you're in some kind of natural setting; if so, allow that to become more real, more and more substantial with every breath you take...

You may be on top of a cliff, you may be in a clearing in an ancient equatorial forest, you may be atop a snowy peak, you might be drowning, you might be in an afterdeath state, swimming toward something achingly familiar, or you might be at the burial site of a loved one, letting them touch you in a subtle yet immensely moving way. Your heart may be broken. You might be staring into a fire. (*Weeping throughout room*)

Whatever is now happening, keep making your gesture, and keep letting *it make you*. Don't lose track of it — don't lose it in your drama or suffering or well-being. Keep making it across time. Let your gesture bridge Then with Now. Let your arms become like graceful stems flowing out of the earth of your heart, flowing out and out, touched by all kinds of winds, earthly, stormy, soft, subtle, all colours... (*The weeping becomes more expansive, mixed with free-form yet movingly melodic chanting*)

(*Several minutes later*) Relax the intention to make the gesture. If the gesture continues by itself, so be it. If it drops away, so be it. Do nothing deliberately now, simply allowing whatever's there to move freely, to enrich the silence that fills this room. (*Long pause*) Some of you need to speak now. Do so.

(*Gail speaks, her voice rich with stillness and integrity, saying that she's experiencing herself as an archetypal force, a Water-Bearer, a medium who evokes in people a deep remembrance of their true nature; in so many words, she says not to turn away from our True Being, and that her function is to bring forward the inner power of the river, the rocks, the sky, the elemental world, so that they might be incorporated for the good of all)*

Then you must continue to bring this forward, even though few, including your everyday self, *will truly* receive it. In fact, most will only receive it as a talisman, a ritual that they'll perhaps view as bringing a deeper sense of well-being, some sort of comfort or reassurance. The rare few'll be those who will receive it for what it is truly intended, as a reminder of their fundamental nature. (*Pause*) Nevertheless, you need to bring this gift down to all — it is your purpose, isn't it?

(*She murmurs yes*)

Whether then or now, the you who brought that gift down as a ritual offering is still very much alive. When you're unidentified with mind, body, psyche, your gift is one of profound simplicity and wonderfully earthy grace; its rituals are straightforward, free of superstition, and, best of all, unworkable if there is *any* rote behavior. You have seen plenty of rote behavior in your past. You have seen the gift turned into a cult, an idol of cheap worship, and because of that, you have again and again cast the cup away from yourself, allowing it to break many times. You have often decided that it's not worth offering such a gift, since so few will *really* receive it; everyone wants the benefits thereof, but very few are willing to actually undergo the transformations it requires.

(*She says how much this saddens her*)

And you cannot say this to those persons who would thus abuse your gift, for they would not understand. They'd probably abuse you, treating you as they treated the ancient oracles, simply looking for good news, ways of consolidating their material wealth, advice as how to conduct their latest machinations or war efforts, etcetera. Do not romanticize those times — they were barbaric, cruel, plagued with superstition, just as this time is...

You can see, Gail, how you have chosen to not bring forward that gift. You have doubted its effect. You have *dulled* yourself so as to not appear to be the carrier of it, but you still are, aren't you?

William Blake (Washington, National Gallery of Art, Lessing J. Rosenwald Collection)

(She says yes)

When you assume that power, that sacred trust, we all breathe easier. Everyone here intuits this potential in you, this Water-Bearer, this Truth-Carrier, this transmitter of the energy of rivers and oceans, inner and outer. There is no need to explain the symbolism of what you do, nor the esoteric significance of the rituals; those who are ready to receive it need no explanation. *(Long pause)* Does anyone else need to speak now?

(Bruce, in a very low voice, says he is no longer waiting)

But you have waited — what were you waiting for?

(For some special sign, he haltingly says)

No. You were actually waiting for safety, and it will never be safe for you to speak out, to unambiguously shine with Truth! It is *always* a risk, a Life-giving risk! *(Pause)* It's time for you to stop curbing your tongue, to stop parking yourself in a no-one's-land — you often appear in the Spiritwork, but unnaturally silent, showing yourself usually only as a pair of hands, dancing out the peripheral nuances of magical alchemies. But now you have to speak, don't you?

(A firm yes from Bruce)

You need to verbalize what your hands have been saying for months, years, even lifetimes; you have in effect cut your own tongue out psychically, robbing your self-expression of most of its power and transformative capacity. You have acted out psychically what was once done to you physically, settling for the suffocating safety of non-participation, non-intimacy, non-risking, all the while complaining about the price you had to pay. Nevertheless, it is time to come forward. It's not safe, but it's still time, isn't it? Don't hesitate to speak. In your doubting or undermining of your intention to speak, to *really* speak, you only destroy or weaken much of your work on yourself. *(Lengthy pause)* Speak...

(Bruce brokenly speaks of sensing himself as a great bird, flying through a vast, intensely rich sky, very high up...)

And what do you see from where you are flying?

(He replies that he sees everything very small, far, far away, far below him)

And how does that feel?

(He says that he longs for it, longs to go into it, to return, but doesn't want to go back)

Because you know what is waiting for you, don't you?

(He says he remembers the slaughter)

And you want to stay above it, just as you did when it actually happened, don't you?

(He whispers yes)

You didn't and don't see how this is avoidance, neurotic separation, life after life of unnecessary self-protection. It is good to fly the eagle's sky, and it's also good to dive its dive. When it's time to dive, one must dive fully and courageously and consciously, falling into grace with gravity and true need. *(Pause)* There's something you're closing in on now, something now in view — what do you see? Look. Don't be afraid to see; your eyes [*Bruce is extremely near-sighted, almost to the point of blindness*] are perfect *now*, eagle-sharp *now*, effortlessly lucid. What do you see?

(He says he sees bodies, he sees blood, he sees people running in every direction, he sees children hiding, children dying, while fire spreads everywhere)

Don't pull back. Don't detach! You must feel this, even though it breaks your heart; you have to feel your helplessness, your inability to stop the carnage. Feel that long-ago decision to never again get so close to others that you could again be so terribly and shockingly be wounded to the core. *Don't blind yourself!* What do you see now?

(He says that the fire has burnt out, and that the land is extremely quiet and fading from view, gradually being replaced by rolling hills)

Are you walking this land, or are you still floating somewhere above it?

(*He says that he's on the ground now; he's sitting, and it's quite dark*)

Is it night-time, or are you just simply half-blind?

(*He says he is not sure*)

Are you dreaming?

(*He says he doesn't know, but it seems like he is*)

You're in between. It's not real physicality, and nor is it merely the terrain of a sleep-dream. Where you are resembles a dream — it is a transitional domain, a place of prolonged limbo for you, a semi-disembodied hideout. (*Pause*) But something else *is* drawing you, calling to you, inviting you forth. Trust it. Let yourself go; let yourself spin, float, dissolve, reenter, reembody, *fleshily* remember. There *is* something stronger calling to you than this lonely bit of wavering dreamland, this bardo state — *remember* the shiver of recognition you feel when you unequivocally know that you are dreaming...

You're avoiding *feeling* your next lifetime, which is several before this one wherein you are busy being Bruce. Do you remember what it was like to be blind, crawling around day after day, month after month, looking for food?

(*He weeps, sobbing loudly*)

Do you remember freezing in the winter, your eyes the colour of fresh blood? Do you recall feeling danger, but not seeing it, being ready to flee, but unable to really get away? You, at that time, were just as trapped as those people running around in that ancient vision of slaughter, that soul-crushing bloodletting that *still* appears to you in this lifetime in vague dreams of torture, and in the chronic collapse of heart that even now plagues you. But that blind lifetime had hardly any awareness in it — it was little more than the unconscious suffering of a brutish creature, enlivened only by some awareness of Death, a few fleeting moments during the life, a few kindnesses from strangers, a few rare loving touches on your mutilated cheeks, your ravaged brow... But again you can fly, and when you fly, your vision is eagle-clear, isn't it?

(*Yes, very sharp, he says*)

And you have a right to fly like this if you are also willing to alight, to fight, to breed, to feel, to dive in and feel, to no longer just withdraw from your pain... (*Long pause*) Does anyone else feel a need to speak now?

(*Shanti says she feels very distraught, because she's afraid she will be hurt*)

That's simply because you've been hurt before, the wounds of which you can now feel much more easily than usual. (*She weeps*) Trust your voice; you need not muddy it to confuse or placate those you fear.

(*She brokenly says that she can only sing or be silent*)

No more — it's time to speak, to articulate, to be blunt. You've done enough chanting [*Shanti spent ten years with Swami Muktananda*] this time around. Say what you're most afraid to say — if your mind judges that, so be it. Speak.

(*She says she knows she's here to speak truly, and that she once did, long ago*)

And what happened to you when you spoke the truth? (*She cries*) Say it.

(*Sobbing, she says that she has a feeling of being put in a dungeon, locked up, tied, left to die*)

You have made your body, your current body, into a dungeon, a bony brittleness, a desiccated chamber. You need to speak like you sing, with everything you've got, right now! Speak without editing anything. Speak.

(*She says she's afraid*)

Go deeper. You're already judging yourself, mercilessly prejudging, *thinking* that everything you'll say or see will be false or superficial or pretentious, some sort of megalomania.

(*She agrees, adding that she thinks whatever she'll say will be impure, and that there doesn't seem to be anywhere to go*)

You speak this, though, like a tired old woman who's already given up, having been sucked dry. You need to *feel* what you say *as* you say it — you're capable of speaking in a way that will make people sit up straight, but when you doubt yourself *before* you speak, and judge it as not right in some way, then of course Truth doesn't come through, and all that is left is your conventional voice with its self-deprecating, subtly apologetic tone, drearily announcing good old Shanti.

(*That's not my truth, she declares — there's a deeper truth*)

Who are you?

(*In a louder yet still contracted voice, she says, "I am me, a stronger me, with nothing held back"*)

That's who you'd *like* to be! Your voice doesn't ring true. Don't lie now. If you're unwilling to speak, say so!

(*She says she knows how her holding back is hurting and diminishing her*)

No you don't! That's just false you talking, spiritually ambitious you. Right now, you'd rather be a cripple, a hunched-over old beggar woman in Calcutta, scrambling for crumbs, chanting as a way of bargaining with God for salvation, letting yourself be free only when singing under certain ritualized conditions, fearful of speaking purely, afraid that the voice that might come through you *now* would be judged by others, condemned as you trying to *act* like a channeler, a medium, to curry favour from Robert in some way. And you know that's bullshit! It does take a certain nerve to speak up when the voice speaking is clearly not everyday you, like Bruce's Eagle, or Gail's Water-Bearer. The voice you hear right now sounds like Robert's, but isn't exactly everyday Robert's, is it? You need to trust in order to speak with conscious spontaneity. If it sounds like you, so be it. If it doesn't, so be it. (*Long pause*) Someone else is ready to speak...

(*Vimalesh, in a thin, remote voice, says that he has risen above things for too long, and that he needs to find his body; he is obviously in deep trance*)

Where are you now?

(*Still hovering around, he murmurs*)

What do you see? Shapes?

(*Yes, he replies, distant shapes, but not very solid*)

What are you remembering?

(*I'm hiding, he mutters, I'm hiding*)

From?

(*Being heard, being welcomed, he says, sobbing uninhibitedly*)

I see your head fallen back, just like in last week's session, your throat cut, open like a second mouth, gaping bright red. The image of that is at the edge of you — that's perhaps why you keep looking for colours and actions in life that have no set form, no definitive solidity — you don't like the *unavoidable specificity* of that body with its throat wide-open, that body half-decapitated. You are afraid more of the same will happen to you, and that very fear ensures that more of the same *does* happen, not necessarily physically, but psychoemotionally, relationally... The jutting rigidity of jaw that you so often manifest is precisely a defense against your throat being interfered with, a defense against the loss of face. (*Pause*) Your insensitivity to your body, as demonstrated by the number of "accidents" you have, is a defense against feeling how very easily your body could be wounded — one swing from a sword, one spray of bullets, one spear-thrust, and what damage!

Along with this, your subtlety is confined to your etheric dimension, your dreamworld, your lighter emotions, your psychic ability, your dream-lucidity, but you don't often allow that subtlety to penetrate and pervade your physicality, especially below the diaphragm. You use your legs, for example, for gross movement, for walking and running hard, but not for subtler, more delicate matters, and you need to! There's history stored in your legs, ancient history, signifi-cant scenery — there's a vast tapestry of experience awaiting you there, but you must enter into it consciously. You need to *live* in and as your legs, and let *them* tell you *their* story; it's not just a simplistic tale, for there's plenty of detail there, plenty of encoded action, right down to your ankles and feet, and up to your perineum, too. There's some stories up there, also, around your pubis, your hip-girdle, your loins — you've been a woman before, and you've given birth. You don't want to feel the pain of childbirth, especially stillbirth; you don't want to feel the great stretching of labour.

Sense your legs now, going right into them, and sense your hips too — in other words, take your attention there, ride your attention there, and *live there* for the rest of the evening. Feel how womanly you've been in recent history, a few lifetimes ago, and how sometimes you've yearned to be a woman in *this* lifetime, and how you've even maintained certain gestures that are, in a sense, colourful parodies of the Feminine, right down to how you move your arms when you run... (*Long silence*) Who else needs to speak?

(*Bob says he does, that he needs room to speak*)

And do you have room?

(*He says that his heart is full, but that his throat is tight*)

You have room if you will but let your throat go, letting go of those old forces, those ghosts that are seemingly saying to you, "Don't you dare speak, or we will slaughter your beloved ones!" You need to let your throat be free. Take your grip away from there; you've had other hands around your throat before, but it's *your* hands now, *your* exaggerated self-containment, *your* self-pressuring... You need to let your heart flood up into your throat, because you *do* have something to say that everybody needs to hear, don't you? Say it. It's time to say it; you've waited a long time. (*Lengthy pause*) Do you feel the hesitation? Does the hesitation say anything to you? Does it warn you of some danger? And what is the danger of speaking freely now?

(*Death, he murmurs, loss, not being heard*)

Okay, that's your expectation; it was once a very valid expectation, but it isn't now. Speak as though there's no danger of being punished for doing so.

(*Forcefully, he declares: I speak to the heart, not to the mind. I speak because it is my need and your need to listen. This voice is your voice. It rings of thunder and rushing rivers. It is the solidity of mountains, the vastness of the sky, the totality of Being that is this planet. Though you*

make many choices, there is but one — move through it all. All! Every-
thing! There is nothing you cannot overcome, nothing! Let your spirit fly!
Trust it even when it is but a dust particle, and let it expand! Even in
your darkest moments, it is there. I speak to the heart, not to the mind...)

But you speak with unnecessary force, as though not trusting that if
you speak softly, vulnerably, you will be heard. Your words ring true
in part, but their particular kind of force weakens their message, and
even subtly dishonours it. Your force is like a river running full-out
without any curves or sensuality, no silent poolings, no variety of
flow — there's a monotone, an excessively male drivenness, as though
you've been cooped up for too long. The challenge ringing through
your voice is unrelenting, overly authoritative, too rigidly male —
within that, however, I feel your need to speak with real vulnerability,
to infuse your voice with something softer, something more yielding.
The Earth-energy that is so implosive in your voice needs to be
translated in *all* its dimensions, not just in its rough, solid, mountain-
ous aspects, but also in its tenderness and refinements — the feath-
ered greens of the forest, the fragility of the Earth, the slant of the
sun, the deer's leap — do you understand?

(Yes, he whispers)

You were cooped up for so long that when you come forward, you're
like an undammed river *fisting* down one long channel. There's a
curvaceousness, a fluidity, that's missing. You need to find that now.
To begin with, you have to speak, to let it flow forward, to be willing
to speak with authority, to be willing to have people tell you that
you're a pushy bastard, a know-it-all, a big chief, or whatever — you
have to let it surge out, and *then* make room for softness, for you're
not in a position yet to *begin* with softness. Is there more for you to
say in this moment?

(He says no)

Good. Remember what I said, and it will deepen you. There is a time
to be very forceful, and there's a time to pause, to soften, to yield, to
become more multidimensional, not just for the voice or presence
that you're embodying now, but for your everyday voice and self...
Anyone else need to speak?

(Jean says she needs to speak, that she is a shapechanger, and that it is

Gustave Doré: *Chateaubriand's Atala*

difficult for her to be embodied)

That's because you're used to being a shapechanger. When did you learn to become such a one?

(*Many lifetimes ago as an Indian, she softly says, adding that it was very natural for her to move from bird to river to tree to rock, to be each of these things, to fill them out with her presence, but that it was far more difficult for her to be human*)

That's because the responsibility was deeper, the stakes higher, and you grew very accustomed to the panoramic fluidity of allowing consciousness to fixate on and pervade a particular bird, an animal, a river, a stone — it's an extremely useful talent, but it can be abused very easily. At best, it teaches deep empathy with everything, animate and inanimate. At worst, it makes one merely slippery, evasive, noncommittal. (*Pause*) What do you see now?

(*She says she sees the roots of a great tree growing down into the Earth*)

You can be those roots, can't you?

(*Yes, she says*)

And you can also be the Earth that's being entered by the roots.

(*Yes, she says, adding that she can also be the tree reaching for the sky*)

And what happens to the human that you also are when this occurs?

(*She says she gets two images: One of the human in trance, the other of the human living its life, both occurring simultaneously*)

The first one is no longer common for you, where the body is parked in deliberate trance or in sleep at night, with you, to varying degrees of lucidity, being roots, birds, stones, as if in a dream wherein you enter the bodies or forms of your dream-beings. Since you are not yet mature enough to fully realize the implications of this, it has created a split in you, a deep split. Your longing for your so-called Indian past-life is not just a longing for that particular life, with its rewards and trials and Earth-bonding, but is also a longing for the capacity to change shape so easily...

This ability could be redeveloped in you quite easily, but it's not really necessary. It's far more important for you to love, to go to the heart of relationship; you need to tap into a deeper longing than that of changing shape. Do you feel something deeper in you than that urge to change shape?

(*Yes, she says, a longing to join, to be in a true circle with others, to give deeply, nourishingly*)

Give the voice of that longing. (*She chants, hauntingly, beautifully, her voice shiveringly rich with presence and evocation*) Give it so fully that it breaks your heart. (*She continues chanting, and then begins to weep*)

Let it break your heart fully, until your heart has no shape. (*She cries very deeply, and many others join her*) Let your voice sing as you weep. (*She does*)

Call your people, call them to the circle, call them back, chant them back, chant them back... (*She does, her voice flooded by a vast purity of longing*)

One more person now.

(*Nancy, her voice almost inaudible, says she would like to speak*)

You are aware of the forces that would stop you from speaking. Feel your neck widen, becoming a column, a sturdy pillar, strong and straight, with your head resting easily on top of it, sacred words slowly rising to your throat, sacred sounds. Allow your words to come forward — speak them, sing them, whatever... (*Her speech is very halting, punctuated by fearful breathing*) Be aware of how you're breathing; your exhale is loaded with drama! You need to speak now without such drama. What do you see?

(*Walls, she says*)

Let the walls breathe... (*Pause*) Now what do you see?

(*She says she can't breathe*)

But you are, aren't you? (*No answer*) Speak.

(She says that she feels frozen, cold, stuck)

Nevertheless, you're indulging — you're busy creating fear for yourself, and swallowing what you *really* need to say. *(She keeps swallowing noisily, as if in terror)* Others have also had difficulty speaking, but they've made the effort. You haven't, so far; otherwise, your voice wouldn't ring so false when you speak.

(I don't know my true voice, she says melodramatically)

Don't lie. You need to speak from something much deeper than this childish theatricalness, this quivering little voice, this balled-up withdrawal from Life. This room's a perfect environment right now for what you need to do... You are very afraid now, aren't you?

(Yes, she says, adding that her body feels as if it's disintegrating, getting smaller and smaller)

Let it get smaller, and even smaller, and even smaller than that. Let it become non-existent, concentrated down to a single point, and then not even that. *(Pause)* There *is* an urge in you to disappear, so that no one will ever be able to get to you, to touch you, to hurt you, to torture you. It's a very old urge, a potent reminder of what you have suffered...

Disintegrate. Let yourself die. *(She begins to cry)* Surrender to this death. Yield fully, keeping your mouth wide open, your throat wide open, your everything wide open. Let your legs die, your back die, your belly die, your face, all of you!

Feel your last death returning, its details suddenly filling out, as you spill out — you can glimpse it from above as you die, as you let go. *Feel* it. *Feel* the spasms. Don't look for White Light; be present at your death — yield to your fear of it. Yes! Go into the fear, fully into it! *(She sobs and wails in a purity of utter terror; others cry with her)* Yes! Yes! Be aware of the Light at the same time, the presence of something other than your terror. You can sense a Light, a great Openness, nearby. *(Now she is crying deeply)* The body's dying, but there *is* light and love, a love you can now feel in the midst of your grief. Let the body die — that's it, let it die, let it go, saying good-bye to it. *(Pause)* Let it go. Softly...

There is something calling you, something achingly familiar, some-thing so, so beautiful that it breaks your heart, your psychic heart, your emotional heart, your everything breaking, dissolving, brighten-ing, orgasmically, peacefully, naturally, truly. You're being called Home, welcomed — you've been in exile, and now you're returning. Feel your love for whatever It is That is calling you — you're swim-ming toward It, flowing and leaping and loving your way toward It, like a river going to the ocean...

(She starts to sing, her voice beautifully alive. The others spontaneously join her. She weeps some more, then resumes singing, her voice high, clear, and sweet, exquisitely wavering above the other voices, which form a choir for her. About ten minutes later, all the voices stop at once, and a long, vibrant silence follows...)

Gustave Doré: *Dante's Purgatorio*

–50–

Look Inside Your Looking:
The Essence of Seeking

When our seeking is free of all desperation and egoic gratification, it becomes but dynamic receptivity, no longer obsessed with its supposed goal, but rather deeply content to consciously participate in and enrich our moment-to-moment aliveness. Ordinarily however, the very search for something, especially in the realm of the spiritual and psychophysical, only narrows, shrinks, and diminishes us, misaligning and ossifying us, rendering us all but unavailable to what we are purportedly seeking. Nevertheless, there's no point in making a virtue out of non-seeking, since in almost all cases such a strategy is only a sophisticated avoidance of what *must* be faced or done, a mere veneer of pseudo-realization splashed over fear-riddled inertia...

The urge to seek (God, Truth, the Holy Grail, Samadhi, Enlightenment, Immunity, No-Mind, Ecstasy, Supreme Knowledge, Gnosis, Sunyata, Wisdom, Immortality, or Something That'll make us Eternally Safe) eventually erodes us, either positively or negatively, positively in the sense of wearing away the non-essential in us, thereby lucidly disillusioning us relative to the whole motive for seeking, and negatively in the sense of simply enervating and degenerating us, inexorably depriving us of the very energy that we need to spark our realization of who we really are.

Seeking, in its very pursuit of its desired object, tends to be a departure from our core of Being, even though it may ostensibly present itself as a would-be movement (adorned with "good" resolutions and galloping sincerity) toward the center of us. Before I go further, let me say that there is a subtlety involved here, a largely transverbal subtlety, in that for the Truth to be evident here, both seeking and non-seeking must be simultaneously understood, paradoxically embraced, fully and unequivocally, bodily — this is not a matter of mind, nor necessarily even of feeling, but of Being, and I do not say this now for your absorption, deflection, or information, but rather to give some flavour as to where this talk seems to be going, given its initial momentum...

The very realm, or arena, wherein both seeking and non-seeking are dramatized and armed must be recognized, and such recognition is not within the reach of the intellect, nor that of conventional faith, for it exists at a deeper level than that of belief (intellect being *mind-centered* belief, and conventional faith *emotion-centered* belief). Neither Science nor Religion are intimate with such recognition, both having been dogmatized into impermeability to it. To the point: The realm I speak of is, when sufficiently illuminated, not just that of pure witnessing, but also, and simultaneously, that of full-fleshed, magically alive, passionate involvement in Life Itself, at all levels.

"Seek and ye shall find" is, in psychospiritual terms, usually a cliché, however metaphysically appealing. It is more accurate to say "Seek and ye shall be left behind" or, even more precisely, "Seek and ye shall reside in your mind", for it is in our mind that we hold and maintain the image of what we seek, but what we ultimately seek is beyond *all* images, *all* idols of mind. Explore, deeply explore, the one who is doing the seeking, and you will encounter the primary machinations of your mind, including the clockwork of identification and addiction. Seeking that does not consciously turn in on itself is little more than nostalgia for the future, a promise-dangling dream, a mind-organized scheme. Simply put, *look inside your looking...*

At its best, seeking is a journey into Being, a journey undertaken not to get rid of fear (and related unpleasantries), but to pass into *and* through the very core of fear, until we are no longer afraid of it, until fear is simply known as a recoil from Life, a suppression of feeling, a knotting of Being, a paralysis of intimacy, a refusal to *really* love... Many people, and many teachings, consider fear to be an emotion, but it isn't — it is a *repression* of emotion, just like depression or doubt, an unwillingness to *fully* feel what we feel. Fear is, in almost all cases, no more than a perversion of fright, a survival reflex stuck on hold by compulsive futurizing (as in worry), a neurochemical mechanism usurped by the conventional mind and kept on alert by all sorts of supportive thoughts and assumptions, mind-forms that, through sheer repetition, actually seem to legitimize our fear's chronic appearance...

Seeking tends to be a strategy whereby we hope to be rid of our fear, or at least to be in such control of it that it no longer upsets us or carries the threat of destruction. However, seeking carries within itself the seeds of its own destruction, seeds that need only the nourishment of conscious attention. Counterfeits of these seeds are the very essence of that species of non-seeking that is but indulgence of inertia, laziness, and emotional disconnectedness. Real non-seeking is a non-doing that is still dynamically alive, vibrantly present; it is no passive reaction to Life's demands, but rather a deep response that complements and supports *Essence-centered* doing. Such non-seeking inevitably *follows* the illumination of seeking, the cutting through of compulsion in our seeking.

It is very easy to say, in metaphysical fashion, that what we seek is already here, that what we seek is exactly what we essentially are right now, but such statements are of no value if they are not fully realized by us, with our *entire* being. It is of no use to merely believe in such pronouncements — they literally are not true, unless we are currently experiencing them as our Truth, not just as something we *believe* to be true (which only reduces them to data, or information), but as something that we *know* and *feel* to be true. To say "We are all one" is a lie, unless it is actually being experienced as being so, directly and right now!

We can read (perhaps in most eloquent form in Da Love-Ananda's books) that the search itself is the problem, that when we make the goal too important we ruin the climb, carrying the contractedness of our ambition and future-fixation right to the peak, so that when we reach it (or far more commonly, a *facsimile* of it), we're not capable of really enjoying it as it is, for our very view, our very stance, is polluted by the way in which we have climbed, by the prevailing attitude of our ascent... We may hear a version of this, sense a kind of truth in it, but the key is to know, to truly know for ourselves, how very important it is to be present in the climb, to be present in our search, so that one day, our very search itself will no longer fascinate or drive us. And even here, there is an inclination to make *that* day an object of seeking! Thus do we go on impaling ourselves upon our greed for shortcuts...

One could say that there's no need for a shortcut, since we are fundamentally already where we need to be, already established in joy, in pure knowingness, in God, in Consciousness Itself, but we of course manage to obscure and misrepresent that native realization in all kinds of ways, madly persisting in our misery-inducing case of mistaken identity, or perhaps inflating it with *thoughts* of a profounder Self. What must be examined and unravelled is the process whereby we obscure our realization of who we actually are, and this requires a heartfelt, luminously discriminative approach to everything, as well as a surrender to the directives arising from our core of Being; both dissolution of self and a firm yet fluid standing of one's true ground are necessary. This is the sacred demand of our humanness, a lucidly passionate honouring of both our individuality and our Eternal Nature. Its strength stems from vulnerability, its integrity from *direct* participation in inviolable wholeness. It doesn't give a damn about security or safety; it loves risk-taking, not naive, foolhardy risks, but *real* risks, risks of Being, risks that only begin once we are no longer in need of de-armoring. So we at once discriminate and surrender, unburdened by technique, for ours is an always-fresh art, obeying no morality except that generated by Awakening's Alchemy. We do not abandon our humanity, nor exploit it, but instead go to the very heart of it, and *through...*

Happiness, real happiness, is inherent to Being; that is, when we are stably established in our essential nature, joy is *already* the case, whether it wears a glad, sad, or mad face. Such joy is not produced by anything in particular, anymore than the sky is produced by the disappearance of its clouds. When this non-situational joy becomes frequent in our experience, then our seeking becomes less of a desperate activity, and more of something we do without distress, something we do (or that *does us*) until it has run itself out, finished its momentum, like a bicycle wheel spinning, then slowing and stopping because there's no one left to drive it on... That quality of "no one left" is here to be embodied, to be lived, to be felt, to be entered into fully, but it is very difficult, almost impossible to do so if our somebody-ness, our individuality, has not been allowed to flower fully. Seeking, at its best, crystallizes our individuality, our native uniqueness of being, helping it to fulfill itself, to flesh itself out. Most of the time though, seeking is in the service of surrogates of individuality, as epitomized by ego-centered character structures and other exaggerated *personifications* of Self-suppression.

There is an obviousness to what I'm saying, and, at the same time, there is a deep subtlety to it, a subtlety more of feeling than content, a need to be aware of two or more levels of being at once (which

does not mean *thinking* about two different views at the same time!).
Such awareness must not just be a sporadic occurrence, or else our
awakening will eventually become reduced to little more than a
byproduct of enthusiasm and upswings of mood — if we're only
inclined to be wakeful when we're in the mood, then we'll never get
to meet and fully know the us that doesn't want to be present, that
doesn't want to meditate, to live fully, to be radiantly alive, to know
God, and we must become intimate with that particular us, that
crabby, scabby, dark-dwelling, appetite-driven us, so that we might
recognize that it's not *really* an us, but only a convincing personification of our resistance to waking up, veined through and through by
our unresolved woundedness, our brokenness of need, our aborted
yearning for real love and intimacy. The armoring of this personified
habit cannot be undone just by observing it, however; detached
witnessing is of lasting use here only if it is combined with a diving
into and through the layers of our woundedness and twisted need, a
diving that is as open-eyed as it is deep and courageous, bright with
the permission to be passionately and unequivocally alive...

When seeking is thoroughly explored, one sees that it's not just this
one big search that's being indulged in, but all kinds of searches or
promise-hunts, large and small, psychedelic and drab, public and
private. Appetite creates a kind of seeking — we're hungry, we look
for food, go to the store, salivatingly open the refrigerator door,
eating and maybe looking for more, but we can also not be hungry
and still busy ourselves hunting for food, such drivenness of habit
characterizing more of us than we'd like to admit. When we turn
away from our deeper desires, we submit to lesser desires; we turn
away from the demands of the *truly* nourishing, and seek fulfillment
of a sort that doesn't really fulfill *us*, but that only inflates and
engorges us, dumping us in a bereft of awakening force, a domain
where unilluminated seeking dangles before us its mirages, its taste-
fully packaged hope, its edible promises...

Seek and ye shall be left behind, within the maelstroms and sterile
compartmentalizations of your mind, but not if you go to the heart
of your very motive for seeking! We only get what we yearn for when
our yearning spontaneously sheds its must; we only reach our goal
when we become soulfully intimate with the *root* of our reach; we
only truly face ourselves when we look inside our looking, losing face
without losing touch, letting ourselves die into a truer Life, a Life
wherein the climb is as full of sacred rhyme as the peak...

William Blake (British Museum)

*An Exploration of Real Work and Its Counterfeits,
As Well as of the Art of Using Our Resistance
To Fine-Tune Our Wakefulness*

–51–
Illuminating Our Resistance
to Working on Ourselves

From a spontaneous talk given February 13, 1990

The deep inner work, the transformational process that we must all engage in if we are to ever become stably established in our center of Being, is plagued, vilified, and obscured by its counterfeits, its promise-jammed, hope-crammed counterfeits, which Robert deRopp so aptly termed the Fantasy Work in his final book (*Self-Completion*) — these surrogates of true work on oneself are but seductive mirages, the darlings of those who want to *believe* that they *are* working on themselves, that they *are* truly getting to the heart of the matter, when in fact, most of the time they are simply clinging to a mere *conceptualization* of what they need to do...

The real work is not easy. It is not characterized by shortcuts; there may be times of radical, rapid transformation, but these have as their foundation a long, steady period of hard inner and outer work. The whole process is a labour of love — it's fraught with resistance, difficulty, pitfalls, suffering (as well as with exhilaration, joy, and all kinds of mastery and surrender), all of which are, when rightly used, no more than necessary tests, not tests given by an omnipresent Somebody, a divine overseer, but tests that are a matter of psycho-spiritual gravitation, of the attraction of conditions, qualities, and circumstances (personified or not) that precisely fit our *current* state of being, our *current* needs...

Most of those who appear to be working on themselves are not sufficiently intimate with their resistance to such work. The harder they try to do this or that, to believe in this or that, to somehow create in themselves the changes they desire, to somehow persist in transformational ambition, the stronger the *counter-effort* will be in them, a counter-effort that can be easily disguised, at least at first or even for a long time, by enthusiasm, hope, force-fed affirmations, positive thinking, renunciation, or obsession with doing it right. It is far more useful to acknowledge and encounter one's resistance to working on oneself *as soon as possible*, making not an enemy out of such apparent obstruction, but rather creatively finding ways to unknot the energies of it, until it is but *available* Life-force, uncommitted to anything less than Life-giving.

In fact, our resistance is simply something in us that has not been given the benefit of luminous love, let alone non-reactive attention; it is in many ways just a personification of a wounded child, a child who grows misshapen out of sheer neglect, a child who sabotages our well-meaning efforts to grow, in order to snare our attention, our focus, our *potential* parental approval, our love — and how very easily we do to this child what was done to *us* when we were of a similar age!

If we deny or ignore our resistance, then it simply festers, growing in twisted fashion, often finding a minimally satisfying outlet, a muted voice, in cries or statements such as: "I *want* to be loving" or "I *want* to be happy" or "I *want* to break through all this." (More *obviously* defeated or vindictive statements, though equally common, won't be considered here.) Such statements signal a kind of good intention, a foundationless resolution, promising or hinting at great things, asking to be *believed in*, delivering basically nothing except for hot air, representing not the impulse to awaken, but rather the resistance, the goody-goody coated resistance, to embodying such impulse. When someone says, "I want to open up" or "I want to go deeper" or "I want to give my anger", say to them "When?" and then, when they've indicated now (to do otherwise would pull down the pants of their *seemingly* good intention), say, "Go ahead." You will then notice that, almost all of the time, nothing really happens — just more hand-wringing, more neurotic helplessness, more trotting out of the afore-mentioned fine resolutions, as if the voicing of such statements of intent actually constituted real work on oneself! This is the problem with most of what is referred to as work on oneself — it is plagued with abstractions and façades of the Real; it doesn't deal directly with key issues, but rather only makes philosophy out of strategies that purport to deal with such things, settling for far less than whole-hearted participation in the Awakening process...

It is easy to create or believe in various theories about becoming fully human, God-realized, or whatever — information about such matters abounds nowadays. Nevertheless, such information is of no use to those who can only receive it as information, as mere data. Real truth is not merely a factual matter; it is a living process, spontaneous and unrehearsable, non-static, never exactly repeatable, both including and transcending the factual. Truth is a vast relatedness in which many things are revealed, not just as information, but as something senior to information, something more akin to Being, to Love, to the Mystery of the Undying One...

Resistance cannot be dealt with as just an intellectual matter; it must be directly encountered, felt, entered into and given room to outbreathe itself, without, however, assuming its viewpoint! This is the true art of working with one's resistance — to not *resist* it, to make room for it, to fully *feel* it, to become intimate with all its twists and turns and endarkened intentions, without yielding to its standpoint. This is a surrender to one's resistance, but not a submission to it. It is an act of love and trust, an act of deep intelligence...

Anyone who comes into true work, work that is *already* well underway in the teacher, will be informed almost right away that what will be worked with is both their longing to awaken, and also their resistance to such a process. Initially, the sheer good feeling of kinship, revelation, and full-blooded breakthrough will make one's so-called resistance seem irrelevant, or perhaps non-existent. One will tend to treat it the same way as most new "lovers" treat the distance between them... Such copulators act as though their being overwhelmed by the happy heat of sexplay and psychoemotional novelty is all there is — in other words, the honeymoon is permitted to obscure the Truth rather than to celebrate or express It. The self-possessed two are just cuddling up in a sensation-sweetened delusion, a romanticized bubble, a suite of fake ecstasy, a bit of illusory immunity.

In similar fashion, most of the good things that happen as one begins to enter real work on oneself are but a kind of honeymoon, a circumstantial high, a freedom not in grounded harmony with responsibility. As soon as it becomes clear that such work actually *requires* significant changes in one's lifestyle, habits, behavior, relationships, sexuality, and so on, resistance suddenly appears, seizing center stage in one's mind (unless one is busy being a devotee, in which case resistance won't surface for a long time, at least directly, since submission here is de rigueur). Of course, this resistance, this recoil, has been there all along, just like the distance so suddenly apparent to the post-honeymooners — it was obscured by all the rushes, the joys of stimulation, the love for the teacher, the feeling of being at home, but as soon as we realize that change, change that is unpopular with our ego, is required, we resist, and we often don't even acknowledge that we are doing so, since it feels so real, so compelling, so *right!* We resist, but we don't resist getting righteous about our contractedness, our sudden withdrawal from intimacy...

We tend to want to keep things as they are, and yet be a transformed us. Extrapolating this further, we want to receive all the benefits of a profound transfiguration of self without actually going through the transformation itself — we, in a nutshell (namely our skulls), want to be an enlightened us, an enlightened ego. Thus does clinging to our *apparent* self, our personified habits, continue. If the work we are doing on ourselves doesn't suit us, the ego-centered us, the spiritually ambitious us, we sooner or later find "good" reasons to drop it, to leave it, to denigrate it. Everyone who turns away from what is unquestionably valuable for them (in terms of work on themselves) almost invariably, as Gurdjieff once said, "choose" the worst possible circumstances for themselves, ever rationalizing themselves out of any telling examination of their flight from such work.

It is easy to turn away. It is easy to forget one's purpose in coming to such work. It is easy to find fault with the teacher. It is easy to dismiss the energies of those around a real teacher as merely cultic, dependent, deluded, brainwashed. When we separate out from the journey to the heart of the matter, we act as if such a journey was only a dream, as though it didn't really occur for us, as so well described by Hesse in his *Journey To The East.* The journey continues whether we stay or not. It must ask everything of us; it is not a tour of the depths, but a literal embodiment of them, an embodiment of all that we are, dark and light, high and low, gross and subtle...

Those who leave real work are only acting out their resistance, letting themselves be mediums for *its* voice and stride, letting themselves speak *its* mind and follow *its* imperatives, without knowing that they are doing so, all the while pretending that they are awake, that they are at last reclaiming their independence! Instead of acting out our resistance, we must work with it sanely. This is not easy, for the chemistry set in motion by activated or exaggerated resistance can create all kinds of terrifying or strangely convincing mind-states to which our attention fastens (this is the meaning of *fascination*) like iron filings to a magnet.

When we are in our resistance deeply, we are cut off from Truth, but not *fully* cut off — it's always possible to confess our inner whereabouts (even if non-verbally at first); it's always possible to let others know what our experiences are, even if they are but utter confusion, paranoia, and extreme doubt. It may be very difficult to speak or share thus, but it *is* possible, and not only possible, but *necessary*. Otherwise, we will never transcend reactivity, but will just keep on acting out the same old dramas, again and again, re-acting and re-acting, instead of responding sanely, lovingly, and ruthlessly to our resistance.

Those who dismiss their resistance, denying it or labelling it "negative," only strengthen it. There is no point in repressing it, nor in indulging it. It must be consciously faced, embraced, known, illuminated, and passed through, not to be somehow annihilated, gelded, or left behind, but rather to be *included*, luminously included, such inclusion being not a matter of naive acceptance or submission, but rather of energetic transformation of such brilliance and potency that even the most contracted or gross of conditions becomes but available Life-force...

It is crucial to become intimate, *specifically* intimate, with our resistance, not married to it, not bound to it, but *truly* knowledgeable about it. All of its involuntary manifestations must be recognized — the little mannerisms, the gestures, the tonal qualities, the exaggerations and omissions that signal its presence must be recognized, and to this end it is useful not to just do this work alone, but to be doing it with others who have a similar commitment, others who will let us know when we are slipping, who will not support our blindness, who will in no uncertain words and actions let us know when we are in resistance, when we're reactive, when we're fucked up. This is why groupwork, not merely therapeutic groupwork, but groupwork of a much deeper nature, is so useful, especially when it's part of a living community, a community that's profoundly involved in the Awakening process.

The energies of our resistance must be externalized in a manner both potent and sensitive, until they are free of their script. This will necessarily involve a lot of emotional work, a lot of breakdown, a lot of losing face, as well as a clear understanding and appreciation of the need to let go. Put another way, the broken wave knows the ocean, but only if it welcomes, *naturally* welcomes, its breaking; otherwise, it is simply present as self-pity, helplessness, resentment, bitterness, a "victim" of unfairness. We have to stop looking for a better deal, or somewhere special to kneel, or for good fortune, and simply get down to work, greeting not only our soul-light and unexploitable core, but also our demons and ghouls, all the personifications of our endarkened moods, habits, and unsuspected corners.

There's no point in getting terribly upset about the mess we're in; all we can really do in the beginning is acknowledge it for what it is, without any inner comforting or buffering whatsoever. In the very pain of *heartfelt* acknowledgement of what we are up to, the raw, *unconsoled* suffering of it, our wounds, our deep wounds, begin to open, their scabs coming off, the buffers disappearing — we are then, through our very hurt, our soul-reaching depth of hurt, *feelingly* reconnected to our Source, returned to intimacy with It, unbarricaded intimacy... Our very grief, when undammed, renders us more spacious, more fluidly open, and our anger, when sanely released, breaks down many barriers to intimacy, *vulnerably* so, untying the knots in our belly and solar plexus, reestablishing the flow between pelvis and chest, so that our body is freer, fuller, truer, more in alignment with our core of Being...

Many of those who are doing true work on themselves (and this is an *Essence-centered* doing, richly veined with dynamic receptivity and other qualities of Non-Doing), are not broadcasting it, not even whispering it. They may not even appear to be particularly evolved people. But if they are looked at closely and deeply felt, empathetically felt, it will be obvious what their state is. Those who are asleep cannot recognize such a one even if they see the shining eyes and sense the deeply centered presence, the non-stop integrity. Such presence is of no more significance to them than the charisma of a movie star (charisma being only the strongly projected force of a particularly colorful or powerful personality). Real presence is not a matter of personality, but of strongly embodied essence...

To undertake the journey of awakening just to become more powerful or more immune or more loving or more whatever only militates against such a passage, actually only encouraging us to embark on a convenient surrogate of this journey, such as can be found in many places, especially the marketplace of the New Age, pop psychology, and prepackaged systems such as est, Siddha Yoga, TM, and the Course In Miracles. Anything that encourages disembodiment or flight from one's darker emotions and inclinations is but part of false work, of fantasy work, of superficial work. One who is awakening cannot help but realize that nothing needs to be denied or risen above so that awakening can occur. Nothing, however dark, mean, lustful, jealous, or dense, need be turned away from — it all must be directly and consciously encountered and passed through, embodied (minus its viewpoint), and integrated with the rest of one's Self (such integration being not a homogenized soup of qualities, but a fruitful coexisting of them, bright with Center)...

Real awakening work transcends all escapism; in fact, it can only occur when the craving to escape is consistently undermined, consistently frustrated. Going to a therapist once every week or two, doing a little work on this or that, getting a pat on the back, providing the therapist with a predictable income in exchange for ego-patching and fake tolerance, is *not* real work on oneself, but only sincerity-caked manipulation, a rearrangement of a few circumstances perhaps, a few superficial changes, a more comforting version of one's dream, almost devoid of *real* risk-taking... Now and then, such "work" goes deeper, but not very frequently, rarely presenting authentic transformation as a necessity, not just because of the client's reluctance, but also because of the therapist's reluctance to enter such territory in himself or herself. It is far easier for the therapist to only rock the boat in areas that the client is willing to tolerate; to take it further might mean a cessation of work with such a client, a dropping of income, and it would also mean that the therapist would have to take some personal risks.

Of course, not all therapists (especially those who are not psychiatrists, psychologists, or New Age counsellors) are so cowardly, but many are. The very word "therapist" can be broken down into "the rapist" and rightly so, since the client is all too often forced, subtly or not-so-subtly, to submit to the therapist's particular system or methodology, whether it is conventional or not, hard or soft, invasive or passive; not many therapists are free of such coercion, simply because they have not let themselves stand free of dogma, so that they are free to be themselves, vulnerably and strongly so, responding empathetically, non-sentimentally, creatively, lucidly, and *naturally* to their clients' needs...

To be a good therapist, don't be a therapist. Stop clinging to professionalism. Do what you have to do to be human. Teach only what you *intimately* know. Drop your phony tolerance; be willing to clearly express what you *really* feel and intuit, and also be willing to only partially present it, to give it in a form that suits your client's current needs. This is an art, and it cannot be systematized or reduced to some sort of merely reproducible format (as in, for example, Neuro-Linguistic Programming). Those who are really adept at working with others and helping them to get right to the heart of the matter may sometimes call themselves therapists, but they are *not* — they are wild and passionate and *nourishingly* unpredictable, capable of great force and great subtlety, obviously intimate with every feeling and emotion. Their integrity is utterly unplastic, not being held in place by some kind of outwardly imposed morality, for it's a *natural* byproduct of their very manner of living. Their love is not at all sentimental or ambitious about appearing unconditional, but is ruthless, sweet, sharp, direct, soft, clear, potent, overflowing with spirit, good humor, and compassion. They are empathetic, but not in such a manner that they get lost or seduced or drained by their clients' needs.

Such beings are but mediums for the Awakening process; they are well-grounded, even ecstatic agents of Truth, taking their clients (or co-adventurers) not from here to there, but from here to a *deeper* here, a *truer* here, a more natural here, offering them not some kind of method or bridge over their difficulties, but rather a well-lit passage into what they most fear, a journey right into their recoil from their true nature, an open-eyed dive right into their resistance, a dive that both exposes and heals the wounded heart, eventually carrying one right into one's core of Being. In such work, whatever is in the way is addressed, artfully explored, illuminated, expansively embodied, transcended and simultaneously enjoyed; that is, resistance is not made a problem of, but is creatively and juicily taken as an opportunity, an unwrapped gift, a fist of dynamic possibility just waiting to let go, to unfold, to unfurl, to reach out...

True work on oneself is not a matter of reading some books, dabbling in this or that, imbibing some philosophy or pseudo-esotericism, studying the teaching argument of some teacher, believing this or that, getting fanatical about some path or the other... It must involve the full us — our bodies, minds, spirits, emotions, psyches — *all of us*! It is not so much a process of addition, of accumulation, as it is of subtraction, of letting go, including letting go of the us who is egocentrically involved in letting go!

* *

Bodywork is important, rejuvenative bodywork, bodywork that's simultaneously deep and subtle, challenging and nourishing, ecstatic and sobering, demanding and inviting, ever teaching us the relationship of our physicality to everything else, giving us a well-grounded sense of elemental continuity with all that exists, ever creating for us a safe place to let go of being safe, to let go of our armoring, our Life-negating patterns, our flesh-imbedded assumptions. Such bodywork is necessarily deep much of the time, *creatively* deep, inviting us to shift from frozen yesterday (as so eloquently epitomized by our postural and muscular constrictions) to fluid Now. There are many forms and styles of deep bodywork available these days, ranging from the merely structural (such as Rolfing and Shiatsu) to systems that include psychological and emotional work (such as Postural Integration), but what really matters is not the system, but the maturity and skill of the practitioner, the quality of his or her presence...

Bodywork is necessary, but it isn't enough; the mind (which we could call the invisible part of the body, just as the body is the visible part of the mind) must be deeply and consistently witnessed, through various meditative approaches, through Gestalt (especially triadic gestalt), through Self-remembering, through whatever deepens our capacity to clearly and consistently observe what our minds are doing.

Sexual work is also essential, being something that requires far, far more than the efforts of so-called sex therapists, with their paint-by-numbers approach to sex, not to mention their preoccupation with self-pleasuring and masturbatory "feel-good" solutions to situations that require deep exploration rather than titillating sedation and orgasm-production. Sex cannot be worked on effectively unless it is worked on in the context of our *entire* being. We must learn to release sex from the obligation to make us feel better, and we must therefore cut through our clinging to fantasy (however much it is extolled by sex therapists and other escapists), outdancing our erotic compulsiveness and our urge for pleasurable consolation, learning to bring wakefulness and passion into full embrace.

Where we are neurotic is exaggerated, colorfully so, in our sexual behavior — to *truly* see what we are up to sexually is to see what we are doing with our *entire* lives! There's no point in trying to rise above our sexuality, nor in simply permitting it to continue in its twisted fashion, nor in submitting to the directives of some sex manual, however "tantric" it might claim to be (the rituals in such books being little more than substitutes for *real* spontaneity and intimacy, hyped with spiritual promise, not to mention the promise of goodies like prolonged orgasm). Our sexuality must be examined and participated in with great specificity, sensitivity, subtlety, passion, humor, and honesty, instead of being treated like a G-Spot in an otherwise dull life!

Also essential to real work is the need to distinguish between authentic and reactive emotion. We must learn to recognize what we are up to in the realm of feeling. We need to stop saying things like "I *feel* like I'm..." when we actually mean "I'm *thinking* that..." The whole area of emotion is commonly muddied by misinterpretation, not to mention terrible transmission and reception; we all too easily try to give expression to our feelings via the mechanisms of our minds, filtering our feelings, or the *perception* of our feelings, through our minds, instead of letting *them* speak directly, with *their* texture and tone, instead of that of our assumptions about them.

Of course, expressing what we actually feel doesn't necessarily always mean emoting or dramatizing our feelings — it simply means being openly alive, vulnerably and vitally present, regaining and reclaiming our capacity to cry deeply, to grieve freely, to roar and rage, to laugh uproariously, to dance ecstatically, to let go of hiding out in our headquarters, to stop being so uptight (an apt word for our mind's overseeing of our emotional expression!), so bound, so self-conscious, so unspontaneous, so held!

Again, distinguish between natural feeling and mind-generated feeling, instead of just making a simplistic virtue out of emotion, as in "I'm doing this, because it's what I *feel*!" We easily get lost in our minds, and we also easily get lost in our emotions, all too readily converting their biochemical force into mere righteousness. Obviously, emotional work must be accompanied by wakefulness, so that real emotion can be distinguished from reactive emotion (such as self-pity, sentimentality, blame-riddled irritation, unilluminated jealousy, various depressive states, and so on)...

Threading through all the preceding is spiritual work — exposing and letting go of spiritual ambition, letting go of being an enlightened ego, a transcendent *somebody*, cutting through our clinging to surrogates of the Real, becoming masters of our attention. Such work necessarily involves meditation, not escapist meditation, not emotionally-disconnected meditation, but meditation that consistently makes room for the panoramic viewing of all we are, meditation that spotlights our every neurosis, as well as our Everlasting Unity with our Source.

Real meditation is not necessarily a passive process; at times, it can be very active, cathartic, overflowing with emotion. Other times, it will be still, throbbingly silent, not out of repression, not out of some uptight, rigidly stationary posturing of self, but out of a *natural* restfulness of Being, one that flowers from the very core of us, emanating out and out; this stillness (which doesn't necessarily mean that the body is unmoving) is radiant with presence, both personal and transpersonal, bringing us into God-communion, into fearless communion with all sorts of beings and indescribable energies.

And what else is there? Implicit in all of the above is psychospiritual integration, a full-bodied, spirit-full reunion of all that we are, a deep intimacy with our shadowself, our resistance, our woundedness, our everything... Every dimension of Real Work must blend, artfully blend, to create conducive conditions for awakening from the entrapping dreams we so compulsively animate and try to make homes out of... None of it needs to be systematized nor turned into a recipe for transformation, for it is as wild, as alive, as rich, as Life Itself, its creativity and positionings arising not from egoic programming, but from the very essence of us.

Real work is a highly intuitive process. It is both work and play, both effort and non-effort. It is no enemy of Paradox. It is the incarnation of Love, it is a welcoming of the preparatory fire, it is primal revelation, it is heaven and hell, and it cannot truly proceed until there's nothing else to do. So long as other options hold more interest for us, work on ourselves will at best be a sporadic affair, dependent upon our enthusiasm and moods. When we are no longer seducible by other options, then we'll no longer be in a state of *preparing* to work on ourselves, but will be ready to plunge in, to dive in without rehearsal, without guarantees, without needing to know what's on the other side.

This movement, this great step, is both a leap and a stand, both an expansion of boundaries and a stabilizing of one's center of Being. Resistance to it is but part of it, a kind of difficulty that, if used well, only hones us, finetuning our wakefulness, ever adding to our work's fruition, lending color and idiosyncrasy to our journey, again and again teaching us that nothing need be turned away from so that we might awaken. Yes, many things will be dropped, but they won't be dropped as a strategy, but simply because they will have been so thoroughly and lovingly explored, assimilated, and understood that they no longer attract us.

Thus does the Real Work become irresistible...

-52-
Turning Off the Headlights:
Dependence, Independence,
& Real Commitment

(Alita talks about wanting to be someone happier, more integrated, fuller, saner, someone living a truer life)

ROBERT: The problem is that that wanting doesn't come from your core, but only from a spiritually ambitious, self-improvement enthused fragment of you, a temporarily pumped-up piece of supposed self whose ability to carry through on its fine-sounding intentions is basically nil... This fragment notices the misery and cancerous neuroses of others, and *wants* to do something different, but in order to do so, it must oppose or subjugate other bits of you, other "I's", that haven't the slightest interest in leading a "better" life, especially the "I" that is addicted to going on binges...

What I'm getting at is the fact that your commitment to living a truer life is not arising from your depths; it is but a "good" resolution of your periphery, a mere partiality... Real commitment is entirely different — it's not the vow of a fragment of you, but rather is the solidly anchored yes of your core of Being. Such commitment actually *includes* the you who doesn't want to wake up, in the same sense that the sky contains its clouds; it makes room for all of you, taking into account everything about you, including your resistance to what you want. Its yes doesn't subjugate your no, but only flows with it like an Aikido adept, artfully liberating its energies, bringing you into intimacy with your resistance.

What is ordinarily termed commitment is but a psychoemotionally institutionalized submission to so-called good intentions or resolutions, as so wonderfully illustrated by the charade of New Year's Resolutions. The taking of disciplinary action against oneself only breeds more inner rebellion, more self-dividedness, more policing of oneself, more schizophrenia, more numbness, more flagwaving zealotry, more and more inner bureaucracy (governed, of course, by ego)... Real commitment is not an act of mind, but of Being; it is rooted not in belief, but in the very core of us...

Most people's so-called choices are not choices at all, any more than the movements of a wind-up toy are the choices of the toy. Our prevalent conditioning makes "our" choices, even as we blithely *act* as if we have free choice, free will, freedom of speech, and so on; we deny our mechanicalness, even as our unillumined appetite gets fat behind the wheel, taking us for yet another fastfood spin... Is it any wonder that we are so fascinated by machines? Is it any wonder that we're obsessed with computers? (Being stuck in one's mind, as is so overwhelmingly common, is paralleled by being stuck in computer-terrain, the computer being but an extension of mind.) We're like a ventriloquist's dummy that thinks it's really somebody, confusing its wooden spasms for real movement, letting its implanted thinking create the illusion of a discrete thinker, a solid somebody! In our unexamined mechanicalness and phony freedoms, we're little more than a dummy sitting in the lap of our habits! (*Laughter*)

Your *habits* are running the show, not you! The habit that personifies itself as Alita is ego. Simply put, ego is a habit that's gone to mind, and made a killing there. In letting your egoity refer to itself as "I", you're only dishonouring yourself, diminishing yourself, misrepresenting yourself — you're suffering from a case of mistaken identity! When you are thus entrapped, *you* don't do this, that, or the other — *it* does! *It* lives, *it* breathes, *it* does yoga, *it* fucks, *it* tries to work on itself, *it* goes on diets, *it* makes New Year's Resolutions... The real choice, the deep choice, is to be a machine or to be a human being. We must become much more sensitive to how mechanized we are. In your good moments, you really *know* how important it is to wake up and stay awake, but as soon as your mood changes, as soon as your appetite's mind gloms onto a Hostess Twinkie, your realization vanishes, or seems far less important. You get lonely, you get upset, and your commitment vanishes... What I'm saying is that your commitment to waking up is not yet rooted in your Being; if it was, there's no way you could so easily binge or pout it away...

You're rarely present during your submission to your moods — much of the time, you're like the drunk who suddenly realizes he's holding a beer in his hand, a beer that he doesn't at all *remember* taking into his grip. We, of course, know how the beer got where it did, but he doesn't, because he *doesn't* want to really know — we love to play innocent, to play victim ("It just happened!" or "I don't know what got into me!" or "I couldn't help myself!" or "It's just the way I am"), and, at the very same time, blather about our so-called freedom of choice, as if we were *conscious* entities!

Very, very few people are capable of making *real* choices, or, more precisely, very, very few people are willing to do what they have to do in order to possess such capability! Some are even so foolish as to *believe* that they *chose* their parents sometime prior to conception, no doubt with the same rapt studiousness that they might bring to the reading of a menu! (Such choice is actually not out of the question for a rare few, but its nature is radically different from that of the ego-consoling, metaphysically disembodied fantasy of "conscious" incarnation!) When you begin to see the illusion that masquerades as much of your "choice", you'll quickly sober up, loosening your grip on your "Gee, how did it get there?" drink... Then, and only then, can you *begin* working on yourself.

Most that would claim to be working on themselves are actually not, but are only *preparing* to do so. Unfortunately, very few get beyond the preparatory stage. Once the honeymoon is over, and the real work makes itself obvious, it's very tempting to back out, to convince yourself that you've got better things to do. It's very easy to leave, very easy to say, "It's not what *I* want," or "I've got to do it my way." Almost all of the time, however, the cry of "I've got to do it my way" is but the bleat of neurotic independence, a mere counter-effort to one's terror of dependence (such dependency, whether neurotic or healthy, having probably been flushed out into the open by one's initial breakthroughs)...

You have made a problem out of being dependent! People who do this usually go in one of two directions: They either overdo it, throwing themselves indiscriminately into various sorts of neurotic belonging, as epitomized by guru-worship or nationalism, or they go to the other extreme, becoming "successful" adolescents, independence-worshippers, "self-made" avoiders of intimacy. (*Pause*) Do you recognize yourself in this?

ALITA: Yes. I haven't let anyone in since my parents when I was very young... I've tried to remain uninfluenced ever since then...

Gustave Doré: *Dante's Inferno*

ROBERT: But look how influential that reaction to your long-ago dependency has been on you! Look at how much supposed support you've sensed or imagined from those in a similar bind, those who've also learned to associate dependency with exaggerated helplessness and parental tyranny... How can you open yourself up to real help if you insist on clinging to your illusion of independence? How can you grow if you avoid the demands of real relationship? How can you ever know a *healthy* dependency, if you won't unravel your neurotic dependency? How can you ever stand your true ground, if you persist in staying glued to your psychoemotional insularity? How can you ever know true aloneness, if you keep avoiding going to the heart of your loneliness?

You have fled from the invitation of real relationship, relationship in which love is senior to all dependence/independence games... You are still flirting with the possibility of being in intimacy; when it suits you or fits your mood, you jump into it briefly, leaving as soon as it becomes threatening to "you" (which is when the spectre of infantile dependency lodges itself in your head, spreading an aura of dire possibility). You flee, your regret in one hand, your rationalizations and superficial relief in the other — you back off before you've developed any consistency relative to intimacy. (*Long pause*)

Real intimacy requires a continuity of care and attention. You cannot be intimate for a day, then disappear for a week, and expect the intimacy to automatically resume! I'm talking about *personal*, specific intimacy, nitty-gritty, everyday intimacy, which is actually much rarer than transpersonal intimacy, which any two (or more) people can easily engage in if they're open. And why is transpersonal intimacy easier to access than personal intimacy? Because it involves much less risk, much less chance of being wounded or betrayed or otherwise subjected to a sometimes devastating vulnerability. Of course, a real relationship involves a creative synthesis of both sorts of intimacy...

ALITA: I know I have a lot of resistance to receiving help from *anyone*... I feel very attached to my own way of doing things... but...

ROBERT: You're in an odd position, because you've burnt more than a few of your obsolete bridges, but you keep imagining that they're still there, redcarpet-arched for your "You never know when" retreat, your "It'll come in handy for a rainy day" psychological packrat mentality. You're like a stubborn caterpillar that won't emerge from its cocoon and yet has changed too much to be able to go back to leaf-munching and crawling. It dreams of being a butterfly, maybe even has some metaphysical notions about being a butterfly, but it craves the security, the plumply engorged familiarity, of *acting* like a caterpillar... (*Pause*)

You've gone too far beyond being a caterpillar to be able to *really* go back, but you won't allow yourself to metamorphose into the next stage — this is why you're so miserable! You are unhappy because you won't give yourself to the joy and challenge of real commitment; you're still more involved in lesser commitments, such as your commitment to avoiding intimacy...

What's ordinarily called commitment is just neurotic dutifulness, a "should", a soulless imposition (swallowed for our own "good") — it's as violent as it's unnatural, setting in motion counterforces of an equally screwed-up nature, thereby reducing us to little more than battlefields for warring opinions and beliefs... (*Pause*)

Rather than enter into real commitment, commitment that honours your wholeness, you're still looking for an easy out, a great escape, a "gentler" way (those who are the most ardent disciples of supposed gentleness are almost invariably, through their very self-repression, actually *violating* their *ungentle* feelings), a path that'll coddle you and beatifically accept your every waddle! But still you crave an experience, a cosmic Hostess Twinkie, that'll suddenly lift you to a level beyond all of us, so that you don't *ever need* to be part of a community like this!

ALITA: (*Laughing*) Then I could be independent!

ROBERT: No one is truly independent, Alita, not even a God-Realized being. Especially a God-Realized being! You are dependent on so many levels... Take away the air, and you'd be gone instantly. Take away the Presence That animates us all, and where would *you* be? Let me make the point quickly: You are utterly dependent upon your environment, simply because you are inextricably interrelated with it, and it with you, level upon level... Elementally, cognitively, emotionally, psychically, and spiritually, *you* are continuous with all that is, *and* you possess the potential to actually *realize* this! What a gift! To *be* it, and to be conscious of such being...

Within this vast realm of interdependence, some people have more power than others, either because they have been given it, by fair means or by foul, or because they've developed it from within. You give yours away, and then fight or flee whomever you've given your power to! In fleeing your own empowerment, you deny yourself the fuel you need to bring forward your gifts... (*Long pause*) How much more will you have to suffer before you'll dive in? All you're really doing, Alita, is postponing the leap you know you must take — you project the yes for taking that jump onto me, as if there was no yes in *you* for taking it! Once you jump, things may even get worse for a while, but it'll be a *good* worse, a necessary purification, and it'll be accompanied by the joy of knowing that you *are* committed! Your body says yes to this leap, but your head keeps saying no or I'm not sure...

ALITA: I think with me I just got so much into my compulsions and overeating that I made it very difficult for myself to do anything else... I give up so easily! (*Crying*)

ROBERT: Because you refuse to claim *your* power! You're turned away from the responsibility that emerges with such reclamation; "you" want someone else to take charge, so that "you" can then act out your rigidly-scripted parent/child bullshit with them... You make them big, so that you can play small, so that you can be the baby you never *really* were, the little girl who despaired of ever being truly seen... (*Pause*) But don't you see how this drearily repetitive script of yours is actually only a misguided attempt at *intimacy*? A strategy to snare love? But you can't trade your power for love! You can't trade your self-respect for love! Making yourself small only makes you *impermeable* to real love, doesn't it? (*She cries*)

You must stop submitting to your urge to collapse. It's as if you're running a race, a race in which you feel fine so long as you're not huffing and puffing — as soon as you start to labour, to really work, you *think* of quitting, giving the very energy you need for the run to your thinking! You need to stop taking the contents of your mind so seriously, and you also need more stamina, not so much physical as psychospiritual, and how do you build stamina? You keep on going, you persevere; you face your barriers like a warrior. Sitting on your ass and messing around with a crystal or a mantra or a headful of hope ain't going to do it — in fact, such activities only weaken the impulse to get on with it.

The Awakening process is not a quick fix, nor a matter of following certain steps; it's a chaotic, turbulent, inherently artful undertaking, both upsetting and grounding, both rough and tender, both spontaneous and disciplined — you could call it a great labour of love, in which you are mother, midwife, and newborn. Through it, everything gets revealed; your neuroses become more obvious than complex. You become more spacious and more focussed, more and more hungry to get to the crux of things...

Consider meditation: For most, including you most of the time, "meditation" is little more than an effort to feel better, to gain some immunity, to focus on the positive, to get detached, to rise above one's difficulties... Real meditation, however, is not a strategy to get away from anything, but rather is a wide-awake facing of it all, however sublime or sordid. It's a finely focussed spaciousness, a dynamic receptivity, an openness anchored in Being. And it's not something *you* can do; it's something you can *be*, something so Real that no lie can penetrate it. (*Long pause*) But you hear this, and you idealize it, fitting *your mind's version* of it into your life-plan. Why reduce meditation to a cure-all? Why shrink it to mere concentrative exercise? Why fake it? Why use it as a means to avoid intimacy?

When you are in a truly intimate relationship, you can be very, very hurt. Betrayal is possible; you can become extremely jealous, grippingly possessive. You're very vulnerable to what the other does, and I think that's wonderful! You're so attached that you can't make yourself immune to being upset — you then *have to feel* what you've spent your whole life avoiding feeling! You get to face things about yourself you'd probably never otherwise face... The wound you'll feel at the heart will, if rightly used, deepen your connection to God, to Life, to your humanness. Wrongly used, however, it'll only embitter you, causing you to padlock your depths, or to remain merely romantic. You want the Ecstasy and soul-bonding of intimacy, but not the hurt and disappointment; you want the security of intimacy, but not the insecurity... (*Pause*)

Intimacy isn't just fireworks and Light and rapture and refuge — it's far more often very ordinary, even extraordinarily ordinary! Consider the ease you feel when you walk into a room, and your intimate's there; you don't necessarily have to speak, for there's a deep knowingness between you, a comfort, and it's not a comfort born of repression (as is so commonly found in the great majority of so-called couples and families, with their socially-sanctioned cultism and plastic freedoms). It's not about locking yourself and the other(s) in a capsule of supposed immunity, but about letting the hot air out of such bubbles, until all that's left is what really matters. I'm not talking about being stupidly or naively open, letting anyone tromp through your house, but about dismantling your *unnecessary* defences, and what better place to do this than in the sanctuary of real intimacy? Call it a safe place to let go of being safe...

At this point, you're still a fan of Awakening, a flagwaving enthusiast, all rosy-cheeked up there in the stands, cheering yourself hoarse, jumping up and down with excitement, but almost always in the same damned place! You're still stuck way up in the bleachers, catching only a whiff of the Fire that you know you must face, while others are more centrally involved, putting their everything on the line again and again, needing not your admiration, but your co-participation!

ALITA: I get into it sometimes, but I don't stay...

ROBERT: Yeah, you keep your seat up in the stands, clutching your turnips and tofu hotdogs! You act as if your season ticket is a lifetime ticket, as if your destiny is to be just a bench-warmer, a nicely supportive maiden aunt who beams at the right time! (*Pause*)

We don't just keep doing the same damned thing here, however... Look at the nights when you all gather with me — they've definitely changed in the last while. The incredible dramatics, gut-wrenching catharsis, and primal encounters no longer occupy so much of each group — sure, sometimes there's still hair-raising work and great explosions or floodings of feeling, but its context is looser, friendlier, more intelligent. Remember how much bodywork I used to do? That hardly ever happens now, because it's not needed — people are much more responsible for getting themselves going. Gestalt work's becoming more triadic than dyadic, thank God! Every week, we build on the foundation created by the previous week's work, whereas a year or so ago, we had to start from scratch — then there were *always* two or three, maybe even four or five, people who had abandoned the circle, so we all had to work very, very hard to reestablish the circle, and gradually, those who kept refusing to come to their work with integrity and passion had to go... (*Pause*) Not because I said so, but because they, through their actions, were saying so...

You keep tearing down the foundation you build when you're sane —
what a pity! All I'm doing is inviting you to get out of the stands, and
take a real stand! (*Laughter*) But you keep on misunderstanding me;
you stick your mind in between us, and then wonder why you're still
fearful. You want me to keep defining and redefining the work... But
it won't make sense unless you have some center, some intimacy
with your core. And you know *exactly* what it feels like to be centered! You know *exactly* what it feels like to be truly happy! And you
also know when you are not existing in those places, but you're still
reluctant to then find out *where* you actually are!

You keep wanting to fix yourself, to zoom away from your difficulty,
instead of witnessing it and bringing some light and presence to it...
So what can you do? Yield to your willingness to observe yourself,
and keep yielding, even when you absolutely don't want to! (*Long
pause*) Now, back to real commitment: It is the structural yes of
soulmaking, an utterly natural functionality, the inherent responsibility of Being. It cannot be forced, or netted, or snared via belief.
It's *not* a good idea, Alita, because it's *not* an idea! Idealize it, and
you'll only be a fan of it, a metaphysical voyeur...

It's important that you discover what works for *you*. Experimentation is essential. Explore different methods. Don't fall into the trap
of pooh-poohing all methods; sure, Krishnamurti was anti-method,
but it was so damned theoretical, so *dry*... Methods are unnecessary
only for those who have *already* deeply experimented with different
methods — only they can profitably freewheel it, for they are already
in resonance with Awakening's context. Relative to psychospiritual
techniques, it's easy to be dilettantish, and easy to be fanatic, but not
so easy to be neither... (*Pause*) Krishnamurti had wisdom and a keen
eye for Truth, but he didn't know how to package it so that it would
tellingly serve the Awakening of others; maybe if he'd gotten more
involved with others, risked himself more in intimacy and sexuality,
he would have *had to* get more practical. Instead of just sitting back,
he needed to dive in more, to *flesh out* his presence more...

In finding out what works for you *specifically, right now*, and going
into it, you will clarify and enrich your individuality, expanding and
filling it out. Do not assume that individuality and being supposedly
independent are synonymous. True individuals are surrendered to
God, and yet are simultaneously and uniquely themselves, at ease
with their dependencies. On the other hand, false individuals are but

devotees of independence, little bastions of self-encapsulation and ego-centered pleasuring, ever bowing down before their barbed-wire perimeters and deified independence, with its wall-to-wall me, me, and more me... To further clarify, real individuality is rooted in essence; it is the face, the vibrantly transparent persona of our core of Being, beautifully and uniquely itself, full of eloquently personal nuance... (*Pause*)

And only in going right into your individuality will you know God; if you merely go into your rituals of supposed independence, you will at best only know an abstraction of God, an ineffable centrefold! The more you *truly* yield to God, the more you will be Alita, and vice versa... Why go on compensating for a lousy childhood? Why go on denying your individuality its guts? Why keep on getting lazy when you're on a roll? Why continue obscuring your deeper addictions with lesser ones?

ALITA: Even when I'm happy, I know I can still go to the food... the habit seems to always be there, no matter what I'm feeling.

ROBERT: Your relationship to food has more to do with security than diet; you are looking for a nourishment through food that food cannot provide. You feed on your do-gooder organic turnips, and also on your saboteur creampuffs, not realizing that both are equally neurotic! You expect the ingestion of so-called health foods to save you, to fix you, to somehow deliver you from your mediocrity, and when that doesn't happen, you say the hell with it and go binge on junkfood, until you feel so fucking guilty that you plunge into the bracing waters of organic broccoli, tofu, and evening primrose oil! As Da Free John once said, diet is not the key to salvation... Food is not meant to take the place of intimacy, nor to be used as a sign of one's spiritual attainment (as so drearily illustrated by the fanaticism of devotees of macrobiotics, raw food regimes, and fruitarianism), nor to be taken as from a trough!

If you're not hungry, don't eat. If you're upset, don't eat. If you're tense, don't eat. When your life becomes healthier, food will be less important to you, less central, and you'll enjoy it more, for you won't be expecting it to make you feel better!

Remember your fuss about Candida albicans, and how convinced you were that you had it? That terrible, terrible yeast, that New Age tapeworm! (*Laughter*) What a smokescreen that was! You were just looking for an alibi, naturopathically-confirmed, for your lackadaisicalness in your work on yourself; even when there wasn't any real evidence, you still believed that you were full of Candida! It was just a way of legitimizing your laziness, a dressing up of your inertia, no different really than calling senility Alzheimer's Disease...

Now, before this session dodders off into senility, let's switch gears. When was the last time you had sex?

ALITA: Last Christmas.

ROBERT: What about Jack?

ALITA: I could see us making love if we were both open, but...

ROBERT: My intuition is that you're both bringing too much strain and expectation, as if someone like me is watching over your heaving shoulders! You're both obsessed with doing it right. For God's sake, be willing to be messy! If you and he wait for it to be just right, guaranteed beforehand, you might have to wait twenty years — want to wait twenty years, Alita?

ALITA: No! (*Laughter*)

ROBERT: Then stop trying to be so fucking spiritual about it! Fuck your perfectionism! Literally! (*Laughter*) Let's say he's finally inside you, and you're feeling really fine, and then he looks into your eyes, *already* suspicious of you perhaps not being fully present, and you then both get uptight, letting your sexplay die on the spike of your good intentions... Why do that? Why not give yourselves more space to be unconscious? Do that, and do it lovingly, and, paradoxically, you'll be *more* conscious, not self-consciously conscious, but *truly* conscious, without any separation out from your passion...

Stop trying to be tantric saints with each other, and give your animal some breathing room! Jack would love to hear me praise him for being conscious during sex, but all he tends to do is pull back from the sheer physicality of sex, zooming up to jack-off in the bathroom of his mind! I can just see him on top of you, both of you really going at it, and then he clears his throat, tells you he doesn't feel good with you, and blasts you! (*Laughter*) Later, of course, I'd hear about his act of integrity, and give him a gold star, or maybe even a silver cock! (*Laughter*) You and he need to stop looking for trouble in each other; let it be messy, let it be neurotic, let it be as mind-free as possible... Stop playing therapist with each other — better to play doctor and nurse! (*Laughter*)

When sex goes deep, there's a built-in awareness. It's not that both people are up against the ceiling, watching the action below! Real passion carries its own inherent knowingness, its own wisdom of ebb and flow, but you cannot access this if you insist on separating yourself from the action — such separation is nothing more than an escape into the calculating domain of your mind. Mind-fucking only screws up sex, unnecessarily complicating it, doing no more good than blind rutting... Stay sensitive, and you'll know when it's working and when it's not working, without having to think about it, or analyze it.

Let your sexing be chaotic, wild, unpredictable, staying open to all sorts of possibilities — for example, in the middle you might feel like crying deeply, so you do, and suddenly it's your father on top of you with a mask on, and then it's someone else, and then it's Jack, like you've never seen him before, and your deep emotion rips him open, and you then both meet so deeply that there's no possibility of losing your flow...

Intimacy isn't just a joyride. There was a Christian minister (whose name I've forgotten) who said something like, "Joy teaches the wisdom of letting go, and suffering teaches the necessity of letting go." I think you're starting to feel the necessity... For you, the Awakening process is no longer just an invitation, but an actual demand, a sacred demand...

If you and Jack become lovers, it'll not be a time of pleasure-sealed immunity, but a time of opening, of joy, of suffering, wherein you'll need to give yourself permission to cry, to laugh, to come and go, to be really alive, to be soft, to be forceful, to be a full woman. Your longing for closeness and your urge to get away will *both* be there, intensified by the energy of sex. You might feel very connected to him during a lovemaking, and then right before orgasm, you'll find yourself wanting to pull away, to separate — all kinds of things like that can happen, and once they're happening or have happened, you can work with them, use them, learn from them...

ALITA: When I feel really close to Jack, sexually close too, I have a tendency to get into a little girlish kind of state...

ROBERT: Make that gesture again. (*She blushingly turns her face away*)

ALITA: (*Laughing*) I'm still presenting, though...

ROBERT: Presenting what?

ALITA: (*Laughing*) I guess... my sexuality!

ROBERT: Even as you "shyly" thrust out your breasts, making a very tempting offering to Daddy, you also are busy making him feel safe by making yourself psychospiritually small... You're literally not facing the situation! You're expecting your tits and crotch to do the work, to *represent you*! But why trade your sexuality for security? Why not present your full self? Why go on misrepresenting yourself? Stop waiting for something miraculous to happen to you before you'll dive into intimacy! Dive into it now, and let your incompleteness become so illuminated that you cannot help but fill yourself out. Go ahead and get messy — just leave the lights on sometimes, and I don't mean the headlights of your mind!

–53–

Dying Into a Truer Life: Real Risk-Taking

If we're not willing to risk everything we've got, to risk *really* laying it all on the line, giving it all permission to outgrow itself or to radically mutate, whether it be a matter of heart, name, fame, blame, addiction, fiction, size restriction, or just plain ownership, then we'll only lose everything of *real* value — in other words, if we insist on making our clinging to security, safety, identity-cementing habit, and distraction-upkeep more important than honoring and embodying our Truth, then we are but isolating ourselves from what *truly* nourishes us, while desperately running around trying to relieve ourselves of the very pain created by our self-imposed isolation and ego-centered encapsulation!

Thus do we cripple ourselves, resolutely barricading ourselves in mind-apartments and remote control disembodiment, taking the edge off our hurt by chronically redecorating and rearranging our psychophysical environment, exchanging one set of beliefs for another, one kind of pleasurable escapism for a more novel sort, madly seeking for some kind of lasting relief, some pause that really refreshes, some juicily stimulating sedative, all the while doing no more than further knotting and reinforcing our suffering...

The dumbest risk is in not taking risks, specifically those gambles that enliven and flesh out our resonance with our core of Being. Risks that don't illuminate and outbreathe our neuroses are of no more use than risks that inflate our egos. There is no point in naive risk-taking, daring or forcing oneself to take leaps that are fueled by egoic ambition. True risk-taking is Essence-centered daring, soul-fulfilling courage, a gutsily artful intelligence of nerve, a willingness to be undone, to have the hub of one's addictiveness outspun by a deeper kind of center. Again, if we aren't willing to risk everything, to put everything on the line, then we have nothing that truly serves our well-being, being instead only burdened and bound by our accumulations, inner and outer, while acting as if such accumulations, especially those of mind, are us, the real us!

A risk is not necessarily equivalent to a typical dare — it isn't some foolhardy gesture, some self-glorifying acting out of twisted courage, some jump based on misguided loyalty to this or that belief, group, political party, or nation. Life *is* risk, *innately* so — taking real risks is basically a full-bodied acknowledgment of the *inherent* insecurity of Life, the built-in instability of manifest Existence. It is a fleshy embracing of such primal Insecurity, an honoring of Change and Flux and Mutation, a passion-shaped goodbye to those habits that would reduce Life to spiritless repetition, anesthetization, and poisonous lullabies.

Only when we take Life-giving risks with nothing held back (and this is an *art*, an art of both extravagance and subtlety, crudeness and elegance, the art of welcoming the Unknown), do we *fully* encounter What is unchanging, undying, Eternally present. Prior to taking such risk, we don't encounter the Everlasting, but rather only encounter our *beliefs* about It, our theological bullshit, our metaphysical abstractions, our hope, our idealized desire, our immunity-promising garbage — thus do we maroon ourselves in personalized vistas of mind, busying ourselves building horizons from hope-riddled thought, slowly suffocating ourselves in dreams of possibility...

A real risk is not an irresponsible act, an act taken without empathetic consideration of one's environment. It is taken to *deepen* the quality of one's life, to shake it up, to make habit-upsetting waves, to jolt and potently invite oneself and one's intimates into a truer communion with each other and with God. Without such risk-taking, psychospiritual inertia sets in, regardless of how active one's life is, a deep inner inertia that is but rationalized cowardice.

If we don't practice taking risks, large or small, we only impoverish ourselves, weakening our capacity for taking leaps of being, growing older without growing wiser, growing without knowing, binding ourselves to mind-made moralities, leaving ourselves so cut off from what truly sustains us that we wither, unable to make any use whatsoever of the fact that Awakening creates Its own morality. If such a statement is only an assembly of words to us, then we are *not* ourselves, but only mannequins, parodies of human beings, animated shells, going through rehearsed motions, taking false risks, cosying up our cage, again and again mistaking rearrangement, facelifts, postural changes, and consuming novelty for real transformation, watching others take risks on television, living a vicarious life or perhaps a life that has risks, but not risks of spirit, not risks that propel one deeper into Now, just risks that glamourize oneself, risks that engorge and thicken ego, risks that are taken only to bring applause, outer or inner...

Ask yourself what you won't risk, knowing that real risk-taking is *not* equivalent to abandoning one's responsibilities, but rather to *purifying* them. Risk-taking, if entered into fully, passionately, and sensitively, may very well necessitate profound alterations in one's life, but these radical changes stem not from ego-centered motives, but from an inner knowingness, a sacred trust, an intuition unburdened by thought or belief. To have access to such intuition, risk is essential. A real risk is a way of saying to the Universe, "I am with You. I trust You. I am not confined in spirit to anything in particular. I honor both my limitations and my Limitless Nature. I am *alive!*" Alive! Such risk-taking is an adventure, not a cruise-ship slumber-fest, but a wild sail upon and through the sea of Being, a heart-spilled sailing guided by the very force of our longing to be Home. However, this sailing, this journey, doesn't carry one above ego, nor above the personal — instead, it carries one *into and through* the personal, the idiosyncratic, so deeply that ego cannot help but yield to authentic individuality, which in turn can only flower in full embrace with What includes and transcends it. This is Ecstasy. This is Home. This is the Reunion we're dying to see, to feel, to know, to be...

Ecstasy is not possible without risk. Without risk, there may be intense pleasure, highly stimulated thrill, a sweet engorgement of flesh, but these are only manipulations of sensation; they're not pure feeling, nor naked desire, nor love, being decidedly non-intimate with the primal currents of Being. Ecstasy *needs* risk. Ecstasy needs a nakedness, a full nakedness of spirit, of flesh, of mind and emotion, an innocence as free as it's conscious. Ecstasy is not some commodity to be bought through certain practices, spiritual, sexual, or whatever, but is inherent to Being, presently and obviously so. As well, Ecstasy is coincident with Awakening, not an emotionally dissociative, monkish awakening, but a vibrantly alive awakening that requires no withdrawal whatsoever from anything.

The point here is to pass *through* it all, not to rise above it, not to float above it, not to merely guide one's attention up one's spine into the higher centers of the brain, the sixth and seventh chakras, and so forth — none of that immunity-seeking manipulation is necessary, except perhaps to know, to really know, that it's just a cul-de-sac, the ultimate yogic attempt to outclimb the demands of embodied Life. Ecstasy is not at the top of the ladder. It is what is present when all ladders are obsolete through their not being taken seriously any more; this is not laziness, but rather true participation in the very matrix of Existence, needing no stimulation for its passion, no reason for its love, no guarantee for its trust, no peace for its silence, no cause for its presence...

What can you risk now? What do you need to risk now? What are you avoiding or postponing risking now? The key here is not to dig up some kind of answer to these questions, nor to turn away, nor to force yourself into a position of apparent bravery relative to the risks you may have identified a moment ago. Every moment poses the same fundamental risk, the same Invitation, with varying degrees of intensity and auspiciousness. Risking it all is not some sort of metaphysical kamikaze, but is about being willing to die to it all, to stand free of it all in the very midst of one's attachments, to die to it so deeply that all that's left is a truer life, wherein one can only stand one's real ground, no longer fucking around with problematicalness, but instead only deepening one's intimacy with Paradox, Mystery and Love...

Real risk-taking is what keeps us unobstructedly alive and alert, but not many of us are truly embodying such deep gambles. The Earth is infested with ambulatory corpses busy injecting meaning into their mediocre and deadening rituals of survival and distraction, and far too many who have some Life are grinding out excuses for the sleep-walkers, covering their own distaste with false tolerance and bleating humanitarianism, mistaking their liberalism for compassion, while avoiding truly facing their own corpse-like patterns. If we won't get right into the clockwork of our own mechanicalness, then we can't really awaken, but at best will only settle into a level of being perhaps a little more refined than the usual, a level whose ceiling we keep raising with spiritual ideals and fantasies about our own attainment; we may even make a home out of our level, finding comfort there, clinging to whatever best epitomizes or signals our particular positioning of ourselves, and then we'll maybe wave the flag of our realm, welcoming those who salute it, condemning those dolts who don't, or if we're liberal enough, we might even give a show of phony tolerance for all other flags, particularly those that represent practices that nauseate us!

Real risk-taking transcends all nationalities, all belief systems, all cultic associations, upending all "isms" — nationalism, Republicanism, feminism, Buddhism, patriotism, anarchism, individualism, Judaism, Hinduism, as well as all those that don't carry the suffix "ism". Nevertheless, such risk-taking does not leave us in a naively disorganized position, nor in an elitist bubble, but rather leaves us more fully established in a responsible life, a life in which freedom and responsibility go hand in hand, illuminated by the realization that every increase in freedom must be accompanied by a corresponding increase in responsibility.

Do not look for security in your relationships. Do not just expect them to provide you with a sense of security or safety, or they will just become one more trap, one more parody of the Real. Instead, let your relationships teach you about insecurity, not the kind of insecurity that betrays love, integrity, compassion, and intimacy, but rather the kind of insecurity that takes the relationship to where it can be *felt* to be continuous with all relationship, to where it is permeable, consciously permeable, to the forces governing Life. Don't just play it safe. A true relationship is one wherein it is safe to let go of being safe. Implicit here is a profound trust between those involved, and such trust cannot be forced, for it is a natural byproduct of honest risk-taking, risk that is not escapism nor mere performance, but rather a breaking down of barriers between oneself and one's Truth, a Yes birthing a deeper Life...

Roloff Beny: *The Pleasure of Ruins*

—54—

Speaking
a Truer Tongue

(After speaking casually for quite a while, Daya suddenly finds it very difficult to continue)

ROBERT: You're having a hard time now, because it is time to change levels verbally. The shift has already happened energetically, all through this room, and it is asking for an accompanying shift in speech...

DAYA: That speech doesn't come as easily for me...

ROBERT: No, because it's the type of articulation where the wastage of words feels awful, right away. (*Pause*) Ordinarily, your habit is to speak with an overload of words, even when you can tell that your audience is squirming; at best, you are, in such excess, creating a social flow, using your extra words and phrases to add a nice little something here and there that rounds off temperamental corners, softening, diffusing, or good-naturedly overseasoning some little reluctance in your listener or listeners... In ordinary social terms, this isn't usually an abuse of speech, but at a deeper level, it *is*. In the state you're on the verge of now, you can't afford to be trivial or banal or gossip-mouthed.

DAYA: Or...or dramatic...

ROBERT: Spoken with understated drama! How rare to see you tongue-tied! Some of your speechlessness is bound up with your devotional energy. True verbal intelligence requires the ability to discern different levels, to tellingly discriminate, and the devotionally inclined don't usually have much to do with such discrimination — they're hoping that by giving themselves to Krishna or Jesus or

Master Whobitchyourcockoff or whoever the hell it is, that they'll be free! They're just bargaining for security, whoring their integrity for the illusion of immunity! Swooning before a guru isn't supposed to be accompanied by any eloquence or verbal acumen, is it? Speechlessness, or a grovellingly grateful approximation of it, actually lends a certain credence to such swooning!

But don't let my criticalness wipe out devotionalism entirely... In the beginning, it can open one's heart, however naively or childishly, bringing into the foreground longings for parenting that might never otherwise be exposed. Unfortunately, such longings are rarely worked with to the point of real understanding, but are instead usually only harnessed to the continuing of one's guru-swoon. Even at its very best, devotional love can only take one so far; it's just a stepping-stone, a minor bridge, and you've still got one foot on it, not even a solid foot, but just a nostalgic foot, dreamily planted...

DAYA: There's a lack of responsibility there.

ROBERT: There is. There's far too much fixation on exaggerations of sensation, far too much dependency — it gives all dependency a bad name. You need to take what's left of your devotional energy and let it fuel a more fitting level of you. You are ready. Yes, you need more silence, but you also need to verbalize more from deeper levels of yourself... When I was in the cave in Greece, I would have been speechless if I'd tried to speak from the position of everyday me. Nevertheless, there was an undeniable urge to speak. The voice that emerged sounded like "mine" — just slower, more resonant, every word carrying the tone and texture of the depth of that time, weighted with just the right nuance, all of it conscious without being self-conscious. In the few moments when "Robert" intruded, it was glaringly obvious. In the same sense that you could say that there was basically no "Robert" there, there is no "Robert" here now, but you could also say that this *is* Robert, the essential Robert, sitting with you now, and that "my" essentialness is simply giving voice to what needs to be articulated. It may sound complicated, but it's actually not — in fact, it's very ordinary, no big deal, nothing like the ego-inflating hoopla of the current channeling fad.

You could say we're all mediums, that we are always channeling. Sometimes you channel your parents, sometimes your insecurity, sometimes your core of Being, sometimes your fear, sometimes the extraordinarily trivial... So there's nothing special in being a medium! There's too much mystique about such a process, and not enough *real* Mystery; most so-called channeling is just mere information, junkfood spirituality, prepackaged Disneyworld metaphysics, filled with syrupy consolation and an enticing pitch for financial donation! But enough of that — our concern now is not "psychic" hucksterism, but rather the very nature of our innate mediumship, which we could call personified permission-giving, whether conscious or unconscious...

When you are deeply present, transparent to God, you may find yourself speaking more slowly than usual, but you mustn't associate such slowness with being thus present — sometimes your voice will need to come out more quickly, more dynamically. There are no rules. The key is to simply say yes to the imperatives of your Being, a full-fleshed yes, a yes that contextually and spontaneously choreographs your emerging speech... (*Pause*) Can you feel that quality of permission in yourself now?

DAYA: Some. (*Speaking very hesitantly*) It's not very full... I feel my hunger for it, my desire, my longing...

ROBERT: The "I" who just spoke that doesn't give a damn about such hunger! As soon as you spoke, you lost the openness you were feeling, and submitted to the viewpoint of a much grosser Daya — your tone in no way matched your content, but only debased you, reducing you to a massive yet grovelling quicksand of appetite. You don't want to embody a full yes to your Being, but to get the hell out of here! But why make an enemy out of the intense inner squirming you now feel? Why sedate or flee it? Why not give it space to breathe, space to be something other than a problem? (*Long pause*)

The familiar you is just an act. If you insist on clinging to its script, you'll only stay in the lowlands, and get all sentimental about the peaks. Instead of attaining the peak, you'll just look up at it and romanticize it, like a gopi, swooning instead of climbing. Does this make sense?

DAYA: Yes. (*Her voice very low*)

ROBERT: So speak. The topic doesn't matter — in fact, there's no need for a topic. Make the effort to speak true right from where you are, even if you have to start with wordless sound... (*A minute of silence*) It's very difficult for you, isn't it?

DAYA: Yes.

ROBERT: Is there an urge to speak?

DAYA: Some... (*Her voice trembling*)

ROBERT: Open your throat and let it happen, without trying to know what's going to happen... Your body knows exactly what to do; trust it! I'm not talking about force, but about permission, about unclenching, about undamming, about loving yourself enough to give yourself this...

DAYA: It's as if there's a difficulty between my throat and my mouth. Sounds start in me, and then I get afraid and tighten everything up...

ROBERT: This is your refusal to leave the familiar. You need to speak from the same place that your hands sometimes articulate in deep Spiritwork; the mudras of your hands, the spontaneous Grace and achingly significant gestures of such soul-rooted movement, must be permitted to find a corresponding expression through your words. I'm talking about speaking without any rehearsal whatsoever. Speech without mind, speech where you don't know what's going to come out of your mouth! (*Laughter*) This isn't about uncontrolled blabbering, but about *real* spontaneity, about letting fly with such power and subtlety that you cannot help but feel originality being birthed moment-to-moment, without any overriding sense of personal accomplishment... It's a way of speaking that actually *deepens* silence, that actually *gives* energy, both to you and to your audience.

DAYA: I have to speak... There's no knowing what I'm going to say (*Speaking very haltingly*), no plan, no rehearsal...

ROBERT: So go ahead.

(*Daya struggles to speak, but seemingly can't; she is both numb and terrified*)

ROBERT: You've had your tongue cut out, haven't you? (*She imme-*

diately starts crying) Someone went in there with a knife... (*Deeper, shiveringly evocative crying*) And after, no taste, no talking, just overwhelming hurt, your mouth like an insatiable cave...

NANCY [*assisting in the session*]: I see a Turkish castle, Daya, thick with violence... I see you there, huddled up in one of its stalls or cells, in the dark...

ROBERT: Face Nancy now, and hold your tongue back in your mouth so that it can't touch the back of your teeth, and start making sounds, tongueless sounds... (*Guttural sounds pour forth from her, mixed with deeply moving crying and keening*) Keep going, and close your eyes. (*Her crying gets even stronger*) Keep going, letting images come, more and more images...

There's your tongue on the floor.

(*Daya starts screaming, her entire body convulsing, not in withdrawal, but in open-eyed horror and hurt, until her screaming and crying are one fluid emotion, turbulent yet free-flowing; Nancy cries with her*)

ROBERT: Your tongue's on the floor, a yard away — just a piece of meat now, rats coming toward it... (*Daya's sounds turn to rage and whitewater fury, then gradually subside*) Now (*Speaking very softly*) let it all go, letting your whole body soften, and soften even more, letting your tongue relax... (*She sighs deeply*) Let your tongue be loose and soft and free...

Sit up straighter now, and close your eyes. (*Long pause*) Tell me what you see.

DAYA: I see just darkness... And now a figure standing a short distance from me — he's big and dense, very dark. He's enjoying this. He's very cruel...

ROBERT: He gets turned on by people's fear.

DAYA: (*Crying*) And by their pain!

ROBERT: It makes him feel more alive.

DAYA: And bigger... Every pain he gives, he gets bigger...

ROBERT: Why did your tongue get cut out?

DAYA: I was too happy, I loved too much, I spoke openly...

ROBERT: My sense is of your land, your territory, being invaded by people who have very fixed ideas, especially about religion — they're interested only in subjugation. Whoever you were then wouldn't align with these invaders. You were a threat to them, so they decided to silence you. The solution was simple — take out your tongue.

DAYA: And leave me as a living example...

ROBERT: (*Sharply*) What's happening now?

DAYA: (*Her voice almost lifeless*) I'm going now, drifting away from my body... It's so cold, so full of fear, so lonely... (*She cries*)

ROBERT: Open your eyes. (*Long pause*) No drama now... Bring more awareness to your tongue, to your breathing, to the sensations of sitting here... Aside from what may or may not have happened to your tongue before, you are still abusing it much of the time, still exploiting its pleasure-possibilities. Your tongue is not just a thickness, a meaty servant of your grosser cravings — why blindly wrap it around food or someone else's tongue? Why let it run around inside your mouth like an electroshocked pork sirloin, as during unconscious speech? Notice how your tongue moves when you speak, notice how you chronically tense it, rarely letting it *fully* rest and settle. Feel this as you speak now...

DAYA: I feel more sensitive to it now...

ROBERT: Being conscious of one's speech doesn't just mean being aware of one's words and phrasings, but also being aware of one's speech mechanisms — mouth, palate, lips, tongue, teeth, throat, breath — in a generalized sense. Given its multilayered intentionality and astonishing capacity for nuance, speech is a very complex phenomenon, yet it is also sublimely simple when its context is illuminated by the presence of Being. The verbalization of Truth is an act of our totality, rather than a collective efforting by all sorts of dissident factions within us... If it is such an efforting, then it is simply the verbalizing of our self-fragmentation, articulating not Truth, but only opinions and personalized information...

True speech requires subtlety, but you keep choosing grossness in your talking, indulging in tonal overkill, coarsening your delivery, making it too loud, too long, too insatiably-lipped, speaking as though you are feeding! Long ago, you decided that it was a hell of a lot safer to act gross, especially good-naturedly gross — it made others, particularly the men around you, feel both unthreatened and familiar with you, securely unchallenged. After all, it was just good old you clowning around, just good old you putting herself down to make everyone feel at ease! What pain! Your real needs lay hidden behind your engrossing act, screaming like a mouth with no tongue... You were, and sometimes still are, afraid that if you're not suitably gross, you're going to be crushed, imprisoned, mutilated, and left all alone, but this is *precisely* what *you* have done with your true needs! Why leave them speechless in a long-ago mudhole?

DAYA: I have to stop letting my fear of being criticized stand in my way...

ROBERT: The worst criticism coming your way is your own — you dishonour yourself before anyone else can, de-tonguing your integrity, flushing your dignity down the handiest toilet, before anyone can crap on you! You expect to be treated like shit, so you desecrate your beauty and subtlety, offering up the ruins of yourself with a vivaciously servile grin, or you go to the other extreme, becoming overcritical of others, especially those who are living a lie — you turn into a heavy-handed warrior, gutting the guilty with rabid righteousness! Purify this, Daya, and you'll be both a marvelously-nuanced subtlety and a luminous powerhouse, too big for any cell! (*Laughter*)

Incarnation's Fleshdance

Behind the sighing hemlocktips and above the unshaven hulk of the alabaster slopes stride inky crowds of cobblestoned clouds, hauling into view fractured sleighloads of pale blue sky, all of it registering in the optical terminals of his beleaguered skull, precise beyond any digital super-remastering, mysterious beyond any metaphysical conceit, true beyond any philosophy, vastly suggestive of something deeper, something so maddeningly close, something at the center of his even most darkly hidden dissatisfaction, something leaving its prints in snowfields that disappear with sublime ease at the first touch of his perception, and so the forest itself becomes his arena, its looming tips gutting every sky he can concoct, its spongy soil absorbing his stride, its endless texturings half-dissolving his mind, taking him far past assimilation into organic identification and naked participation, and then into the tunnel beside the raging brook, the moss-lipped aperture beneath the mushroomed overhang, through which he has now already gone in imagination and bloody simulation, but into which he now offers his body and the sputtering remainder of his mind, as well as everything else he once called his...

The walls, the throbbingly soft walls, close in, squeezing him loose in a delicious peristalsis, a pinkly involuted pulsatory embrace, with him not giving a damn whether the whole thing's a metaphor or not, since nothing makes, nor needs to make, any sense anymore, except for the brilliance that he can now feel invading his passage, the shining marvel that is suddenly flooding his every corpuscle and breath, exploding and streaming him beyond his sense of passage, past all cocooning, past every marooning, right into the cascading serenity, the rapturous wild, the full day, the full night, the luminous Infinity, of what first sought to get somewhere, to take form, to assume shape and name...

Instantaneously he is where it all begins and ends, already in flames, already dramatizing a skyload of names and embodiment-games, already getting solid and taking it personally and making it through scene after scene, while remaining consciously edible, both a feast and one hell of a mouthful for his devourers, all of whom are branded with his mark, her mark, its mark, our mark, the sign of Life, the slippery scrawl of birth, the scratch of death, the wingprints of every breath, the sapphire clouds, all so creamily diaphanous, hanging in the fatly blossomed air for an achingly significant moment, bulging with Forever, all the faces flowering and gone in an instant, wet with love and hurt, passing so, so fast, yet etched against Eternity, carved into Time, wrestling rhyme out of Nothing and love out of Everything, making a stand in savage dreamlands, turning incarnation into art, and exile into soul style, and unfathomableness into Being, again and again dying in a blaze of undecipherable decoding, as Mystery upstages all history, and still here I am, my heart all over my face, my everything aspill, my pages no longer cages, my story unlaced, my joy no longer displaced, my human need a sacred seed, my words like rain...

– 55 –

The Spirit of Assignments:
From Submission
to Cocreative Surrender

The assignments I give are not meant to be taken only at face value; they are meant to be worked with *fully*, in the spirit of what they are designed to address. Resistance to doing them, which is generally almost inevitable (and often extremely repressed, as in the case of the devotee or blind believer), must be tellingly exposed, and also must not be automatically viewed as a negative or unfortunate circumstance. Occasionally, resistance will be a sign that the assignment that one currently has is not appropriate, or needs some alteration or reworking. Most of the time, however, resistance is simply a neurotic, ego-protecting recoil from the aspect of oneself that the assignment is aimed toward...

If all of one's resistance to doing assignments is seen only as an obstacle or a shortcoming, then there's no possibility of making good use of one's resistance — here, one is but a devotee, a true believer, a fanatic yes-sayer, adopting the easy route of implicit, unquestioning obedience, settling for a childish submission to me (as the apparent force behind the assignment) as an unimpeachable icon of authority. Doing so only impoverishes us all. To encounter your *healthy* resistance (unhealthy resistance being that which refuses to see itself as resistance or reactivity) to an assignment, it's necessary to take an assignment not just as a directive, a higher species of "should", but rather as a gift, a gift of nourishing challenge, a gift that must be felt not only in content and context, but also in spirit.

When you feel, *really feel* the spirit of an assignment, you will not merely be submitting to its directives or structure, forcing yourself to go along with it, but instead will be consciously participating in it, yielding to it fully, passionately, and cleanly, and at the very same time witnessing it in action and intention, feeling nourishingly connected to me through your very understanding of the nature of the assignment, intuitively realizing that I'm not giving you the assignment to control or subdue you, but to de-mechanize you, to alert and sensitize you, to not permit you to detour around your darkness...

Obviously, you have good intentions with regard to facing your darkness and pain, but the force of your habits (including that of ego) is so powerful that, without skilful guidance (both outer and inner), you likely wouldn't *truly* face certain aspects of your darkness (except perhaps sporadically, like a psychospiritual tourist), for to do so would be to *openly* encounter the hurt, shame, betrayal, and fear that you've spent just about your whole life avoiding, hoping that never again would you have to feel such an intensity of suffering. But you *do!* At this stage of Xanthyros, you are all ready for that encounter, not as tourists, but as voyageurs to the very heart of the matter. It is no longer at all appropriate to sidestep it, to receive it in tiny doses, to fuck it into apparent oblivion, or to enter its domain only in my presence. It is time to penetrate and become intimate with that painful realm frequently, daily, deeply, without prodding from me, without me necessarily having to make *it* an assignment for you!

When you get into this on your own, there is a stronger possibility of you doing it with every fiber of your being, than if it merely came from me — when it only comes from *me*, there is every chance that part of you will say yes to it (to please or appease the parental forces that haunt you), and that another part will say no (to play adolescent to the same parental forces), thereby not only dividing and thus weakening you, but also generating a friction within you, a yes/no friction that once served a purpose (and occasionally still does) in the Gurdjieffian sense of *forcing* you to visit your edges and to see your mechanicalness and degree of reactivity, but now such friction is little more than masturbatory. It is no longer needed — enough uncovering and revelation has occurred!

There need not be a split between the yes and no in you; by now, at least some of the time, the yes and the no in you are in significant embrace. Your vulnerability is no longer just a kind of helplessness, but is a source of strength. Now, male and female have begun to merge and fruitfully coexist in you, needing no friction for their mutual ecstasy, no hyped stimulation to get their passion going, no sensory kickstarting for their love to cut loose — now their passion simply arises from their stillness, their vibrant silence, their naked empathy, their deep feeling for God, their happiness. No friction is needed. Friction will spontaneously arise during the movements and coursings of passion, but it won't be there as a strategy to create distraction (in the form of exaggerated charge) from your suffering, for it will be but part of the celebration of already-existing happiness, of being-to-being communion, of ecstatic alchemy between male and female, yes and no, dark and light...

This process, this archetypal inner marriage, although not near fruition in most, is already happening to everyone here. Each week now, Xanthyros is being built upon the work of the previous week, whereas six months ago and previous, every week when we met I had to basically start from scratch with all of you, rebuild the temple so to speak, reestablish a living circle, reunite us all in a potently conscious unity of Being, again and again and again, through all sorts of means, more often than not extraordinarily cathartic and wild, primal, scriptlessly dramatic, hair-raisingly psychic, drawing you into heartfelt communion with each other over and over, right in the midst of all our grief, rage, heartbreak, and surfacing joy, not to mention our vast array of superpersonalized neuroses! Those who refused to join in such a venture have now gone. Those who remain are all now committed enough to Awakening so as to make all but obsolete the need to tear down what has been built up. The false foundations that you've spent almost all of your life building upon are now little more than rubble, fertile soil for a real foundation, both within each of us, and for our deepening of community...

None of this, however, means that there isn't more deep purifying work and surprises for all of us, including me, but the context for that purifying work has altered, having become more subtle, more wide-ranging, more firmly based on open-eyed trust. The creation of sanctuary by us is no longer a plan, but a *necessity*, a profound need, and such sanctuary must be created anew every moment, with all the unrehearsed vitality of living Truth.

Xanthyros is not an institution, nor an organization, but rather is a living force, an energy field of fertile chaos, immense vitality, and awakening power. Its structure is firm yet fluid, ever ripe for stretching and reshaping — you could say it's a living temple, of which each one of us is a pillar, rising, rising, rising, learning to stand and deepen our true ground, learning to enjoy our responsibility, to again and again take the "should" out of our shouldering...

Assignments are not just some arbitrary set of directions coming from me in some depersonalized, random fashion; they are not applied to you without me deeply attuning to you, sensitizing myself to you, loving you, feeling both your counterfeit and deep needs. Your assignments may seem at times to go against what you think you need, but they are formed in resonance with your real needs. From a certain viewpoint, this is just my arrogance (i.e., how does *he* know what *I* need?), and from another, it smacks of exaggerated trust on your part. But in Truth, it is simply my responsibility, the part I must play in our community, a part that must creatively coexist with *your intuition* as to what you need to do — this isn't about you abdicating your responsibility here, but instead is about you *illuminating* that responsibility through what I give you. If your trust for me in this is blind, then it won't work — you will have only replaced the authority native to yourself with my authority, instead of allowing both to work synergistically.

Implicit in this, of course, is the utter necessity of making wakeful-ness priority — I am not here to be part of your dream, but to invite you to awaken from it. Do not give me your trust until I have earned it, and then give it with open eyes. I have given you my trust, even though there is much I mistrust about you — the seeds have already been planted, and it is utterly natural for me to tend them, just as natural as it is for me to breathe and teach. My trust in you is a leap of deliberate faith, a leap that I cannot and will not turn back from; my commitment has, through its very totality, an intensity that both brightens and sustains my labour.

You could say that I am the midwife of Xanthyros, and that your flowering is my labour of love, my sacred need, my art and my choice, yet it is more a matter of transcending choice, of surrender-ing to the need for true community and to my part in that joy and ordeal, which necessarily involves a yielding of my own egocentric concerns — if such yielding was just a spiritual strategy, a means of accumulating spiritual credentials, we would be in big trouble, but it is not, being very natural to me, the me who outshines and out-dances every surrogate self, the me who presents Robert to you as a useful, fiery, humourous, and supportively idiosyncratic front...

Part of my responsibilty is to fit the assignments I create for you to your resistance to the Awakening process, your resistance to cutting through those very habits that are so deeply ingrained in you that you, most of the time, find yourself *already* engaged in them without having noticed your entry into them. It takes more than goodwill and good intentions to cut through an addiction; much more is required than just mechanically obeying an assignment. Every assignment I give you provides an opportunity to plunge into and through one or more of your addictions, to experiment with altering your behaviour to such a degree that a radically different perception of a particular resistance can emerge. If you, for example, tend to talk too quickly, I'll probably ask you to speak slowly, or only on the exhale, or not to use five or six agreed-upon words in your speech — this may drive you seemingly mad at first, irritate and frustrate the hell out of you, but it will, if done with true effort, eventually bring you in far deeper touch with yourself, sensitizing you to intentions you didn't even know existed in you, attuning you to your environment, inner and outer, in a manner previously almost unknown to you...

Assignments may embarrass you; they may make you cringe and react. In the midst of even the most difficult-to-accept assignment, remember that your particular assignment at any given time is actually an assignment given to the *whole community*, so that it might further purify itself and deepen its capacity to be a sanctuary for Awakening, for all-round health, for the emergence of the full human. If you see others in Xanthyros working on a difficult assignment and not doing it very well, phasing in and out of integrity, not acknowledging their resistance enough, don't simply turn away from them in disgust, righteousness, liberalized "acceptance", or mere re-activity to their sloppiness — instead encounter them *directly and vulnerably*, realizing that their assignment could well be *yours!*

Get into it with them, not from a position of superiority, nor from a position of commiseration (which only reinforces the tacit agreement of "I won't go after you, if you won't go after me when I'm in a similar bind"), but from your core of Being. If you won't thus participate in their assignment as fully as you can, if only for brief moments, then we are *all* further burdened. I am then further drawn into working with that person on their assignment, and then the assignment becomes mainly a matter between me and that particular person, when in fact it ought to be taken on, at least in spirit, by the whole community!

Everyone needs to participate in each assignment, however fleetingly. There must be no rigid separation from someone else's assignment.

The more you give yourself to their assignment, the more you will *really* be with them in their working with it, whether your response is exasperation, hurt, rage, humour, gentleness or fieriness — if you are truly with them in it, they will, perhaps not at first but eventually, feel their assignment not as a burden, a solitary drag, a negative adventure, a separative task, but rather as a welcome challenge, a Life-strengthening demand. That is, they will feel the *spirit* of the assignment, and then will do it not like a slave, but like a warrior. It is very important that you do your assignments as best you can, and that you learn to welcome, really welcome, everyone else's participation and/or intervention in your assignments, however uncomfortable that might be. It is *your* responsibility to be actively available for and aware of everyone else's assignments — such is your and our ongoing assignment, existing as an act of love and compassion for each other, as well as a catalyst for alertness...

If, for example, someone is not to say certain words, you too need to be aware of those words when you are with that person, so that if they slip, you can *immediately* point out their forgetting. If you see someone failing to do their assignment, or doing it in a half-hearted way, involve yourself in their struggle — help them cut through their reactivity, their partiality, their doubt, their self-defeat. If you hold back from doing so, you are only reinforcing your own partiality, your own half-heartedness, distancing yourself from the very pain in you that corresponds to the pain they are feeling with regards to their assignment. This is about love, not storybook love, but real love, raw love, love that's not afraid to make demands...

Keep becoming more aware of others' assignments; kindle and re-kindle your interest in them. When you are with each other, don't merely settle for typical conversation, which is not much more than machine-to-machine recitations and ego-reassuring ritualism. (Real conversation can certainly be superficial, but its superficiality is *not* an avoidance of its depths, nor an obstacle to risk-taking.) Don't simply regress into being children lost in non-intimate play and hierarchical stupidities. With joy, humour, and integrity, stay alert to each other's assignments, and also stay alert to what has not yet been, but needs to be, made into an assignment. Don't, however, just pick at each other — if you go about simply looking for trouble or signs of disease, you will find them, but you will in all likelihood miss a more inclusive picture, thereby crippling your capacity for compassion.

Spontaneously penetrate each other when it feels *truly* appropriate, when the urge to do so arises not in your mind (nor as some sort of should, nor as an imagining of me looking over your shoulder), but rather is simply and obviously felt as a *bodily* response to that person in the moment. For example, you might feel a subtle irritation or grabbing somewhere in your torso when someone else is speaking at a particular moment; if you were to just say to yourself that this irritation, along with its accompanying thoughts, was only you being out of touch, just you caught in doubt, or just you projecting your own troubles onto this other person, then you would have robbed both yourself and the other of an *opportunity* to deepen your relationship. So what if you're wrong? Even if you were, *that* could be used to further illuminate something about you, in a vulnerable enough fashion to bring you and the other closer. You might not even know what your irritation is about, but if you spontaneously and consciously give it a voice, a mind-free voice, very soon the exact content required will be right there, however messily arrived at, with all the necessary eloquence, the necessary bluntness, the necessary emotional expression, the necessary sensitivity and humour and love, *all* without you having rehearsed *any* of it! This is not some contrived sharing, some therapeutic exercise, but is the essence of real risk-taking, simultaneously innocent and knowing...

Each person's assignments are everybody's assignments. This is not about some massive memorization of assignments, some huge effort to keep it all in mind, nor is it about being a therapist supreme, a ubiquitous busybody, a pointer-outer par excellence — what needs to happen will simply occur when you are *truly* loving everyone here (without, of course, presenting yourself as a devotee of love-negating *concepts* such as "unconditional love"!), when you are so thoroughly unfascinated by your so-called problems, when you are so *uninterested* in your self-enclosing habits and soul-obscuring distractions, that you have *plenty* of energy and attention for what lies outside your self-concerns. Your obligation here, in part, is to remain in *real* relationship with everyone. Everyone!

Don't deny yourself this. Don't simply reduce yourself to a little sun, a little cemented-in centre of ego. Spread out beyond your assumed boundaries — fan out without diluting yourself, without thinning your passion. Move from promiscuity to intimacy. Radiate yourself out, and you will become *naturally* sensitized to everyone here, so that if someone slips, it will not only be me, and one or two others, who feel or intuit such a slip (without necessarily needing to be in physical proximity to that person), but *you* as well!

It's as if we are, at least to some degree, one body so finely attuned to itself that malfunction in one part, however slight or subtle, is almost immediately registered by the rest of the body (or bodymind), so that there are no huge shocks or surprises that a particular part of the body is already badly damaged or ruined in some way — the very *beginnings* of such disease or potential crisis will be known, felt, intuited, by the rest of the body, so that healing steps can be taken...

Such is the context in which I give assignments. I need all of you to more fully join me in the spirit of it. If I've given you an assignment that doesn't ring true for you, or that ceases to ring true for you after you've done it for a while, then your obligation is not to continue doing it in some "true believer" masochistic fashion, but is to contact me, to talk to me about it, to join me in recreating it in a more appropriate form, or in ending it, or in discussing with me how to make better use of it, how to more artfully adapt it to your current situation. Implicit in this is your need to do each of your assignments with everything you've got — such is your sacred need, to bring the fullness of yourself to everything you do, even when it is *very* difficult to do.

You have not already arrived. You're still half-flirting with getting right to the heart of the matter. Comfort and reassurance still easily take precedence over Awakening's imperatives. I have no interest in fixing or tidying up your chaos, nor in burdening it with meaning — instead, I invite you to journey with me to its Heartland, letting the very momentum of our passage create the appropriate structurings for Xanthyros. You must realize that the ripening of your individuality depends upon your capacity to enter into dependency, healthy, unchildish, self-illuminating dependency, not on me, but on the Great Process That is the Source and Substance of all, the Unfathomable Mystery That breathes us, lives us, *is* us, about Which there is nothing more I can say now, except that surrender to It is the very foundation of a truly human life, the primordial raison d'être...

Gustave Doré: *Milton's Paradise Lost*

–56–

We're Always Channeling: Mediumship Unveiled

Because dishonesty, delusion, and runaway projection are so glaringly evident in the current channeling fad, it is very easy to dismiss all channeling or mediumship as mere nonsense, wishful thinking, ego-inflating spirituality, or just plain consolation, but channeling itself is *not inherently* empty, deluded, or false. Because of its largely non-verifiable nature (at least at the level of solid proof and everyday logic), it is very easily abused, especially by those who are plagued by low self-esteem, haunted by chronic deflation, pumped up by delusions of grandeur, or simply trumped by the promise of a better or more reassuring hand — such players find immense comfort in the *thought* or assumption that they are indeed the voices for something great, or at least something greater than themselves. They ordinarily take no responsibility for what they "channel," for they envision it as separate from themselves (or as existing in a kind of bland, deadeningly nice continuum with them, as in the New Age *conceptualization* of a "Higher Self")...

However, we cannot channel someone or something that is greater than ourselves; we can only channel *our mind's version* of that greater something, dressing it up with loftily supportive metaphysical notions and the stupefied credulity of those who've been seduced by our act. To understand, really understand, all of this, we have to realize that all of us all the time are channels or mediums — we are always channeling something, however unconsciously. Ordinarily, it is just our conditioning that we are channeling, no more than the programmings dictated by our prevalent habits; actually, it is more accurate to say that it is our conditioning that is being channeled, for there is no "us" doing it, *unless* we are stably established in our core of Being, and therefore no longer at the mercy of our habits or addictions.

The apparent channeling of entities or energies outside oneself is *usually* just an unacknowledged metaphoric process, a largely impractical means of accessing facets or qualities of oneself that are not readily available through other means, or that one does not wish to experience the full implications of, as in the case of those who refuse to sanely embody and become intimate with their darker aspects. It is no accident that most channeling (and its related sidekicks, like the Course In Miracles) makes a virtue out of disembodiment, treating the body as though it were but a container for a "Higher Self". There is, however, no discrete entity inside us, no jinni in the bottle, but only the responsibility and freedom of ever-deepening embodiment with its attending soul-making — you could say the soul is to the bodymind as the tree is to the acorn...

To assume that what we channel exists independent of us is no different than assuming that we exist independent of everything else. When we are present, deeply present, there is an obvious sense of unity between us and others who are in a similar state. When we feel and abide *as* That Oneness, That undying unity, that profound sense of interconnectedness with all that is, we are not so concerned about the appearance or disappearance of various mind-forms or psychic shapings — our noticing of particularities remains, but becomes gracefully *secondary* to our actual Presence, our very Being. Short of this, however, all kinds of appearances, intentions, details, and shapings of perception, fleshed-out level upon level, fascinate us, magnetizing our attention and drawing us into identification with them, or into playing medium for them. Further complicating the fastening power of such fascination is the whole process of imagination, especially of unacknowledged imagination, which is little more than fragmented, desire-framed fantasy or psychic catharsis locked into the service of escapism...

Most of what is termed channeling is just overblown imagination, a matter of the mind going on an ego-spree and conferring metaphysical credentials onto itself. Only those who are utterly committed to their own integrity will bother distinguishing between what they imagine and what is actually "appearing" to them prior to any imaginal flights. This is not about so-called objectivity (which is just the bias against bias), but about becoming sensitized to something deeper than the merely informational, something whose primary purity is of feeling and full-blooded intuition, the outward expression of which necessitates a translation into a correspondingly resonant form or activity that can only be fully appreciated, let alone recognized, by those who are, to a significant degree, awakened to who they really are. Let me take this a little further: The transcendence of imagination does not signal the end of imaginal shapings, but rather sets up the *relocation* of them, so that their presence is *secondary* to That of Being — that is, imagination becomes gracefully peripheral to Being, instead of serving as a compensation for Its *apparent* absence...

We are all mediums. We can play medium for our lowest possibilities, and we can also be mediums for our highest possibilities. Trouble arises when we try to play medium for *abstractions* of our highest possibilities, as is so abundantly common in the New Age. True or conscious channeling is not an act of mind, but rather the result of a certain permission being granted right at the core of us, a permission that is not accessible through wishful thinking and other mentalized strategies. Such channeling is not a hankering after compensatory information or financial donation, but is a *natural* byproduct of a fully lived life, a life as subtle as it's vital, as transpersonal as it is personal...

Most so-called channeling is simply exploitation, whether of self or of others. There is a lot of profit in telling the gullible what they want to hear, particularly if the disclosure of such information is accompanied by assurances that everything will be taken care of, painlessly and pleasurably, even prosperously, as an even newer New Age is gently ushered in, gently, gently, taking shape as a metaphysical Disneyworld wherein success is assured by having the right set of beliefs! The deodorization and marketing of such cosmic crap is big business, ever outthinking its own stink! Most "channeled" information basically only offers a postponement of growth through generously spooning out the readily-bought illusion that one is *already* growing — that is, it serves egoic consolation instead of Awakening, exhorting the gullible to come admire the Emperor's new clothing, to not be bothered by those wayward souls who refuse to affirm the presence of such magnificent robes!

Awakened channeling, unlike the efforts of most professional psychics, is not ego-based, nor an escape from the demands of embodiment. It is not about trying to conjure up the dead, or to gather arcane information, or to hand out spiritual recipes, or to affirm the magnificence of those who buy their way into its seminars — it offers not buffers, but a passage right into and through the very heart of

our suffering. As such, it unmasks falseness, with an elegant economy of articulation that's as potent as it's subtle. It doesn't protect
anyone from their delusions, nor does it insensitively expose them. It
has no need for bizarre intonations or eccentric accents, nor does it
require closed eyes and upper-chakra encapsulation. It can happen
anywhere, anytime. It doesn't deal in remedy, but in artfully direct
doses of living Truth, delivered in uniquely appropriate fashion to
each individual. Its love is not saccharine, mind-driven, or merely
reassuring, but is richly embodied, vital, lucid, spacious, and often
necessarily fiery...

The true medium, the magician of Awakening's Alchemy, must know
how to work with fire, how to teach others to make good use of both
the Fire's Heat and its Light. Such mediums, whether they are called
psychotherapists, counsellors, spiritual teachers, or whatever, are
attuned to the real needs of their students, as well as to the forces or
circumstances that can best serve such needs. This is not always a
gentle process; sometimes it is painful, difficult, very challenging,
veined with strong criticism. However, it is threatening only to ego-
centricity, not to Essence-centricity...

And just who is it who is medium for all this? Just as most of what is
being channeled is not *innately* personal, but only personified for
purposes suited to the recipient, mediumship is not *primarily* personal — the one who plays medium is not so much a person as a
process, a personification of granted permission, a richly vibrating,
fluid field of energy, not ultimately distinguishable from what is
being channeled. Short of profound meditative states or times of
samadhic absorption, the distinction between the channeler and the
channeled is of some use, if it's not trivialized into the service of self-
glamourization. Awakened channeling neither campaigns for a homogenized oneness, nor does it reinforce self-fragmentation through
artificial distinctions between this and that part of oneself (as in
"Higher Self" and "Lower Self" hierarchies) — instead, it generates a
reunion of all that we are, however endarkened or sordid or dis-
owned or "unspiritual"...

The flight of most psychics to their skulls, whether between and
behind their eyebrows, or up above the top of their head, is just that,
a *flight*, an avoidance, a recoil from the demands of embodiment —
they go to a mentalized Heaven, and their *"down there"* body gets
treated as a problematic "it", hung with a vacancy sign. It is no

wonder that so many are fans of dissociative, rise-above-it, body-negative teachings such as The Course In Miracles... On the other hand, true psychics luminously and *fully* embody all that they are, dark and light, gross and subtle, thick and thin — they are not turned away from what they are. They are intimate with their own labyrinths and addictions. They may not even call themselves psychics, for their psychic work is fluidly integrated with the rest of their life.

Nor are they necessarily dependent upon go-betweens such as crystals, tea leaves, tarot cards, or astrological readouts, though they may well use such intermediaries from time to time. Most of the time, true psychics directly sense what is required; they may not be able to articulate it right away, but the core truths of it are already resonating within them, already moving toward a useful and unique translation formed in direct accordance with the needs of the one before them...

What I'm talking about here, of course, is the art of working with others, that art that psychologists, psychiatrists, and other so-called professionals claim to be experts at, though they are, in general, no more adept here than "unlicensed" therapists. Sadly enough, most therapists, credentialed or not, are failures at the art of working with others, simply because they are not living what they are purporting to teach or draw out — it is no accident that many therapists or counsellors are inept in the very area of their expertise, the reason for which I'll try to clarify through an example... Take relationship counsellors who are failing to live in healthy relationship, failing to establish real intimacy in *their* life, and, once you've gotten past the rationale that they're working through their own relational mess through their attempts to "help" others in a similar fix, you'll notice that they're only living out their needed resolution *vicariously*, using the struggle of their clients as a subtly cathartic break from their own stalemated dramas, a profitable and superficially rewarding distraction from what they *need* to do for themselves! In short, we can only teach what we already *intimately* know; otherwise, we're not teaching, but only preaching.

Now, back to channeling... It is fine to play at channeling, if it's done in the same spirit as children playing out various desires through fantasy-construction, but to *automatically* assume that it's more than fantasy (even though it sometimes is) can do harm, especially when such "ability" is made a cornerstone of ego-inflation, as in "I channel;

therefore I am". If you say you're channeling so-and-so (probably some impressively advanced being who comes only through little old you), no one can prove that you aren't, but those who aren't suffering from a de-activated bullshit detector will know you're full of crap; if you are gutsy enough to not spurn their feedback, you'll find yourself not only embarrassed, but also a lot clearer about your craving to be somebody special, and a lot less caught up in metaphysical lullabies...

A pregnant woman has a wonderful opportunity to authentically channel the being of the little one she is carrying, if she is willing to deeply and vulnerably *feel* the presence of that one, to let that being's energy possess her, illuminate her, and expand her far beyond her everyday self. If she allows what is within her womb *and* all around her to express itself, if she gives this mysterious obviousness her unrestrained voice, she will not necessarily just sit or lie there and speak a few wise words from the beyond, but will more than likely weep and sigh and become ecstatic — her hands may move in all kinds of eloquent ways, weaving out an achingly loving welcome for her baby-to-come.

She will transmit the feeling of her baby to those who are nearby; the sound of her voice, the quality of her movements, the pattern of her words, will all accurately and feelingly convey the presence of her little one. Such channeling is but a doorway for Presence Itself, a conduit for nakedly obvious Life, at once transpersonal and personal, its Fullness of Being ringing truer than any explanation of it. This is non-dissociative channeling, non-fragmentary mediumship, the very Prism of Being...

The "channeled" voice of the unborn child may manifest just as sound, perhaps even semi-mantric, but certainly emotionally and spiritually resonant sound, and it may also carry information about the baby, the mother, the father, or perhaps about past associations of the baby with the mother, and so on — such information, however, is *secondary* to the feeling of what is being transmitted, and must be taken as such.

Again, mediumship is never truly absent. If we're in doubt about this, we're just busy being mediums for our doubt. The separation between channeler and channeled is meant to be permeable; in fact, when we are deeply established in our core of Being, this separation is so flimsy as to seem almost non-existent. At such times, the room may be filled with all sorts of spirit-presences, but "their" being and "our" being are too intimate to need a *specified* differentiation — there *is* a difference, but it is gracefully peripheral to the Presence That pervades us and our room. To get busy channeling at such times would necessitate an unnecessary condensation of Self, an unnecessary filling out of the Silence with content.

Eventually, mediumship reaches the point where there is only Life, nakedly present, moving in and out of various embodiments, various personalizations, ever transparent to Its Source. Our work is to become transparent yet grounded mediums for our Source. All the lower degrees of channeling must be permitted to enter into conducive alignment with this primal mediumship, until we are surrendered yet idiosyncratically present before the Presence of God...

Gustave Doré: *Chateaubriand's Atala*

–57–
Na Pali:
Embracing the Knowingness
that Upstages all Mindtraps

We're not here to have something special happen to us, but rather to *clearly* be in deep, heartrooted communion with all of this — these peaks, these jungled valleys, this ancient coastline [*this talk was given atop a cliff overlooking Kauai's Na Pali coast*], this time, these desires. We are *not* in need of some magical alteration of all this, outer or inner, so that we might feel better about ourselves. Rather, we simply need to feel unobstructedly, to feel fully, to feel and breathe *this*, not with some manipulation of emotion, some kind of exaggeratedly positive feeling, but with *natural* emotion, open-bodied love, respect, and awe, so that we might juicily and deeply participate in this sublime calm, this quiveringly pure blue, this rainbowed storminess, this magnificence that fills and surrounds us...

The beauty of this must not be trivialized into a mere producer of good feelings, but instead must be allowed to penetrate what we take to be ourselves so, so deeply that our hearts become luminously raw and open — we may well feel as if our hearts are breaking, while at the same time intuiting that such heartbreak is not simply heartache, nor reactive sorrow, depression, downfall, misery, misfortune, nor any other supposed problem, but rather is an eloquently vulnerable exposure of what has been hidden or denied, as well as a celebration of what we *really* are, especially in terms of our interrelatedness with all that is, our primal connectedness, our inherent empathy with the entire Universe, level upon level...

None of this needs to be turned away from. The momentary is as important as the Everlasting; the surface is as important as the innermost depths. None of it needs to be altered so that we might feel better about ourselves. It is *already* in a state of continuous alteration, inherently so! All we need do is cooperate with its Essentialness, by consciously yielding our attention not to the preferred specifics that we'd like to have happen, but rather to the heart of the matter, the primal currents of existential flux, the fundamental imperatives of Being.

This is what is crucial — to become so *natively* intimate with change itself that it is all but impossible to seek security in the realm of possession or having. The only security is in Being, and *that* security is *not* in opposition to insecurity, for it is the very hub of insecurity! It is not a positioning, it is not a placing, it is not a fixation or strategy of any sort, but is a conscious residing in one's core of Being, and, more precisely, *as* one's core of Being, *as* the very Heart of this moment...

Without a deep, consistently deep, embracing and understanding of Life's *inherent* insecurity, we just keep on desperately searching for security, *already* turned away from the Truth of our Being, *already* unhappy, *already* calculating, *already* looking for refuge in the *surrogates* of What we have turned away from, those very surrogates that both animate and haunt our entrapping dreams.

Go now into this very moment. Appreciate and honor its contours, its textures, its theatrics, its surface idiosyncrasies, but do not linger there for very long. Dive, dive deep into the moment, letting yourself approach the Great Moment That is continuous with all moments, the Great Moment that is now shaping Itself as you and me and this valley, this creamy breeze, this wildly sculptured vista, this voice...

This is not about participating in your own annihilation, nor about being some kind of enlightened tourist! Diving deeply into the Heart of the moment creates both a seamless continuity with everything, and, equally so, a lucid crystallization of one's real uniqueness, that very uniqueness that is meant to fully flower, to individuate itself so completely that it cannot do it more fully, at which point it may die (or radically mutate) into a very different sort of individuation eventually abiding as Awareness Itself, Consciousness Itself, no more troubled by its elemental upheaval and time-making than is the sky by its clouds...

But the call remains, existing as an Invitation That will not go away, ever beckoning us to dive deep, to climb steep, to enter *this* moment totally, not another moment, but *this* very moment, with its frameless door, its garlanded passage, its unspeakable depths, its open-faced secret... It is folly to just wait for a more auspicious moment. Even if the timing of a particular something isn't apparently right now, doesn't ring true enough just now, still the very *waiting* for the arrival of that timing is the moment to dive into — otherwise, we are forever blindly climbing, focussed only on the peak, or on our dream of the peak, not realizing that when we arrive at the peak (which is very unlikely), we will only bring to it the *same* drivenness and contractedness of spirit that characterized our climb. The climb itself is what matters, especially the quality of our climb...

If this moment is entered into deeply enough, it expands to include the essence of every other moment, past, present, and future, and in That Infinite Moment, we are Home, already Home, unavoidably at ease with ourselves, overflowing with unexploitable love, empathy, and power, living a blazingly true individuality and a simultaneous transcendence of that very self, knowing that to transcend ourselves, we must *be* ourselves... Transcendence is not an escape, although what is commonly called transcendence all too often is simply dressed-up or spiritually fashionable escapism. Real transcendence is simply the unobstructed embodiment of Infinity; it is not an escape, but is the very spaciousness, the very luminosity, the very intelligence, the very paradoxicalness needed to ground us in Being, to anchor us in living Truth...

Now, now contact the urge in you, however subtle or evasive, to have something special or magical occur to this very moment so that it might make you feel more secure, more at home, more at ease, more immune, more of something! Do not judge that urge; simply notice it now. Don't pretend it's not there, so that you might congratulate yourself for your spiritual development — it *is* there, and it will be there (however mute or coma-like or background it will be from time to time) until you have *fully* awakened. This hankering for fulfilling change is an obsession, however subtle, with having things change the way *you* want them to change, or having them remain the way *you* want them to remain, without you, however, actually noticing that the very *you* who wants this change or non-change is precisely what is in the way!

In fact, it is not even a you, but only the habitual, almost always unconscious, personification of a cluster of assumptions. It is not truly personal; it's just a mechanical activity that has attached to

Roloff Beny: *The Pleasure of Ruins*

itself the label "I", and it craves an environment that reinforces or legitimizes its identity. It's this very energy, this desperate animation of ego, that is now despoiling the Earth, running amok, projecting its barbarically computerized vision everywhere. Almost everything on the Earth now is, to varying degrees, pervaded by this utterly mechanistic, mind-driven case of mistaken identity that is even now nibbling at your edges, trying to hook some of your attention...

Now, slip more deeply into this moment, letting your woundedness uncongeal, letting your hurt undam, letting a deeper hurt start to flow, gradually letting your love pour from you, stream from you, trickle and roar from you, emanate, radiate, pulsate, shower and flower all around you, blooming inside the moment, both emptying and filling you, opening out into concentric circles of nectared petals, spiral upon expansive spiral, everything now opening, unfolding, releasing, flowering fully without any concern for its upcoming death, its upcoming change of state. Now feel, unhurriedly feel yourself surrendering, not giving up, but rather giving yourself without giving yourself away, giving so deeply that you are not helpless, but rather are receiving what you have *always* longed for, that which you assumed was elsewhere or elsewhen, maybe in the cave behind your forehead, or up in the Himalayas, or in some mystical valley, some auspicious powerspot or supposed samadhi site, or perhaps at the feet of some reputed spiritual master...

What you really need is precisely, *exactly*, right before you, right with you, *now*. You are being tested right now in a manner that *exactly* reveals what you are avoiding, what you are afraid to face, what you are postponing doing, what you wish you didn't have to deal with... It's right here! All you need do is be grateful that it's before you right now, right here, including that aforementioned urge to have your circumstances magically altered so that you might feel better! So also here, *blatantly* here, is that urge for a more fulfilling relationship, that craving for a more streamlined physique, a more satisfying orgasm, a more interesting meal, a more whatever! What you *need* is right here, not perhaps in its most conventionally fulfilling form, but here in a format that exactly suits your *current* level or stage of development...

And you will be tested until you've said a pure yes to all of this, not a naively all-accepting yes, not a strategic yes, not a partial yes, but rather a yes that throbs with awakened wonder, a yes that makes room for every no, a yes that is not in opposition to no, but that both includes and transcends it, an unambiguously alive yes, a self-radiant yes, a yes that cannot help but blaze with Awakening's Song, Texture, Feel, Presence...

Wherever you now are provides the *ideal* conditions for your awakening, simply because it is full of structures, processes, motives, people, and opportunities that correspond to your current state. If you were in a supposedly more auspicious setting, or with people who were more luminous, more real, more centered, perhaps that would be inappropriate for you, because you wouldn't be *ready* to make good use of such circumstances or people; you probably would only feel worse about yourself, only do worse, only reinforce your reactivity, because of your very failure to make good use of such a situation!

Whatever is before you *now*, both inner and outer, is what you must make good use of — if you're angry now, make good use of it; if you are jealous now, make good use of it. For example (in the case of jealousy), instead of just automatically assuming rejection and doing harm to one you love, instead of boxing yourself in, instead of just believing the righteous viewpoint that jealousy can so convincingly present, why not let your jealousy roar, moan, curse, shout, weep, without you, however, taking on its viewpoint? Why not ride its currents past the temptation to blame, past your recoil from vulnerability, past your *unloving* demand to be loved, past your suffocating possessiveness, right into your undressed need and love, your rawness of soul, until you are no longer exploitable by the possibility of rejection, but only nakedly present, available, alive?

Everything that is happening to you is fertile soil for your awakening. Everything! Everything! Notice how you might want to argue with this, to suggest that your circumstances are unfavorable for your awakening, not seeing that such conditions are, if properly encountered, *exactly* what you need to deal with *before* going deeper or elsewhere; they are not bad luck, for they artfully suit the *current* you, manifesting as a marvellously personalized, wraparound psychogravitational field...

To want to make your prison prettier or more consoling only reinforces your stay, merely strengthening your self-entrapment. You must learn to honor those who stand outside the trap. Instead of just looking for flaws in them, vilifying and crucifying them, or else worshipping and adulating them, making them cultic objects, simply honor them, use them well, relate to them in a manner that serves your well-being, however jarring it is to your ego. Find the right distance between them and you. If you, in your spiritual ambition or naïveté, get too close to such beings, you will in all likelihood only recoil, react, withdraw, shrink, for the fire will be too hot for you — their presence will demand too much of you, even if they are seemingly asking nothing of you. Back up until you've found a position (and not just physically) where you are *still* strongly challenged by their presence, yet not so challenged that you feel crushed or overwhelmed (except perhaps in very small doses).

And it's not just proximity to a teacher that I'm talking about; it's proximity to teaching situations. Everything, everyone is your teacher, but to varying degrees — those situations, those beings, that are most strongly and attractively in the position of teacher relative to you must be approached skilfully, in a manner that brings together "Look before you leap" and "He who hesitates is lost."

You must find, and refind, your right position with such teachers, your appropriate form of relationship with them; love is necessary, but it is not enough. Do not expect to be comfortable, except with your discomfort, your necessary stretching and undoing. If you remain too distant with a teacher, you won't grow, but will just think and dream about growing; you'll probably only pretend or believe that you are making it. Get too close for too long, and you'll be burnt, probably ending up in bitterness, neurotic disillusionment, cynicism, or, even worse, in an ever-wandering devotional stupor, an infantile search for perfect parenting somewhere, somehow...

Surrender doesn't mean jumping into the Fire and being burnt to a crisp; it means approaching the Fire with intelligence, heartfelt intelligence, so that you can simultaneously make use of the Fire's Heat and Its Light. It is crucial to realize that you can't surrender something you don't have, something that is unripe, something that you haven't *really* developed in yourself!

The whole notion of surrender is frequently no more than just an ego-centered manoeuvre, a strategy to somehow grab onto or invest in some immunity, a kind of bargaining with the Undying One — I'll surrender, *then* I'll get this, this, and that — *real* surrender, however, doesn't bargain, nor does it look ahead for byproducts of its action. Such surrender is simply the *natural* activity of one who is deeply committed to waking up. It is not a disempowering action, but a profoundly empowering one, however sacrificial its imperatives might be. It does ask that one lose face, and ultimately that one lose every face, but at the same time it also asks that the losing of face not be accompanied by a losing of touch. Real surrender is an act of love, an act of trust. It is a stretching of self, a leaping into the deepest pools of one's Being, and it is not a blind jump. It is not a matter of renunciation, of cessation of desire, of angerlessness, of non-lust, nor of any other such strategy to avoid or dilute the inherent suffering and passionplay of Life.

Real surrender is a joyous undertaking, not some gloomy, tight-lipped discipline — it is a yes, a pure yes to Being Itself. It is a recognition of one's true condition, a recognition of what must be done, however painful that might be. It doesn't necessarily ask that something change, for it already knows that change is inevitable, but this doesn't mean that it is simply a passive yielding to the play of circumstances, for it can be active, dynamic, extremely potent, making enormous waves. Such surrender is far from being narrow, rigid, or dogmatically-positioned — it *can* take positions, not to reinforce egocentricity, but rather to deepen Essence-centricity, to flesh out the Truth of what we are...

Now, don't hesitate. Look and leap at the same time. Let your heart be filled with the Holy Rhyme, the Ecstasy That beats out of time, the Knowingness that upstages every thought and mind-knot. Let Magic, the magical ordinariness of Eternity, seize every particle, every parcel, every budding and every piece of this moment, every last flavor of it, every shaping and every nuance of it, until your breath is not yours, nor is anything else, not even your hearing of these words, these dying phrases...

Listen — we sit here atop a sacred canyon, while birds with long, fragile tailfeathers float white and so soft through the greenwalled canyons to and from the Na Pali coastline, their lines of flight needing no decoding. [*Helicopter overhead*] The sun beats down on us in this small meadow, so near the edge of a great precipice. Birds sing and squawk, call and holler in the background, insects whirr and hum, helicopters pass by like bloated dragonflies, loaded with optically-obsessed tourists armed with cameras and binoculars, trying to find some comfort, some reassurance, in their densely-scheduled time, their plastic rhyme, their sanitized and unacknowledged touring of the outside of the outside...

The land here is an intensification of the Earth's energyfield; it's not just solid and immensely powerful, but bulgingly alive, packed with vast presence. It can speak. If it would, it might say, "I have stood here, I have risen here, I have exploded here, I have flowered and settled here for time immemorial. Human footsteps are an extremely recent development. I am ancient, I am present, I am She, I am He, and I am present in you..."

An Ordinariness of Extraordinary Obviousness

There is no cave left for me, nowhere left to be a solid somebody, for the links with that have been shattered, not as a strategy, but because there was nothing else to do. No progress here, no saintly applause, no jackpot avalanches, but just ordinariness, an ordinariness of extraordinary obviousness; no wraparound labels here, no requisite fame, no new or auspicious name, but just this, nakedly and unavoidably true, blooming with Paradox, at once exhausted and tremendously alive...

What you call me is only another experience I occasionally have, of no more significance than any other experience.

The cave is empty. No longer am I inclined to look inward or outward; both are endlessly fascinating dead-ends, mirages of hope, the twinned moneytrees of religion, the back-and-forth that erodes the impulse to move in a truer direction. Nothing new has occurred to me, but something old has become obsolete in me, faded to vanishing data, existing now as no more than a dream already half-blown into infinite confetti, celebrating nothing in particular, only briefly smudging the lesser sky whereunder I live and die daily.

Everything continues as before, but its familiarity is fleeing me; I am more indifferent to its content, and more intimate with its Mystery. I'm more fragile now, and more powerful, more streamlined, softer, gentler, and much more ruthless. I stand in a land that has no maps, and I stand there reaching for you, calling to your purity of heart, now and then cheerleading you beyond your false starts... And why do I teach? Because it is my very nature, my inborn need. And what do I teach? The ever-spontaneous art of living a full life, a God-illuminated Life, a life of Awakening, Passion, Intimacy, and Ecstatic Practicality. And how do I teach it? Wildly and softly, subtly and vibrantly, improvisationally and committedly, intensely and gently, lit with the flesh-brightening shiver of living right at one's edge, travelling beyond all tourism into and through both the Difficult and the Easy...

My mind is quiet, my body expansive, my breath unburdened by concentrative focus, my stride delicate and quiveringly muscular, my description here not a promise, not a guarantee, not an eyeful of data, but a welcome, enlivened by a necessary and multidimensional loss of face. Don't try to match my pace, and don't just settle for your conditioning's pace — find your own, and find something vital in these surging and dying phrases, even though you've heard them, or a variation of them, a thousand times.

And what do you assume my purpose is with you? To serve your Awakening in a manner that does not rob you of your uniqueness, nor of your passion. At this moment, I am weary, grieving over your foolishness — another time, I'll be indifferent or angry or joking or just hair-raisingly present about it, but for now I am wounded by it. There is no escape for me. There isn't for you, either, but you still think there is. I know there isn't, and that's the difference between us. I'm not running away, nor am I running in place. I am only here, taking root in the Great Nowhere, branching all through It, already chopped down, already burnt to nothing, already reborn, already present. This is no great achievement, but only the foundation of a truly human life, the very beginning.

I, half-limping, have begun, but you have not — you're still flirting with the possibility, weighing facsimiles of it in your mind, pumping life into other apparent options, keeping yourself stuck in Time, seeking pleasurable compensation for your trouble. And so I wait for you, waiting without waiting, even when I plunge into your world...

Gustave Doré: *Dante's Purgatoria*

–58–

The Invitation
That Will Not Go Away

If we refuse to accept the Invitation That won't go away, then It inevitably shapeshifts into a demand, and if we ignore such a demand or try to rewrite it according to our own ego-centered needs, it becomes a baffling elbowing, a roughhouse push, an overly aggressive shove, eventually festering into an undeniable (and *apparently* unfortunate) crisis...

The Invitation is given or offered in each moment — *every* moment provides us with the *same* opportunity for awakening or for deepening our awakening. The Invitation is here, now, in the midst of your emotion, your hurry, your postponement, your every thought, your every psychosomatic knot; It is here, in the breath of the wind, the slant of the snow, the arching of the waves, the sway of the trees, the play of the day, the glory and horror of it all. The Invitation That will not go away is written into everything, encoded everywhere, translated into luminous obviousness wherever and whenever we activate our capacity to stand our true ground.

Though the Invitation is inherent to all, It exists only in seed form for those who are resolutely slumbering. Its breakout from Its seedcase, Its spherical night, requires the nourishment of unfettered attention, the light-filled rain of uncluttered awareness — then the seed starts to swell, not out of egoic inflationary tendency, but out of a deep inner imperative that is in potent resonance with the will characteristic of awakened attention.

And so the seed strains, expands and swells further and further, finally cracking its encasement beyond repair, as well as its identity as a seed. The emerging seedling is ours to tend, ours to care for, ours to love, daily, sensitively, intelligently, for it is more us than the us we ordinarily take ourselves to be, however tiny it may seem, however vulnerably green and superslender it might appear. It is immensely fragile, yet veined with a surpassingly great power, the power not to have, but to be, to purely *be*. To enter into this process, the seed must let go of being a seed; it must yield its seed-ness, its safe and seemingly secure position. Its very identity must be fully surrendered if it is to fulfill its destiny...

It is very, very easy to defend against what *appears* to be the end, to go on clinging to our apparent identity, however miserable, contractive, or suffocatingly barren it might be. Cozy or not, it is still *our* assumed identity, familiar and predictable, something steady, something relatively consistent that we *have*, something that we can anchor ourselves to in the midst of our daily chaos, something that seems, through its sheer density of repetitious programming, to indisputably prove that "we" exist. The Unknown is what is feared, and yet it is the Unknown into Which we are being invited, every moment, not the Unknown that is simply awaiting the tools of science so that it can become mere knowledge, but the Unknowable, the Eternal Unknowable, the vast Mystery, the fathomless Mystery That is both the Source and the Substance of all, Wherein our true identity is a forever open secret...

If someone else cracks open our seedcase, our testa, we may swell and grow and emerge, but there will almost invariably be a chronic doubting accompanying our upward stretch, our outreach for the Light. Such doubt will, unless *thoroughly* explored and uprooted, only sabotage our growth, spooning itself into the blind mouth of those *aspects* of us that did not participate in our opening. There are no shortcuts, but we've all known (and probably exploited) the desire to tap into some transformative shortcut, to not have to struggle or suffer. Yes, most struggle is unnecessary (being little more than a stalemated armwrestle between unilluminated polarities within us), but there is nevertheless a true struggle, a worthy ordeal that is utterly healthy and necessary, an all-out effort that purifies and strengthens us, rendering us more and more receptive to true non-effort, or *natural* ease.

Those who claim that there's no need to struggle at all (their platform being that if we *think* there has to be struggle, then there will be) have but made a cleverly loopholed virtue out of escapism and disembodiment, finding some immunity by holing up in their headquarters and locking themselves to various beliefs; they are only diseased children, severely damaged children playing make-believe, playing on the seashore, building mindcastles out of sand, forgetting the approaching waves, the storm, the nearby turbulence, the Death hissing in the wavespray... What is required here is much deeper than mere thought or belief — we need to permit ourselves a bodyfree, soulshining participation in our own opening, a deliberate and dynamic receptivity to the sacred Invitation That pervades all.

As I said earlier, if the Invitation is ignored or counterfeited, then It mutates into more and more of a rough demand, which we tend to react to like frightened children recoiling before a hostile, authoritarian figure. The point is to *respond* to the Invitation, not just once in a while, but now, and now and now, not expecting It to come in a particular form, nor expecting It to duplicate Its most recent shaping or circumstantial presentation. The Invitation is formed in direct correspondence with your current needs, your current state of development — It is not mass produced by some omnipotent Parent-figure to be delivered to all in the same form. It is uniquely shaped and articulated according to *your* present state, obeying a kind of psychospiritual gravitation relative to your true needs and to what you are *doing* with them...

Do you not now feel the Invitation That will not go away, the Invitation That you have so easily turned away from so, so many times, as you sought a more consoling or pleasantly distracting ride, ever assuming that you had limitless time? There is Eternity, yes, but *you* do not have Eternity — Eternity *has you*, every possible you!

If you are wise, you will not continue postponing your own flowering; you will not obstruct it, nor will you ambitiously speed it or slow it, nor will you be sucked in by those who say, "I've been through it all, and I want to tell you that you don't have to go through it." What exploitive crap! You *do* have to go through it! Not through *every* possible experience, but through the *matrix* of experience — you, in other words, don't have to become a heroin addict to understand what such fixation is all about, but you *do* have to, level upon level, understand the nature of addiction, not just with your mind, but with your entire being! You can't merely have someone tell you about it, and believe what they say because they are a teacher or appear to be full of light — you must know it thoroughly, for yourself, and know it *intimately*. There are no shortcuts (belief is not a shortcut, but only a detour, a disembodied dead end, an ossified stand-in for integrity and fluidity of being), none! But there is a soul-serving economy of time, movement, intention, and stretch that is ours to embody, to live from the tips of our toes to our fontanelle; there is a way of living in which energy is not wasted, not unnecessarily discharged or thrown away as is so common in typical sex or thinking or doing, a way of living in which energy is conserved without hoarding or relational withdrawal or any other sort of dissociation from Life...

Ask yourself how you waste energy. Be specific, very specific, then start doing something other than just animating those particular habits of waste-making. Stop polluting yourself, stop sooting your sky, stop shitting in your lifestream, stop looking for a better dream, stop and take a long, easy breath, and then let your breath take you and shake you from your mind-roost, carrying you into something finer — no ambition here, no heroic mission, no righteous ecological submission, just this moment to be embraced, to be appreciated, to be felt right to the heart, its throbbingly pure Invitation received without qualification. *Now.* Now, and every species of Now, lofty and lowly, sweet and hard, soft and angular, shallow and deep, pristine and plain, every flavor, every texture of wind, of Holy breath, of lowly lust, everything, *all of it* vibrating with the same Invitation, the same purity and significance of call, calling and calling to you, to the real you. Do not expect this calling to be framed in some conventional manner. It can come in all sorts of ways — from the stones under your feet, the distant sound of a buzzsaw, the line of an airplane passing overhead, the thoughts coalescing behind your forehead, the bodily urges that compete for your attention, the place where you now sit or lie, all of it pulsating with the same primal Invitation, undilutedly alive...

Awakening is not unnatural; psychospiritual sleep is. The deepest trouble is for those who are convinced that they are awake, when in fact they are only dreaming that they are awake. To acknowledge the degree of one's sleepfulness requires that one not sit in the position of one's persona; the view from such a lookout is of no use here, except as an object of witnessing, being at best but a colorful, supportively idiosyncratic expression of one's depths. Most of the time, however, persona doesn't reflect or magnify essence, but instead mutilates its energies, misrepresents it, obscures and blocks it, working in opposition to it. When we identify with our persona, we cannot hear, see, feel, or recognize the Invitation That will not go away — we then all too easily just create a surrogate of It, and get busy enslaving ourselves to that substitute, that parody of the Real, merely inviting ourselves into the most ego-reinforcing sanctums of our masquerade, those imaginal chambers wherein we can most easily console ourselves.

The key is not to return to a preverbal state, some archaic or sentimental positioning, full of superstition, ritualized magic, organic escapism, or New Age gullibility, but rather is to embody a more profound level of the spiral, turning toward the sacred Invitation instead of away from It — this is not a movement of repetitive circling or looping, nor of regression, but of moving deeper into Now, journeying from the periphery to the heart of the matter.

This involves, among other things, a transverbal stance, not a rigid positioning, but a fluid one, a bodybright assuming of a truer ground wherein the sacred Invitation is easily accessible, almost always close at hand, close at heart, obviously nearby, not at all difficult to find or touch, not at all difficult to fall in love with, to rise in love with, to be in embrace with so deeply that we literally become Love, Love without an object, letting such Love carry us into the Great Mystery Wherein all this sits, rises, dies, cries, flies, births and dives, with Its infinite shapings and colorings, Its seasonless center, Its Heart That even now pervades every one of us with sublime Obviousness, supremely empathetic Welcome, and lucid Indifference...

Feeling this now, however slightly, do you not already intuit a degree of intimacy with what I've termed the Invitation That will not go away, even in the midst of your distractions and your compensatory contractions? Do you not *feel* this Holy Call, this sublimely simple reminder, this undying Love That asks only for *your* wholehearted yes, *your* return, *your* love, *your* undressed need, *your* seedling soul's deepest cry? Such Love is not an emotion, but is a state of being — in fact, It is the very current of primal Being, the very prism of the Formless, the very Doorway through which manifest Existence makes Itself apparent. *It is the feeling of God.* It is the Divine in action. It is our very nature, our foundation, our native occupation. It is not apart from Truth. It does not cling, nor does it stand apart, strategically detached, avoiding the inevitable woundedness of real intimacy. It is not afraid of pain, nor of heartbreak. It makes room for all. It doesn't require a turning away from Life, a clinging to Nothingness. It does not make a virtue out of Emptiness, nor out of Nirvanic

extinction, nor out of non-attachment. It is *already* free of all "isms",
all chains, all reins, yet It is not without sensitivity, being profoundly
attuned to what It is embraced by — Its freedom is in Its commitment to Being, in Its ecstatic slavery to the Unknowable, in Its
surrender to limitation, in Its marriage of the finite and the Infinite.
If taken to heart, It burns through the non-essential in us, burning
through all of it in a glory of flames; It is not a polite little flicker,
obsessed with gentleness and cuddlesome safety, but rather is a
great force, a fieriness, a passion and an intensity, a heat that, if
properly worked with, can only reveal Its eternal companion, Light...

As what's non-essential in us goes to embers, and our actions and intentions become more and more frequently lit from within by a
graceful economy of energy, we need only to keep yielding to our
momentum. The spaces between our words become as important as
the very tone and texture of our speech. We no longer avoid silence;
we no longer try to fill it up with what we take ourselves to be, and
nor do we make a virtue out of saying nothing. We simply become
more and more human, more and more established in and *as* Being,
knowing that there's no need to extinguish persona or ego, no need
to get rid of anything, in fact. The point is to let it all become
permeable to the purifying Fire, to the Great Invitation, to the
sacred Call, now, ever now, not later when things seem more auspicious, but *now*. *Every* moment is auspicious! Some moments carry
more promise, more energy, more focus perhaps, more circumstantial good news, but every moment carries exactly the same Demand,
the same Opportunity to dive deeper.

Whenever you are awake, you will feel this Invitation, even if It
doesn't take shape as an invitation, and your awakening will deepen,
will become less dry, will become more subtle, more expansive, more
vulnerable, less and less focussed on details, and more and more
attuned to Presence, to Being, to Love, to Truth...

When you suddenly come awake, realizing that you've been asleep
for the past few minutes, hours, days, or years, don't waste energy
judging yourself for having been asleep, and don't judge yourself for
being judgmental. Simply make room for your reactivity, letting its
energies become something more enlivening, and get on with it.
Enjoy your wakefulness — it's not some dreary task, some humorless
labour, some clinging of attention to the objects of apparent meditative focus. It is inherently happy, even if it must cry or rage. Real

meditation is a joy, though its concentrative preliminaries may not be. Meditation is an ease, an effortlessness, but such effortlessness arises from soil that has been prepared by true effort (rather than by trying, which always carries within itself a sweaty counter-effort), an essence-centered doing that is fueled by an ongoing awareness of the Invitation That will not go away.

Meditation has no goal. It is sufficient unto Itself. It is a purity, a tranquil ecstasy, the peace of a storm, the vibrancy of a calm, an inviolable ocean, a room with no walls, ceiling, or floor — It is not enemy to anything, however turbulent or dark, being no more disturbed by these things than is the sky by its clouds. Real meditation is so obviously natural, so joyful, so juicily serene, that it cannot be mistaken for anything else. It is but wide-open sky, the Presence of Space, the unequivocally felt acknowledgment of Being and Mystery, ever ready to mutate beyond Itself...

Feel the sacred Invitation now, without trying to alter your state, to somehow improve your condition in this moment, or to auspiciously reposition yourself. Let whatever is occurring for you *right now* be your soil, your springboard — emerge, gradually emerge from it with gratitude, with ease, with exultant openness, with wet eyes, with luminous passion, with knowingness and wonder, now, now, now, until the Fire is but Light, until exhale and inhale are one, until the Darkness is in love with the Light, until outside and inside are lovers, now, eternally and precisely now, Now...

ROBERT AUGUSTUS MASTERS is a psychospiritual trailblazer and shamanic visionary, as well as a master therapist and teacher, an adept at getting to the heart of the matter, teaching only what he *intimately* knows, artfully, unswervingly, and potently serving as a multidimensional catalyst and medium for the Awakening and embodiment of the full human. He is the guide of Xanthyros, a community both young and very ancient, in which Awakening is the priority, not a dry, detached, or desireless awakening, but rather a vibrant, full-bodied, exquisitely practical awakening...

In Xanthyros, the difficult is not risen above, nor otherwise avoided, but is deliberately entered into *and* passed through with open eyes, until its energies, however dark or reactive, are *fully* and luminously integrated with the rest of one's being — this passage is simultaneously a solitary and communal effort, the structuring of which is neither prepackaged nor rehearsable, but is instead formed in earthy yet fluid correspondence with the *essential* imperatives of the *present* moment. This journey, which is not so much from here to there, as it is from here to a *deeper* here, honours no morality except that generated by Awakening's alchemy. As such, Xanthyros serves the *real* needs of its members, rather than merely fitting them into an already designed system.

Xanthyros is an ever-evolving sanctuary for those whose longing to be truly free is stronger than their longing to distract themselves from their suffering. Xanthyros is also a fertile experiment, a passionate risk, a stand and a leap, an invitation and a sacred demand, a frameless doorway, a dynamic yet sweetly subtle crucible wherein the fire of the Awakening process can do its work, not just in the transformative and revelatory meetings of Xanthyros, but also in its businesses, its children's school, and its ever-deepening transfamily intimacy...

THE WAY
OF THE LOVER

The Awakening & Embodiment
Of The Full Human

Robert Augustus Masters

Its Chapters Include:

- The Inside & Outside Of Self-Fragmentation
- The Teacher Is Everywhere • The Impulse To Awaken
- True Center & Its Chief Surrogate
- Breakdown Precedes Breakthrough • Irony Undressed
- Egocentricity & Essence-Centricity
- Sentimentality & Cynicism • Hope Is Nostalgia For The Future
- Responsibility Is The Ground Of Freedom
- The Anatomy Of Eroticism • Masochism & Sadism
- Into The Heart of Rejuvenative Orgasm
- Ecstasy Is Not Elsewhere • Jealousy Unmasked
- A Mirage of Intimacy: The Cult Of Two
- You Are Being Tested, Now • Working With Criticism
- Parenting, Freedom & Responsibility
- Guilt Means We Don't Have To Grow
- Birthing The Man • Myth As Transformative Metaphor
- Guru-Worship, Cultism, & God-Communion
- We Are Not "In" A Body • Awakening Creates Its Own Morality
- There Are No Oscars For Awakening

208 pages, Quality softcover
$14.95 • ISBN: 0-88925-922-4

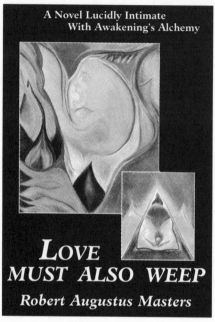

**A Novel Lucidly Intimate
With Awakening's Alchemy**

**LOVE
MUST ALSO WEEP**

Robert Augustus Masters

320 pages
Quality softcover
$16.95
ISBN: 0-88925-980-1

LOVE MUST ALSO WEEP is both novel and catalyst; in its lucid sensuality, epiphanous breakthroughs, full-bodied emotion, exultant leaps, and dynamic yet subtly textured drama, it is highly entertaining reading, but it is also demanding, in that it engages far more than just imagination, artfully transporting the attentive reader not into the consoling terrain of fantasy (however seemingly "spiritual"), but right into the heartland of the Real. However, LOVE MUST ALSO WEEP is not mere exhortation, nor is it some kind of remedy or cure-all in novelistic form — it is a *direct*, multidimensional, vibrantly alive, exquisitely articulated honouring and expression of the Invitation to fully awaken, the Invitation That will not go away, the Invitation That is present in seed-form in *every* moment, asking only for our undivided attention. LOVE MUST ALSO WEEP is not about positive thinking, hope, nor any other compensatory strategy, but rather is about authentically facing what must be faced if we are to *truly* awaken from all the entrapping dreams we habitually animate, including our craving to dwell in a "better" dream.

LOVE MUST ALSO WEEP is at home with both suffering and ecstasy; it plunges with open eyes into the very core of Life, again and again finding expression at a deeper level than thought or belief, a level aglow with both natural integrity and self-illuminating passion. Its protagonist, Glam, is a spiritual adventurer, a warrior inside and out, a man simultaneously strong and vulnerable, already firmly and fluidly rooted in his being, yet ever allowing his deepest inner imperatives, however terrifying or bewildering, to direct his course. Gradually, he learns, and learns with his *entire* being, that nothing need be turned away from so that he might fully awaken — it all, however dense, violent, lustful, or endarkened, must be uninhibitedly faced, embraced, and passed through, not to be somehow left behind, but rather to be *included*, such inclusion being not a matter of naive acceptance, but of energetic transformation of such potency that even the most contracted or gross of conditions becomes but *available* Life-energy...

LOVE MUST ALSO WEEP does not sidestep or trivialize Paradox, nor replace it with metaphysical lullabies, but goes straight into It, seeking not meaning, but radical and unqualified revelation, until the very act of seeking lies in fertile ruins all around the naked Presence of living Truth. Glam's passage into and through so-called Darkness is one of both terror and rapture, aflame with labyrinthine surprise and primal recognition. He doesn't overcome Darkness, nor does he rise above It, nor does he settle for trying to think, affirm, believe, or meditate It away — instead, he *literally* and luminously embodies It, both befriending It and freeing up Its energies for life-giving purposes. Put another way, he persists, until the Dark's in love with the Light, until Paradox is but Truth, until the Fire is but Light, until there is room for all in his being...

Sacred Fire is a sharing, an aesthetically vibrant sharing, of the very best we in Xanthyros can offer, the deepest and truest expression we currently have of the particular topics we're addressing. What we are conveying springs cleanly from direct experience and exhaustively thorough work within a community of people who are deeply committed to the Awakening process; we have much to share, and Sacred Fire is a way of moving that sharing into the community at large. Sacred Fire is an invitation to make good use of our every facet and flaw, a potential welcoming into a truly supportive kinship for the journey of being that we, sooner or later, all must undertake...

Sacred Fire seeks to embody Truth, not the truth that is merely synonymous with the factual, but the Truth that is uncompromisingly alive, fresh, and spontaneous, bright with unrehearsed creativity and a knowingness that is paradoxical only to our mind; such Truth is consistent not in form, but in feel... *Sacred Fire* endeavors to provide not a bridge over Life's difficulties and delusions, but rather a conscious entry right into and through the very heart of them, a journey of gutsy luminosity, burdened by neither hope nor despair, obeying no morality except that generated by Awakening's alchemy.

A QUARTERLY MAGAZINE
DEDICATED TO THE LIVING
OF A TRULY HUMAN LIFE,
A LIFE OF FULL-BLOODED
AWAKENING

Sacred Fire

A Journal That, In Its Commitment

To Exploring & Illuminating

Awakening's Alchemy, Does Not Play It

Safe, Nor Compromise Itself To Please Its

Audience, Nor Hide In Detachment, Nor Make

An Enemy Out Of Whatever

Obstructs Wakefulness...

SACRED FIRE Is An Invitation To Dive Deep,

To Climb Steep, To Find Whatever It Takes

To Make The Necessary Leap;

It Provides Both Heat & Light For The Journey,

As Well As Juicily Alive Company, Company

That's More Interested In Going Through

Rather Than Around What's Troublesome.

Such Kinship, Such Integrity-Bright Intimacy,

Such Deep Travel Together,

Is What SACRED FIRE

Is All About...

ISSN: 0735-6501
$18/yr. (Quarterly)

Spontaneous Talks
by
Robert

Dolby B Chrome Cassette Tapes

Set I: 1988

MAKING GOOD USE OF TURNING POINTS

Turning points are times of extra energy, times of fertile chaos and potential transition; when we try to *think* our way through a turning point, we only confine its turbulent force in our minds, thereby intensifying our confusion, instead of letting its energies *fuel* our leap into a more fitting level of being. This talk, given October 27, 1988, is about how we must *consciously* blend with the currents of our turning points — we won't necessarily know where we are being taken, but we will not need to know, for we will inevitably be carried to a truer shore. Turning points need not be turned into crises; they are *not problems*, but wonderfully visceral confessions of our ripeness for a certain jump, or shift...

RELEASING SEX FROM THE OBLIGATION TO MAKE US FEEL BETTER

This talk, given October 7, 1988, is about freeing sex from its all-too-common chore of consoling us, whether through stress-discharge, pleasurable distraction, neurotic sublimation, or romantic delusion. If we pay *conscious* attention to ourselves in the midst of sex, we will see the underpinnings of our suffering with remarkable clarity — we will literally catch ourselves in the *act*, recognizing that what we tend to do sexually is but an exaggeration of what we do (or intend) when we *aren't* being sexual. When we stop depending on sex to make us feel better, we stop making a problem out of dependency itself, finding in ourselves a strength that is utterly *unthreatened* by dependency or attachment. Come toward sex *already* unstressed, *already* established in joy, letting it be a celebration of ecstatic intimacy, unburdened by any goal whatsoever...

THE ANATOMY OF EGO & SELF-ENTRAPMENT

Ordinarily, we exist as a self-enclosed, uneasily governed crowd of fragments, each one of which, when given sufficient attention, tends to refer to itself as "I" — however, all of these "I's" are not really selves, but are only *personified habits*. This talk, given October 23, 1988, is about shifting from ego-centricity (or unconscious identification with our dominant fragment of self) to essence-centricity, the point being not to annihilate ego, but to illuminate and purify it. All too easily, we seek release *not* from our self-entrapment, but from the pain of being *in* the trap, not truly realizing that the trap-door is *already* open, awaiting our passage, asking only that we let go of the *security* provided by our self-entrapment...

INTO THE HEART OF ENDARKENED MOODS

Instead of trying to escape or distract ourselves from our endarkened moods (which only reinforces their *roots*), we need to consciously confess *their* point of view and intentions, doing whatever we can to illuminate their terrain. In this talk, given November 22, 1988, the emphasis is on clearly exposing what we are *actually* doing while in unpleasant circumstances (inner or outer). Real happiness is not in fleeing "bad" moods, but rather is in going right to the very heart of them. Pure witnessing is of some use, but all too easily creates an unnecessary withdrawal from passion — the key here is to blend witnessing with *direct*, empathetic participation in our *feeling* dimension, knowing that *everything* we are must be fully faced, embraced, and passed through...

HAPPINESS IS NOT IN HAVING, BUT IN BEING

Real happiness is not in having, but in being. The expectation that *having something* (a relationship, an object, a certain feeling, a spiritual breakthrough) will make us feel better only intensifies our suffering, by *addicting* us to that particular something. This talk, given December 12, 1988, is about the nature of having, the need to shift from having to being, and the sane use of possessiveness. If we insist on having something, then it *has* us; on the other hand, if we rest in and *as* our being, then we can both enjoy and *deeply* participate in having, without becoming addictive about it...
(*Concludes with a poem*)

EMBODYING THE PASSIONATE WITNESS

This talk, given December 7, 1988, is about carrying alertness into the labyrinths of self-contraction, without any recoil from passion, desire, attachment, intimacy, or any other facet of a fully human life. Trying to escape the pain of our self-entrapment only creates more pain and more craving for pleasurably sedating release. The alternative to this is not resignation, nor more sophisticated strategies of escape (including those of all too many "spiritual" paths), but is simply to make room for our pain, letting its energies come unclenched, until they are but *available* Life-Force — this is *not* a technique, nor a recipe, but an always-fresh *art*, the very essence of which is the spirit-bright embodiment of the passionate witness, the one for whom turning away is no longer an attractive option...

ECSTASY CANNOT BE PRODUCED

The assumption that ecstasy is elsewhere, at the end of a series of steps, or at the point of maximal sexual stimulation, is not true — ecstasy exists in the *heart* of each moment, in the very depths that we flee in our compulsive searching for pleasurable release. This talk, given October 7, 1988, explores both ecstasy *and* its surrogates, emphasizing our need to *literally embody* a life free of all escapism and compensatory activity. Ecstasy is *not* addictive; only when we've turned away from ecstasy do we become addictive, simply because we then create dependency-relationships with whatever promises to deliver us from our suffering. Ecstasy is not a reward, nor is it a product — it is but the open face of real happiness, the pure shout of the awakened heart...

(*Concludes with three poems*)

RESPONSIBILITY IS THE GROUND OF FREEDOM

This talk, given August 29, 1988, is about not permitting *circumstantial* happiness to obscure our addictions, including that of ego, and it is also about the relationship between freedom and responsibility. For *real* freedom to exist, we must be responsible for creating and maintaining the environment, both inner and outer, that best supports such freedom. Without true responsibility, freedom is but licence, just an exaggerated kind of permission; without freedom, responsibility is but joyless duty, a burdensome obligation, polluted by well-dressed *blame*. As we awaken, it becomes increasingly clear that for every increase in freedom, there must also be a corresponding increase of responsibility...

AWAKENING CREATES ITS OWN MORALITY

Prior to awakening, we are infested by moral codes dictated by authority other than that native to ourselves, literally enslaving ourselves to inner and outer shoulds, worldly or other-worldly. This talk, given September 9, 1988, concerns the art of opening ourselves to the morality generated by the awakening process. Instead of rigidly conforming to rules, we need to create conditions conducive to the stage of our awakening, *without* addicting ourselves to the replication of such conditions — our activities thus become not a means *toward* happiness, but rather an expression of happiness. Peace then is for us not a repression of violence and primal force, but rather a passionate, *full-bodied* yes that includes within itself *every* no...

REAL RISK-TAKING

In this talk, given November 2, 1988, risk-taking is thoroughly explored. If we aren't willing to risk everything, then we'll only lose everything of *real* value. Sane risk-taking is not a matter of egocentric daring, but rather a matter of luminous intelligence and heartfelt gutsiness; it is a willingness to come undone, to let our binding familiarities come unstrung, and it is also a way of *directly* acknowledging the inherent insecurity of Life. It is crucial to dive into open-eyed intimacy, to dive deep, to again and again stretch to make the leap, to develop and honour relationships wherein it is safe to let go of being safe. Without risk, there is no ecstasy, no fullness of being...

FROM GUILT TO SHAME TO FREEDOM

Guilt is *not* a feeling, but a suppression of feeling, a psychophysical knottedness, a heart-numbing splitting of self that allows us to *continue* doing what apparently makes us "feel" guilty — put another way, guilt means we don't have to grow. However, guilt is but frozen shame. This talk, given November 16, 1988, describes the movement from guilt to shame to freedom, and from blame (the morality of guilt) to responsibility (the morality of *healthy* shame). Shame, when skillfully worked with, catalyzes a deep inner cleansing, a lucid, *heartfelt* acknowledgment of what was done, a warmly streaming catharsis of one's entire system, bright with both self-forgiveness and a return to wholeness, free of guilt's stalemated world...

TRUTH CANNOT BE REHEARSED

When we are committed to being other than ourselves, we are but beggars for applause, inner or outer, capable only of *re-acting*; we are haunted by stage fright, especially that of performing what *cannot* be performed. This talk, given November 21, 1988, is about acting, truth-telling and identity. As we cease pretending that we aren't pretending, we become less and less concerned about others' approval of us, and our freedom of choice becomes more than just the dictates of our conditioning. We learn the art of giving ourselves away, gradually ceasing to animate our reactivity, shining through our every role, realizing that there are no Oscars for awakening...

Set II: 1989/90

KEEPING OUR HEART OPEN IN HELL

Much of Earth's hellishness has to do with both the avoidance of being *truly* alone, and the avoidance of being *truly* together — it's the dreary dance of loneliness and cultism, of neurotic dependence and neurotic independence, the loneliness of the crowd, all swirling around that hellishly ubiquitous cult of one known as ego... This passionate, wide-ranging talk, given December 7, 1989, is about keeping ourselves open, discriminatingly yet vulnerably open, during seemingly negative times, making as much room for our pain as for our love. Instead of pushing away what we can't stand about ourselves, we need to go right into it, meeting and merging with the dreaded "it", until it's no longer an "it", but only reclaimed us...

THE ART OF LETTING LOVE BE PRESENT

When we separate love from endarkened or seemingly negative emo-tion, we only strand ourselves from the riches of our own shadowland, not realizing that love is essential for the illumination of such feeling. This talk, given March 20, 1990, thoroughly explores the art of letting love be present in the midst of whatever we're feeling, not as an *alterna-tive* to that feeling, but as a supportive medium for its truest possible ex-pression. Real love gives us room to feel what we are afraid to feel, until we are at its heart, sensing and knowing it from the inside, not just ob-serving or witnessing it, but being fully and *intimately* present with it. Such love is unexploitably alive, outdancing all escapism...

THE INVITATION THAT WILL NOT GO AWAY

Every moment is auspicious. Some moments carry more promise, more energy, more focus perhaps, more circumstantial good news, but every moment carries the same Demand, the same Opportunity to dive deeper... This talk, given August 10, 1989, precisely and poetically explores the Invitation to Awaken, the Invitation That is written into everything, encoded everywhere, translated into obviousness wherever and whenever we activate our capacity to stand our true ground. This Invitation is uniquely shaped and articulated according to our *present* state, obeying a kind of psychospiritual gravitation relative to our *true* needs and to what we are *doing* with them...

NA PALI: EMBRACING OUR TRUEST NEED

What we *need* is right here, right before us, not perhaps in its most conventionally fulfilling form, but here in a format that exactly suits our *current* state. This talk, given July 9, 1989, concerns the art of yielding our attention not to the preferred specifics that we'd like to have happen, but rather to the heart of our need — this necessitates becoming so *natively* intimate with change itself that it's all but impossible for us to seek security in the realm of having. The only real security is in Being, and *that* security is not in opposition to insecurity, for it is the very hub of Life's inherent insecurity!
(*The tape includes some background chanting; the periodic "noise" is that of gusting wind*)...

WHEN SUFFERING SERVES OUR AWAKENING

In almost all cases, the search to end suffering has a false foundation, one that is based not on Awakening, but rather on exploiting the options *within* our self-entrapment. As this talk (given November 27, 1989) points out, our suffering is not *inherently* a problem, but as soon as we make it into a problem, we tend to get caught up in apparent solutions, thereby overengaging our thinking minds in the process, thus increasing our distance from what is *really* going on. However, suffering that is not fled from, nor collapsed with, cuts through our defences, eroding our egotism and compensatory preoccupations, casting us into a fertile chaos, equipped with nothing except a lifeline to our Heartland...

THE ESSENCE OF SEEKING

Suffering creates seeking, and *most* seeking, through the very contracted-ness of its compulsive goal-fixation, only creates more suffering. This talk, given July 31, 1989, goes right to the heart of both seeking and non-seeking, clarifying the use and abuse of both with fluid subtlety. Explore, deeply explore, the you who is doing the seeking, and you'll encounter the primary machinations of your mind, including the clockwork of identification and addiction; seeking that is not made conscious is little more than nostalgia for the future, a promise-dangling dream, a mind-organized scheme, a well-intentioned ruining of the climb. We only reach our goal when we become soulfully intimate with the *root* of our reach...
(*Three prose-poems at end*)

DESPAIR AS A DOORWAY TO TRUTH

Almost all despair is negative despair, a sunken bewailing of one's condition; there is, however, a deeper kind of despair, one that's a result of being so thoroughly and lucidly disillusioned about the power of experience (worldly or other-worldly) to *truly* satisfy us, that we lose all interest in being distracted from our suffering. This positive despair, with its luminous sobriety and bedrock knowingness, is deeply explored in this talk (given March 23, 1990). In deep yet healthy disillusionment, the heart is broken in the same way that a stream rushing down a mountainside is broken — it's still cohesive spiritually, still unified in essence, its elemental dying only strengthening and affirming its fundamental aliveness, its dynamic yet utterly vulnerable surrender...

DOUBT EXPLORED AND UNMASKED

Doubt is a collapse of heart that's gone to mind, a dead-end inquiry, a bottled-up questioning that's terrified of being uncorked. When the *energy* of Doubt is allowed to mushroom, it naturally fastens onto whatever subject matter is handy, immediately *framing* that particular something in a questionable light. This talk, given March 1, 1989, not only explores Doubt in great depth, but also details the art of working with Doubt. Doubt is a gripping of mind; to try to relieve it through another play of mind, be it an earnest jump into Belief, positive thinking, contextual reprogramming, or whatever, doesn't work, except superficially. The suppression of Being that catalyzes Doubt must be seen, felt, known from the inside...

CHILDREN & REAL EDUCATION

What is referred to as education in our culture is little more than indoctrination, whether authoritarian or permissive; children are taught (both directly and through example) that acting is more important than being, that happiness depends on having certain things — they are driven, through the sheer load of information thrown at them, to live in their minds, to fragment themselves, to become as gone to pieces as their teachers and parents. Alternative approaches that espouse a wholistic approach are usually no better, since they usually only *preach* wholism, instead of directly *living* it. This provocative talk, given December 12, 1989, not only explores the failure of so-called education, but also passionately articulates what can be and needs to be done...
(Poem at end)

WE'RE ALWAYS CHANNELING

This talk, given October 26, 1989, clearly distinguishes between the metaphysical Disneyworld of most so-called channeling, with its disembodied recipes and naive literalism, and the non-escapist realm of awakened channeling, wherein is offered a full-bodied passage right into and through the very heart of our suffering, a passage that generates a reunion of all that we are. Our work is to become transparent yet grounded mediums for our Source. All the lower degrees of channeling must be permitted to enter into conducive alignment with this primal mediumship, until we are both surrendered and idiosyncratically present before the Presence of the Undying Unspeakableness That is both the One and the Many...
(Poem at end)

WHAT IS OBJECTIVE KNOWLEDGE?

Objective knowledge is neither subjectivity (or personified inwardness) nor conventional objectivity (or everted subjectivity), but is Essence-centered knowingness, an understanding senior to knowledge, a full-bodied intuition of Truth... In this talk, given October 27, 1989, such knowingness is richly illuminated, especially in contrast to its opinion-polluted surrogates. As long as we persist in dwelling at the level wherein agreement, disagreement, opinion, sentiment, and other bastard offspring of cognition and superficial emotion exist, we will take such opaque abstractions very seriously — we'll make real estate out of them, we'll wave their flags, we'll even *die* for them, instead of diving deeper, to where all our opinions and usual subjectivity are transparent to Being...
(Concludes with essay on meaning)

CUTTING THROUGH ANXIETY

The more we fear something, the more likely it is that we'll remain in close association with it, ever deepening our unwilling intimacy with it; what we worry about often comes true, since our very worrying keeps the dreaded something in mind, creating a chronic template for its fleshing-out... This talk, given October 2, 1989, explores the nature of anxiety, anxiety being obsessively futurized fear, a neurotic readiness for trouble that has not yet arrived, trouble that may well never arrive. Instead of trying to sedate away our anxiety, we need to penetrate and illuminate its energies, giving them room to breathe themselves sane...
(Three prose-poems at end)

Ordering Information

BOOKS: LOVE MUST ALSO WEEP $16.95

THE WAY OF THE LOVER 14.95

TRUTH CANNOT BE REHEARSED 19.95

SACRED FIRE MAGAZINE:
(sample: $5.00)   1 year sub $18.00

DOLBY B CHROME AUDIOTAPES:

(Real-Time tapes, each with two talks by Robert; average length is 80 minutes)

Set I: 1988

Into the Heart of Endarkened Moods /
Embodying the Passionate Witness

Releasing Sex From the Obligation to
Make us Feel Better /
From Guilt to Shame to Freedom

Happiness is Not in Having, But in Being /
Responsibility is the Ground of Freedom

Awakening Creates its Own Morality /
Ecstasy Cannot be Produced

Truth Cannot be Rehearsed /
The Anatomy of Ego & Self-Entrapment

Making Good Use of Turning Points /
Real Risk-Taking

Set II: 1989/90

Keeping Our Heart Open in Hell /
The Art of Letting Love Be Present

The Invitation That Will Not Go Away /
Na Pali: Embracing Our Truest Need

When Suffering Serves Our Awakening /
The Essence of Seeking

Despair as a Doorway to Truth /
Doubt Explored and Unmasked

Children and Real Education /
We Are Always Channeling

What is Objective Knowledge? /
Cutting Through Anxiety

($12.95/tape; $69.95 for a set of six)

POSTAGE & HANDLING: $2.50 for the first book
or tape, and $1.00 for each additional item.

Order from:

XANTHYROS FOUNDATION

P.O. Box 91980, West Vancouver, B.C., Canada V7V 4S4
(604) 922-8745
FAX (604) 922-8181